Recipes from an Ecological Kitchen

Recipes from an Ecological Kitchen

Lorna J. Sass

William Morrow and Company, Inc.
New York

This book was printed on recycled paper.

Copyright © 1992 by Lorna J. Sass

Grateful acknowledgment is made for use of the following:

Polenta, page 79. Adapted from *The Complete Whole Grain Cookbook* by Carol Gelles (New York: Donald I. Fine, Inc.: 1989).

Thumbprint Cookies, page 376, and Peanut Butter–Granola Cookies, page 373. Adapted from *The Natural Foods Cookbook* by Mary Estella (New York: Japan Publications, 1985).

Wild Rice with Chestnuts, page 140, previously appeared in *International Food and Wine* magazine.

It is the policy of William Morrow and Company, Inc., and its imprints and affiliates, recognizing the importance of preserving what has been written, to print the books we publish on acid-free paper, and we exert our best efforts to that end.

Library of Congress Cataloging-in-Publication Data

Sass, Lorna J.
    Recipes from an ecological kitchen / Lorna J. Sass.
        p.   cm.
    Includes bibliographical references (p.   ).
    ISBN 0-688-10051-1
    1. Vegetarian cookery. 2. Pressure cookery. 3. Stir frying.
I. Title.
TX837.S266   1992
641.5′636—dc20   91-40662
                                                          CIP

Printed in the United States of America

First Edition

1 2 3 4 5 6 7 8 9 10

BOOK DESIGN BY RICHARD ORIOLO

to Mother Earth

Acknowledgments

Many dear people have worked behind the scenes to make my dream of this book come true.

First I would like to offer heartfelt thanks to everyone at William Morrow, most particularly to Ann Bramson, my editor, for her patience, good cheer, and vision; Laurie Orseck for so respectfully separating the wheat from the chaff; Sarah Rutta for cheerfully juggling manuscripts and sending up the messengers; Sonia Greenbaum for such diligent copy editing; Deborah Weiss Geline for so kindly extending galley deadlines; Richard Oriolo for creating such an organic interior design; and Ursula Brookbank for another winning jacket.

Friends, both old and new, became enthusiastic members of the "Eco-Elves Club." Qualifications for membership involved retesting my recipes and reporting the results. Many eco-elves made delicious suggestions for improvements and variations. Thanks go to Barbara Aimes, Pat Baird, Myrna Baye, Ann Brady, Sheila and Irwin Burnstein, Barbara Campbell-Moffitt, Steve Chamberlain, Jane Cooper, Lucille Corrier, Joyce Curwin, Charlie Davidson, Marilyn Einhorn, Bess Ezekiel, Larry Gianneschi, Ellen Goren, Heidi Guber, Shelley Hainer, Jane Head, Dana Jacobi, Beth Johnson, Jeanette Miller, Leslie Miller, Margaret Mills, Jennifer Phillips, Eleanor Sass, and Joanne Zitko. Special hugs and kisses go to Super Elves Judy Bloom, Joan Carlton, Beth Johnson, and Roberta Chopp Rothschild.

Numerous colleagues have come to my aid, answering questions, offering moral support, and making valuable contributions to the manuscript. My gratitude to Frank Arcuri, Pat Baird, Gabriella Bengis, Bev Bennett, Mary Estella, Carol Gelles, Barbara Kirschenblatt-Gimlet, Meredith McCarty, Jane Rockhold, Richard Sax, Elizabeth Schneider, Debora Sperling, and Rebecca Wood. I would also like to acknowledge the many talented instructors at the Natural Gourmet Institute for Food and Health and especially founding director Annemarie Colbin and associate director Lissa De Angelis for inspiration and practical know-how. Any mistakes, of course, are my own.

And special thanks to:

My agent, Phyllis Wender, for her nurturing support;

Marc David and Lynne Tanzman (Manisha) for finding me a very special writer's retreat in the Berkshire Hills;

Pam Hunter for a magnificent edible tour of Anderson Valley, California;

The many organic farmers and gardeners for sharing with me their love of the land and their joy in growing our food;

Professor Joan Dye Gussow of Columbia University Teachers College for her inspirational course in Nutritional Ecology;

Professor Marion Nestle of New York University for sharing her files on vegetarian nutrition;

Silvia Blandon for keeping my kitchen so tidy;

Neighbors Christian Dorbandt, Dennis Hunsicker, Betsy Lawson, and Bobby Troka for sheltering the world's pestiest cat;

Miguel Hernandez for being such a super super;

The School of Practical Philosophy in New York City and Kripalu Center for Yoga and Health in Lenox, Massachusetts, for providing refuge from the storms;

Paul Hess for his love, support, and patience in helping me learn that I can have it all.

Contents

Introduction

This book documents how I cook and eat. When I changed my diet a number of years ago, I discovered a beautiful symmetry: What is good for our health is also good for the health of our planet.

It is therefore with great hope and enthusiasm that I invite you to share the delicious and exciting world of the ecological cook. Among the recipes, you'll be introduced to a wide variety of new dishes and will also find low-fat, high-fiber versions of many familiar favorites. The section called Ingredients A to Z can serve as your ready reference to all of the ingredients.

You can dip into this book on many levels. Learn some quick and satisfying ways to prepare vegetables, or discover a nutrition-packed grain that has recently come on the market. Turn a soul-satisfying lentil soup out of the pressure cooker in 7 minutes, or retrieve your wok from the attic for a quick stir-fry. Cholesterol-watchers are rewarded with a kaleidoscope of alternatives to meat, dairy, and eggs.

I would like to acknowledge two books that inspired me to eat the way I do. The first is Frances Moore Lappe's *Diet for a Small Planet*, first published in 1971. Lappe proved to me that I could get adequate protein by combining beans and grains, and the book launched me on a happy round of healthful vegetarian cooking.

In retrospect, however, I realize that by focusing on the "Diet" part of the title, I had missed Lappe's real point. That my personal eating habits could have any effect on our "Small Planet" just didn't register. At the time, it was difficult for me to grasp that people in the third world were starving as a consequence of the first world's food and life-style choices. And so I blithely went on to graduate school and ate soybean loaves until they went out of style.

Almost two decades passed before I picked up John Robbins's *Diet for a New America*, published in 1987. I cried when I learned in detail about the devastating effects that our meat-centered diet was having on our health and on the health of the ecosystem. As Lappe did before him, Robbins provides mind-boggling statistics that reveal the waste of grain and the devastation of land, water, and human resources resulting from large-scale cattle rearing. He shows that by moving to a plant-based diet, we can make a significant contribution toward bettering the environment.

As I pondered these convincing arguments, what had previously been an on again–off again personal dietary preference gradually became aligned with a much larger vision and purpose. I began to seek ways to express my concern for the planet in my daily life, and I decided to begin by turning my attention to what was showing up on my dinner plate.

Over time I developed the following guiding principles for an ecological kitchen:

- Focus on whole grains, fruits, and vegetables.
- Buy organic food as much as possible.
- Favor regional, seasonal produce.
- Reduce garbage by buying in bulk and opting for minimally packaged goods.
- Eliminate waste by menu planning and creative recycling of leftovers.
- Use fuel-efficient cooking equipment like the pressure cooker and the wok.
- Find nontoxic solutions for kitchen cleaning and pest control.

All well and good, you may be thinking, but does the food coming out of an ecological kitchen taste good? I'll be the first to admit that vegetarian cooking has gotten a pretty bad rep—most of it well deserved—for being tasteless, uniformly brown, time-consuming to prepare, and heavy enough to sink an ocean liner.

I promise you that right from the outset, I made it my personal mission to dispel all of these timeworn images. In my cooking, I aim for sophisticated flavor and strong visual appeal. And what's more, I like to get a healthy, well-balanced meal on the table in record time—and that can easily be done by using the pressure cooker and wok.

Aside from all of these practical advantages, keeping ecological principles in mind has enriched the quality of my life considerably. I feel more in harmony with the seasons as I shop in farmers' markets and plan menus around just-harvested fruits and vegetables. As a result, I'm eating fresher, more flavorful food and I feel more joyful about cooking it.

One day I found myself spontaneously joining hands with my friends before dinner and giving thanks to Mother Earth for her bounty. This felt so good that I've been saying a blessing before meals ever since.

I welcome you to the ecological kitchen. Let's join hands and together give thanks to Mother Earth.

LORNA J. SASS
New York City

RECIPE REQUEST

If you'd like to share your recipes or eco-tips for future editions of this book, please write to me at

Recipes from an Ecological Kitchen
Box 704
New York, New York 10024

Long before institutionalized religions came along—and temples, and churches—there was an unquestioned recognition that what goes on in the kitchen is *holy*. Cooking involves an enormously rich coming-together of the fruits of the earth with the inventive genius of the human being. So many mysterious transformations are involved. . . . In times past there was no question but that higher powers were at work in such goings-on, and a feeling of reverence sprang up in response. I wonder sometimes whether the restorative effects of cooking and gardening arise out of similar—though quite unconscious—responses.

—Laurel Robertson, Carol Flinders,
and Brian Ruppenthal, *The New Laurel's Kitchen*
(Berkeley: Ten Speed Press, 1986).

Stocking the Ecological Pantry

The great advantage of having a larder well stocked with whole grains, beans, and condiments is that you can create an endless variety of meals at a moment's notice—shopping only for fresh vegetables, salad greens, and other perishables to fill in the gaps.

Although you may feel a bit daunted by the list of ingredients that follows—some of them unfamiliar—rest assured that you can proceed gradually, introducing a few new items at a time.

In this shopping list, which includes just about all you'll need to prepare the recipes in this book, each category is divided into three: staple, specialty, and esoteric. Begin by purchasing the staples and then move into the specialty and esoteric items as the spirit (or a recipe) moves you. Opt for organic products when they're available. (If you need convincing on this subject, see "Why Buy Organic?" on page 5.)

For descriptions of the ingredients as well as tips on how to select and use them, turn to Ingredients A to Z.

ECO-TIP: The fuller your freezer, the more energy-efficient it is. Store all of your raw grains and flours in the freezer. Mark the date of purchase, and arrange them in alphabetical order.

Grains

Staple: short-grain brown rice, long-grain brown rice or brown basmati, quinoa, medium or coarse bulgur, pearl or hulled barley, extra-long-grain, white rice or white basmati. *Specialty:* amaranth, buckwheat, whole wheat couscous, millet, wheat berries, Arborio rice (for risotto), wild rice. *Esoteric:* Job's Tears (not always readily available), kamut, spelt, rye berries, triticale berries. *Storage:* freeze (preferably) or refrigerate in a well-sealed container for up to 4 months.

Pasta/Noodles

Staple: whole grain fettuccine and spirals or other small pasta, whole wheat or brown rice udon. *Specialty:* buckwheat soba. *Esoteric:* kuzu kiri, harusame, somen. *Storage:* keep at room temperature in a well-sealed container for a year or longer.

Flours

Staple: whole wheat pastry, unbleached white. *Specialty:* brown rice, high-lysine cornmeal, oat, barley. *Esoteric:* kamut, spelt, quinoa, soy, blue cornmeal. *Storage:* freeze (preferably) or refrigerate in a well-sealed container for up to 4 months.

Beans and Legumes

Staple: chick-peas, brown lentils, black beans, pintos, red kidneys, navies, black-eyed peas, split peas, large limas. *Specialty:* adukis, red lentils, anasazis, Great Northerns, black soybeans. *Esoteric:* scarlet runners, Christmas limas, Black Valentines, favas, etc. (see mail-order sources). *Storage:* store at room temperature in a cool, dry place away from the light in a well-sealed container for a year or longer.

Sea Vegetables

Staple: kombu (kelp), nori sheets, hijicki, arame. **Specialty:** dulse, wakame (alaria). **Storage:** store at room temperature in a well-sealed container indefinitely.

Dried Fruits

Staple: raisins, currants, apricots, prunes, dates. **Specialty:** bananas, cherries. **Storage:** refrigerate (preferably) or keep in a cool place in a well-sealed container for 6 months.

Nuts and Seeds

Staple: sunflower seeds, unhulled sesame seeds, walnuts. **Specialty:** pine nuts, almonds, pumpkin seeds, raw cashews. **For Sprouting: Staple:** alfalfa, sunflower seeds. **Specialty:** radish. **Storage:** freeze (preferably) or refrigerate for up to 4 months.

Nut Butters

Staple: almond, sesame tahini, peanut (if desired). **Specialty:** cashew, hazelnut, pistachio. **Storage:** keep in a cool place; refrigerate (after opening) for up to 4 months.

Beverages

Staple: herbal teas, grain-based coffee substitutes. **Storage:** store at room temperature. **Specialty:** apple juice, amasake, soy milk. **Storage:** refrigerate (after opening) for up to 5 days.

Oils

For Sautéing: olive, peanut. **For Baking:** canola or high-oleic safflower. **For Salads:** olive, high-oleic safflower, toasted sesame. **Specialty:** walnut, hazelnut. **Storage:** keep in a cool place; refrigerate (after opening) for up to 4 months.

Condiments

Staple: sea salt, sesame seasoning salt (gomasio; purchased or homemade; page 454), barley miso, tamari soy sauce (organic mansan tamari is a personal favorite), apple cider vinegar, umeboshi plum vinegar. **Specialty:** chick-pea, millet, and other varieties of light and dark miso, Bragg Liquid Aminos, brown rice vinegar, balsamic vinegar, natural mustard, horseradish, soy mayonnaise, natural ketchup, pickles, sauerkraut. **Esoteric:** umeboshi plum paste, pickled ginger, pickled daikon root. **Storage:** store vinegars at room temperature; refrigerate all others after opening.

Dried Herbs and Spices

Staple: oregano, thyme, rosemary, marjoram, bay leaves, dillweed, mint. **Specialty:** sage, tarragon, chervil. **Staple:** black pepper,* chili powder, curry powder, whole cumin seeds, whole coriander seeds, dry mustard powder, cinnamon, cloves,* nutmeg,* allspice,* ginger, cayenne (ground red) pepper, crushed red pepper flakes. *Specialty:* cardamom,* fennel seeds,* turmeric, anise seeds,* paprika, caraway seeds. *Esoteric:* juniper berries,* fenugreek,* star anise,* mustard seeds,* Szechuan peppercorns,* ancho and chipotle chili peppers. *Storage:* store in a cool place *away from light* in a tightly sealed container.

Sweeteners

Staple: maple syrup, barley malt syrup. *Specialty:* rice syrup. *Storage:* store at room temperature, refrigerate maple syrup after opening.

Miscellaneous

Staple: pure vanilla extract, dried mushrooms, dried chestnuts. *Specialty:* kuzu or arrowroot (for thickening sauces), agar sea vegetable flakes (for gelling glazes). *Storage:* store at room temperature in well-sealed containers.

*Buy whole if possible and grind as needed.

Flavorprints

When it comes to creating your own recipes, it's helpful to know which seasonings and oils are characteristic of each of the world's cuisines. By selecting a few from a particular category to cook with vegetables or grains you can confidently create an infinite variety of new dishes.

Here is a brief list, with thanks to the American Spice Trade Association and *The Flavor Principle Cookbook* by Elisabeth Rozin.

Italian: basil, bay leaves, garlic, fennel seeds, marjoram, oregano, parsley, crushed red pepper flakes, rosemary, sage, olive oil, salt and pepper

French: bay leaves, chervil, garlic, rosemary, tarragon, thyme, olive oil, salt and pepper

Mexican: chili peppers, cinnamon, cumin seeds, fresh coriander, oregano, olive oil, salt and pepper

Chinese: fresh ginger, garlic, star anise, peanut oil, soy sauce

Middle Eastern: cinnamon, cumin seeds, garlic, mint, oregano, parsley, olive oil, salt, sesame tahini

Indian: cardamom, coriander seeds, cumin seeds, fenugreek, fresh ginger, mustard seeds, turmeric, curry powder

Greek: cinnamon, garlic, mint, oregano, olive oil, salt

Organically Speaking

Why Buy Organic?

In addition to the fact that organically grown food is more healthful and just plain tastes better, here are some of the far-reaching contributions you make to society and the world when you buy organic food:

1. You are supporting a farmer in maintaining the health of the soil. Naturally healthy soil nourishes food crops more completely than chemical fertilizers, and provides a broad spectrum of micronutrients and trace minerals. Healthy soil is the foundation of life for all of the inhabitants of our planet.

2. You are protecting our supply of clean air and water, both of which are polluted by chemical-dependent agriculture.

3. You are encouraging the use of composting—the recycling of plant and animal wastes into fine-quality soil fertilizer. Full-scale, properly organized composting could reduce the garbage ending up in our landfills by 70 percent.

4. You are helping to reverse global warming, as 15 percent of the global-warming gases are caused by chemical agriculture.

5. You are providing wildlife habitats, since organic farms coexist nonviolently with animals.

6. You are encouraging crop diversity in a rotation system of planting that is at the heart of organic agriculture. Such diversity is much needed to ensure our future food and seed supply.

7. You are honoring the value of the small American farm and are helping to provide safe and wholesome work environments for those who are working to grow your food.

(Information provided by the Committee for Sustainable Agriculture, Colfax, CA)

High Cost

Organically grown food usually costs more for a variety of reasons. First, organic farmers initially need to lay out a considerable amount of capital to build up and maintain their soil. For the first few years, their yields may be lower than normal. However, as yields improve and more and more people opt for organic produce, prices are likely to drop.

Many people committed to the idea of purchasing organic produce are rightfully concerned that some products labeled "organic" may, in fact, not be. Confusion has reigned in this arena because to date there has been no federal agency determining national certification standards and only a handful of states have addressed the issue.

There is a strong movement afoot to have national standards in place by October 1993. Hopefully by that time, any label stating "certified organic" would mean that an independent third party verified that the national standards for certification had been met.

To Peel or Not to Peel

Until organic produce is competitively priced and more widely available, many of us are confronted with the challenge of how best to avoid pesticide residues in our food. While the skin (and just below) on fruits and vegetables contains the highest concentration of undesirable chemicals, it is also a fine source of fiber and nutrients. Each time we are about to cook or eat an apple or a potato, many of us wonder whether or not to take out the peeler.

Here is the way I approach this frustrating dilemma.

1. I don't peel organic fruits and vegetables. I just scrub them lightly with a vegetable brush.

2. I peel all fruits and vegetables that are not organically grown, most especially those that are waxed (like cucumbers or rutabagas). Since I eat a high-fiber and nutrient-rich diet, I don't feel concerned about the losses incurred when I remove the peels. (Instead of peeling, I can opt to scrub them with a few drops of vegetable-based soap or soak them in water containing a bit of Clorox, but both of these approaches are unappealing to me.)

3. With vegetables that grow in bunches or heads, I discard the outer leaves and wash the inner ones.

4. I soak in water and rinse thoroughly produce that cannot be peeled or scrubbed, such as cauliflower florets or blueberries. When using tomatoes of unknown origin, I generally peel them (page 463). If peppers are waxed, I often roast them to remove the skins (page 451) and enjoy a special taste treat.

5. I use only organic orange and lemon peel.

6. I try to feel peaceful about what I'm eating, knowing that I'm doing my best to give my body the good-quality fuel it deserves.

For more information on these issues, I recommend *Safe Food: Eating Wisely in a Risky World*, by Michael Jacobson, Lisa Lefferts, and Anne Witte Garland.

This we know; the Earth does not belong to humanity; people belong to the Earth, this we know. All things are connected. Whatever befalls the Earth, befalls the people of the Earth. We did not weave the web of life, we are merely a part of it. Whatever we do to the web, we do to ourselves.

—Chief Seattle, leader of the Squamish Tribe, 1854

Cooking from This Book

Almost all of the recipes in this book (with the exception of the dessert and quick-bread chapters) can be prepared in a pressure cooker or a wok, two cooking methods that offer optimum time and fuel efficiency. (A large skillet can replace the wok, and for those who don't own a pressure cooker, standard stovetop instructions are provided.)

The pressure cooker cuts down cooking time to one third or less than normal, and the wok, with its large cooking surface, is the most efficient way to make quick stir-fries. They both offer a nice balance for meal planning, as the pressure cooker is great at producing soups, grains, beans, and all manner of comfort food in record time, while the wok is excellent for making crisp-cooked vegetables.

Since the pressure cooker can double as a steamer (see page 12) and spaghetti pot, I need in addition only a 1½-quart enameled saucepan for making sauces, and a large cast-iron skillet for miscellaneous stovetop and baked dishes. I've eliminated all other pots from my kitchen. Using only a few pieces of equipment streamlines my cooking and minimizes washing up. Besides, it's a joy to live without clutter.

The Basics of Pressure Cooking

I can assure you that this single pot will dramatically improve your cooking and eating life. What other appliance can seal in nutrition while producing 2-hour taste in 20 minutes?

If you've heard stories of lids blowing off, fear no more. The newly designed, second-generation pressure cookers are totally safe to use. If you're planning to buy one, look for a heavy pot with a stationary pressure regulator rather than an old-fashioned removable jiggle-top. The new type is more expensive, but it is safer, more versatile, and well worth the price.

If you already own a pressure cooker but haven't used it in a long time, you'll need to replace the rubber gasket that sits in the rim of the lid. If it's a jiggle-top cooker, be sure to follow special instructions in the recipes and respect the limitations suggested by the manufacturer. In addition, always stay within earshot of the kitchen. If you ever hear any very loud hissing sounds, turn off the heat and set the cooker under cold running water to release the pressure. Remove the lid, clean out any food clogging the vent, and then proceed with cooking.

If you bought your cooker during the last fifteen years, it probably has an overpressure plug and at least one safety back-up feature. If in doubt, ask the manufacturer. If your cooker is of unknown age and origin (or if it's the one Aunt Tillie used when her pea soup shot up to the ceiling), I advise you to consider buying a new one that you can trust.

The recipes in this book will work in a 6- or an 8-quart cooker. If you are using a smaller model, be sure that the ingredients don't fill the cooker beyond the manufacturer's recommended maximum. If they do, either halve the recipe or cook it in two batches.

How the Pressure Cooker Works

The pressure cooker turns out a lentil soup in 7 minutes and a steamed bread pudding in well under an hour because it cooks food at higher-than-standard boiling-point temperature. Once the lid is locked into place, the cooker is set over high heat and the boiling liquid produces steam. Since the steam is sealed inside, pressure builds and the internal temperature rises, increasing the boiling point from the standard 212° to 250° Fahrenheit. Under high pressure, the fiber in the food is softened and flavors mingle in record time.

Since food cooks so quickly in the pressure cooker, certain ingredients can easily become overcooked if you lose track of the time. For this reason, a timer is indispensable.

The Language of Pressure Cooking

Here is an explanation of the phrases you will find in pressure-cooker recipes:

Set the Rack in Place: Most cookers come with a rack for steaming vegetables. Place the rack on the bottom of the cooker. In some recipes, a heatproof casserole is set on this rack to raise it slightly. If your appliance doesn't come with a rack, you can substitute a steaming basket when cooking vegetables or a trivet when using a casserole. (A makeshift trivet can be created by smashing aluminum foil into a log and shaping the log into a ring that will fit in the cooker; after cooking, air-dry it and save for future use.)

Lock the Lid in Place: Follow the manufacturer's instructions. If the lid is not locked properly, the pressure won't rise.

Over High Heat, Bring to High Pressure: Depending upon the quantity and type of food you are cooking, it will take anywhere from 30 seconds to 20 minutes to bring the pressure up to high. You can speed up this process by having the liquid heat up in the cooker as you prepare and add other ingredients. Apply maximum heat to reach high pressure as quickly as possible.

Lower the Heat Just Enough to Maintain High Pressure: Once high pressure is reached, reduce the heat to medium-low to maintain it; otherwise pressure will continue to build, creating loud hissing noises. After using the cooker a few times, you'll have a good idea of the amount of heat required to maintain high pressure. (If you reduce the heat too much, the pressure will start to drop.) If your stove is electric, move the cooker to another burner for a minute or two after reaching high pressure, since the coils are slow to cool down.

Under High Pressure: The manufacturer's instruction manual explains how to recognize when maximum (13 to 15 pounds) pressure has been reached. All recipes in this book have been tested under high pressure.

Unless otherwise noted, cooking time begins from the moment that high pressure is reached. For example, above each recipe is a phrase such as "3 minutes high pressure." This means that as soon as the cooker reaches high pressure, you set the timer and cook under high pressure for 3 minutes.

Total Cooking Time: This term is used almost exclusively in connection with quick-cooking vegetables. Since these vegetables can so easily be overcooked, set the timer from the moment the lid is locked into place. If the recipe states "3 minutes *total cooking time*," this means you should release any pressure that has built up—*whether or not* high pressure has been reached—after 3 minutes have elapsed. Release the pressure and remove the lid immediately.

Use a Quick-Release Method: When the timer goes off, bring down the pressure by placing the cooker under cold running water, or use an alternative method suggested by the manufacturer. (If the latter method causes sputtering at the vent, bring down the pressure under cold running water instead.) Recipes for preparing vegetables and other quick-cooking foods *require* the quick-release method.

Let the Pressure Drop Naturally: When the timer goes off, turn off the heat and let the cooker sit until the pressure drops of its own accord; depending upon the quantity and type of food in the pot, this can take 3 to 20 minutes. The food continues to cook as the pressure drops; and it is a gentler way to bring down the pressure—an advantage when cooking beans (which otherwise tend to "lose their skins") and grains, which benefit from a final steaming.

When the recipe says "Let the pressure come down naturally for 5 minutes," keep the lid in place for as long as indicated, whether or not the pressure has already dropped. Release any remaining pressure before attempting to remove the lid.

Remove the Lid, Tilting It Away from You to Allow Excess Steam to Escape: Even when the pressure is completely released, there is residual steam in the pot, so make it a practice to tilt the lid away from your face when removing it.

Replace the Lid and Cook for a Minute or Two in the Residual Heat: When delicate foods such as rice or fresh vegetables are only slightly underdone after the pressure is released, set (don't lock) the lid in place and let the food cook in the heat that remains in the pot, without applying any additional heat.

With the Aid of a Foil Strip: To move a heatproof casserole both in and out of the pressure cooker, cut an aluminum foil strip measuring 2 feet long by 1 foot wide (the width of standard foil) and double it twice lengthwise. Center the casserole on the strip and gently lower it into the cooker. Loosely fold the ends of the foil strip over the top of the casserole. After cooking, air-dry strip and save for future use.

Transfer to a Heated Flame Tamer: A flame tamer is an inexpensive heat-diffusing device that prevents scorching. It is particularly useful when cooking grain pilafs, which require relatively little liquid and have a tendency to stick to the bottom of the pot. Flame tamers are readily available in housewares stores. To use one, first set the cooker directly on the heat to bring it up to high pressure. Shortly before high pressure is reached, set the flame tamer on a second burner over high heat. As soon as high pressure is reached, transfer the cooker to the hot flame tamer. Lower the heat just enough to maintain high pressure and continue as directed in the recipe.

A Few Extra Tips

Cooking Times: I usually give a range of cooking times, since doneness is often a matter of taste and timing is always approximate at best. To avoid overcooking, release pressure after the minimum recommended time. If the food is only slightly undercooked, finish it off by simmering, covered, over low heat. If considerably more cooking is required, return to high pressure for another few minutes.

Gas Versus Electric: Timing of the recipes is based on cooking over gas. Owners of electric stoves may need to make minor adjustments. Always move the cooker to a cool burner when releasing the pressure.

Browning: If a recipe calls for sautéing onions or garlic before adding liquid, be sure to scrape up any browned bits sticking to the bottom of the cooker before setting the lid in place. If left in place, they have a tendency to scorch and impart a burned taste to the dish.

The Basics of Wok Cooking

The ancient Chinese technique of wok cooking is quick, convenient, and fun. With considerable stirring, vegetables are cooked until tender-crisp over high heat for a brief time. Although the shape of the wok allows for maximum cooking surface, stir-frying can also be done in a large (12- to 14-inch), heavy skillet, preferably cast iron. Once you get the hang of wok cooking, you can create new dishes based on any combination of fresh vegetables you like.

Wok cooking comprises two basic techniques: stir-frying and wok-steaming. Quick-cooking vegetables, such as onions or thinly sliced zucchini, can be stir-fried in a bit of oil just until tender-crisp. (A long wooden paddle shaped to the wok or oversized chopsticks work best for stir-frying.) Longer-cooking vegetables, or those cut into chunks rather than slices, require a second step that I call wok-steaming. After the vegetables are stir-fried in an open wok to sear them, a small amount of liquid (water or a mixture of water and tamari soy sauce) is added and the wok is covered. This allows the vegetables to steam until tender at the center.

You can combine stir-frying and wok-steaming in several ways to cook a variety of vegetables together:

1. Stir-fry longer-cooking vegetables and wok-steam them until just short of being done. Then add quick-cooking vegetables and stir-fry until all of the ingredients are tender-crisp.
2. Slice all vegetables very thin. Stir-fry longer-cooking vegetables, like squash, first, and add quick-cooking vegetables, such as mushrooms, shortly before the squash is finished.
3. Cut quick-cooking vegetables thick, and longer-cooking vegetables very thin. Stir-fry and wok-steam them together.

Here's a partial list of short-cooking and long-cooking vegetables. The main difference between them is density, which is related to their water content. In general, the denser the vegetable, the less water it contains and the longer it will take to cook.

Mind you, even the long-cooking vegetables don't really take very long. Figure on 2 to 5 minutes for quick cooking, and 6 to 12 minutes for long cooking.

Short Cooking	Long Cooking
Bean sprouts	Brussels sprouts
Snow peas	Chopped kale
Spinach	Diced winter squash
Mushrooms	Sliced broccoli stalks or florets
Shredded cabbage	Sliced carrots
Thinly sliced zucchini	Sliced potatoes

Some More Tips

Chop up all of the vegetables before you begin, and have all of the condiments and additional ingredients within arm's reach. Once you heat the pot, you'll need to act quickly.

For successful searing with a minimal use of oil, first heat the pot over a high flame until a bead of water cast on the surface evaporates immediately. Then add the oil, and tilt and swirl the pot so that the oil lightly coats the surface. As soon as the oil begins to sizzle, add the first ingredients and stir-fry to coat them with oil. If the ingredients are browning very quickly, lower the heat to medium or remove the pot briefly from the source of heat while continuing to stir. Adding a few drops of liquid (such as water or soy sauce) will also quickly bring down the temperature of the cooking surface.

To avoid overcooking, remove the pot from the heat while doing any final adjustments to the seasoning.

The Basics of Steaming

Steaming is so simple a process that we tend to take it for granted. And yet, for retaining the purest taste and best texture of a perfectly fresh vegetable, there is perhaps no better cooking technique.

For steaming a small amount of vegetables, a metal steamer basket on legs set into a large pot will do the trick. To cook a substantial quantity of vegetables, or for large vegetables like artichokes, it's more practical to use a rack.

If you own a pressure cooker, chances are that it has a perforated rack. Set the rack on a trivet—or you can create a raised platform by bunching up aluminum foil into a long rod and shaping the rod into a circle. The idea in either case is to raise the vegetables at least ¾ of an inch above the boiling water.

One of the handiest ways to steam vegetables—particularly when you want to cook two or three kinds at one time—is to use a Chinese bamboo steamer set. Put a different vegetable in each basket and set the baskets on top of a large stockpot or your pressure cooker and steam away. Place the quicker-cooking vegetables in the top baskets for easy removal when done.

Here are a few other things to keep in mind when steaming:

1. Always bring the water to a rolling boil before you set the vegetables into the pot. (All timings in Ingredients A to Z are calculated from this point.)
2. Be sure the pot is large enough to leave a few inches between the vegetables and the lid. For proper steaming, the hot air must be able to circulate freely.
3. Make sure that the lid of the pot fits tightly so that little to no steam escapes.
4. When removing the pot lid, always tilt it away from you to avoid being burned by steam.
5. To safely lower and raise the steaming basket or rack to and from a large pot, use a foil strip (page 10).

Menus

Sit-Down Holiday Feast

Mushroom Spread with Thinly Sliced Whole Grain Bread
Creamy Cauliflower Soup
Nosmo King's Moroccan Chili
Herbed Bulgur Rice
Butternut Squash and Parsnip Puree
Sesame Biscuits
Tossed Green Salad with Sweet Potato Vinaigrette
Steamed Cranberry Pudding

International Party Buffet

Moroccan Carrots
Eggplant Caponata
Lima Beans à la Grecque
Red Bean Salad Olé
Barley Salad with Carrots and Dill
Marinated Pan-Fried Tempeh
Quick Pickled Beets
Lemon Poppy Seed Cake

Sunday Brunch

Black Bean Skillet Casserole with Cornbread Topping
Marinated Broccoli
Mixed Salad with Moroccan Vinaigrette
Gingered-Prune Drop Scones

Quick Sunday Supper for Chilly Days

Curried Yellow Split-Pea Soup with Squash and Raisins
Skillet-Fried Brown Rice
Tossed Salad with Toasted Sesame Vinaigrette
Thumbprint Cookies

Quick Sunday Supper Any Time of Year

Mom's Tofu Curry in a Hurry
Pistachio Rice
Mixed Green Salad with Avocado Vinaigrette
Fresh Fruit

20-Minute Gourmet

Sun-Dried Tomato Dip with Whole Grain Crackers
Tarragon Risotto with Mushrooms and Leeks
Vinaigrette-Wokked Brussels Sprouts
Orange and Fennel Salad with Walnuts
Anise-Pignoli Dipping Cookies

Middle Eastern Summer Lunch

Babaghanoush
Tabbouleh
Hummus
Middle Eastern Pita Salad
Summer Fruit Compote

Picnic in the Park

Summer Pasta Salad for a Crowd
Eggplant Caponata
Celery Slaw
Carrot Cake

Bracing Winter Dinner

Smoky Chestnut Soup
Whole Grain Bread with Tahini Miso Spread
Mushroom Barley Pilaf
Gingered Acorn Squash
Apple Pie

Rustic Italian

White Bean Soup with Escarole
Polenta Plus
Basic Sautéed Greens
Anise-Hazelnut Thumbprint Cookies

Time for Thai

Thai Vegetable Soup
Coconut Rice with Lemongrass
Zesty Thai-Style Broccoli
Pineapple Granita

Plantation Dinner

Black-eyed Pea Soup with Collards
Creole Brown Rice
Red Cabbage Slaw with Maple-Mustard Dressing
Pecan Pie

We give thanks to Life.
May we never lose touch with the simple joy and
wonder of sharing
a meal.

—Rabbi Rami M. Shapiro, in *Earth Prayers*,
Elizabeth Roberts and Elias Amidon, eds.
(San Francisco: Harper, 1991).

The Lazy Cook's Guide to Menu Planning

It's nice to be able to look at menu suggestions, write out a shopping list, gather the ingredients, and then spend an hour or two cooking. Then there's real life.

Meetings, deadlines, laundry, and other intrusive aspects of the daily round have inspired me to fall into what I call "The One-Thing-Leads-to-Another Method of Menu Planning." The basis of this lazy technique is creating leftovers on purpose.

I start the whole scheme in motion by making a double batch of beans, say Spicy Black-eyed Peas and a grain—for example, Basic Brown Rice. For the evening meal I serve half of the beans mounded over half of the rice along with a steamed vegetable or a green salad. The leftover beans and grains then inspire my next menu.

The choices are endless. With the beans, I can make Empanadas, Curried Rice Muffins, a spread, or a Hoppin' John Salad. With the rice, I can whip up some Sushi Rolls, or if there are some steamed vegetables left over too, I'd be more likely to make a grain salad, following the guidelines in What's Available Bean-and-Grain Salad.

Here's another example. Say I make a double batch of Zesty Black Bean Soup and serve it with Basic Quinoa and a green salad. The next day I might toss the quinoa, drained black beans, and some cooked corn kernels with Coriander Pesto and serve the salad hot or cold. Or I could drain the beans and make a Black Bean Skillet Casserole with Cornbread Topping. I'd then use the leftover quinoa as the basis for a grain salad or Tabboulleh, using the quinoa instead of bulgur wheat.

If I cook double batches of one or two basic dishes each day—occasionally freezing some to use a few weeks down the line—I find myself with a kaleidoscope of ready-to-use ingredients that keeps me in motion day after day. When all else fails, I just throw everything into the wok with some fresh ginger and a drizzle of tamari and call it Stir-fry du Jour.

As you may suspect from the above suggestions, a cardinal rule of this method is that you be quite irreverent about the recipes in this book. After you have followed the directions once or twice, let your imagination run wild and start substituting like crazy. If you fancy Skillet-Fried Brown Rice but only have cooked millet on hand, substitute millet for the rice and go happily on your way. Or if you have white beans instead of adukis, make the Aduki-Watercress Salad anyway.

Most of all, have fun, be happy, feel peaceful and chew well.

Soup, Beautiful Soup

When it comes to cooking, there is nothing I enjoy more than inventing a new soup. Surely there is no other category of food preparation that invites such wanton experimentation.

For the soup-maker, there are rewards at every step. First, there's the fun of foraging in the pantry and refrigerator to see what's on hand and what's screaming for immediate attention. I always reach for the soup pot when I spy lots of tired-looking vegetables in the bin: It gives me great satisfaction to use up what would otherwise go to waste.

Once I've assembled the available ingredients, I ask myself some pretty basic questions:

Will these ingredients go together?

What herbs and spices will meld the flavors so that the whole becomes greater than the sum of its parts?

What can I stir in at the end to surprise the taste buds and add a flash of color?

If the soup is to be the focal point of the meal, I serve a large bowlful along with a big salad, whole grain bread, and a bean spread. If it's going to be an appetizer, I make the portions smaller and serve a regular meal to go along with it (see pages 13–16 for menu suggestions).

Almost all of the soups in this chapter were made in the pressure cooker because it's the quickest and tastiest way I know to get the job done. Cooking food under pressure causes flavors to mingle in record time; you'll find that these soups develop deep, rich flavor in 10 to 20 minutes—homemade tastes you've been longing for, but didn't think you had the time to create. For those who don't have a pressure cooker, I've included standard stovetop timings and directions.

. . . Food reveals our connection with the earth. Each bite contains the life of the sun and the earth. The extent to which our food reveals itself depends on us. We can see and taste the whole universe in the piece of bread!

—Thich Nhat Hanh, *Peace Is Every Step*
(New York: Bantam, 1991).

Basic Vegetable Stock

Makes about 1½ quarts

Vegetable stock is the city cook's best alternative to the compost pile. Don't throw away all of those vegetable peels (if organic) and trimmings, corncobs, limp carrots, celery sticks, those half-used onions and unused herb stalks. They still have good flavor. Get in the habit of collecting them in the refrigerator (up to 4 days) or freezer (up to 3 months) until you have enough bits and pieces to make a tasty broth.

Although you don't need a strict recipe for vegetable stock, the following will give you some guidelines. Once you've become a confident stock-maker, you can graduate to the (Almost) Anything Goes stock recipe on page 23.

The basic stock tastes best when used within 2 to 3 days. It can be frozen for up to 3 months, but there will be some loss of flavor (see Cook's Notes). I find it convenient to freeze stock in different quantities and defrost as needed. For a big batch like this, I usually put half in a 1-quart container and the remainder in 2-cup portions that are suitable for cooking grains and beans.

Pressure cooker: 10 minutes high pressure, optional natural pressure release
Standard stovetop: 60 to 90 minutes

8 cups water
8 cups coarsely chopped miscellaneous vegetables (see Candidates for the
*   Stock Pot, page 23)*
2 medium onions, coarsely chopped (include skins for a darker stock)
1 to 2 cloves garlic, peeled and crushed (optional)
3 large carrots, cut into 3 to 4 chunks
4 large ribs celery, cut into 3 to 4 chunks
1 to 2 parsnips, cut into 3 to 4 chunks (optional; makes the stock sweeter)
2 bay leaves
¼ to ½ cup tightly packed minced fresh parsley stalks and leaves
A few sprigs of fresh thyme or oregano, or ½ teaspoon dried thyme or dried
*   oregano (optional)*
Sea salt to taste (see Cook's Notes)

1. Place the water in the cooker and over high heat begin bringing to the boil as you prepare and add the remaining ingredients except for the salt.

continued

2. Lock the lid into place. Over high heat bring to high pressure. Lower the heat just enough to maintain the pressure at high and cook for 10 minutes. If time permits, allow the pressure to come down naturally. Otherwise, reduce pressure with a quick-release method. Remove the lid, tilting it away from you to allow any excess steam to escape.

3. Allow the stock to cool slightly. Pour the stock through a strainer into one or more storage containers. Smash the vegetables against the sides of the strainer to extract all of the liquid. Cool and refrigerate for up to 3 days or freeze up to 3 months.

Standard Stovetop: Finely chop the vegetables. In a large soup pot, proceed as directed in step 1. Bring to the boil, reduce heat and simmer, partially covered, until the vegetables have given up their flavor, about 60 to 90 minutes. Follow step 3.

Cook's Notes: I prefer to make my stocks free of fat and extra labor, but you'll attain a richer and more intensely flavored stock by browning the vegetables 10 to 15 minutes in a tablespoon or two of oil before adding the water. Also, because fat absorbs flavor, sautéing the vegetables enables you to freeze the stock with less loss of taste.

You'll have more options later on if you cook the stock without salt, then add salt as desired in individual recipes. Salted stock used in a bean soup, for example, will toughen the bean skins and lengthen cooking time.

Instant Homemade Stock

The greatest almost-instant stock I know is kale cooking water (page 253). It is full flavored and perfect for any hearty soup. (Be sure to taste it first: On occasion it can be too strong or slightly bitter.) Kale stock can be refrigerated for up to 3 days and frozen for up to 3 months (with some loss of flavor).

Here's an idea: Before storing the stock, pour some in a mug and stir in a few drops of tamari soy sauce or Bragg Liquid Aminos for a mineral-rich potion to heal what ails you.

(Almost) Anything Goes Vegetable Stock

This is not really a recipe, but a reminder to make stock with any vegetables and peelings that might otherwise end up going to waste. Just toss them into the cooker, cover with water, and away you go, following the directions in the Basic Vegetable Stock recipe.

Scrub all vegetables well if you plan to use the peelings for stock. If possible, use organic vegetables.

Pressure cooker: 10 minutes high pressure, optional natural pressure release
Standard stovetop: 60 to 90 minutes

CANDIDATES FOR THE STOCK POT

Asparagus and broccoli stalks
Bay leaf or a few pinches of dried herbs (if you're feeling magnanimous)
Celery, parsnip, and carrot chunks, peelings, and trimmings
Corncobs and husks
Garlic (unpeeled, crushed)
Kale stalks (for a strong, distinctive flavor like cabbage)
Leek greens and roots
Onions (unpeeled for a darker stock)
Potatoes and potato peelings (remove any green spots)
Scallions (including root ends)
Sweet potatoes, apples or pears (for a slightly sweet stock)
Tomatoes or lemon slices (for a slightly acid stock)
Turnips (peel to avoid bitterness)
Wilted celery, lettuce, and watercress
Winter squash (avoid waxed peels)
Zucchini

AVOID

Beets and beet peelings (unless you want a magenta-colored stock)
*Green peppers, eggplant, and leafy greens such as collards and mustard
    (they can impart a bitter taste)*
*Most members of the cabbage family, such as cabbage and Brussels
    sprouts (they easily overpower the stock)*
Turnip peels (they're bitter)

Variations: For a stock with an Oriental twist, add a tablespoon or so of freshly grated ginger, and use soy sauce instead of salt. A few pieces of star anise are a wonderful addition if you're partial to the licorice-like flavor.

East Meets West Vegetable Stock

This stock is ideal for cooking grains that will be served with an Oriental-style vegetable dish, such as the Chinese-Style Stir-fry with Kale, Onions, and Marinated Tofu on page 258. It's also very tasty as a light broth on its own, with perhaps a few of the cooked shiitake and some thinly sliced scallions floating on top.

Pressure cooker: 10 minutes high pressure, 10-minute natural pressure release
Standard stovetop: 50 to 60 minutes

6 cups water
1 bunch scallions, coarsely chopped
3 to 4 large cloves garlic, peeled and coarsely chopped
8 quarter-sized slices fresh ginger
1 ounce dried shiitake (see Cook's Notes) or Chinese dried mushrooms,
*   rinsed*
2 cups shredded bok choy or cabbage
1 large bunch coriander, including well-washed roots, coarsely chopped
*   (about 2 cups loosely packed)*
1 tablespoon dried lemongrass or 1 stalk fresh, chopped (optional)
2 to 3 tablespoons tamari soy sauce
2 to 3 teaspoons toasted (Oriental) sesame oil

1. Place the water in the cooker and over high heat begin bringing to the boil as you prepare and add all of the ingredients except the soy sauce and sesame oil.

2. Lock the lid in place and over high heat bring to high pressure. Lower the heat just enough to maintain high pressure and cook for 10 minutes. Allow the pressure to come down naturally for 10 minutes. Remove the lid, tilting it away from you to allow any excess steam to escape.

3. Allow the stock to cool slightly. Pour the stock through a fine-meshed strainer into a storage container, leaving in the pot any sandy dregs that have sunk to the bottom. Smash the vegetables against the sides of the strainer to extract all liquid. Cool and refrigerate for up to 3 days or freeze up to 4 months. Add soy sauce and sesame oil to taste just before using.

Standard Stovetop: In a large soup pot, proceed as directed in step 1. Bring to the boil, reduce heat and simmer partially covered, until the stock is richly flavored, about 50 to 60 minutes. Follow step 3.

Cook's Notes: If you use shiitake mushrooms, after cooking remove them from the strainer and discard the stems. Slice the mushrooms and toss them into cooked grains or add them to soups.

Double Mushroom Stock

When your leek greens have lost their sprightly good looks and your mushrooms are begging for attention, try making this intense and luscious stock. When cooked with mushroom stock rather than water, grains and pilafs are transformed from simply pleasing to extraordinary.

> **Pressure cooker:** 15 minutes high pressure, optional natural pressure release
> **Standard stovetop:** 40 to 50 minutes

5 cups water
½ cup (½ ounce) loosely packed dried mushrooms, swooshed in water to remove surface sand and grit, then drained
4 to 6 ounces fresh mushrooms, thinly sliced
5 to 6 leek greens or 1 large onion, peeled and coarsely chopped
2 large ribs celery, coarsely chopped
6 sprigs parsley or 10 to 12 stems
5 whole black peppercorns
2 large cloves garlic, peeled and finely chopped (optional)
½ teaspoon dried tarragon, marjoram, oregano, or rosemary
Sea salt to taste

1. Place the water in the cooker and over high heat begin bringing to the boil as you prepare and add all of the ingredients.

2. Lock the lid in place and over high heat bring to high pressure. Lower the heat just enough to maintain the pressure at high and cook for 15 minutes. Use a quick-release method or allow the pressure to come down naturally, if time permits. Remove the lid, tilting it away from you to allow any excess steam to escape.

3. Set aside to cool slightly. Pour the stock through a fine-meshed strainer into a storage container, leaving in the pot any sandy dregs that have sunk to the bottom. Smash the vegetables against the sides of the strainer to extract all liquid. Cool and refrigerate for up to 3 days or freeze up to 4 months.

Standard Stovetop: In a large soup pot, proceed as directed in step 1. Bring to the boil, reduce heat and simmer, partially covered, until the mushrooms have given up their flavor, about 40 to 50 minutes. Follow step 3.

Variations
- Use flavorful shiitake or porcini mushrooms to replace all or part of the supermarket-type dried mushrooms.
- For an elegant "cream" of mushroom soup, add some soy milk to the strained stock. Float a few slivers of the cooked dried mushrooms on top.

Bonus Bean Stock

Here's a great way to cook up a tasty pot of beans and make a flavor-packed stock at the same time. Since bean stock freezes very well, I always make some when I am preparing beans for a salad or side dish. It makes a wonderful soup base, and adds a depth of flavor and nutritional boost to grains. (I use one part bean stock to one part vegetable stock or water when cooking grains.)

Please consider this recipe a general rule of thumb. Feel free to add or subtract ingredients according to what's in your vegetable bin. Even plain-cooked beans automatically yield a tasty stock.

One caution: After soaking the beans, taste the water. If it's slightly bitter, forget about making the stock—it's likely to have a faint bitter edge too.

Pressure cooker: 5 to 20 minutes high pressure (depending upon type of bean)
Standard stovetop: 45 to 90 minutes

2 cups beans, soaked 4 to 8 hours in ample water to cover
5 cups water
1 large onion, peeled and halved from top to root end
2 large cloves garlic, peeled and halved (optional)
1 large carrot, cut into thirds
1 large rib celery, cut into thirds
1 large bay leaf
2 to 3 whole cloves
6 sprigs parsley or 10 to 12 parsley stems
½ teaspoon dried thyme, marjoram, or oregano
6 whole black peppercorns
1 tablespoon oil

1. Drain and rinse the beans. Place the water in the cooker and over high heat begin bringing to the boil as you prepare and add the beans and remaining ingredients. (Don't omit the oil; it controls the foaming action of the beans.)

2. Lock the lid in place and over high heat bring to high pressure. Lower the heat just enough to maintain the pressure at high and cook for the recommended time. (Check the bean cooking chart on page 175.) Use a quick-release method or allow the pressure to come down naturally, if time permits. Remove the lid, tilting it away from you to allow any excess steam to escape. If the beans are quite undercooked, return to high pressure for another few minutes. If they are just short of done, simmer, covered, until they achieve the desired consistency.

3. Strain the stock into a storage container. Discard the vegetables (or see Cook's Notes), bay leaf, cloves, parsley, and peppercorns.

4. Cool the beans to room temperature and refrigerate up to 3 days or freeze up to 4 months.

Standard Stovetop: In a large soup pot, proceed as directed in step 1, omitting the oil if you wish. Bring to the boil, reduce heat and simmer, covered, until the beans are tender (check the bean cooking chart, page 177, for approximate timing). Follow steps 3 and 4.

Cook's Notes: Instead of discarding the vegetables, puree them, thin the puree with some stock, then add a few beans and season to taste. In other words, have a cup of soup—cook's reward!

White beans—such as cannellinis, French navies, limas, and white runners—produce the best light stocks. Black beans and black soybeans yield wonderfully rich, dusky potions.

Since salt makes bean skins tough, add it to the stock after the beans are tender, if desired.

Instant Broth Mix: Buyer Beware

I always keep some instant broth mix on hand in case homemade stock is not available. Health food stores carry a variety of brands with names like vegetable broth mix, vegetable bouillon, and vege base. A few broth mixes are pastes, but most come in powdered form, which I find more convenient to use.

The tastes of the broths vary dramatically, ranging from bitter and salty to an acceptable facsimile of the real thing. In a comparative tasting of six brands, my colleagues and I found Vogue's Instant Vege Base the freshest and fullest flavored. If you can't find it in health food stores, write or call the company for retail sources (437 Golden Isles Drive, Suite 15G, Hallandale, FL 33009. Tel.: 305-458-2915).

The instant broths sold in supermarkets usually contain MSG. Read the label carefully. If hydrolyzed vegetable protein is an ingredient, contact the manufacturer to determine if MSG was used in the manufacture of the vegetable protein itself; unfortunately, lax United States labeling laws do not make it mandatory to itemize the constituents of all listed ingredients.

Spring Asparagus–Celery Stock   Makes about 2 quarts

This is a lovely, delicate stock to make when asparagus is in season: Just throw the woody base-parts of the stalks and any peelings into the stockpot instead of throwing them out.

I like to use this stock for making Lemon-Scented Asparagus Risotto (page 152) and as a base for cold summer soups.

Pressure cooker: 10 minutes high pressure, optional natural pressure release
Standard stovetop: 50 to 60 minutes

2 quarts water
Tough stalks of a large bunch (about ¾ pound stalks) asparagus, scrubbed
    and cut into 2 to 3 pieces
4 large ribs celery, sliced
1 large onion or the greens of a large leek, coarsely chopped
1 large carrot, sliced
10 to 12 parsley stems or whole sprigs
1 teaspoon dried marjoram or tarragon or ½ teaspoon fennel seeds
3 to 4 thin slices lemon, preferably organic
2 bay leaves
6 whole peppercorns
Sea salt to taste

1. Place the water in the cooker and over high heat begin bringing to the boil as you prepare and add the remaining ingredients.

2. Lock the lid in place and over high heat bring to high pressure. Lower the heat just enough to maintain the pressure at high and cook for 10 minutes. Use a quick-release method or allow the pressure to come down naturally, if time permits. Remove the lid, tilting it away from you to allow any excess steam to escape.

3. Allow the stock to cool slightly. Pour the stock through a strainer into a storage container. Smash the vegetables against the side of the strainer until they release all of their liquid.

4. Cool the stock completely, then cover and refrigerate for up to 2 days. (This stock loses most of its flavor if frozen.)

Standard Stovetop: In a large soup pot, proceed as directed in step 1. Bring to the boil, reduce heat and simmer, covered, until the vegetables become very soft, about 50 to 60 minutes. Follow steps 3 and 4.

Variation: Use ½ pound of broccoli stalks instead of asparagus for a heartier stock more suitable to winter soups.

Pea Pod–Corncob Stock

½ pound empty pea pods
produces about 2 cups stock

It's such a pity to throw out mounds of crisp, green pea pods that I decided to see what kind of stock they would produce. The result? A gentle, slightly sweet stock that makes a lovely base for cold summer soups and adds a pleasing taste to vegetable risottos and white rice pilafs. (It's too delicate for use with brown rice.) You'll need at least ½ pound of empty pods to make the stock.

Freeze corncobs and tender inside husks and toss them into the stockpot for an added flavor dimension.

Pressure cooker: 10 minutes high pressure, optional natural pressure release
Standard stovetop: 40 to 50 minutes

Empty pea pods, thoroughly washed
Corncobs and husks (optional)
Water
Sea salt to taste

1. Place the pea pods, corncobs, and husks (if using) in the cooker with water to cover, plus 1 inch. Add salt, if desired.

2. Lock the lid in place and over high heat bring to high pressure. Lower the heat just enough to maintain the pressure at high and cook for 10 minutes. Use a quick-release method or allow the pressure to come down naturally, if time permits. Remove the lid, tilting it away from you to allow any excess steam to escape.

3. Set aside to cool slightly. Pour the stock through a strainer into a storage container. Cool and refrigerate for up to 2 days. (This stock loses most of its flavor if frozen.)

Standard Stovetop: In a large soup pot, proceed as directed in step 1. Bring to the boil, reduce heat and simmer, covered, until the pea pods give up their flavor, about 40 to 50 minutes. Follow step 3.

Man at his best, like water,
serves as he goes along.
—Lao-tzu

Soups

Most soups consist of three components: liquid, body, and flavor. The liquid may be water or stock. The body is provided by the solid ingredients, such as vegetables, beans, and grains. The flavor derives from all of the above plus complementary herbs and spices.

Some pointers for creating full-flavored soups:

1. Use stock (or half stock and half water) for a more complex flavor, if the soup has relatively few ingredients, or if the ingredients are mild in taste.
2. If no stock is on hand, you can always use an instant broth mix (see page 27). If you're not sure that the broth mix is needed, you can always stir some in at the end of cooking. Or you can build stock into the soup by adding generous portions of onions, carrots, and other vegetables that would normally go into an already prepared stock.
3. For richer flavor (whether or not you're using stock), brown the onions and briefly sizzle the spices before adding the other ingredients.
4. For soups using a variety of vegetables with different cooking times, cut slow-cooking vegetables into thin slices and quick-cooking vegetables into thick slices. Cook the soup for the time required by the slowest-cooking ingredients.
5. Before adding salt, consider the following alternatives for building in additional flavor:

   - miso (fermented soybean paste), stirred in at the end, adds saltiness plus a complex winy flavor.
   - tamari soy sauce and Bragg Liquid Aminos both add saltiness and a rich "beefy" taste.
   - a dash of vinegar brings up flavor and contributes piquancy.

6. To add vibrant color and flavor, stir in fresh herbs at the end, or divide the herbs and cook half with the soup and stir in the remainder at the end.
7. If a soup is too thick, thin it with water or stock. If it is too thin, puree a cup or two of the solid ingredients and stir them back in.

"In a batch of vegetable soup, it's not right for the carrot to say, I taste better than the peas, or the pea to say, I taste better than the cabbage. It takes all the vegetables to make a good soup!" Miriam said.

—Sue Bender, *Plain and Simple*
(New York: Harper & Row, 1989).

7-Minute Mushroom Barley Soup

The trick to making this old favorite so quickly is using barley flakes, barley's equivalent to oatmeal. They're readily available in health food stores and have become a great favorite in my household for making quick soups and breakfast porridge. (By the way, they have none of the gooeyness of oatmeal.)

This soul-satisfying soup thickens on standing; thin it with vegetable stock or water if you like.

Pressure cooker: 7 minutes high pressure, optional natural pressure release
Standard stovetop: 40 to 50 minutes

¾ *cup dried baby lima beans, picked over and rinsed, soaked 4 to 8 hours*
    in ample water to cover
1 tablespoon oil
2 large leeks (white and green parts), thoroughly rinsed and chopped,
    or 2 large onions, coarsely chopped
2 cloves garlic, peeled and finely chopped
5 cups water
2 large ribs celery, cut into ½-inch slices
2 large carrots, cut into ½-inch slices
2 slender parsnips, cut into ½-inch slices
½ cup (½ ounce) loosely packed dried mushrooms, swooshed in a bowl of
    water to remove sand, then drained
½ pound fresh mushrooms, thinly sliced
¾ *cup barley flakes or pearl barley (see Cook's Notes)*
1 bay leaf
⅓ *cup tightly packed minced fresh dill*
Sea salt to taste

1. Drain the limas and discard any loosened bean skins. Heat the oil in the cooker and sauté the leeks and garlic for 1 minute, stirring frequently. Add the limas, water, celery, carrots, parsnips, dried and fresh mushrooms, barley flakes, and bay leaf.

2. Lock the lid into place. Over high heat bring to high pressure. Lower the heat just enough to maintain the pressure at high and cook for 7 minutes. Allow the pressure to come down naturally or use a quick-release method. Remove the lid, tilting it away from you to allow any excess steam to escape. If the barley or limas are not sufficiently cooked, simmer covered for a few more minutes.

3. Remove the bay leaf and stir in dill and salt to taste before serving.

continued

Standard Stovetop: In a large soup pot, proceed as directed in step 1. Bring to the boil, reduce heat and simmer, covered, until the dried mushrooms, limas, and barley are very soft and the soup is intensely flavored, about 40 to 50 minutes. Follow step 3.

Cook's Notes: You can substitute pearl barley for barley flakes if you soak it for 4 to 8 hours along with the limas. Add 2 minutes to the cooking time under pressure and 10 minutes to the standard cooking time.

The link between quality food and family farmers is worth recalling: It's us.
—Mark Kramer, "Are Farmers an Endangered Species?"
in Robert Clark, ed., *Our Sustainable Table* (Berkeley: North Point Press, 1990).

Creamy Cauliflower Soup

Elegant and delicate—very creamy despite being fat-free, and very simple to prepare—this soup has the subtleness of cauliflower sweetened and burnished by the autumnal orange of the carrots or butternut squash. Good cold as well as hot.

Pressure cooker: 3 minutes high pressure, optional natural pressure release
Standard stovetop: 20 to 30 minutes

1 small head (1½ pounds) cauliflower
2 cups water
2 cups vegetable stock
¾ pound carrots or butternut squash, scrubbed and coarsely chopped
    (peeling not necessary, particularly if organic)
1 medium (about ½ pound) potato, peeled and coarsely chopped
1 teaspoon dried tarragon
1 to 2 tablespoons light miso or sea salt to taste (see Cook's Notes)

GARNISH
3 radicchio leaves, cut into thin strips (looks especially striking),
    or 4 to 6 tablespoons chopped watercress leaves

1. Cut the cauliflower into medium-sized florets and set aside. In the cooker, combine the water, stock, carrots, potato, and tarragon. Bring to the boil. Add the cauliflower.

2. Lock the lid in place and over high heat bring to high pressure. Lower the heat just enough to maintain the pressure at high and cook for 3 minutes. Reduce pressure with a quick-release method or allow the pressure to come down naturally. Remove the lid, tilting it away from you to allow any excess steam to escape.

3. Puree the soup in two batches in a blender (for a smoother texture), food mill, or food processor, adding miso or salt. Return to the pot to rewarm. Adjust seasonings and garnish before serving.

Standard Stovetop: In a large soup pot, proceed as directed in step 1. Return to the boil, reduce heat and simmer, covered, until the vegetables are very soft, about 20 to 30 minutes. Follow step 3.

Cook's Notes: I prefer using miso rather than salt because it adds a complex and winy flavor to the soup. I rarely peel organic potatoes, so the vitamins and minerals remain intact. But in this instance, peeling them will assure that the soup has a pleasing color.

Autumn Gold Carrot-Yam Soup

Serves 6

My good neighbor and pressure-cooker buddy Judy Bloom created this beautiful fall soup. If you can find garnet yams, with their smooth-as-silk texture and candy-sweet taste, this dish is extraordinary. With everyday sweet potatoes, it's just plain delicious.

Pressure cooker: 6 minutes high pressure
Standard stovetop: 25 minutes

5 cups vegetable stock or water
1½ pounds carrots, scrubbed and cut into ½-inch slices
1½ pounds yams or sweet potatoes, peeled, halved, and cut into ½-inch
    slices (see Cook's Notes)
1 medium onion, peeled and coarsely chopped
2 large apples, peeled, cored, and coarsely chopped
⅓ cup old-fashioned oatmeal (rolled oats)
1 tablespoon mild curry powder
Sea salt or tamari soy sauce to taste

GARNISH
¼ cup tightly packed minced fresh coriander or parsley

1. Combine all ingredients except the coriander in the cooker.
2. Lock the lid into place. Over high heat bring to high pressure. Lower the heat just enough to maintain the pressure at high and cook for 6 minutes. Reduce pressure with a quick-release method. Remove the lid, tilting it away from you to allow any excess steam to escape.
3. Puree the soup in two batches in a blender (for a smoother texture), food mill, or food processor, adding salt to taste.
4. Return to the pot to rewarm and serve with a garnish of fresh coriander.

Standard Stovetop: In a large soup pot, proceed as directed in step 1. Bring to the boil, reduce heat and simmer, covered, until the vegetables are quite soft, about 25 minutes. Follow steps 3 and 4.

Cook's Notes: Sweet potatoes can be tricky to peel using a vegetable peeler. I advise using a sharp pairing knife.

Smoky Chestnut Soup

Perfect for serving at Thanksgiving or any time you have a yen for elegant taste and texture, this soup is made in less than 15 minutes.

I am very partial to cooking with dried chestnuts. They have a distinctive smoky taste that I find irresistible, and it's most convenient that they are already skinned. Dried chestnuts are available in most health food stores and gourmet shops, and by mail order.

In this recipe, the chestnuts are cooked in the water used to soak them overnight. If you haven't presoaked the chestnuts, see Cook's Notes.

Pressure cooker: 9 minutes high pressure, optional natural pressure release
Standard stovetop: 40 to 50 minutes

1¾ cups dried chestnuts, rinsed and soaked overnight in the cooker in 5½
     cups water
1 large butternut squash (2¾ pounds), scrubbed, halved, seeded, and cut
     into 6 to 8 large chunks (peeling not necessary, especially if organic)
1 rib celery, cut into ½-inch slices
½ teaspoon ground cinnamon
½ teaspoon sea salt

GARNISH
Freshly grated nutmeg

1. Rub off any chestnut skins that have become loosened and discard any that have floated to the top of the soaking water. Add the remaining ingredients.

2. Lock the lid into place. Over high heat bring to high pressure. Lower the heat just enough to maintain the pressure at high and cook for 9 minutes. Reduce pressure with a quick-release method or allow the pressure to come down naturally. Remove the lid, tilting it away from you to allow any excess steam to escape. If chestnuts are not tender, either return to high pressure for a few minutes or simmer covered until they are quite soft.

3. Let the soup cool slightly, then puree in a blender (for smoothest texture) or food processor, or pass the mixture through the finest blade of a food mill. Add salt, if desired, and thin with water or vegetable stock if required. Reheat and serve, with a few gratings of nutmeg on top of each portion.

Standard Stovetop: In a large soup pot, proceed as directed in step 1. Bring to the boil, reduce heat and simmer, covered, until the chestnuts are very soft, about 40 to 50 minutes. Follow step 3.

continued

Cook's Notes: For an impromptu chestnut soup, bring the chestnuts and 5½ cups water to the boil, cover, and let sit off heat for 1 hour. Then proceed as directed.

Variation: Stir in a tablespoon or two of maple syrup before serving to bring out the sweetness of the squash and chestnuts.

Dilled Broccoli Soup

Serves 5 to 6

An elegant soup that couldn't be simpler to prepare. If using dried dill, be sure that it has vibrant flavor. Instead of adding salt, stir in a tablespoon or two of light blond miso at the end for a complex, winy taste.

Pressure cooker: 3 minutes high pressure
Standard stovetop: 15 to 20 minutes

1 large bunch (about 2 pounds) broccoli
4 cups vegetable stock
1 large onion, peeled and coarsely chopped
⅓ cup old-fashioned oatmeal (rolled oats)
Sea salt or blond miso to taste
¾ cup tightly packed minced fresh dill (preferred) or 2 tablespoons dried dillweed

GARNISH
3 tablespoons minced fresh dill (optional)

1. Cut the broccoli tops into large florets. Trim and peel the stalks, removing any fibrous or woody parts. Cut the stalks into 1-inch chunks. Place the broccoli, stock, onion, oatmeal, and salt (but not the miso) into the cooker. If using dried dillweed rather than fresh dill, add it at this time.

2. Lock the lid into place. Over high heat bring to high pressure. Lower the heat just enough to maintain the pressure at high and cook for 3 minutes. Reduce pressure with a quick-release method. Remove the lid, tilting it away from you to allow any excess steam to escape.

3. Puree the soup in two batches in a blender (for a smoother texture), food mill, or food processor. Return the soup to the pot and stir in fresh dill and miso to taste (if using). Simmer just long enough to reheat the soup. Garnish with fresh dill (if using) just before serving.

Standard Stovetop: In a large soup pot, proceed as directed in step 1. Bring to the boil, reduce heat and simmer, covered, until the broccoli is quite soft and the oatmeal is cooked, about 15 to 20 minutes. Follow step 3.

Orange Squash Soup

The lively color and tangy orange taste give this soup double appeal. You'd never guess that this recipe is virtually fat-free, since the rolled oats provide such a pleasing creaminess and sheen.

Pressure cooker: 5 minutes high pressure
Standard stovetop: about 25 minutes

2½ pounds butternut, kabocha, or delicata squash, scrubbed, seeded, and
    cut into ½-inch chunks (peeling not necessary, particularly if organic)
1 small onion, peeled and coarsely chopped
2 cups water
1 cup freshly squeezed orange juice (see Cook's Notes)
¼ cup old-fashioned oatmeal (rolled oats)
1 tablespoon freshly grated ginger
1 tablespoon finely minced or grated orange peel (colored part only,
    preferably organic)
½ teaspoon ground cinnamon
¼ teaspoon ground coriander seeds
½ teaspoon sea salt, or to taste
1 to 2 tablespoons maple syrup

GARNISH
Toasted pumpkin seeds

1. Place all ingredients except the maple syrup in the cooker.

2. Lock the lid into place. Over high heat bring to high pressure. Lower the heat just enough to maintain the pressure at high and cook for 5 minutes. Reduce pressure with a quick-release method. Remove the lid, tilting it away from you to allow any excess steam to escape.

3. Puree the soup in a blender (for a smoother texture), food mill, or food processor. Add maple syrup to taste. Return the soup to the pot to rewarm. Thin slightly with water or orange juice, if necessary. Garnish with toasted pumpkin seeds.

Standard Stovetop: In a large soup pot, proceed as directed in step 1. Bring to the boil, reduce heat and simmer, covered, until the squash is very soft, about 25 minutes. Follow step 3.

Cook's Notes: Remove the orange peel before squeezing out the juice.

Heavenly Carrot Soup

A gentle reminder of life's simple pleasures. Wonderful served either hot or chilled.

Pressure cooker: 5 minutes high pressure
Standard stovetop: 25 to 30 minutes

1 tablespoon oil
3 medium leeks (white part only), thinly sliced and thoroughly rinsed
    (about 3 cups)
1 pound carrots, thinly sliced
½ pound small thin-skinned potatoes, scrubbed and quartered
2 large ribs celery, thinly sliced
5 cups vegetable stock
1¼ teaspoons dried tarragon
1 to 2 tablespoons light miso or sea salt to taste

GARNISHES
¼ cup finely chopped watercress or a pinch dried tarragon
Whole Grain Herb-Garlic Croutons (page 419)

1. Heat the oil in the cooker. Sauté the leeks for 2 minutes. Add the carrots, potatoes, celery, stock, tarragon, and salt. (If using miso, do not add it at this time.)

2. Lock the lid in place and over high heat bring to high pressure. Lower the heat just enough to maintain the pressure at high and cook for 5 minutes. Reduce the pressure with a quick-release method. Remove the lid, tilting it away from you to allow any excess steam to escape.

3. Puree the soup in batches in a blender or food mill. Blend 1 tablespoon of miso (if using; see Cook's Notes) into the final batch. Return to the cooker to reheat. Blend in additional miso or salt if desired. Garnish with watercress and croutons before serving.

Standard Stovetop: Cut the potatoes into thin slices or chop them coarsely. In a large soup pot, proceed as directed in step 1. Bring to the boil, reduce heat and simmer, covered, until the vegetables are very soft, about 25 to 30 minutes. Follow step 3.

Cook's Notes: Miso is especially delicious in this recipe; it adds complex flavor that has a suggestion of wine.

Thai Vegetable Soup

All the Thai-style foods in this book, including this memorable soup, were inspired by the wonderful dishes that emerge from the kitchen of my dear friend, cookbook author Pat Baird.

Pressure cooker: 1 minute high pressure, 1 minute simmering
Standard stovetop: 5 to 8 minutes

6 cups vegetable stock
1 tablespoon freshly grated ginger
1 tablespoon dried lemongrass, placed in a large aluminum tea ball
2 jalapeño peppers, trimmed, seeded, and cut into thin strips lengthwise
    (wear rubber gloves when handling; for a hotter dish, leave some or
    all of the seeds in)
2 slender carrots, cut into ⅛-inch slices on the diagonal
½ pound firm tofu, drained and cut into ½-inch cubes
¾ pound broccoli
¼ pound small mushrooms, halved
½ pound Napa or Chinese cabbage (bok choy), shredded
¼ cup tightly packed minced fresh coriander
¼ cup thinly sliced scallion greens
Tamari soy sauce to taste

1. Combine the stock, ginger, lemongrass, jalapeño peppers, carrots, and tofu in the cooker and set over high heat.

2. Trim and peel the broccoli stalks. Cut the thin stalks lengthwise in half and the thick ones into 4 spears. Cut the spears into ¼-inch slices and add to the pot. Cut the broccoli tops into small florets. When the soup has come to the boil, add the florets, mushrooms, and cabbage.

3. Lock the lid in place and over high heat bring to high pressure. Lower the heat just enough to maintain high pressure and cook for 1 minute. Reduce the pressure with a quick-release method. Remove the lid, tilting it away from you to allow any excess steam to escape.

4. Remove the tea ball. Stir in the coriander, scallions, and soy sauce and simmer for 1 minute before serving.

Standard Stovetop: In a large soup pot, proceed as directed in steps 1 and 2. Return to the boil, reduce heat and simmer, covered, until the broccoli is tender-crisp, about 5 to 8 minutes. Follow step 4.

Bean Soup for Beginners

For the novice soup-maker, creating a bean soup is a great way to begin. It's easy to keep the basic ingredients on hand, and bean soups are delicious, nutritious, and very filling.

Just follow the basic formula given below. By varying the type of bean and the seasonings, you can have a different soup for almost every day of the year.

Seasoning Base

Heat 1 tablespoon of oil in a pressure cooker or heavy soup pot. Sauté 1 large chopped onion and 1 large clove of minced garlic for a few minutes. (The oil also keeps the beans from foaming while they cook.)

Beans

To serve 4 to 6, use about 2 cups of dried beans, soaked 4 to 8 hours, then rinsed and drained.

Liquid

Use three times more liquid. For example, if you begin with 2 cups of dry beans, use 6 cups of water. For a richer soup, you can use vegetable stock.

Vegetables

Sliced carrots add nice color and flavor. Chunks of parsnip lend a delicate sweetness. Add these firm, longer-cooking vegetables at the beginning of cooking.

Use spinach, chard, mustard, or beet greens for their sprightly green color. Since these greens cook so quickly, you need only chop them and simmer them in the soup for 2 to 3 minutes at the end of cooking.

Seasonings

Choose herbs and spices that will complement the beans, and add them at the beginning of cooking: cumin and chili powder with pinto beans for a Southwest flavor; or oregano and basil with cannellini beans for an Italian-style soup. Check the recipes in this section for other ideas and for appropriate amounts.

Remember to add salt *after* the soup has cooked so that the beans will cook properly.

Add ¼ to ½ cup of finely chopped fresh herbs to the cooked soup for vibrant color and flavor.

Timing

Check the bean cooking chart on page 175 or 177 for approximate cooking time.

Final Touches

If the soup is too thick, thin it with water or stock. If too thin, puree a cupful of cooked beans and stir them back in.

Adjust seasonings before serving.

Garnish each portion with a sprinkling of chopped fresh herbs.

Collards and Black-eyed Pea Soup

A combination of soul-food favorites makes for an earthy and very satisfying dish. It quickly thickens upon standing; thin it with water or stock as needed. And don't forget to pass the hot sauce.

Pressure cooker: 10 to 12 minutes high pressure
Standard stovetop: 45 to 55 minutes

6 cups water or vegetable stock
1 tablespoon oil (to control foaming)
2 cups black-eyed peas, picked over and rinsed
1 small bunch (about 1 pound) collard greens
2 large onions, peeled and coarsely chopped
2 ribs celery, finely chopped
4 large cloves garlic, peeled and finely minced
½ teaspoon dried thyme
Pinch cayenne or crushed red pepper flakes
Sea salt or miso to taste

1. Bring the water, oil, and peas to the boil in the cooker. Meanwhile, thoroughly wash the collards. Discard any thick, tough stems and discolored leaves. Chop the remaining leaves and stems into 1-inch strips. Add the collards, onions, celery, garlic, thyme, and cayenne to the cooker.

2. Lock the lid into place. Over high heat bring to high pressure. Lower the heat to maintain the pressure at high and cook for 10 minutes. Reduce pressure with a quick-release method. Remove the lid, tilting it away from you to allow any excess steam to escape. If the peas are not quite done, return to high pressure for another minute or two.

3. Stir in salt or miso to taste.

Standard Stovetop: In a large soup pot, proceed as directed in step 1. Bring to the boil, reduce heat and simmer, covered, until the peas are tender, about 45 to 55 minutes. Follow step 3.

Cook's Notes: Like lentils, black-eyed peas cook quickly and do not require presoaking.

Variations
- Use 1 to 2 large leeks (including the greens), thinly sliced, instead of the onions.
- Try finely chopped mustard greens or kale to replace the collards. Since these greens take less time to cook, add them at the end and simmer until cooked, about 3 to 5 minutes for the mustard greens and 5 to 8 minutes for the kale.

Aduki Bean Soup
with Chestnuts and Apricots

Serves 6

A wonderfully colorful, festive soup with the sweet-tart hint of apricots and the luscious richness of chestnuts.

Pressure cooker: 15 minutes high pressure
Standard stovetop: 60 to 90 minutes

1 cup dried, peeled chestnuts, soaked 4 to 8 hours in the cooker in 5 cups water
2 cups aduki beans, picked over and rinsed, soaked 4 to 8 hours in ample water to cover, drained and rinsed
1 tablespoon safflower or canola oil
1 large onion, peeled and coarsely chopped
2 large carrots, cut into 1-inch chunks
2 ribs celery, finely chopped
¼ cup tightly packed minced dried apricots
¼ to ½ teaspoon ground cardamom
Sea salt to taste

GARNISH
Freshly grated nutmeg

1. Lift the chestnuts up with a slotted spoon and cut them in half. Return them to the pot. Discard any loose chestnut skins. Bring the chestnuts and their soaking water to the boil as you prepare and add all remaining ingredients except salt to the cooker.

2. Lock the lid into place. Over high heat bring to high pressure. Lower the heat to maintain the pressure at high and cook for 15 minutes. Reduce pressure with a quick-release method. Remove the lid, tilting it away from you to allow any excess steam to escape. If the beans are not quite soft, return to high pressure for a few more minutes.

3. Add salt to taste. Stir well. Pour into a tureen or individual serving bowls, and sprinkle with a few gratings of nutmeg.

Standard Stovetop: In a large soup pot, proceed as directed in step 1. (Eliminate the oil if you wish.) Bring to the boil, reduce heat and simmer, covered, until the aduki beans and chestnuts are tender, about 60 to 90 minutes. Follow step 3.

Cook's Notes: Sometimes I create a thicker soup by pureeing about ½ cup of the beans and stirring them back in.

Garlicky Chick-pea Soup with Greens

Serves 4 to 6

Fans of chick-peas and garlic will find this irresistible: Three tablespoons of chopped garlic suffuse the soup with lovely flavor; 4 tablespoons create paradise for the impassioned. A hint of orange peel adds a surprising lilt.

This soup is a meal in itself.

Pressure cooker: 16 to 18 minutes high pressure, optional natural pressure release, 2 to 8 minutes simmering
Standard stovetop: 90 minutes

1½ cups dried chick-peas, picked over and rinsed, soaked 8 hours in
ample water to cover
1 to 2 tablespoons olive oil
3 to 4 tablespoons finely chopped garlic (make sure it's fresh and
unblemished)
1 large leek (white and green parts), carefully rinsed and thinly sliced
(2 cups), or 1 large onion, peeled and coarsely chopped
6 cups water
2 large carrots, cut into ½-inch slices
2 large ribs celery, cut into ½-inch slices
1¼ teaspoons dried oregano
¼ teaspoon dried rosemary leaves
2 bay leaves
½ pound beet greens, spinach, Swiss chard, escarole, or kale, finely
chopped
2 to 3 teaspoons finely minced orange peel (colored part only, preferably
organic; optional but yummy)
Sea salt to taste

1. Drain the chick-peas and discard any loose skins. Set aside. Heat the oil in the cooker and sauté the garlic and leek for 1 minute, stirring frequently. Add the water, reserved chick-peas, carrots, celery, oregano, rosemary, and bay leaves.

2. Lock the lid into place. Over high heat bring to high pressure. Lower the heat just enough to maintain high pressure and cook for 16 minutes (or 18 minutes if you like your chick-peas very soft). Allow the pressure to come down naturally or use a quick-release method. Remove the lid, tilting it away from you to allow any excess steam to escape. If the chick-peas are not sufficiently tender, return to high pressure for a few minutes or simmer covered until done.

continued

3. Remove the bay leaves and stir in the greens, orange peel (if using), and salt. Gently simmer, uncovered, until the greens are cooked, about 2 to 3 minutes for beet greens, spinach, and chard, and about 5 to 8 minutes for escarole and kale.

Standard Stovetop: In a large soup pot, proceed as directed in step 1. Bring to the boil, reduce heat, and simmer covered for 1 hour, then partially covered until the chick-peas are very tender, about a half hour longer. Follow step 3.

Cook's Notes: You can create a very thick soup by pureeing about a cupful of chick-peas before adding the greens, then stirring them back into the pot.

Eating is an agricultural act. Eating ends the annual drama of the food economy that begins with planting and birth. Most eaters, however, are no longer aware that this is true. They think of food as an agricultural product, perhaps, but they do not think of themselves as participants in agriculture.
　　　　—Wendell Berry, "The Pleasures of Eating,"
　　　　in Robert Clark, ed., *Our Sustainable Table* (Berkeley: North Point Press, 1990).

Squash-Aduki-Corn Chowder

A delicate soup sporting the colors of fall. The squash becomes meltingly soft, its bright orange dotting the sea of red aduki beans and yellow corn.

Pressure cooker: 10 to 12 minutes high pressure, 3 to 4 minutes simmering
Standard stovetop: 60 to 90 minutes

1½ cups aduki beans, picked over and rinsed, soaked 4 to 8 hours in
    ample water to cover
1 tablespoon oil
2 medium leeks (white and green parts), carefully rinsed and thinly sliced
    (about 4 cups), or 3 cups chopped onion
4 cups water or vegetable stock
1½ pounds butternut or kabocha squash, scrubbed, seeded, and cut into
    2-inch chunks (peeling unnecessary, particularly if organic)
2 teaspoons dried tarragon or ¾ teaspoon dried thyme, approximately
2 cups fresh or frozen (defrosted) corn kernels (see Cook's Notes)
¼ cup thinly sliced scallion greens
Sea salt or tamari soy sauce to taste

1. Drain and rinse the aduki beans. Set aside. Heat the oil in the cooker and sauté the leeks for 2 minutes, stirring frequently.

2. Add the water, adukis, squash, and tarragon.

3. Lock the lid into place. Over high heat bring to high pressure. Lower the heat just enough to maintain high pressure and cook for 10 minutes. Allow the pressure to come down naturally or use a quick-release method. Remove the lid, tilting it away from you to allow any excess steam to escape. If the adukis are not tender, return to high pressure for a few more minutes, or simmer covered until done.

4. Stir in the corn, scallions, and salt to taste. Add a bit more dried herb, if desired. Simmer, uncovered, until the corn is tender, about 3 to 4 minutes.

Standard Stovetop: In a large soup pot, proceed as directed in steps 1 and 2. Bring to the boil, reduce heat and simmer, covered, until the adukis are tender, about 60 to 90 minutes. Follow step 4.

Cook's Notes: If you are using fresh corn kernels, cook the stripped cobs with the soup for extra flavor; remove them before serving. For a thicker soup, puree a cupful of the adukis and stir them back into the pot.

White Bean Soup with Escarole Serves 6 to 8

Escarole is a light green leafy vegetable related to endive. It has a slightly bitter taste, which is much loved by Italians. I love it, too.

Pressure cooker: 12 to 15 minutes high pressure, 10 minutes simmering
Standard stovetop: 60 to 90 minutes

*1 cup dried cannellini or Great Northern beans, picked over and rinsed,
    soaked 4 to 8 hours in ample water to cover*
1 to 2 tablespoons olive oil
1 large onion, peeled and coarsely chopped
4 large cloves garlic, peeled and finely chopped
3 ribs celery, finely chopped
1 large carrot, finely chopped
6 cups water
¼ cup tightly packed minced fresh parsley
1½ to 2 teaspoons fennel seeds
1 head escarole (about 12 ounces), coarsely chopped
2 tablespoons Tomato Paste (page 306, optional)
¼ cup tightly packed minced fresh basil or 1 tablespoon dried basil
Sea salt and freshly ground pepper to taste

1. Drain and rinse the beans. Set aside. Heat the oil in the cooker and sauté the onion and garlic for 3 minutes, stirring frequently. Stir in the beans, celery, carrot, water, parsley, and fennel seeds. If using dried basil, add it at this time.

2. Lock the lid into place. Over high heat bring to high pressure. Lower the heat just enough to maintain the pressure at high and cook for 12 minutes. Allow the pressure to come down naturally or reduce pressure with a quick-release method. Remove the lid, tilting it away from you to allow any excess steam to escape. If the beans are not tender, return to pressure for a few more minutes or simmer, covered, until done.

3. Stir in the escarole, tomato paste (if using), and fresh basil. Add salt and pepper to taste. Simmer with the lid slightly ajar until the escarole is tender, about 10 minutes.

Standard Stovetop: In a large soup pot, proceed as directed in step 1. Bring to the boil, reduce heat and simmer, covered, until the beans are tender, about 60 to 90 minutes. Follow step 3.

Variation: You can substitute almost any green for the escarole. Try 1 pound of spinach, trimmed and coarsely chopped, or ½ pound kale or mustard greens, finely chopped. Cook the greens just until tender.

Lima Bean Vegetable Soup

Little flecks of quinoa and the faint licorice taste of fennel give this luscious vegetable soup an exotic twist. The mixture thickens considerably on standing; thin as needed with a little extra water or vegetable stock.

Pressure cooker: 7 minutes high pressure, 2 to 3 minutes simmering
Standard stovetop: 40 to 50 minutes

*1 cup baby limas, picked over and rinsed, soaked 4 to 8 hours in ample
water to cover*
5 cups water
1 tablespoon oil (to control foaming; see Cook's Notes)
2 large carrots, cut into 1-inch slices
3 large ribs celery, cut into ½-inch slices
1 large onion, peeled and coarsely chopped
*½ cup (½ ounce) loosely packed dried mushrooms, swished in a bowl of
water to remove sand, then drained*
½ cup quinoa, thoroughly rinsed (page 95)
½ teaspoon fennel seeds
1 bay leaf
Sea salt or light miso to taste

1. Drain the soaked limas and rinse them. Discard any loose skins. Place the limas and all of the remaining ingredients except the salt in the cooker.

2. Lock the lid into place. Over high heat bring to high pressure. Lower the heat just enough to maintain the pressure at high and cook for 7 minutes. Reduce pressure with a quick-release method. Remove the lid, tilting it away from you to allow any excess steam to escape.

3. Remove the bay leaf and add salt or miso to taste. Simmer for 2 to 3 minutes before serving.

Standard Stovetop: In a large soup pot, proceed as directed in step 1, adding all ingredients except quinoa and salt. Bring to the boil, reduce heat and simmer, covered, for 20 minutes. Add the quinoa, cover, and continue to simmer until the limas and quinoa are tender, about 20 to 30 additional minutes. Follow step 3.

Cook's Notes: Please don't be tempted to omit the oil when pressure-cooking this soup: It controls the foaming action of the limas. You can eliminate the oil for standard stovetop cooking.

continued

Variations

- For extra color and taste, cook 1 to 2 stripped corncobs with the soup and add the fresh corn kernels when you stir in the salt. Simmer the soup an additional few minutes until the corn is tender-crisp.
- Add some finely chopped beet greens or spinach at the end of cooking, and simmer until tender, about 2 to 3 minutes.

Green Split-Pea Soup with Parsnips   Serves 6 to 8

Parsnips—the unsung heroes of the soup pot—add a subtle sweetness to this hearty pea soup.

Pressure cooker: 6 minutes high pressure
Standard stovetop: 30 to 40 minutes

1 tablespoon oil
1 large onion, peeled and finely chopped
1 large clove garlic, peeled and finely chopped
1 tablespoon whole cumin seeds
2 tablespoons freshly grated ginger
2 teaspoons ground coriander seeds
6 cups water
2 cups green split peas, picked over and rinsed
3 slender parsnips, cut into 2-inch chunks
Sea salt and freshly ground pepper to taste

1. Heat the oil in the cooker and sauté the onion and garlic for 2 minutes, stirring frequently. Stir in the cumin, ginger, and coriander and sauté an additional 10 seconds. Add the water (watch for sputtering oil!), split peas, and parsnips.

2. Lock the lid into place. Over high heat bring to high pressure. Lower the heat just enough to maintain the pressure at high and cook for 6 minutes. Reduce pressure with a quick-release method. (If much sputtering occurs, let the pressure come down naturally or set the cooker under cold running water.) Remove the lid, tilting it away from you to allow any excess steam to escape.

3. Stir in salt and pepper to taste and simmer a few minutes. If the soup is too thick, thin it slightly with water or vegetable stock.

Standard Stovetop: In a large soup pot, proceed as directed in step 1. Bring to the boil, reduce heat and simmer, covered, until the peas are soft, about 30 to 40 minutes. Follow step 3.

Curried Yellow Split-Pea Soup with Squash and Raisins

Serves 6 to 8

Split peas marry beautifully with Indian seasonings and the sweetness of squash and raisins.

> **Pressure cooker:** 6 minutes high pressure
> **Standard stovetop:** 30 minutes

1 tablespoon oil
1 large onion, peeled and coarsely chopped
2 tablespoons freshly grated ginger
2 ribs celery, thinly sliced
1½ pounds butternut or kabocha squash, scrubbed, seeded, and cut into
1-inch chunks (peeling not necessary, particularly if organic)
2 cups yellow or green split peas, picked over and rinsed
⅓ cup raisins
6 cups water
1 tablespoon plus 1 teaspoon mild curry powder
¾ to 1 teaspoon fennel seeds
¾ teaspoon ground cinnamon
1 bay leaf
1 teaspoon sea salt, or to taste

1. Heat the oil in the cooker and sauté the onion and ginger for 2 minutes. Stir in all of the remaining ingredients except the salt.

2. Lock the lid into place. Over high heat bring to high pressure. Lower the heat just enough to maintain high pressure and cook for 6 minutes. Reduce pressure with a quick-release method. (If much sputtering occurs, let the pressure come down naturally or set the cooker under cold running water.) Remove the lid, tilting it away from you to allow any excess steam to escape.

3. Add salt, remove the bay leaf, and simmer for a few moments. Stir well and thin with additional water if necessary.

Standard Stovetop: In a large soup pot, proceed as directed in step 1. Bring to the boil, reduce heat and simmer, covered, until the peas are very soft, about 30 minutes. Follow step 3.

Variation: Substitute an equal amount of red lentils for the split peas.

Multibean Minestrone

A good recipe for all those little bits left in various bean bags. Soak all of the beans together, then pressure-cook the soup until the longest-cooking bean is done (check the bean cooking chart on page 175 for timing). Avoid lentils, black-eyed peas, split peas, and other quick-cooking beans.

This soup is full of good flavor—a meal in itself.

Pressure cooker: 12 to 14 minutes high pressure, 5 to 10 minutes simmering
Standard stovetop: 75 to 90 minutes

1 cup mixed beans, picked over and rinsed, soaked 4 to 8 hours in ample
    water to cover
1 tablespoon olive oil
2 cups coarsely chopped onions or leeks (white and green parts)
2 large cloves garlic, peeled and finely chopped
6 cups water
2 large carrots, cut into 1-inch slices
2 large ribs celery, cut into ½-inch slices
½ cup (½ ounce) loosely packed dried mushrooms, swooshed in a bowl of
    water to remove sand, then drained
2 bay leaves
1½ teaspoons dried oregano
¾ teaspoon fennel seeds
½ teaspoon dried thyme or marjoram
½ teaspoon dried rosemary leaves
Generous pinch crushed red pepper flakes
2 cups coarsely chopped tomatoes, preferably plum tomatoes
½ cup small uncooked pasta (such as elbows; optional)
2 cups shredded cabbage
½ pound green beans, trimmed and cut into thirds
1 cup fresh or frozen (defrosted) corn kernels (see Cook's Notes)
1 to 2 tablespoons balsamic vinegar
1½ to 2 teaspoons sea salt, or to taste
Plenty of freshly ground black pepper

OPTIONAL GARNISH
Parsley Pesto or Coriander Pesto (pages 185 and 298)

1. Drain and rinse the beans and set aside. Heat the oil in the cooker and sauté the onions and garlic for 2 minutes. Add the water carefully (watch for sputtering oil!), reserved beans, carrots, celery, mushrooms, bay leaves, oregano, fennel, thyme, rosemary, and crushed red pepper flakes.

2. Lock the lid in place and over high heat bring to high pressure. Lower the heat just enough to maintain high pressure and cook for approximately 12 minutes (or for the length of time required by the longest-cooking bean). Allow the pressure to come down naturally, or use a quick-release method. Remove the lid, tilting it away from you to allow any excess steam to escape. If the beans require more cooking, either return to high pressure for another 2 to 3 minutes or simmer, covered, until done.

3. When the beans are tender, stir in the tomatoes and pasta (if using) and cook until pasta is half done (check package for timing). Then add the cabbage, green beans, corn, and just enough vinegar to make the flavors pop. Add salt and pepper to taste and simmer until the vegetables and pasta are tender, about 4 to 5 minutes. Remove the bay leaves and corncob (if used; see Cook's Notes) before serving. Pass the pesto (if using) in a small bowl at the table or set a dollop on top of each portion.

Standard Stovetop: In a large soup pot, proceed as directed in step 1. Bring to the boil, reduce heat and simmer, covered, until the beans are tender, about 75 to 90 minutes. Follow step 3.

Cook's Notes: If using fresh corn, cut off the kernels with a serrated knife and set them aside. Add the corncob to the soup pot at the beginning of cooking for added flavor.

Variations

- For beautiful color and a nice touch of sweetness, add ½ pound butternut squash, cut into ½-inch cubes, with the fresh vegetables.
- Try diced zucchini as a replacement for the green beans.
- Substitute ½ pound sliced, fresh mushrooms for the dried mushrooms.
- Add ½ pound chopped beet greens, spinach, or chard to the other fresh vegetables or use instead of cabbage.
- Puree 3 to 4 cloves of roasted garlic and stir into the cooked soup.

I have always believed that a restaurant can be no better than the ingredients it has to work with. . . . As a restaurant, we are utterly dependent on the health of the land, the sea, and the planet as a whole, and [the] search for good ingredients is pointless without a healthy agriculture and a healthy environment.

—Alice Waters,
"The Farm-Restaurant Connection,"
in Robert Clark, ed., *Our Sustainable Table*
(Berkeley: North Point Press, 1990).

Fruited Lentil Soup

Fruited Lentil Soup first made an appearance in *Cooking Under Pressure* as Lentil Soup with Prunes and Pears. This slightly revised version cuts the cooking time by two thirds and turns up the spices a few notches.

Pressure cooker: 7 minutes high pressure
Standard stovetop: 40 to 50 minutes

6 cups water
2 cups dried brown lentils, picked over and rinsed
1 tablespoon olive or canola oil (to control foaming)
1¼ teaspoons ground coriander seeds
¼ teaspoon ground cloves
1 cup pitted prunes, halved
3 ripe pears, peeled, cored, and cut into large chunks
1 teaspoon sea salt, or to taste

1. Pour the water into the cooker and set it over high heat as you prepare and add the lentils, oil, coriander seeds, cloves, prunes, and pears.

2. Lock the lid into place. Over high heat bring to high pressure. Lower the heat just enough to maintain high pressure and cook for 7 minutes. Reduce the pressure with a quick-release method. Remove the lid, tilting it away from you to allow any excess steam to escape.

3. Add salt to taste and thin with a bit of water if the soup is too thick.

Standard Stovetop: In a large soup pot, proceed as directed in step 1, adding all of the ingredients except the pears and salt. Bring to the boil, reduce heat and simmer, covered, for 15 minutes. Add the pears and continue to simmer, covered, until they and the lentils are very soft, about 25 to 35 minutes. Follow step 3.

Variations
- Substitute apricots for the prunes and apples for the pears.
- Add a cinnamon stick, broken in two.

What this power is, I cannot say. All I know is that it exists . . . and it becomes available only when you are in that state of mind in which you know exactly what you want . . . and are fully determined not to quit until you get it.

—Alexander Graham Bell

Quick Lentil Soup with Chestnuts   Serves 4

The ingredients for this fine dish are easy to keep on hand, and the complex taste belies the ease of preparation. The chestnuts add a subtle sweetness and smokiness, perfectly complementing the peppery brown lentils.

Pressure cooker: 7 minutes high pressure
Standard stovetop: 35 to 40 minutes

½ cup dried chestnuts, soaked about 8 hours in the cooker in 3 cups water
1½ cups brown lentils, picked over and rinsed
1 tablespoon olive or canola oil (to control foaming)
3 cups additional water
2 large carrots, cut into ½-inch slices
1 medium onion, peeled and coarsely chopped
½ teaspoon ground cinnamon
⅛ to ¼ teaspoon ground cardamom (optional)
Sea salt to taste

1. Remove any dark brown skins that have floated to the top or are still clinging to the soaked chestnuts, and discard them. Drain the chestnuts, reserving the soaking liquid. With a large chef's knife, cut the chestnuts into quarters. (To cut the hard ones, pound on the top edge of the knife with your fist.) Place the chestnuts, soaking water, lentils, oil, additional water, carrots, onion, cinnamon, and cardamom (if using) in the cooker.

2. Lock the lid into place. Over high heat bring to high pressure. Lower the heat just enough to maintain high pressure and cook for 7 minutes. Allow the pressure to come down naturally or reduce pressure with a quick-release method. Remove the lid, tilting it away from you to allow any excess steam to escape.

3. Add salt to taste before serving.

Standard Stovetop: In a large soup pot, proceed as directed in step 1. Bring to the boil, reduce heat and simmer, covered, until the lentils and chestnuts are soft, about 35 to 40 minutes. Follow step 3.

Lentil Soup Italiano Serves 6

Imprinting the lentils with traditional Italian seasonings—garlic, thyme, oregano, crushed red pepper, and tomato—gives them a totally different character than they have in the previous soup recipe.

Pressure cooker: 7 minutes high pressure, 2 to 3 minutes simmering
Standard stovetop: 35 to 40 minutes

6 cups water
2 cups brown lentils, picked over and rinsed
1 tablespoon olive oil
1 large onion, peeled and coarsely chopped
2 large cloves garlic, peeled and minced
4 ribs celery, cut into 1-inch slices
2 large carrots, chunked
¼ pound mushrooms, sliced
2 bay leaves
1 teaspoon dried thyme or marjoram
¾ teaspoon dried oregano
Pinch crushed red pepper flakes
3 tablespoons Tomato Paste (page 306) or 2 large tomatoes,
*   coarsely chopped*
1 to 2 tablespoons balsamic vinegar
Sea salt to taste

GARNISH
¼ cup finely minced parsley or watercress

1. Combine all ingredients except tomato paste, vinegar, and salt in the cooker.

2. Lock the lid into place. Over high heat bring to high pressure. Lower the heat just enough to maintain high pressure and cook for 7 minutes. Reduce pressure with a quick-release method. Remove the lid, tilting it away from you to allow any excess steam to escape.

3. Remove the bay leaves. Dissolve the tomato paste (if using) in a cup of the soup and stir this mixture back into the pot. Alternatively, add the tomatoes. Stir in enough vinegar to perk up the flavors. Add salt to taste, if needed. Simmer for 2 to 3 minutes. Transfer soup to a serving bowl and garnish with parsley or watercress.

Standard Stovetop: In a large soup pot, proceed as directed in step 1. Bring to the boil, reduce heat and simmer, covered, until the lentils are tender, 35 to 40 minutes. Follow step 3.

Cook's Notes: To create a slightly richer, more complex soup, sauté the onions and garlic in 1 to 2 tablespoons of olive oil before adding the other ingredients.

Variation: After overnight refrigeration, the soup will thicken considerably and can be transformed into a spread. Puree with mustard to taste and additional herbs or vinegar as needed. You can stretch the amount by blending in a few tablespoons of soft tofu.

Hot and Zesty Black Bean Soup **Serves 4 to 6**

A simple soup with a Southwestern flair. For an elegant presentation, place a dollop of Roasted Red Pepper Sauce (page 301) in the center of each portion and swirl it through gently to create an orange ribbon.

Pressure cooker: 10 to 12 minutes high pressure, optional natural pressure release
Standard stovetop: about 90 minutes

2 cups black beans, soaked 4 to 8 hours in ample water to cover
1 tablespoon olive oil
1 large onion, peeled and coarsely chopped
4 large cloves garlic, peeled and finely chopped
1 fresh jalapeño pepper, trimmed and thinly sliced (wear rubber gloves
        when handling), or generous pinch crushed red pepper flakes
1½ to 2 teaspoons whole cumin seeds
2 teaspoons dried leaf oregano
½ teaspoon ground cinnamon
5 cups water
2 large carrots, thickly sliced
3 large ribs celery, thickly sliced
2 bay leaves
2 teaspoons sea salt, or to taste
Mesquite or hickory smoke flavoring, or hot sauce to taste (optional)

OPTIONAL GARNISHES
⅔ cup Roasted Red Pepper Sauce (page 301)
¼ cup minced fresh coriander or parsley

continued

1. Drain the beans, rinse, and set aside. Heat the oil in the cooker and sauté the onion, garlic, and jalapeño or crushed red pepper for 2 minutes, stirring frequently. Add the cumin, oregano, and cinnamon, and sauté another minute. Add the water (watch for sputtering oil!), reserved beans, carrots, celery, and bay leaves.

2. Lock the lid in place and over high heat bring to high pressure. Lower the heat just enough to maintain high pressure and cook for 10 minutes. Allow the pressure to come down naturally or use a quick-release method. Remove the lid, tilting it away from you to allow any excess steam to escape. If the beans are not cooked, return to high pressure for another minute or two.

3. When the beans are tender, remove the bay leaves and stir in salt and a drop or two of mesquite smoke flavoring or hot sauce (if using). Puree 1 to 2 cups or more of the soup, depending upon if you want it chunky or smooth. Return the puree to the cooker and simmer another 1 to 2 minutes to reheat thoroughly before serving. Garnish with roasted red pepper sauce or fresh coriander, if desired.

Standard Stovetop: In a large soup pot, proceed as directed in step 1. Bring to the boil, reduce heat and simmer, covered, until the beans are very soft, about 90 minutes. Follow step 3.

Cook's Notes: Since the heat of jalapeño peppers is variable, the soup may not be hot enough for you. If so, add a pinch of cayenne before serving, or set some hot sauce on the table for those who like a tongue-lashing with their black beans.

Cold Soups

When it's ninety degrees in the shade, every cook's mind turns to cooling foods, and there is perhaps no more refreshing hot weather meal than a chilled soup. It quenches thirst, hunger, and heat all at the same time and brings you a taste redolent of summer's harvest.

In addition to the three recipes that follow, Creamy Cauliflower Soup (page 33) and Heavenly Carrot Soup (page 38) are delicious served cold.

Gazpacho

Serves 4 to 6

Perhaps the most famous cold soup of all is the Spanish "liquid salad" known as gazpacho. At its best, it is a truly great summer soup that wakes up a hot and tired palate with its unforgettable contrasts of flavor and texture. The secret, of course, is using vine-ripened tomatoes that are bursting with flavor. What follows is one of my favorite versions.

3 large ripe beefsteak tomatoes (about 1½ pounds), peeled, cored,
    and quartered
1 large cucumber, peeled, halved, and seeded (see Cook's Notes)
1 rib celery, cut into chunks
1 small green bell pepper, seeded and cut into eighths
1 small red bell pepper, seeded and cut into eighths
2 to 3 tablespoons finely chopped Spanish or Vidalia onion
3 tablespoons fruity olive oil
1 cup tomato juice, approximately
2 to 3 tablespoons finely minced parsley
1 small clove garlic, peeled and finely minced (optional)
1 teaspoon red wine vinegar, approximately
Sea salt and freshly ground pepper to taste

GARNISH
Whole Grain Herb-Garlic Croutons (page 419)

continued

1. In a food processor, combine all of the ingredients, using the pulsing action to create a coarse puree. (For a smoother gazpacho, spin the processor at full speed or use the blender.)

2. Add extra tomato juice, if needed, to thin the soup. Add sufficient vinegar to perk up the flavors.

3. Chill well before serving, garnished with croutons.

Cook's Notes: If Kirby cucumbers are available, opt for 2 small ones instead of the 1 large one called for in the recipe. Kirbies are sweet, dense in texture, and don't need to be seeded. An added bonus is that they are generally unwaxed.

Every choice we make that consciously aligns our daily life with our vision of a better future makes us more powerful people. We feel less victimized. . . . The less victimized we are by forces outside us, the freer we become. For freedom is not the capacity to do whatever we please; freedom is the capacity to make intelligent choices.

—Frances Moore Lappe, *Diet for a Small Planet*
(New York: Ballantine, 1982).

Creamy Sorrel Soup

Sorrel is also known as sour grass, and with good reason—it has the puckery tartness of lemon. There's nothing like it to cut through the heat of a hot summer's day.

Pressure cooker: 4 minutes high pressure, optional natural pressure release
Standard stovetop: 20 minutes

3½ cups water
¾ pound sorrel, stripped of thick stems and browned leaf tips
1 large onion, peeled and coarsely chopped
3 medium (1¼ pounds) thin-skinned potatoes, scrubbed and coarsely
    chopped
2 ribs celery, thinly sliced
2 large carrots, coarsely chopped
½ to 1 teaspoon sea salt, or to taste

GARNISH
½ cup finely chopped, peeled cucumber

1. Place the water in the cooker and over high heat begin bringing to the boil as you prepare and add the remaining ingredients.

2. Lock the lid in place and over high heat bring to high pressure. Lower the heat just enough to maintain the pressure at high and cook for 4 minutes. Use a quick-release method or allow the pressure to come down naturally. Remove the lid, tilting it away from you to allow any excess steam to escape.

3. Allow the soup to cool slightly. Puree in a blender (preferred for a smoother texture), food processor, or food mill. While still warm, add salt as desired. Cool to room temperature, then chill before serving.

Standard Stovetop: In a large soup pot, proceed as directed in step 1. Bring to the boil, reduce heat and simmer, covered, until potatoes and carrots are quite soft, about 20 minutes. Follow step 3.

Cook's Notes: Sorrel soup loses tartness when frozen. If you freeze leftovers, add a tablespoon or two of freshly squeezed lemon juice before serving.

Vichyssoise (Potato-Leek Soup)

Serves 6 to 8

This classic always is a hit. Serve it hot for a warming opener to a winter meal; serve it chilled to refresh on a hot summer's night.

For a luscious creamy texture (without a drop of cream!), use thin-skinned potatoes instead of Idaho baking potatoes.

Pressure cooker: 4 minutes high pressure, 10-minute natural pressure release
Standard stovetop: 25 minutes

1 tablespoon olive oil
3 large leeks (white part plus 3 inches of green), thinly sliced, thoroughly
    rinsed to remove all sand, and drained (6 cups)
1½ pounds (6 medium) thin-skinned potatoes, scrubbed or peeled
    (for a lighter-colored soup), and coarsely chopped
2 ribs celery, thinly sliced
4 cups water
¼ cup finely minced fresh parsley
3 teaspoons dried tarragon
1 teaspoon sea salt, or to taste
Freshly ground black pepper
Additional sea salt or tamari soy sauce

GARNISH
⅓ cup chopped chives or thinly sliced scallion greens

1. Heat the oil in the cooker. Sauté the leeks for 2 minutes, stirring frequently.
2. Add the potatoes, celery, water, parsley, tarragon, and salt.
3. Lock the lid in place and over high heat bring to high pressure. Lower the heat just enough to maintain high pressure and cook for 4 minutes. Allow the pressure to come down naturally for 10 minutes. Remove the lid, tilting it away from you to allow any excess steam to escape.
4. Puree the soup in 2 to 3 batches in a blender (preferred for a silky-smooth texture) or a food processor. (Do not overprocess or the soup may become gummy.) Add black pepper and salt or tamari to taste (see Cook's Notes). Return to the pot to rewarm or let cool to room temperature and then chill thoroughly.
5. Garnish with the chopped chives or scallions.

Standard Stovetop: In a large soup pot, follow steps 1 and 2. Bring to the boil, cover, reduce heat and simmer until the potatoes are very soft, about 25 minutes. Follow steps 4 and 5.

Cook's Notes: For a pretty effect, pour a few drops of tamari in the middle of each portion of soup and swirl it lightly to create a pattern.

Amber Waves of Grain

Those amber waves of grain that make America beautiful may be primarily wheat and corn, but the shelves of any well-stocked health food store quickly reveal that a magnificent array of cereal grains is now available to us. Since each grain has a different nutritional profile, eating a variety ensures a well-balanced diet and more fun at the dinner table.

In addition to rice, barley, corn, and oats, there are such exotic imports as teff from Ethiopia, quinoa and amaranth from the Andes, and Job's Tears from China. More recently, the "new ancient" grains known as spelt and kamut have been revived, much to the delight of those with wheat sensitivities.

Although grains are easy to become acquainted with, each has its own special characteristics. Rather than overwhelming yourself by trying out many new varieties at once, why not focus on one or two and then branch out as the spirit moves you. You'll be amazed at how quickly whole grains become a regular part of your diet. I find that if I let a day of two go by without brown rice or quinoa, I feel as if I haven't really been eating. And once you get used to whole foods, your body becomes less willing to settle for anything less.

It becomes fun to cook and eat grains if you can relax and accept the fact that they never come out precisely the same way twice. The amount of time it takes for a grain to cook, the quantity of water it absorbs, how fluffy your final product will be—all of these factors depend upon the age of the grain and the conditions under which it has been grown and stored.

Having said all that, I can now reassure you that by following the basic recipes in this chapter, you will have very respectable results every time. If one batch falls short of ideal, adjust the liquid or cooking time slightly to meet your particular requirements the next time.

The Anatomy of the Whole Grain

Most of the foods that we commonly call grains are actually the edible seeds of plants in the grass family. These seeds (kernels) are loaded with nutrients—so much so that they have provided the backbone of the human diet for millennia.

Each kernel of grain is made up of four parts:

1. The *outer husk (hull)* is a hard inedible covering that protects the seed. It is removed by grinding or threshing.

2. Beneath the husk is the *bran*, which offers a few additional layers of protection and is an excellent source of minerals and B vitamins as well as fiber.

3. Beneath the bran is the *germ*, which holds the life force of each kernel and is rich in protein, enzymes, and oil. The germ also contains some vitamins and minerals.

4. The *endosperm* is the starchy center of each grain and is primarily made up of carbohydrates.

Since whole grains contain the bran, germ, and endosperm, while such refined grains as white rice, couscous, or pearl barley are the endosperm alone, a dramatic loss of nutrients occurs when whole grains are refined.

Buying Grains

I was amazed the first time I tasted organically grown and recently harvested millet. I had purchased it from a mail-order source on the strong recommendation of a knowledgeable colleague. I am not exaggerating when I tell you that this millet bore little resemblance to the stuff that had been occupying space in my cupboard over the previous six months. It was sweet and delicate, with none of the faintly bitter aftertaste that I had come to associate with this grain.

Whole grains are living foods that must be handled with respect. If they aren't, the oils (located primarily in the germ) will quickly go rancid. We are so accustomed to leaving our white rice and pearl barley indefinitely on the pantry shelf that it takes some adjustment to remember that grains with their germs intact have different storage requirements.

If this were the best of all possible worlds, every health food store would refrigerate its entire stock of whole grains, but I have never been in one that does; it's just too expensive. The best that most of us can hope for is to shop in a clean establishment that is air conditioned in the hot weather and has a quick turnover. If you are dubious about the freshness of the grains sold in your local health food store, consider mail-ordering grains from a reputable source (see page 475). And go for organic grains whenever possible: You'll be as amazed as I was by the difference in quality and taste—a strong indicator of enhanced nutritional value.

Storing Grains

The best way to keep grains is to freeze them in Ziploc bags, which you can use over and over. Label each with the date of purchase. They will remain fresh for 4 to 5 months. You can also store the grains in the refrigerator for up to 4 months. It's not a good idea to store them at room temperature for more than a week or two, especially in hot weather.

To test the freshness of whole grains presently in your cupboard, open the bags and take a sniff. Fresh grains should have either no smell or a faint sweet aroma. Toss them out if they give off a slightly musty odor. Grains that appear to be clinging together indicate the imminent arrival of baby moths. Although theoretically moth eggs are harmless and can be rinsed off, my inclination is to throw out the grains.

Cooking Whole Grains

Rinsing

Unlike white rice, which has been cleaned as part of the refining process, whole grains *must be rinsed thoroughly* to remove dust and any natural coatings that may impart a bitter taste. For many packaged grains, one good dousing will suffice; grains bought in bulk often require more vigorous rinsing. Clean only the amount of grain that you are planning to cook.

Here is an efficient and effective way to clean grains:

1. Measure the amount of grain you need.
2. Pour the grain into a strainer and plunge the strainer up and down about ten times in a large bowl filled with cold water. If the grain is very dirty, twirl it around with your fingers while it is immersed. Lift out the strainer and throw out the water.
3. Fill the bowl with clean water and repeat the process of plunging and replacing the water until the water remains almost clear. (It's sometimes impossible to get the water completely clear.)
4. While twirling the grains, give them a quick rinse under cold running water.
5. Let the grains drain in the strainer while you proceed with the recipe.

Optional Pretoasting

Before pressure-cooking or boiling grains, you have the option of browning them in a heavy skillet or in your cooking pot, if it is heavy-bottomed enough to prevent scorching. Browning brings out the nutty quality of grains. It also opens their pores, allowing the grains to absorb liquid more readily and therefore cook more evenly through to the center.

Toasting a cup or two of grains can take as long as 10 to 15 minutes. Frankly, I think it's rarely worth the effort—with two major exceptions:

The flavor of millet is considerably improved by pretoasting. Millet also cooks more thoroughly and develops a much fluffier texture when it is pretoasted.

Pretoasting is essential for cooking Job's Tears, which otherwise end up with unpleasant hard centers and a slightly grassy taste.

The basic recipes for these two grains include the pretoasting step, and the liquid has been adjusted accordingly. If you decide to pretoast any of the other grains, add 2 to 3 more tablespoons of liquid to compensate for greater absorption. To toast grains:

1. Heat a large, heavy skillet (cast iron is ideal) over a medium flame.
2. Add the rinsed grain and stir it in figure eights with a long-handled wooden paddle until all of the rinse water has evaporated. **Note:** At this point you can add a few teaspoons of oil to the grains to hasten the toasting process slightly and coat each grain, helping to keep the cooked grains separate.
3. Lower the heat slightly and continue stirring until the grains begin to pop and emit a faint roasted aroma like popcorn. By this time, some of the grains will probably have darkened a shade or two.

Presoaking

Soaking long-cooking grains overnight reduces their cooking time approximately by half. I usually presoak wheat berries, rye berries, triticale, oat groats, and hulled barley. If you're cooking any of these grains in combination with brown rice, you must presoak them so their cooking time will be the same as the rice's. (Except for oat groats, the other whole grains will remain pleasantly chewy, offering a nice contrast to the texture of the rice; oat groats are likely to become very mushy.)

Doubling and Tripling Basic Recipes

It can be a bit tricky to double grain recipes because the amount of liquid is not automatically doubled as well. For general guidelines, refer to the Brown Rice

Cooking Chart on page 121 when cooking amounts that are larger than those indicated in the basic recipes for barley, Job's Tears, and millet. Use the White Rice Cooking Chart on page 143 when cooking larger amounts of buckwheat, cracked wheat, or couscous. See the instructions in the grain cooking chart on page 67 when preparing oat groats, triticale, spelt, kamut, rye, and wheat berries.

Cooking Tips

- If you're not using a pressure cooker, use the heaviest pot you own and be sure it has a tight-fitting lid.
- Measure the grains in a dry-cup measure (the cups that nestle inside each other) and level off the top.
- Measure the liquid using a glass measuring cup held up to eye level.
- If the grains are not sufficiently cooked when the time is up and all of the water has been absorbed, stir in a few tablespoons of boiling water. Cover the pot and continue to cook over very low heat until done.
- If there is excess water after the grains are tender, simply drain it off and return the grains to the pot to reheat them.
- If the grains burn or stick to the bottom, plan to use a heat diffuser for future batches (see page 10).

To Salt or Not to Salt

Most people prefer to cook grains with salt, which enhances flavor and is thought to improve their digestibility. Thanks to the painstaking labors of my colleague Carol Gelles, author of *The Complete Whole Grain Cookbook*, I learned that amaranth, wheat berries, triticale, and Wehani brown rice do not absorb liquid properly if salt is added during cooking. For these grains, it's best to add salt (or tamari) after cooking. All other grains cook effectively with salt.

Serving Ideas

Figure on ¾ to 1 cup of cooked grain per person. Here are some ideas for giving plain grains a face and taste lift:

- Toss them with toasted sesame seeds, coarsely chopped nuts, or fresh minced herbs.
- Top them with a sauce or salad dressing (pages 291–305).
- Stir in some tamari soy sauce or Bragg Liquid Aminos.
- Mix nuts and seasonings into moist-cooked grains, then shape into patties. Pan-fry them in a heavy skillet lightly brushed with oil, or heat them in the oven.
- Stuff grains into baked squash.
- Press moist-cooked grains into small, lightly oiled individual ramekins; run a knife along the edges and then unmold.

Storing and Reheating Cooked Grains

You can let grains cool uncovered, and store them at room temperature in the pot with the lid slightly ajar for up to 6 hours.

For longer storage, refrigeration is the best choice, although it tends to dry out and harden grains. If this happens, place them in a heatproof bowl and set the bowl on a rack in a pot over a few inches of boiling water. Set the lid in place and steam, stirring once or twice, just until the grains are rehydrated and heated through, about 2 to 3 minutes.

Chew on This

Unlike pasta or other refined foods, most of the grains in this chapter require more chewing than you may be accustomed to. Herein lies an opportunity to relax more at mealtime, slow down, and pay closer attention to what you are eating.

It takes a bit of getting used to, but well-chewed grains will reward your taste buds with a subtle sweetness and your body with good digestion and a sense of well-being.

I have come to terms with the future.
From this day onward I will walk
easy on the earth. . . . Use no more of its resources than I need.
And listen to what it is telling me.

—M. J. Slim Hooey, in *Earth Prayers*,
Elizabeth Roberts and Elias Amidon, eds.
(San Francisco: Harper, 1991).

Pressure Cooker
Grain Cooking Times at a Glance

For basic cooking instructions, see pages 63–65
and check Index under individual listings.

Grain (1 cup)	Cups Liquid	Optional Salt	Minutes under High Pressure	Yield in Cups
Amaranth	1½–1¾	½–1 t*	4 plus 10-minute npr[§]	2
Barley (hulled)	3[†]	½–1 t	35–45	3½–4
Barley (pearl)	3[†]	½–1 t	18–20	3½
Buckwheat	1¾[†]	½–1 t	3 plus 7-minute npr[§]	2
Bulgur	1½	½–1 t	5 plus 10-minute npr[§]	3
Job's Tears[‡]	2½	½–1 t	16 plus 10-minute npr[§]	3
Kamut	3[†]	½–1 t*	35–45	2¾
Millet[‡]	1¾–2¾	½–1 t	10 plus 10-minute npr[§]	3½–4
Oats (whole groats)	3[†]	½–1 t	25–30	2–2½
Quinoa	1½	½–1 t	0 plus 10-minute npr[§]	3–3½
Rye berries	3	½–1 t	25–30	2½
Spelt	3	½–1 t*	35–45	2¼
Triticale	3	½–1 t*	35–45	2–2½
Wheat berries	3	½–1 t*	35–45	2¼

*To ensure proper absorption of water, add salt after cooking.
[†]Add 1 tablespoon oil to control foaming action.
[‡]Toast before boiling.
[§]npr = natural pressure release

ECO-TIP: Soak the grains overnight and reduce cooking time by 30 to 40 percent.

Standard Stovetop
Grain Cooking Times at a Glance

*For basic cooking instructions, see pages 63–65
and check Index under individual listings.*

Grain (1 cup)	Cups Liquid	Optional Salt	Standard Cooking Time	Yield in Cups
Amaranth	2½	½–1 t*	20–25 minutes	2
Barley (hulled)	3	½–1 t	1½ hours plus 10 minutes standing	3½–4
Barley (pearl)	3	½–1 t	50 minutes plus 10 minutes standing	3½
Buckwheat	2	½–1 t	10–12 minutes plus 5 minutes standing	2
Bulgur	2	½–1 t	20 minutes plus 5 minutes standing	3
Couscous	2	½–1 t	1 minute plus 5–10 minutes standing	3
Job's Tears†	2½	½–1 t	50–60 minutes plus 5 minutes standing	3
Kamut	3	½–1 t*	2 hours plus 15 minutes standing	2¾
Millet†	2–3	½–1 t	20–25 minutes plus 5 minutes standing	3½–4
Oats (whole groats)	2¼	½–1 t	1 hour plus 10 minutes standing	2–2½
Quinoa	2	½–1 t	15 minutes plus 5 minutes standing	3–3½
Rye berries	3	½–1 t	2¼ hours plus 10 minutes standing	2½
Spelt	3	½–1 t*	2 hours plus 15 minutes standing	2¼
Triticale	3	½–1 t*	1¾ hours plus 10 minutes standing	2–2½
Wheat berries	3	½–1 t*	2 hours plus 15 minutes standing	2¼

*To ensure proper absorption of water, add salt after cooking.
†Toast before boiling.

Amaranth

While steaming away in the pot, this ancient Aztec grain releases an irresistible aroma reminiscent of its South American cousin, fresh corn. Amaranth also tastes vaguely like corn, but its texture is unique: crunchy and slightly porridgy at the same time.

Amaranth is a better source of protein and calcium than many cereal grains and is now widely available in health food stores. Unlike most other grains, it releases so much starch during cooking that it creates its own silky sauce, making it more akin to grits or risotto than to a fluffy pilaf. It's definitely an acquired taste, but one worth cultivating for its unusual flavor, texture, and high nutritional profile.

Forget about plain-cooked amaranth, at least the first time around. Add a tablespoon of freshly grated ginger or some toasted sesame seeds and snipped smoked dulse. Try it cooked with garlic and onion for a gritslike side dish (page 70) or mixed with other vegetables (page 71). Because amaranth is slightly soupy, plan to serve it in small bowls.

Two unusual details about amaranth are worth mentioning: First, it is one of the tiniest grains—about the size of mustard seeds—so it is impractical to rinse it before cooking—a fact that doesn't trouble me in the least, since packaged amaranth always seems very clean. Second, if you add salt to the cooking water, amaranth won't absorb sufficient water to become tender.

If the amaranth sticks to the bottom of the pot toward the end of cooking, simply stir in 1 to 2 tablespoons of water to loosen it. For further information on selecting, storing, and cooking, see Ingredients A to Z under Amaranth and Grains.

Our life is frittered away by detail. . . . Simplify, simplify.
—Henry David Thoreau, *Walden*, 1854.

Amaranth Grits

Here's a simple way to prepare amaranth for an unusual grain side dish. Serve these grits in small bowls, accompanied by a bean dish and a steamed green vegetable or salad.

Pressure cooker: 4 minutes high pressure, 10-minute natural pressure release
Standard stovetop: 20 to 25 minutes

1 cup amaranth
1 small clove garlic, peeled and finely chopped
1 medium onion, peeled and finely chopped
*1½ to 1¾ cups vegetable stock or water (use the larger amount if you have
    a jiggle-top cooker; see Cook's Notes)*
1 tablespoon oil (to control foaming)
Sea salt or tamari soy sauce to taste
Hot sauce to taste (optional)

GARNISH
2 plum tomatoes (preferably) or 1 large beefsteak tomato, finely chopped

1. Combine the amaranth, garlic, onion, stock, and oil in the cooker.
2. Lock the lid in place and over high heat bring to high pressure. Lower the heat just enough to maintain high pressure and cook for 4 minutes. Allow the pressure to come down naturally, about 10 minutes. Remove the lid, tilting it away from you to allow any excess steam to escape.
3. Stir well. If the mixture is too thin or the amaranth not quite tender (it should be crunchy, but not gritty or hard), boil gently while stirring constantly until thickened, about 30 seconds. Add salt or tamari to taste.
4. Stir in a few drops of hot sauce, if desired, and garnish with chopped tomatoes.

Standard Stovetop: In a heavy, 2-quart saucepan, follow step 1, using 3 cups of liquid and omitting the oil. Return to the boil, then reduce the heat and simmer, covered, until most of the liquid has been absorbed, about 20 to 25 minutes. Follow steps 3 and 4.

Cook's Notes: Since amaranth absorbs water better if salt is added after cooking, it's best to use only a lightly salted or unsalted stock.

Amaranth, Bean, and Corn Medley

Colorful, crunchy, and full of good flavor. And quite filling—a heaping half cup goes a long way. Serve with a big green salad and some steamed broccoli or Brussels sprouts.

Pressure cooker: 4 minutes high pressure, 10-minute natural pressure release
Standard stovetop: 20 minutes

1 tablespoon olive oil
1 large clove garlic, peeled and thinly sliced
½ teaspoon dried oregano
1 cup amaranth
1½ to 1¾ cups vegetable stock (use the larger amount if you have a
    jiggle-top cooker)
¾ cup cooked or frozen (defrosted) corn
¾ cup cooked beans, such as red kidneys, pintos, or Great Northern
¼ cup finely minced fresh parsley
¼ cup thinly sliced scallion greens or fresh chopped chives
Sea salt to taste

1. In the cooker, heat the oil and sauté the garlic for 30 seconds, stirring continuously. Stir in the oregano and amaranth, coating the grains with the oil.

2. Add the vegetable stock (watch for sputtering oil!).

3. Lock the lid in place and over high heat bring to high pressure. Lower the heat just enough to maintain high pressure and cook for 4 minutes. Allow the pressure to come down naturally, about 10 minutes. Remove the lid, tilting it away from you to allow any excess steam to escape.

4. Stir in the corn, beans, parsley, scallion greens, and salt to taste. If the mixture is too thin or the amaranth not quite tender (it should be crunchy, but not gritty or hard), boil gently while stirring constantly until the mixture is thickened and all of the ingredients are heated through.

Standard Stovetop: In a 2-quart saucepan, follow steps 1 and 2, using 3 cups of liquid. Return to the boil, then reduce the heat and simmer, covered, until most of the liquid has been absorbed, about 20 minutes. Follow step 4.

Barley

Barley has a sweet, mellow taste and a delightfully chewy texture. It's easy to cook as it doesn't turn to mush in a matter of seconds as some grains do. You can choose between hulled barley (only the outer husk has been removed), which is quite chewy, and pearl barley (devoid of the husk and most or all of the bran), which is less chewy and seems slightly more starchy. If you opt for pearl barley, buy the type sold in health food stores, as it usually has a thin layer of bran to protect the germ. Barley is a good source of fiber and minerals, including iron, calcium, and potassium. The less refined form of barley, the larger amount of fiber and minerals.

Barley expands considerably in cooking: 1 cup dry will produce 3 to 4 cups cooked. To prepare it plain, follow directions for Basic Wheat Berries, page 101. Also see Ingredients A to Z under Barley and Grains.

Mushroom Barley Pilaf

Serves 6

A variation of that Old World treasure, mushroom-barley soup. The recipe calls for hulled barley, the chewier and less refined cousin of pearl barley. To reduce cooking time, the barley is soaked overnight. For a pearl barley version, see Variations.

For a comforting cold-weather meal, serve soup as a first course, then Mushroom Barley Pilaf, accompanied by a steamed vegetable and a salad.

Pressure cooker: 9 minutes high pressure
Standard stovetop: 45 to 50 minutes plus 10 minutes standing

1 tablespoon oil
2 large onions, peeled and coarsely chopped
2 large cloves garlic, peeled and minced
2 cups hulled barley, rinsed and soaked overnight in 5 cups water
2 large carrots, cut into half-moons
4 ribs celery, cut into ¼-inch slices
*½ cup loosely packed (½ ounce) dried mushrooms, swooshed in water to
     remove sand (see Cook's Notes)*
2 bay leaves
¾ teaspoon sea salt, or to taste
*½ cup finely minced fresh dill, divided, or 2½ tablespoons dried dillweed
     added all at once*

1. Heat the oil in the cooker. Sauté the onions and garlic, stirring frequently, until the onions are nicely browned, about 5 to 8 minutes.

2. Add the barley with its soaking water (watch for sputtering oil!) plus the remaining ingredients except for ¼ cup of fresh dill (if using dried dill, add it all at this point). Stir well, taking care to scrape up any bits of browned onion sticking to the bottom of the cooker.

3. Lock the lid into place. Over high heat bring to high pressure. Lower the heat just enough to maintain high pressure and cook for 9 minutes. Reduce the pressure with a quick-release method. Remove the lid, tilting it away from you to allow any excess steam to escape. If the barley is not quite tender, set the lid back into place and allow it to steam in the residual heat for another few minutes.

4. When the barley is cooked, drain off any excess liquid (reserve for stock) and return the pilaf to the cooker to dry out and fluff up as you stir it over medium heat. Remove the bay leaves and stir in remaining ¼ cup of fresh dill (if using) just before serving.

Standard Stovetop: In a heavy 4-quart saucepan, follow steps 1 and 2. Bring to the boil, then reduce the heat and simmer, covered, until the barley is almost tender, about 45 minutes. Turn off the heat and let stand, covered, for 10 minutes. Follow step 4.

Cook's Notes: I usually use chopped dried mushrooms. If your dried mushrooms are whole, follow the preparation instructions for SHIITAKE MUSHROOM PILAF variation below.

Variations
- MUSHROOM PEARL BARLEY PILAF: Follow step 1. Follow step 2, using 2 cups of unsoaked pearl barley and 5 cups of water. Pressure-cook for 18 minutes under high pressure. Follow step 4.
- SHIITAKE MUSHROOM PILAF: Soak about 8 to 10 medium-sized dried shiitake in just-boiled water until soft, about 15 minutes. Remove and discard the stems. Slice the mushrooms and cook them with the pilaf. Use the mushroom soaking water to replace an equivalent amount of the barley soaking water.

Barley Salad
with Carrots and Dill

Serves 5 to 6

This simple yet filling salad is easy to throw together with ingredients you have on hand. It has become a favorite among my friends, perhaps because it has lots of familiar tastes that live together as comfortably as happily married folks.

This salad lasts up to 3 days in the refrigerator, but will need to be perked up with extra lemon juice before serving. Present it on a bed of greens with some hearty whole grain bread and an interesting spread (pages 309–316). For newcomers to whole grains, or if you have company coming to dinner, I suggest using pearl barley, which requires less chewing.

3½ cups cooked barley (pearl or hulled), drained and cooled
5 medium (¾ pound) carrots, coarsely grated
⅓ cup dried currants or raisins
⅓ cup toasted sunflower seeds
¼ to ⅓ cup olive oil
3 tablespoons lemon juice or mild wine vinegar (sherry is nice),
*   approximately*
1 cup loosely packed, finely minced fresh dill or 3 to 4 tablespoons dried
*   dillweed*
Sea salt to taste and pinch freshly ground black pepper

1. In a large serving bowl, combine the barley, carrots, currants, and sunflower seeds.

2. Prepare the dressing by combining ¼ cup olive oil, lemon juice, dill, salt, and pepper in a jar or food processor and blend well.

3. Pour the dressing over the barley and toss well. Taste, and add salt, pepper, additional olive oil or lemon juice, if desired.

Oats, peas, beans, and barley grows,
Nor you, nor I, nor anyone knows
How oats, peas, beans, and barley grows.
                    —Traditional nursery rhyme

Buckwheat

Buckwheat is a quick-cooking, nutrition-packed grain—a fast food that deserves more attention than it gets. It's rich in protein (especially lysine, which is uncommon in most cereal grains) and loaded with vitamins B and E as well as iron, calcium, and phosphorus. I prefer the white, untoasted groats, which have a milder taste than the pronounced, earthy flavor of the toasted ones, commonly known by their Russian name, kasha.

Buckwheat is available in numerous grinds. I like to use the coarse grind, which has more texture. Rinse the buckwheat quickly to avoid extra water absorption, which might result in a mushy dish. For additional information on selection and storage, see Ingredients A to Z under Buckwheat and Grains.

Small changes are beautiful. Small changes that seem insignificant in isolation can be great contributions when they are simultaneously undertaken by many others.

The character of a whole society is the cumulative result of countless small actions, day in and day out, of millions of persons. . . .

—Duane Elgin, *Voluntary Simplicity*
(New York: Bantam, 1982).

Basic Buckwheat

The following recipes work for either white or toasted groats (kasha). While the pressure-cooker method is convenient, I find that standard stovetop cooking is almost as fast and produces the best results more reliably. Carol Gelles, author of *The Complete Whole Grain Cookbook*, offers this tip:

"When cooking kasha, always remember to remove it from the heat just as soon as most of the water has been absorbed and holes appear on the surface. Tilt the pan to determine that there is very little water left, then remove from the heat. The small amount of water that remains will be absorbed during a few minutes of standing time. (This vigilance will also prevent a difficult clean-up job, as the kasha and pot seem to be inseparable if the kasha is cooked until every last drop of water has been absorbed.)"

Pressure cooker: 3 minutes high pressure, 7-minute natural pressure release
Standard stovetop: 10 to 12 minutes plus 5 minutes standing

1 tablespoon oil (optional; see Cook's Notes)
1 cup white (untoasted) or toasted buckwheat groats, quickly rinsed
1¾ cups boiling water or vegetable stock
Generous ½ teaspoon sea salt (less if using salted vegetable stock)

1. Heat the oil in the cooker and toast the grains over medium-high heat, stirring constantly, until dark brown spots appear on the white buckwheat or the toasted buckwheat becomes darker in color, about 2 to 5 minutes. Add the boiling water (watch for sputtering oil!) and salt.

2. Lock the lid into place. Over high heat bring to high pressure. Lower the heat just enough to maintain high pressure and cook for 3 minutes. Allow the pressure to come down naturally for 7 minutes. Reduce any remaining pressure with a quick-release method. Remove the lid, tilting it away from you to allow any excess steam to escape.

3. If the mixture seems dry and the buckwheat is still too chewy, stir in a few extra tablespoons of boiling water or stock, replace the lid, and allow the grains to steam in the residual heat for another few minutes.

Standard Stovetop: In a heavy 2-quart saucepan, follow the first instruction in step 1. Turn off the heat and pour in 2 cups of boiling water (watch for sputtering oil!) and salt. Return to the boil, then reduce the heat and simmer, covered, until almost all of the liquid has been absorbed, about 10 to 12 minutes. Turn off the heat and let stand, covered, until all of the water has been absorbed, about 5 minutes longer. Fluff up with a fork.

Cook's Notes: Except for those using jiggle-top cookers, the oil is optional. If you don't use oil, dry-toast the buckwheat in a hot skillet: stir it constantly to avoid scorching.

Triple Brown Buckwheat

Usually I try to underplay the "brownness" of whole grain cooking, but in this dish I went full steam ahead: browned onions, browned buckwheat, and brown mushrooms. A heart-warming dish for cold-weather appetites.

Pressure cooker: not recommended
Standard stovetop: 10 minutes plus 5 minutes standing

1 tablespoon oil
1 large onion, peeled and coarsely chopped
1 cup white buckwheat groats or kasha, quickly rinsed
1¾ cups boiling vegetable stock or water
¼ pound mushrooms, quartered
1 large carrot, cut into ¼-inch slices on the diagonal
2 ribs celery, cut into ¼-inch slices on the diagonal
½ teaspoon dried rosemary leaves
¾ teaspoon sea salt (less if using salted stock)

1. Heat the oil in a heavy 3-quart saucepan and sauté the onions until they are lightly browned, about 4 minutes. Stir in the buckwheat and continue to sauté, stirring frequently, for 2 additional minutes.

2. Stir in the boiling stock (watch for sputtering oil!), and remaining ingredients.

3. Return to the boil, then reduce the heat and simmer, covered, until the buckwheat is tender and most of the water has been absorbed, about 10 minutes. Turn off the heat and let stand, covered, for 5 minutes. Fluff up with a fork and serve.

We're all in this together. We're not alone. It's not like your body can go to hell on chemicals and mine won't. If there's one juvenile delinquent we've all failed in raising our children.

—Elizabeth Berry, organic specialty produce gardener,
Abique, New Mexico

Dried Corn

Various forms of dried corn—whole sweet corn, grits, and hominy—are increasingly available in health food stores. My experiments with whole sweet corn and hominy did not win accolades, but I have certainly grown fond of yellow corn grits, which are made by grinding dried sweet corn into small bits.

Basic Polenta

Serves 4

Polenta is a wonderfully satisfying and versatile Northern Italian form of corn porridge that deserves to be better known in this country.

The pressure cooker produces a terrific polenta in a jiffy with little effort—a far cry from the 30 minutes of continuous stirring required in the traditional method. But purists may want to revert to the standard stovetop method since the pressure-cooked version calls for yellow corn grits rather than cornmeal; these grits create a slightly chewy, coarse porridge rather than the delicate, smooth one produced by cornmeal.

Serve a mound of plain hot polenta instead of rice. Top it with a ladleful of Nosmo King's Moroccan Chili (page 188), douse it with Roasted Red Pepper Sauce (page 301), or try some alternative Polenta Possibilities (page 81).

Pressure cooker: 5 minutes high pressure, 10-minute natural pressure release
Standard stovetop: 35 minutes

4⅓ cups water
1 teaspoon sea salt
1 cup yellow corn grits (so labeled in health food stores)
1 tablespoon olive oil
½ teaspoon dried rosemary leaves

1. Bring the water and salt to the boil in the cooker. Gradually sprinkle in the yellow corn grits while stirring with a long-handled spoon or whisk. Stir in the oil and rosemary.

2. Lock the lid in place and over high heat bring to high pressure. Transfer the cooker to a heated flame tamer, lower the heat just enough to maintain high pressure, and cook for 5 minutes. Allow the pressure to come down naturally for 10 minutes. Quick-release any remaining pressure. Remove the lid, tilting it away from you to allow any excess steam to escape.

3. Stir the polenta well to incorporate any liquid on top. If the mixture is too watery, boil it over medium-high heat, stirring vigorously until the excess liquid evaporates.

4. Serve polenta in small bowls or pour into an oiled 9-inch pie plate to cool.

Standard Stovetop: Traditional polenta can be tricky to make because in addition to the workout your arms get from stirring, it has a tendency to get lumpy. Here's Carol Gelles's foolproof technique, which she learned from her friend Lucia Sciorsci. This recipe makes enough to serve 8; you can divide it in half, if you wish.

In a heavy 4-quart saucepan, bring 5 cups of water and 1 to 2 teaspoons salt to the boil. Meanwhile, stir together 3 additional cups of water and 2½ cups yellow cornmeal. (You can also shake these together in a jar.) When the water comes to a boil, add the cornmeal batter all at once and stir like crazy until the entire mixture is well blended. Add 1 teaspoon rosemary, if desired.

Reduce the heat so that the mixture is simmering and cook, stirring constantly, until the polenta pulls away from the side of the pot, about 35 minutes. Serve in small bowls or pour into two 10-inch oiled pie plates and cool.

Variation: CASSEROLE POLENTA: Polenta sticks to the bottom of some cookers; you may find it more convenient to pressure-cook polenta in a heatproof casserole, as described in the recipe for Polenta Plus on page 80. For 1 cup of yellow corn grits, use 3½ cups water and 1 teaspoon of sea salt. The olive oil and rosemary are optional. Cook for 20 minutes under high pressure, then allow the pressure to come down naturally for 15 minutes.

The earth is the Mother, a living entity whose milk is the corn from which the human body is made.

—Ancient Hopi wisdom

Polenta Plus

Serves 4

Here's a gussied-up version of polenta using classic Italian ingredients: garlic, mushrooms, tomatoes, and olives.

Pressure cooker: 20 minutes high pressure, 15-minute natural pressure release
Standard stovetop: 35 minutes

1 large onion or leek (white part only), peeled and coarsely chopped
1 large clove garlic, peeled and finely chopped
3½ cups water
½ to 1 teaspoon sea salt
1 cup yellow corn grits (so labeled in health food stores)
*Generous ¼ cup (½ ounce) chopped, dried mushrooms, swooshed in water
    to release all sand*
½ teaspoon dried oregano
Pinch crushed red pepper flakes (optional)
2 large plum tomatoes, coarsely chopped
1 to 2 tablespoons olive oil (optional)

GARNISH
¼ cup oil-cured black olives

1. In a 2-quart heatproof casserole (that will fit into the cooker with at least a ½-inch space around the perimeter), combine the onion, garlic, water, salt, yellow corn grits, mushrooms, oregano, and red pepper flakes (if using).

2. Place 2 cups of water in the cooker and set the rack or trivet in place. Lower the uncovered casserole into the cooker and set it on the rack with the aid of a foil strip (page 10).

3. Lock the lid in place and over high heat bring to high pressure. Lower the heat just enough to maintain high pressure and cook for 20 minutes. Allow the pressure to come down naturally for 15 minutes. Remove the lid, tilting it away from you to allow any excess steam to escape. If the grits are not quite tender, replace the lid and continue to steam them in the residual heat for a few more minutes.

4. When the grits are done, remove the casserole from the cooker with the aid of the foil strip. (Reserve the strip for future use.)

5. Stir the polenta well—there is likely to be a layer of liquid on top—while adding the tomatoes, olive oil (if using), and extra salt if needed. The polenta will seem quite thin, but will thicken considerably as it cools.

6. Serve in small bowls. Alternatively, pour into an oiled 10-inch pie plate to cool and serve at room temperature in slices. Garnish with olives before serving.

Cook's Notes: If you prefer grits more tender than this recipe produces, soak the grits in the water for 8 hours before cooking.

Standard Stovetop: Follow the instructions for standard stovetop Basic Polenta (page 78), using half the quantity of water, salt, and cornmeal. Once the mixture is blended, add the onion, garlic, mushrooms, and crushed red pepper flakes (if using). Proceed as directed. When the polenta is done, stir in the tomatoes, olive oil (if using), and extra salt, if needed. Follow step 6.

Variation: Instead of fresh tomatoes, use ⅓ cup finely chopped sun-dried tomatoes that have been marinated in oil.

Polenta Possibilities

1. Serve it hot from the pot, in small bowls as a slightly porridgy side dish, rather like grits. For luscious richness and flavor, stir in 1 to 2 tablespoons additional olive oil. For a more complex and slightly winy flavor, omit the salt and blend in a bit of light miso after the polenta has cooked.

2. Pour it while hot into a pie plate, smooth the top with a spatula, and let it cool. Once set, cut the polenta into slices and serve at room temperature, pan-fry in a little olive oil, or brush with a thin film of oil and bake or broil until slightly crisp. Its taste and texture are interesting enough to stand alone as a bread or grain substitute, but you may want to top the polenta with some Tomato Sauce (page 304), a dollop of Coriander Pesto (page 298), or sautéed mushrooms and leeks (page 310).

3. To make POLENTA PIZZA: pour hot polenta into an oiled 8- or 10-inch cast-iron skillet. Top with fresh mushroom and tomato slices, diced bell or hot peppers, olives, garlic slivers, and seasonings of your choice (dried rosemary and oregano are nice). Drizzle with olive oil, cover, and bake in a 350° oven until the vegetables are soft, about 15 minutes. Set under the broiler to brown the top, if desired.

Job's Tears

Job's Tears are a relative newcomer to natural food stores and are not always easy to find. Also known as hato mugi barley, this Oriental grain looks like oversized pearl barley except for the light brown indented stripe running down its middle. Job's Tears have the chewiness of barley, but release more starch in cooking, giving them a slight stickiness.

I think Job's Tears are best either in combination with brown rice (use 1 part Tears and 3 parts rice) or in a well-seasoned dish. Served plain, they have a slightly grassy taste. But a few rules must be observed to guarantee good taste and texture:

1. Pick over the grains and remove any tan ones as they have an unpleasant flavor. (In a high-quality batch, you probably won't find any tan grains.)
2. Wash the grains thoroughly (see page 63) to diminish the characteristically grassy taste.
3. Toast the grains to ensure that they will absorb water properly and be cooked through.

Job's Tears taste best when freshly cooked. After an overnight stay in the refrigerator, the grains become unpleasantly hard. To heat and rehydrate them, follow the basic instructions for reheating cooked grains on page 66. For additional information, see Ingredients A to Z under Job's Tears and Grains.

Each thought, each action in the sunlight of awareness becomes sacred. In this light, no boundary exists between the sacred and the profane. . . . Washing the dishes is at the same time a means and an end—that is, not only do we do the dishes in order to have clean dishes, we also do the dishes just to do the dishes, to live fully in each moment while washing them.

—Thich Nhat Hanh, *Peace Is Every Step* (New York: Bantam, 1991).

Basic Job's Tears

Job's Tears benefit dramatically from a quick pretoasting, which enhances the flavor and, more important, enables the grains to absorb liquid and cook evenly through to the center.

Serve Basic Job's Tears to accompany an interesting stir-fry, toss it into a soup or salad, or sprinkle it with a bit of tamari soy sauce.

Pressure cooker: 16 minutes high pressure, 10-minute natural pressure release
Standard stovetop: 50 to 60 minutes plus 5 minutes standing

1 cup Job's Tears
2½ cups boiling water or vegetable stock
½ teaspoon sea salt

OPTIONAL FLAVORINGS
3 to 4 quarter-sized slices of fresh ginger
1 clove garlic, peeled and thinly sliced

1. Look over the Job's Tears and remove any that are distinctly tan. Swoosh the grains vigorously in a small bowl of cold water. Drain. Repeat rinsing the grains several times in fresh water and draining until the water is clear. This may take as many as 5 to 6 changes of water. Drain well.

2. Place the grains in the bottom of the cooker and turn the heat to high. (If your cooker is not heavy-bottomed, use a heavy cast-iron skillet for this step.) Stir continuously as the water evaporates and the grains begin to dry out and start to toast. Continue to stir, scraping up any bits that stick to the bottom of the pot, until the grains begin to make crackling sounds (you may have to stop stirring for a few seconds to hear them) and emit a popcornlike aroma when you sniff up close. This process should take about 3 to 5 minutes. (The grains will actually not look much darker than when you started cooking.)

3. Turn off the heat and add the boiling water and salt. Stand back to avoid getting splattered. Add one of the optional flavorings, if desired.

4. Lock the lid in place and over high heat bring to high pressure. Lower the heat just enough to maintain high pressure and cook for 16 minutes. Allow the pressure to come down naturally for 10 minutes. Remove the lid, tilting it away from you to allow any excess steam to escape. If the Job's Tears are not quite done (they should be chewy but not hard in the center), replace the lid and steam for a few more minutes in the residual heat.

5. Fluff up with a fork before serving.

Standard Stovetop: Follow step 1. In a heavy 2-quart saucepan, follow steps 2 and 3. Return to the boil, cover, and simmer until the Job's Tears are tender and most of the liquid has been absorbed, about 50 to 60 minutes. Turn off the heat and let stand for 5 minutes. Follow step 5.

Quick Sesame-Scallion Tears

Serves 4 to 6

Job's Tears get transformed in no time into a colorful dish with decided Oriental flavors. Since the grain is native to China, it has a natural affinity to toasted sesame oil and tamari soy sauce. Serve with a crisp vegetable stir-fry.

> **Pressure cooker:** 16 minutes high pressure, 10-minute natural pressure release
> **Standard stovetop:** 50 to 60 minutes plus 5 minutes standing

1½ cups Job's Tears
3½ cups boiling water
2 to 3 teaspoons tamari soy sauce, or to taste
⅓ cup thinly sliced scallion greens
2 to 3 teaspoons toasted (Oriental) sesame oil

1. Pick over the grains and remove any that are tan. Swoosh the Job's Tears vigorously in a small bowl of cold water. Drain. Repeat swooshing in fresh water and draining until the water is clear. This may take as many as 5 to 6 changes of water. Drain well.

2. Place the grains in the bottom of the cooker and turn the heat to high. (If your cooker is not heavy-bottomed, use a heavy cast-iron skillet for this step.) Stir continuously as the water evaporates and the grains begin to dry out and start to toast. Continue to stir, scraping up any bits that stick to the bottom of the pot, until the grains begin to make crackling sounds (you may have to stop stirring for a few seconds to hear them) and emit a popcornlike aroma when you sniff up close. This process should take about 3 to 5 minutes. (The grains will actually not look much darker than when you started cooking.)

3. Turn off the heat and stand back a bit to avoid getting splattered as you add the boiling water and 2 teaspoons of tamari.

4. Lock the lid in place and over high heat bring to high pressure. Lower the heat just enough to maintain high pressure and cook for 16 minutes. Allow the pressure to come down naturally for 10 minutes. Remove the lid, tilting it away from you to allow any excess steam to escape. If the Tears are not quite done (they should be chewy but not hard at the center), replace the lid and steam them for a few more minutes in the residual heat.

5. Stir in the scallions, toasted sesame oil, and additional tamari to taste as you fluff up the Job's Tears with a fork.

Standard Stovetop: Follow step 1. In a heavy 2-quart saucepan, follow steps 2 and 3. Return to the boil, cover the pot, reduce the heat, and simmer until most of the liquid has been absorbed, about 50 to 60 minutes. Turn off the heat and let stand for 5 minutes. Follow step 5.

Variations

- Add 2 tablespoons toasted sesame seeds with the scallion greens for a double dose of sesame flavor and some delightful crunch.
- Stir in 1 cup of cooked or frozen (defrosted) green peas or corn, or a mixture of the two, while the Job's Tears are still very hot. Cover and cook over very low heat just until the vegetables are heated through.

Job's Tears with a Mexican Accent   Serves 4 to 6

Since Job's Tears stand up nicely to strong flavors, they work well with some of the herbs and spices of the Mexican kitchen: chili pepper, oregano, and cumin seeds. If Job's Tears are unavailable, try this approach with pearl barley (see Variations).

Pressure cooker: 16 minutes high pressure, 10-minute natural pressure release
Standard stovetop: 50 to 60 minutes plus 5 minutes standing

1½ cups Job's Tears
1 tablespoon olive oil
2½ teaspoons whole cumin seeds
1 large onion, peeled and coarsely chopped
3 large cloves garlic, peeled and chopped
1 large red pepper, seeded and diced
2 ribs celery, thinly sliced
¼ teaspoon crushed red pepper flakes
2 teaspoons dried oregano
3 medium (1 pound) tomatoes, pureed (about 2 cups)
Water
½ teaspoon sea salt, or to taste
⅓ cup tightly packed, finely minced coriander or parsley
Hot sauce (optional)

1. Look over the Job's Tears and remove any that are distinctly tan. Swoosh the grains vigorously in a small bowl of cold water. Drain. Repeat swooshing in fresh water and draining until the water is clear. This may take as many as 5 to 6 changes of water. Drain well.

continued

2. Place the grains in the bottom of the cooker (or in a cast-iron skillet) and turn the heat to high. Stir continuously as the water evaporates and the grains begin to dry out and then start to toast. Continue to stir, scraping up any bits that stick to the bottom of the pot, until the grains begin to make crackling sounds (you may have to stop stirring for a few seconds to hear them) and emit a popcorn-like aroma when you sniff up close. This process should take about 3 to 5 minutes. (The grains will actually not look much darker than when you started.) Transfer the toasted grains to a bowl and set aside.

3. Heat the oil in the cooker. Sauté the cumin seeds, stirring, for 5 seconds. Add the onion, garlic, red pepper, celery, red pepper flakes, and oregano, and sauté for 2 minutes, stirring frequently.

4. Add the tomato puree and enough water to equal a liquid total of 3½ cups. Bring to the boil.

5. Stir in the reserved toasted Job's Tears and the salt.

6. Lock the lid in place and over high heat bring to high pressure. Lower the heat just enough to maintain high pressure and cook for 16 minutes. Allow the pressure to come down naturally for 10 minutes. Remove the lid, tilting it away from you to allow any excess steam to escape. If the grains are not quite done (they should be chewy but not hard at the center), replace the lid and steam them for a few more minutes in the residual heat.

7. Add the coriander, stirring the grains well. Adjust the seasonings before serving, adding hot sauce, if desired.

Standard Stovetop: Follow step 1. In a heavy 2½- or 3-quart saucepan, follow steps 2 to 5, adding an additional ¼ cup water. Cover the pot, reduce the heat, and simmer until most of the liquid has been absorbed, about 50 to 60 minutes. Turn off the heat and let stand for 5 minutes. Follow step 7.

Variations
- BARLEY WITH A MEXICAN ACCENT: Substitute 1½ cups pearl barley for the Job's Tears and add an extra ½ cup of water. Cook for 16 minutes under high pressure plus a 10-minute natural pressure release. For standard stovetop, increase water by ¾ cup and simmer for 45 minutes, followed by 10 minutes standing time off heat.
- For color and a nice crunch, stir in 1½ cups cooked corn at the end.
- Garnish each portion with a tablespoon or two of chopped green olives.

Kamut

Kamut, also referred to as Egyptian wheat, is about three times larger than wheat berries or triticale. It's a wonderfully buttery grain, so dishes in which it plays a prominent role require little to no fat to taste quite rich.

Kamut, like wheat berries and triticale, retains its chewiness, even when thoroughly cooked. (A good way to check doneness is when about 20 percent of the berries in the pot have burst open.) To cook kamut, follow the instructions for cooking Basic Wheat Berries, page 101.

Like spelt (another ancient grain that is making a comeback), kamut is a welcome alternative for many people who are sensitive to wheat. For additional information on selection and storage, see Ingredients A to Z under Kamut and Grains.

Kamut with Limas

Serves 4

A delicate dish, lovely when prepared with just-cooked grains and served warm. It also makes a fine room-temperature salad. The chewiness of the kamut berries creates an appealing contrast with the softness of the limas.

2 cups cooked kamut, wheat berries, spelt, or triticale berries
½ cup tightly packed minced fresh dill (preferred) or 1 to 2 tablespoons
*   dried dillweed*
1 cup firm-cooked baby limas
1 to 2 tablespoons olive oil (see Cook's Notes)
2 to 4 tablespoons lime or lemon juice
½ teaspoon sea salt, or to taste

1. In a medium-sized serving bowl or storage container, combine the kamut with the dill, limas, olive oil, lime juice, and salt.

2. Serve warm or at room temperature.

Cook's Notes: If you're using a grain other than kamut, you'll probably need to add some more olive oil.

If the dish sits for a few hours or overnight, it may need perking up with a bit more lime juice or lemon juice before serving.

Variation: Toss the salad with Avocado Vinaigrette (page 297) instead of the oil–lime-juice dressing.

Millet

It's worth becoming acquainted with millet because it is a nutritional giant, with an impressive protein profile and generous amounts of B vitamins as well as iron, potassium, magnesium, and phosphorus. And it's easier to digest than many other grains.

If you think millet is for the birds, you're in for a nice surprise. Hulled millet is a versatile grain which, when dry-cooked, makes a fluffy and wholesome alternative to couscous. When moist-cooked, it is nice for stuffings or savory burgers.

The problem with most millet dishes is that they're flooded with water and cooked to death. In the recipe that follows, you'll discover a fluffy grain with a mildly crunchy texture and the faint aroma of popcorn. The latter comes from toasting the millet before cooking—an essential step in eliminating this grain's faint bitterness and helping it to cook thoroughly in a limited quantity of water. (Without pretoasting, the outside of each grain usually turns to mush by the time the inside loses its crunch.)

Millet stands up to strong flavors and is a good grain to serve with assertively flavored entrées. For further information, see the Millet entry in Ingredients A to Z.

Little drops of water,
Little grains of sand,
Make the mighty ocean
And the pleasant land.

—Julia A. Fletcher Carney,
Little Things, 1845.

Reliably Fluffy Millet

Because this millet recipe results in a dry, fluffy grain, plan on serving it with a sauce (pages 301–305) or topping it with a soupy dish like chili.

For MOIST-COOKED MILLET, see Variations.

Pressure cooker: 10 minutes high pressure, 10-minute natural pressure release
Standard stovetop: 20 to 25 minutes plus 5 minutes standing

1 cup millet, rinsed and thoroughly drained
1¾ cups boiling water or vegetable stock
½ teaspoon sea salt, or to taste

1. In the bottom of the cooker (or in a cast-iron skillet if your cooker does not have a heavy bottom), set the rinsed millet. Over high heat, dry out and then toast the millet, stirring almost constantly. The millet will be done when it emits a toasted aroma resembling popcorn and begins dancing around in the pan. This may take as little as 2 to 3 minutes and as long as 8 to 10 minutes. If at any point the millet seems to be toasting too quickly, lower the heat slightly. (Do not be concerned if the bottom of the cooker starts to turn brown, but if the millet begins to scorch, turn off the heat immediately and stir vigorously to cool.)

2. When the millet is toasted, turn off the heat. Stand back to avoid sputtering and add the boiling water and salt.

3. Lock the lid into place. Over high heat, bring to high pressure. Lower the heat just enough to maintain high pressure and cook for 10 minutes. Allow the pressure to come down naturally for 10 minutes. Remove the lid, tilting it away from you to allow any excess steam to escape.

4. Immediately fluff up the millet with a fork.

Standard Stovetop: In a heavy 2-quart saucepan, toast the millet as directed in step 1. Follow step 2, increasing the water to 2 cups. Return to the boil, then reduce the heat and simmer, covered, until all of the water has been absorbed, about 20 to 25 minutes. Turn off the heat and let stand, covered, for 5 minutes. Follow step 4.

Variations
- Once the millet has "dried" out in the initial minute or so of toasting, add a tablespoon of oil and continue toasting. This will result in a slightly richer taste.
- To prepare MOIST-COOKED MILLET, increase the water to 2¾ cups (or 3 cups for the standard stovetop method) and proceed as in main recipe. Moist millet, mixed with some olive oil, salt, and lots of freshly grated black pepper, makes a good substitute for mashed potatoes. I also like to prepare it for a breakfast porridge and then use the leftovers for making Millet Burgers (page 90).

Millet Burgers

A great way to use leftover millet, especially if it was moist-cooked (page 89). Before starting the recipe, check to see if the millet will mold properly by squeezing it into a ball. If it doesn't hold together, set it in a heatproof casserole and steam it in a covered pot on a rack over boiling water until moist and sticky, about 3 to 4 minutes.

These tasty burgers are nice for lunch or a light dinner, served "naked," or on a whole wheat bun with soy mayonnaise, mustard, and sprouts. For tang and crunch, serve a slaw (pages 282–286) on the side.

2 cups tightly packed Moist-Cooked Millet (page 89)
⅓ cup grated carrots or beets (which tint the millet red)
3 tablespoons whole wheat, oat, or barley flour
¾ teaspoon ground cumin seeds
½ teaspoon ground coriander seeds
1 tablespoon oil plus oil for shallow frying
2 to 3 tablespoons minced fresh herbs such as parsley or dill, or ½ to ¾
    teaspoon dried leaf oregano
3 tablespoons toasted sunflower seeds
Sea salt and lots of freshly ground black pepper to taste

1. Blend together the millet, carrots, flour, spices, the tablespoon of oil, herbs, sunflower seeds, salt, and pepper. Taste and adjust seasonings. (The mixture should be assertively flavored.)

2. With moistened hands, shape the mixture into patties about 3 inches round by ½ inch thick.

3. Brush a large cast-iron skillet or griddle lightly with oil and fry the patties until browned on both sides, pressing down with a spatula to flatten them. (Alternatively, the burgers can be baked on an oiled baking sheet at 425° until heated through and lightly browned, about 8 to 12 minutes.)

4. Serve warm or at room temperature.

Variations
- Make the burgers very tiny for hors-d'oeuvres or snacks.
- Make the burgers with any slightly sticky or moist-cooked grain, such as brown rice, quinoa, or bulgur. If the grains don't want to hold together, pulse them a few times in a food processor, adding a few tablespoons of boiling water if necessary.

Casserole Millet with Herbs

In this foolproof and flavorful recipe especially recommended for millet newcomers, toasted millet is steamed with dried herbs in a heatproof dish set right into the cooker, then fluffed up and tossed with toasted sesame seeds and a bit of fruity olive oil.

This dish goes well with warm Eggplant Caponata (page 250), and a large green salad dressed with a simple vinaigrette. Leftovers are delicious when moistened with Avocado Vinaigrette (page 297) and served at room temperature.

Pressure cooker: 20 minutes high pressure, 10-minute natural pressure release
Standard stovetop: 20 to 25 minutes plus 5 minutes standing

1½ cups millet, picked over and rinsed
1 small red bell pepper, seeded and diced
1¾ cups water or vegetable stock
1 teaspoon sea salt (less if using salted stock)
1 large bay leaf
½ teaspoon dried leaf oregano
½ teaspoon dried rosemary leaves
½ teaspoon dried basil
⅓ cup tightly packed, finely minced parsley or dill
1 to 2 tablespoons olive oil

1. In a heavy skillet, toast the millet as instructed on page 89.

2. In a 1½- to 2-quart heatproof casserole, combine the toasted millet, red pepper, water, salt, bay leaf, and dried herbs.

3. Pour 2 cups of water into the cooker and set a rack or trivet in place. With the aid of a foil strip (page 10), lower the casserole into the cooker and set on the rack.

4. Lock the lid in place and over high heat bring to high pressure. Lower the heat just enough to maintain high pressure and cook for 20 minutes. Allow the pressure to come down naturally for 10 minutes. Remove the lid, tilting it away from you to allow any excess steam to escape.

5. If the millet is not tender, replace the lid and allow it to steam for a few additional minutes in the residual heat. When the millet is tender, remove the casserole from the cooker with the aid of the foil strip.

6. Remove the bay leaf. Fluff up the millet while stirring in the parsley and olive oil.

continued

Standard Stovetop: In a heavy 2-quart saucepan, toast the millet as directed on page 63. Turn off the heat, stand back to avoid sputtering, and stir in 3 cups of boiling water and the red pepper, salt, bay leaf, and herbs. Return to the boil, then reduce the heat and simmer, covered, until all of the water has been absorbed, about 20 to 25 minutes. Turn off the heat and let stand, covered, for 5 minutes. Follow step 6.

Variations

- Cook 2 cups of fresh corn along with the millet.
- Substitute ½ cup quinoa for ½ cup of the millet.
- Use 2 to 3 teaspoons toasted sesame oil instead of olive oil.
- Brown a large chopped onion in a little oil after you've toasted the millet. Cook the browned onion along with the millet.

Lemon-Scented Millet with Kale   Serves 4

The millet in this recipe is cooked with more than the usual amount of liquid to develop a moist consistency that provides a very homey backdrop to the kale. A soul-satisfying dish.

Pressure cooker: 10 minutes high pressure, 10-minute natural pressure release
Standard stovetop: 25 to 30 minutes plus 5 minutes standing

4 cups water
½ pound kale, finely chopped
1 tablespoon olive oil
1 cup millet, picked over and rinsed
*1 medium leek (white and green parts), thoroughly rinsed and thinly
    sliced, or 1 large onion, peeled and coarsely chopped*
5 large cloves garlic, peeled and minced
1½ teaspoons dried marjoram or 1 teaspoon dried tarragon
1 teaspoon sea salt, or to taste
*1 tablespoon grated or finely minced lemon peel (colored part only, organic
    if possible)*
Freshly ground black pepper
1 to 3 tablespoons freshly squeezed lemon juice

1. Bring the water to the boil in the cooker.

2. Add the kale and cook covered until it is tender, about 3 to 6 minutes. Check for doneness frequently and stir every minute or two. When kale is cooked, drain it in a strainer or colander set over a large measuring cup to catch the cooking liquid. "Shock" the kale under cold running water to set the color; set aside. Either pour off or add water to the kale cooking liquid to achieve a total of 3 cups liquid. Rinse out and dry off the cooker.

3. Heat the oil in the cooker and toast the millet, stirring frequently, until the grains begin to turn brown and pop, about 3 to 4 minutes.

4. Stir in the leek and garlic and continue to sauté for 2 minutes, stirring frequently. Add the marjoram, salt, and kale cooking liquid.

5. Lock the lid in place and over high heat bring to high pressure. Lower the heat just enough to maintain high pressure and cook for 10 minutes. Allow the pressure to come down naturally for 10 minutes. Remove the lid, tilting it away from you to allow any excess steam to escape. If the millet isn't quite cooked, replace the lid and allow it to steam in the residual heat.

6. Stir in the cooked kale, lemon peel, pepper, and just enough lemon juice to perk up the flavors. Serve warm.

Standard Stovetop: In a 3-quart saucepan, follow steps 1 to 4. Bring to the boil, then reduce the heat and simmer, covered, until all of the water has been absorbed, about 25 to 30 minutes. Turn off the heat and let stand, covered, for 5 minutes. Follow step 6.

Each day, I look for something small that I can do in my environment. . . . I use a wood-burning stove for most heat and plant at least two trees a year for each one I've burned. . . . Everything I don't buy is a gift to myself. Every unessential task which I avoid is an offering to my life and the lives of others. . . . Simplicity and being present are twin stars.

—Deena Metzger, "Aspiring to Integrity,"
*In Context, A Quarterly of Humane
Sustainable Culture*, No. 26, Summer 1990.

Quinoa

This tiny Andean seed—considered the Mother Grain by the Incas—has become one of my all-time favorites. Not only is it quick to cook, easy to digest, and delightfully versatile, it has a more impressive protein profile than that of wheat, and contains numerous amino acids (lysine, cystine, and methionine) not normally found in grains.

Cooked quinoa looks like a fluffy couscous except that each grain sports a distinctive tiny white filament. I like quinoa best when it retains a slight crunch. Cooked too long or in too much water, it turns to mush.

There are many varieties of quinoa, including black quinoa, a personal favorite available by mail order from the Colorado organic farmer Ernie New (see page 476). Some varieties have an unappealing, slightly grassy taste. Thorough washing helps diminish this quality, as does cooking this grain with a smashed clove of garlic or substituting stock for water. Use stock if you plan to serve quinoa as a substitute for rice. Switch to water if using quinoa as the base for a cold salad that will be seasoned with a vinaigrette.

For further information, see the Quinoa entry in Ingredients A to Z.

Basic Quinoa

Makes about 4 cups

In its natural state, quinoa is coated with a bitter substance called saponin—a natural insect repellent. Most packaged quinoa has been thoroughly cleaned, but there is some variation among the brands. To avoid a bitter taste in your cooked dish, thorough washing is a must unless directions on the package indicate otherwise.

To Wash Quinoa

Place the tiny grains in a large, *very fine-meshed* strainer and bounce it up and down vigorously in a bowlful of cold water. Occasionally stir the quinoa vigorously with one hand when the strainer is submerged in the water. Change the water each time it gets dark and cloudy. Continue to bounce the strainer and change the water until the water remains completely clear. Drain well.

> **Pressure cooker:** 2 minutes *going up toward* high pressure, 10-minute natural
>   pressure release
> **Standard stovetop:** 15 minutes plus 5 minutes standing

2¼ cups vegetable stock or water
1½ cups quinoa, thoroughly rinsed and drained
½ teaspoon sea salt (or season to taste with tamari soy sauce or Bragg
*   Liquid Aminos after cooking, very yummy)*

1. Bring the stock or water up to the boil in the cooker. Stir in the quinoa and salt to taste (if using).

2. Lock the lid in place and immediately set the timer for 2 minutes. Over high heat bring toward high pressure. Turn off the heat after 2 minutes (whether or not high pressure has been reached). Allow the pressure to come down naturally for 10 minutes. Remove the lid, tilting it away from you to allow any excess steam to escape.

3. If the quinoa is not quite done (it should be slightly crunchy, but not hard), replace the lid and allow it to steam in the residual heat for another minute or two (but don't forget about it, or you'll have mush).

4. When done, fluff up quinoa with a fork, and season with additional salt, tamari, or Bragg Liquid Aminos if desired. If there is any unabsorbed liquid, use a slotted spoon to serve the quinoa.

Standard Stovetop: Bring 3 cups of stock or water to the boil in a 2-quart saucepan. Add the quinoa and salt. Return to the boil, then reduce the heat and simmer, covered, for 15 minutes. Turn off the heat and let stand, covered, for 5 minutes. Follow step 4.

Cook's Notes: If you like your quinoa crunchier than this recipe produces, reduce the liquid by 2 tablespoons and reduce the time for natural pressure release to 8 minutes.

So far I haven't found toasting quinoa before cooking worth the effort.

Quinoa and Potatoes with Caraway

Serves 4 to 6

A dish made with potatoes and quinoa seems natural, since both these ingredients are indigenous to the Andes—and they sure do taste like they belong together.

Pressure cooker: 2 minutes high pressure, 10-minute natural pressure release
Standard stovetop: 15 minutes plus 5 minutes standing

1 tablespoon olive oil
2 large cloves garlic, peeled and finely chopped
1 large onion, peeled and finely chopped
½ pound thin-skinned potatoes (such as new potatoes or fingerlings),
*   scrubbed and cut into matchsticks approximately ¼ inch × 1 inch*
1¼ teaspoons caraway seeds
1½ cups vegetable stock
1 cup quinoa, thoroughly rinsed (page 95) and drained
¾ teaspoon sea salt (less if using salted stock)

1. Heat the oil in the cooker and sauté the garlic, onion, potatoes, and caraway seeds for 1 minute. Stir in the vegetable stock (watch for sputtering oil!) and bring to the boil. Take care to scrape up any bits of onion or potato that have stuck to the bottom of the cooker. Stir in the quinoa and salt.

2. Lock the lid into place. Over high heat bring to high pressure. Lower the heat just enough to maintain high pressure and cook for 2 minutes. Turn off the heat and allow the pressure to come down naturally for 10 minutes. Remove the lid, tilting it away from you to allow any excess steam to escape.

3. If the potatoes are not quite tender, set the lid back into place and allow them to steam in the residual heat for an additional 1 to 2 minutes. (But don't leave the lid on for too long or the quinoa will become mushy.)

4. Stir well before serving.

Standard Stovetop: In a 3-quart saucepan, follow step 1, increasing liquid to 2 cups. Return to the boil, then reduce the heat and simmer, covered, for 15 minutes. Turn off the heat and let stand, covered, for 5 minutes. Follow steps 3 and 4.

Scarlet Quinoa

If there was ever an elegant-but-easy dish to prepare, this is it. The just-cooked quinoa is turned into a crimson grain salad by stirring in some raw grated beets and adding a vinaigrette. It's best served warm or at room temperature.

After you get raves about its gorgeous appearance, sit back and enjoy the requests for second helpings.

3½ to 4½ cups just-cooked quinoa (page 95)
1 cup (about ½ pound) grated raw beets (see Cook's Notes)
½ cup tightly packed minced fresh parsley or coriander
⅓ cup finely chopped scallion greens
2 to 3 tablespoons fruity olive oil
⅓ to ½ cup freshly squeezed lemon juice
Sea salt to taste

GARNISH
A bed of leafy greens
Carrot sticks

1. While fluffing up the just-cooked quinoa, stir in the beets until all of the grains turn scarlet.

2. Stir in the parsley, scallion greens, olive oil, ⅓ cup lemon juice, and salt.

3. Serve warm or refrigerate until shortly before needed and bring to room temperature. Add more lemon juice to perk up the flavors, if desired.

4. To serve, set onto one large or several individual beds of lettuce. Surround with carrot sticks.

Cook's Notes: Scrub the beets well before grating; it's not necessary to peel them.

What is hateful to you do not do to your fellowman. That is the entire Law: all the rest is commentary.

—The Talmud

Quinoa with Corn

Serves 4

These two south-of-the-border natives cook up in the same amount of time and taste delicious together.

Pressure cooker: 2 minutes *going up toward* high pressure, 10-minute natural pressure release

Standard stovetop: 15 minutes plus 5 minutes standing

1 tablespoon olive oil
1 large onion, peeled and finely chopped
1½ cups water or vegetable stock
1 cup quinoa, thoroughly rinsed (page 95) and drained
2 cups fresh corn kernels (see Cook's Notes)
Scant ½ teaspoon dried tarragon, leaf oregano, or summer savory
½ teaspoon sea salt, or to taste

1. Heat the oil in the cooker. Sauté the onion for 2 minutes. Add the water (watch for sputtering oil!) and bring to the boil. Stir in quinoa, corn, choice of herb, and salt.

2. Lock the lid in place, and immediately set the timer for 2 minutes. Over high heat bring toward high pressure. Turn off the heat after 2 minutes (whether or not high pressure has been reached). Allow the pressure to drop naturally for 10 minutes. Remove the lid, tilting it away from you to allow any excess steam to escape. If the quinoa is not quite cooked, replace the lid and allow it to steam in the residual heat for a few more minutes. (Don't leave the lid on for too long or the quinoa will turn to mush.)

3. Fluff up with a fork and adjust seasonings. If there is a bit of liquid left in the bottom of the pot, lift the quinoa and corn with a slotted spoon to serve.

Standard Stovetop: In a 2-quart saucepan, follow step 1, increasing the liquid to 1⅔ cups. Return to the boil, then reduce the heat and simmer, covered, for 15 minutes. Turn off the heat and let stand, covered, for 5 minutes. Follow step 3.

Cook's Notes: Two large ears of corn will produce about 2 cups of kernels. Slightly more or less will work just fine. To remove the kernels, first strip off the husks and corn silk. Working over a large plate and holding the corn vertically, use a serrated knife with a sawing motion, working your way down each ear in strips until the cobs are stripped bare. You can use the cobs to add flavor to soups and vegetable stocks; they can be frozen until needed.

Variations: After the quinoa and corn are cooked, stir in 1½ cups of asparagus steamed tender-crisp and cut into ½-inch pieces. Alternatively, add 1 cup of cooked green peas.

Inscrutable Quinoa Pilaf

Serves 3 to 4

Quinoa cooks up surprisingly well with Oriental seasonings. Familiar flavors make this lesser-known grain more accessible to the uninitiated.

> **Pressure cooker:** 2 minutes *going up toward* high pressure, 10-minute natural pressure release
> **Standard stovetop:** 15 minutes plus 5 minutes standing

2½ *cups water*
¼ *pound snow peas, trimmed*
1 tablespoon toasted (Oriental) sesame oil
1 small clove garlic, peeled and finely chopped
1 small onion, peeled and finely chopped
6 scallions, thinly sliced (keep white and green parts separate)
1 tablespoon freshly grated ginger
1 to 3 tablespoons tamari soy sauce
1½ *cups quinoa, thoroughly rinsed (page 95) and drained*
1 tablespoon toasted sesame seeds
⅛ *to* ¼ *teaspoon freshly ground Szechuan peppercorns or black pepper*
Additional toasted sesame oil, if desired

1. Bring the water to the boil in the cooker. Blanch the snow peas for 1 minute. Remove with a slotted spoon and refresh under cold water. Cut into thin slivers and set aside. Pour 2 cups of the cooking water into a Pyrex measuring cup and discard the rest. Wipe the cooker dry.

2. Heat the oil in the cooker and sauté the garlic, onion, and scallion whites for 2 minutes. Add the ginger, 2 cups of reserved water (watch for sputtering oil!), and 1 tablespoon of tamari. Scrape up any bits of onion that are sticking to the bottom of the cooker. Return to the boil and stir in the quinoa.

3. Lock the lid in place, and immediately set the timer for 2 minutes. Over high heat, *bring toward* high pressure for 2 minutes.

4. Turn off the heat after 2 minutes (whether or not high pressure has been reached); then let the pressure drop naturally for 10 minutes. Remove the lid, tilting it away from you to allow any excess steam to escape. If the quinoa is not quite cooked, replace the lid and allow it to steam in the residual heat for a few more minutes. (Don't leave the lid on for too long or the quinoa will turn to mush.)

5. Fluff up the quinoa, stirring in the reserved snow peas, scallion greens, sesame seeds, and pepper. Add more tamari and toasted sesame oil to taste. Serve hot or at room temperature.

continued

Standard Stovetop: In a 2-quart saucepan, follow steps 1 and 2, increasing the liquid to 2¾ cups. Return to the boil, then reduce the heat and simmer, covered, for 15 minutes. Turn off the heat and let stand, covered, for 5 minutes. Follow step 5.

Variation: This combination of Oriental seasonings does great things for bulgur; check Basic Bulgur (page 104) for the amount of grain, liquid, and cooking time.

"What is enough?" is the key to bringing our lives into alignment with what the Earth can sustain. It can also be the key to personal fulfillment—to a life that is simpler, less cluttered, yet rich with purpose and meaning.

—In Context, A Quarterly of Humane
Sustainable Culture, No. 26, Summer 1990.

Wheat Berries

Wheat berries are whole kernels of wheat with only the outer inedible hull removed. Like other whole grain berries (such as rye or triticale), they are somewhat chewy, even when thoroughly cooked. Because of this "resistance to the tooth," it's probably not a good idea to set a bowl of wheat berries out for your guests. It's best to combine them with vegetables or other grains in such a way that the chewiness becomes an asset. Whole grain berries are especially nice in mixed-grain salads.

To dramatically reduce the cooking time of wheat and other whole grain berries, soak them overnight in ample water to cover. Use the soaking water for cooking and save any that you drain off for use in soups and stocks. It is full of starch that will add body and a subtle sweetness to other preparations.

One piece of advice: Wait until after wheat berries are thoroughly cooked before adding any salt, which interferes with their absorption of water.

Basic Wheat Berries Makes about 2½ cups

These cooking instructions can be used for other whole grain berries, including rye, triticale, spelt, kamut, hulled (and pearl) barley, and oat groats. Check the chart on pages 67 and 68 for recommended timing.

Pressure cooker: 35 to 45 minutes high pressure
Standard stovetop: approximately 2 hours

1 cup whole wheat berries, picked over and rinsed
3 cups water
1 tablespoon oil (to control foaming)

OPTIONAL SEASONINGS
Sliced fresh ginger and/or halved garlic cloves, and/or ½ teaspoon dried
herbs, and/or 1 bay leaf (during cooking)
Sea salt (after cooking)

1. Place the wheat berries, water, oil, and choice of seasonings in the cooker.
2. Lock the lid in place and over high heat bring to high pressure. Lower the heat just enough to maintain high pressure and cook for 35 minutes. Allow the pressure to come down naturally or quick-release by running cold water over the lid. Remove the lid, tilting it away from you to allow any excess steam to escape.

continued

3. If the grains are still very chewy, lock the lid back in place and return to high pressure for 5 to 10 more minutes; if the grains are slightly underdone, replace the lid and simmer over low heat for a few more minutes.

4. When the grains are cooked, drain off any excess liquid and reserve it for stock, if desired. For drier, fluffier grains, immediately return the wheat berries to the pot, replace the lid, and steam in the residual heat for a few minutes.

Standard Stovetop: In a heavy 2-quart saucepan, follow step 1, omitting the oil. Bring to the boil, then reduce the heat, cover and cook until the wheat berries are tender, about 1½ to 2 hours. Follow step 4.

Cook's Notes: Cooked whole grain berries always retain some chewiness. When about 20 percent have burst open, you can consider them properly cooked.

Wheat Berry–Bean Stew

Serves 6

A wonderful cold weather dish, full of good flavor and stick-to-the-ribs heartiness. Serve in bowls, accompanied by a big salad and a crusty loaf.

Pressure cooker: 20 minutes high pressure, 10-minute natural pressure release
Standard stovetop: 60 to 90 minutes plus 15 minutes standing

1 tablespoon olive oil
2 large cloves garlic, peeled and finely chopped
2 large onions, peeled and coarsely chopped
1½ cups wheat berries, soaked overnight and drained
¾ cup anasazi or pinto beans, picked over and rinsed, soaked overnight in
    ample water to cover, drained, and rinsed
2 ribs celery, cut into 1-inch slices
2 large carrots, cut into large chunks
1 pound unpeeled thin-skinned potatoes, scrubbed and cut into 1-inch dice
½ pound medium mushrooms, quartered
2 cups water
2 teaspoons dried leaf oregano
2 bay leaves
Cayenne (ground red) pepper or crushed red pepper flakes to taste
    (optional)
1 to 2 tablespoons Dijon mustard
Tamari soy sauce or sea salt to taste
1 to 2 tablespoons toasted (Oriental) sesame oil

1. Heat the oil in the cooker and sauté the garlic and onions for 1 minute. Stir in the wheat berries, beans, celery, carrots, potatoes, mushrooms, water, oregano, bay leaves, and pepper (if using).

2. Lock the lid into place. Over high heat bring to high pressure. Lower the heat just enough to maintain high pressure and cook for 20 minutes. Allow the pressure to come down naturally for 10 minutes. Remove the lid, tilting it away from you to allow any excess steam to escape. If the wheat berries are not quite done (they should be tender but still chewy), replace the lid and steam in the residual heat for a few more minutes.

3. Remove the bay leaves. Stir in the mustard, soy sauce, and sesame oil, and simmer a few minutes to allow the flavors to mingle.

Standard Stovetop: In a heavy 3-quart saucepan, follow step 1. Bring to the boil, then reduce the heat and simmer, covered, until most of the liquid has been absorbed. Check after 60 minutes, and if the wheat berries are not yet tender continue to simmer until they are almost done, about 15 to 30 more minutes. Stir in ¼ cup boiling water if the mixture seems dry. When the berries are almost tender, turn off the heat and let stand, covered, for 15 minutes. Follow step 3.

Variation: This dish can also be made with triticale or rye berries, but keep in mind that these whole grains remain slightly chewy even when they are properly cooked.

. . . I pledge allegiance to the soil
    of Turtle Island
    one ecosystem
    in diversity
    under the sun—
With joyful interpenetration for all.

—Gary Snyder, in *Earth Prayers*,
  Elizabeth Roberts and Elias Amidon, eds.
  (San Francisco: Harper, 1991).

Bulgur/Cracked Wheat

Bulgur and cracked wheat are refined forms of the whole wheat berry. Unlike the whole grain, they cook very quickly and are easy to chew. Both have the pleasant, mild, and familiar taste that we associate with wheat.

To make bulgur, wheat berries are stripped of their hull and bran and then steamed, dried, and crushed into grits. Cracked wheat is made by cracking whole wheat berries into small pieces. Because bulgur is the more readily available of the two, I have used it in the recipes that follow.

For further details, check Ingredients A to Z under Bulgur, Cracked Wheat, and Grains.

Basic Bulgur   **Makes about 4 cups**

Here's a quick-and-simple way to pressure-cook bulgur in a 1½-to 2-quart heat-proof casserole. Bulgur comes in different grades (see Ingredients A to Z). I use medium or coarse bulgur in this recipe because of its hearty texture.

Pressure cooker: 5 minutes high pressure, 10-minute natural pressure release
Standard stovetop: 20 minutes plus 5 minutes standing

1½ cups medium or coarse bulgur, rinsed and drained
2 cups boiling water or vegetable stock
½ teaspoon sea salt, or to taste

OPTIONAL SEASONINGS TO ADD DURING COOKING
1 clove garlic, peeled and thinly sliced; ½ teaspoon dried herbs, such as leaf oregano, tarragon, rosemary, or thyme; 1 bay leaf

OPTIONAL INGREDIENTS TO STIR IN AFTER COOKING
1 tablespoon finely minced or grated lemon or orange peel; ¼ cup finely minced green olives; ¼ cup toasted pine nuts; ¼ cup dried currants

1. Place 2 cups of water in the bottom of the cooker and set the trivet or rack in place.

2. Place the bulgur in the casserole. Pour the 2 cups of boiling water over it and stir in the salt and any optional seasonings. Lower the casserole into the cooker with the aid of a foil strip.

3. Lock the lid in place and over high heat bring to high pressure. Lower the heat just enough to maintain high pressure and cook for 5 minutes. Allow the pressure to come down naturally for 10 minutes. Remove the lid, tilting it away from you to allow any excess steam to escape.

4. Taste the bulgur and if it is not sufficiently tender, quickly stir the grain, adding a few tablespoons of boiling water if the mixture seems dry. Set the lid back into place and continue to steam it in the residual heat for a few more minutes. Alternatively, if the bulgur is tender but has not absorbed all of the water, pass the mixture through a strainer.

5. When the bulgur is done, stir in any optional postcooking ingredients, and fluff up with a fork.

Standard Stovetop: In a heavy 2-quart saucepan, bring 3 cups of water and ½ teaspoon salt to the boil. Stir in 1½ cups medium or coarse bulgur plus optional seasonings. Return to the boil, then reduce the heat and simmer, covered, until almost all of the liquid has been absorbed, about 20 minutes. Turn off the heat and let stand, covered, for 5 minutes. Follow step 5.

Variation: Toast the bulgur first in a heavy cast-iron skillet to bring out its nutty aroma. For additional instructions on toasting grains, see page 63.

On personal integrity hangs humanity's fate.
—Buckminster Fuller

Bulgur-Potato Pilaf

A substantial dish with a moist texture, somewhat like stuffing. One nice way to serve it is to mound it into one large (or several small) baked squash.

Leftovers made into patties and heated in the oven or fried in a bit of oil are delicious. For best results, use thin-skinned potatoes with a creamy texture, such as new potatoes, fingerlings, or yellow Finns.

> **Pressure cooker:** 4 minutes high pressure, 10-minute natural pressure release
> **Standard stovetop:** 20 minutes plus 5 minutes standing

1 tablespoon oil
1 large onion, peeled and finely chopped
3 large cloves garlic, peeled and finely chopped
1½ cups medium or coarse bulgur, quickly rinsed
½ pound thin-skinned potatoes, scrubbed and cut into ¼-inch dice
2 large carrots, coarsely chopped
2 ribs celery, thinly sliced
2½ cups boiling water or vegetable stock
1 bay leaf
¾ teaspoon dried rosemary leaves
1 teaspoon sea salt, or to taste
½ cup tightly packed minced fresh parsley
Freshly ground black pepper

1. In the cooker, heat the oil. Sauté the onion and garlic for 3 minutes, stirring frequently. Add the bulgur and stir to coat with the onion-garlic mixture. Add the potatoes, carrots, celery, boiling water (watch for sputtering oil!), bay leaf, rosemary, and salt.

2. Lock the lid into place. Over high heat bring to high pressure. Lower the heat just enough to maintain high pressure and cook for 4 minutes. Allow the pressure to drop naturally for 10 minutes. Remove the lid, tilting it away from you to allow any excess steam to escape. If the bulgur is not quite tender, replace the lid and let steam in the residual heat for an additional minute or two.

3. Remove the bay leaf. Stir in the parsley, adjust seasonings, and add pepper.

Standard Stovetop: In a heavy 3-quart saucepan, follow step 1, increasing liquid to 3 cups. Return to the boil, then reduce the heat and simmer, covered, until the potatoes and bulgur are tender and almost all of the liquid has been absorbed, about 20 minutes. Turn off the heat and let stand, covered, for 5 minutes. Follow step 3.

Variation: Substitute ½ teaspoon whole caraway seeds for the rosemary. After cooking, add more caraway seeds if needed.

Tabbouleh

In the United States, bulgur appears most commonly in tabbouleh, a Middle Eastern grain-based salad that American cooks have embraced with gusto.

To my mind, a great tabbouleh has to have lots of fresh parsley and be very lemony—and that's what you'll get with this recipe. Since lemons vary in potency, I suggest you have at least 3 large ones on hand before you begin assembling the salad.

Tabbouleh is best made a few hours in advance and allowed to marinate at room temperature. In the unlikely event that there's any left over, refrigerate it and liven it up the next day with additional lemon juice.

4 cups cooked coarse bulgur (page 104), cooled slightly
1 large carrot, grated or finely chopped
1½ to 2 cups tightly packed minced fresh parsley leaves (2 to 3 large
*   bunches; see Cook's Notes)*
2 tablespoons dried currants (optional)
3 to 4 tablespoons fruity olive oil
4 to 5 (or more!) tablespoons freshly squeezed lemon juice
1 teaspoon Dijon mustard
1 large clove roasted garlic (page 425), peeled and mashed, or 1 to 2 small
*   raw cloves garlic, peeled and finely chopped*
⅓ cup tightly packed minced fresh mint or 1 to 2 teaspoons dried mint
*   (see Cook's Notes)*
1 tablespoon finely minced or grated lemon peel (colored part only, organic
*   if possible)*
½ teaspoon sea salt, or to taste

GARNISHES
½ cup small cherry tomatoes
½ cup peeled, diced cucumbers

1. In a large bowl or storage container, combine the bulgur, carrots, parsley, and currants (if using).

2. In a jar, combine 3 tablespoons of the olive oil, 4 tablespoons of lemon juice, mustard, garlic, fresh or dried mint (start with 1 teaspoon), lemon peel, and salt. Shake well to blend. Pour the dressing over the bulgur mixture and toss to thoroughly coat the grains.

3. Taste and add more olive oil, lemon juice, dried mint (if using) or salt as needed.

continued

4. Let tabbouleh sit at room temperature for a few hours, or refrigerate until shortly before needed. Bring to room temperature before serving, garnished with tomatoes and cucumbers.

Cook's Notes: Use flat-leafed parsley when available. Mince the thin stems to which the leaves are attached. The thick stems below the leaves should be cut off and saved for stock.

If you're using dried mint, be sure it's peppermint and not spearmint. I once used the latter by mistake and ended up with a dish tasting like toothpaste!

Variation: Tabbouleh is delicious when prepared with cooked quinoa (page 95) instead of bulgur.

Unless we become conscious, we eat by habit. We are so far removed from the land. Can we be nourished when we are so far out of touch?

—Louise Frazier, biodynamic farmer and cook,
Housatonic, Massachusetts

Couscous

Most commercially available couscous is a highly refined form of durum wheat. First the bran and germ are stripped from the wheat berry, then the starchy endosperm is ground, steamed, and dried to form tiny pellets. Recently a whole grain couscous has become available, with bran and germ intact. I've enjoyed using it in the recipes that follow. With its mild flavor, couscous is very versatile and easily becomes the backdrop for a wide variety of seasonings.

Basic Couscous
Makes about 3 cups

Because it is so quick-cooking, light, and fun to eat, couscous is a terrific grain to have on hand for quick salads and suppers—especially on hot summer days when whole grains can weigh heavily on the digestion.

Standard Stovetop: 1 minute plus 5 to 10 minutes standing

2 cups water or vegetable stock
1 cup whole wheat couscous
½ teaspoon sea salt, or to taste

1. In a heavy 1½- to 2-quart saucepan, bring the water to a boil. Reduce the heat to medium.
2. Whisking steadily, sprinkle in the couscous. Cook for 1 minute, whisking continuously.
3. Cover the pot, turn off the heat, and let steam until all of the liquid is absorbed, about 5 to 10 minutes.
4. Fluff up couscous with a fork before serving.

Variations
- For a quick pilaf, cook the couscous with one or more of the following ingredients: 3 tablespoons toasted pine nuts; 2 tablespoons raisins, dried currants, or cherries; 1 tablespoon finely minced or grated orange peel (colored part only, preferably organic); ½ teaspoon ground cinnamon; ¼ teaspoon ground cardamom or allspice.
- For a sweeter pilaf, use 1 cup fruit juice and 1 cup water.

Whole Wheat Couscous with Lentils Serves 4 to 6

A moist combination with a stuffinglike consistency, this makes a fine filling for baked squash. Leftovers can be pressed into patties and baked or fried.

Pressure cooker: 6 minutes high pressure, 5 to 10 minutes simmering and standing
Standard stovetop: 30 to 45 minutes plus 5 to 10 minutes simmering and standing

1 tablespoon oil
1 clove garlic, peeled and minced
1 medium onion, peeled and finely chopped
3¼ cups water or vegetable stock
¾ cup lentils, picked over and rinsed
2 large carrots, coarsely chopped
1 bay leaf
½ teaspoon ground cinnamon
½ teaspoon ground coriander
½ teaspoon ground allspice
1 cup whole wheat couscous
⅓ cup dried currants
¾ teaspoon sea salt, or to taste
¼ cup tightly packed minced fresh parsley

GARNISH
¼ cup toasted almonds, coarsely chopped

1. Heat the oil in the cooker and sauté the garlic and onion for 2 minutes, stirring frequently.

2. Stir in the water, lentils, carrots, bay leaf, and spices.

3. Lock the lid into place. Over high heat bring to high pressure. Lower the heat just enough to maintain high pressure and cook for 6 minutes. Reduce the pressure with a quick-release method. Remove the lid, tilting it away from you to allow any excess steam to escape.

4. Stir in the couscous, currants, and salt. Simmer uncovered for 3 minutes, stirring occasionally. Turn off heat, cover, and let stand until the couscous is tender and all of the water has been absorbed, about 5 to 10 minutes.

5. Remove the bay leaf, stir in the parsley, and garnish with toasted almonds before serving.

Standard Stovetop: In a heavy 3-quart saucepan, follow steps 1 and 2, using 4 cups water. Return to the boil, reduce the heat, and simmer, covered, until the lentils are just short of tender, about 30 to 45 minutes. Follow steps 4 and 5.

Crunchy Couscous Salad

In this salad, created by Beth Adams Smith, the crunch comes from raw apple and toasted sunflower seeds. The dish tastes best when made a day ahead and refrigerated overnight, to give the flavors a chance to mingle. It's a great recipe to prepare for a crowd.

Standard stovetop: 1 minute plus 10 to 15 minutes standing

2 cups water or vegetable stock
¾ teaspoon ground cinnamon
½ teaspoon ground ginger
½ teaspoon ground cumin
¼ teaspoon ground turmeric
¼ cup olive oil, divided
1 cup whole wheat couscous
1 large carrot, finely diced
1 Granny Smith apple, peeled, cored, and diced
1 cup cooked chick-peas
¼ cup minced chives or scallion greens
½ cup dried currants
¼ cup toasted sunflower seeds
¼ cup freshly squeezed lemon juice, approximately
½ teaspoon sea salt, or to taste
½ teaspoon lemon pepper, or to taste

1. In a 1½- or 2-quart saucepan, whisk together the water, spices, and 2 tablespoons of the oil. Bring to the boil and whisk in the couscous slowly. Stir 1 minute, cover, remove from the heat, and let sit until all of the liquid has been absorbed, about 15 minutes.

2. Fluff with a fork and transfer to a large serving bowl, continuing to fluff until the couscous releases all of its steam.

3. Toss in the carrot, apple, chick-peas, chives, currants, and sunflower seeds.

4. In a small jar, combine remaining 2 tablespoons olive oil with the lemon juice, salt, and lemon pepper. Pour over the couscous and toss until thoroughly blended. Taste and add more salt or lemon juice, if needed. (The salad should taste lively and pleasantly puckery.)

5. Chill for at least 4 hours. Bring to room temperature, toss, and adjust seasonings before serving.

Grain Salads

It's a great advantage to have odds and ends of cooked grains in the refrigerator as they can become the base for a terrific salad. Even dried-out grains become soft and plump when doused with dressing and allowed to sit at room temperature for a few hours.

If you lack the ingredients to prepare any of the recipes that follow, take a look at the What's Available Bean-and-Grain Salad (page 209) and have fun inventing your own.

Basil Grain Salad

Serves 4 to 6

A terrific and versatile summer salad to make when basil, zucchini, and corn are abundant. It works well with quinoa, bulgur, rice, Job's Tears, millet, or barley.

3 cups cooked grains
1 pound small zucchini, halved and cut into ¼-inch slices
2 cups cooked corn kernels
¾ cup tightly packed minced fresh basil
¼ cup thinly sliced scallion greens
¼ cup olive oil
3 tablespoons freshly squeezed lemon juice or balsamic vinegar,
*   approximately*
1 teaspoon Dijon mustard
½ teaspoon sea salt, or to taste

1. Place the cooked grains in a large serving bowl.
2. Add zucchini, corn, basil, and scallion greens and toss.
3. In a food processor or jar, prepare the dressing by combining the remaining ingredients.
4. Pour the dressing over the grain mixture and toss well. Taste and add more lemon juice and salt if needed.

Variation: Substitute fresh dill or coriander for the basil.

Dilled Grain and Broccoli Salad

Serves 4

This dish is made by lightly dressing any cooked grain—millet, barley, couscous, and rice work well—and tossing it with crisply steamed broccoli. It looks particularly pretty served on a bed of Boston lettuce.

1 medium bunch broccoli (about 1½ pounds)
3½ to 4 cups cooked grain
1¼ cups tightly packed minced fresh dill (preferred) or 3 to 4 tablespoons
*   dried dillweed*
⅓ cup tightly packed, finely chopped (oil-marinated) sun-dried tomatoes or
*   pitted black olives, preferably oil-cured*
¼ cup olive oil (use some of the oil from the sun-dried tomatoes)
2 tablespoons balsamic vinegar
¼ teaspoon sea salt, or to taste
Freshly ground black pepper
2 to 4 tablespoons freshly squeezed lemon juice
Umeboshi plum vinegar to taste (optional)

GARNISH
¼ cup toasted sunflower seeds

1. Peel the broccoli stalks and cut off any tough, woody sections. Cut the stalks into ½-inch dice. Divide the florets into small pieces. Steam the diced stalks on a rack in a covered pot over high heat for 1 minute. Then add the florets and continue to steam until crisp-tender, about 2 additional minutes. Immediately run broccoli under cold water to set the color, then drain thoroughly.

2. In a large bowl, combine the grain, broccoli, dill, and tomatoes.

3. In a small jar, combine the oil, balsamic vinegar, salt, pepper, and 2 tablespoons of lemon juice. Shake well, pour over the salad, and toss until thoroughly blended.

4. Taste and add more salt and a few sprinklings of umeboshi vinegar (if using) or additional lemon juice to make the flavors pop.

5. Garnish with sunflower seeds before serving.

> **The supreme reality of our time is the vulnerability of our planet.**
> —John F. Kennedy

Triple Grain Waldorf Salad

Serves 4 to 6

This is a great dish to make when you have small quantities of various grains in the refrigerator. Better yet, plan ahead: Prepare an additional cup or two of different grains for a few days in a row and store them in well-sealed containers until you make the salad.

Nice combinations are wild rice, brown rice, and barley, or bulgur, brown rice, and Job's Tears. You can also make a tasty version using 3 cups of any single grain (pearl barley is especially good).

> *3 cups cooked grains (see Cook's Notes)*
> *2 large tart apples, such as Granny Smith (peel if not organic),*
>   *cored and diced*
> *½ cup coarsely chopped walnuts*
> *2 ribs celery, thinly sliced on the diagonal*
> *1 small carrot, finely chopped*
> *⅓ cup dried currants or raisins*
> *½ cup tightly packed chopped fresh dill or 2 to 3 tablespoons dried dillweed*
> *⅓ to ½ cup soy mayonnaise*
> *2 to 3 tablespoons freshly squeezed lemon juice, approximately*
> *Sea salt and freshly ground pepper to taste*

1. In a large bowl, combine the grains, apples, nuts, celery, carrot, currants, and dill.

2. Blend in enough mayonnaise to moisten and add 2 tablespoons of lemon juice, salt, and pepper to taste. If needed to perk up flavors, add more lemon juice.

Cook's Notes: If the grains have gotten hard and dried out sitting in the fridge, place them in a vegetable steamer and steam them over a few inches of water for a minute or two in a covered pot until they become tender. Cool before assembling the salad. If using dried dillweed, it's best to assemble the salad at least 1 hour before serving.

Variations
- For an un-Waldorfy variation of this recipe, use Lime-Curry Vinaigrette (page 292) instead of mayonnaise.
- Substitute ⅓ cup toasted pumpkin or sunflower seeds for the walnuts.
- Add ½ cup seeded grapes.

Citrus Grain Salad

Try this salad with cooked bulgur (my personal favorite), wild rice, or long-grain brown rice—or a combination of all three.

4 cups cooked grains
1 large navel orange, peeled and chopped (remove pits)
½ cup tightly packed minced fresh parsley
1 large carrot, finely grated
½ cup finely chopped celery
⅓ cup dried currants or raisins
2 tablespoons olive oil
2 tablespoons safflower or canola oil
1 tablespoon wine vinegar (sherry is nice)
3 tablespoons freshly squeezed lemon juice, approximately
1 tablespoon finely minced or grated orange peel (colored part only,
   preferably organic)
¾ teaspoon sea salt, or to taste
Freshly ground black pepper

GARNISH
2 tablespoons additional minced fresh parsley

1. In a large serving bowl, combine the grains, orange, parsley, carrot, celery, and currants.

2. In a food processor or jar, prepare the dressing by combining the remaining ingredients. Pour dressing over the grains and toss until thoroughly blended. Taste and add more salt or lemon juice, if needed, to perk up the flavors. (A few drops of umeboshi plum vinegar will also do wonders!)

3. Garnish with additional parsley before serving.

Only that day dawns to which we are awake.
—Henry David Thoreau

We often speak of "producing food," but farmers do not produce the food of life. Only nature has the power to produce something from nothing. Farmers merely assist nature.

—Masanobu Fukuoka, The Natural Way of Farming
(New York: Japan Publications, 1985).

Rice and Risotto

Although there are more than forty thousand different varieties of rice grown worldwide, there are only approximately twenty kinds grown in the United States. These are divided into three main categories, depending upon their size and shape: long grain, medium grain, and short grain. Within each of these categories, you will find brown rices, white rices, and aromatic rices.

Brown rice is the whole grain from which only the inedible hulls have been removed. It is not polished as white rice is, and therefore retains a natural coating of bran that gives it a delicious nutlike flavor and a wonderfully chewy texture.

Because the bran layer acts as a barrier to heat and moisture, brown rice takes about twice as long to cook as white rice, and some cooks find it tricky to get it to come out just right—a problem I intend to solve for everyone once and for all.

Brown rice contains more protein, calcium, phosphorus, potassium, niacin, and vitamin E than white rice; for this reason—in addition to its good taste—it is a staple in my kitchen. There are times, however, when I just don't want to take the time to cook brown rice or chew quite as much as the whole grain requires. That's when a bowl of white rice (especially white basmati), or a healthy portion of risotto really hits the spot. For information on white rice, see pages 141–158. For selection and storage of rice, see the Rice entry in Ingredients A to Z.

How to Make a Perfect Pot of Brown Rice

Some people think it's difficult to cook rice, so they avoid the enterprise altogether. This is particularly true of brown rice, which has a longer cooking time and therefore a greater chance of scorching. Such trepidation is a shame because brown rice is so full of good taste and nutrition, and it's actually very easy to prepare if a few simple rules are followed.

First and foremost, use a heavy pot with a tight-fitting lid. A good-quality stainless-steel pressure cooker fits the bill perfectly. For standard stovetop cooking, I favor the porcelain enameled pots made by Le Creuset, but any well-made heavy-bottomed pot will do.

If your pot does not have a layer of copper or aluminum sandwiched into the base, or if you find that the rice consistently sticks to the bottom after cooking, set the pot on a flame tamer and your problems will dissolve. (A flame tamer is an inexpensive heat diffuser available in any good housewares store. See page 10.)

Rice is slightly unpredictable in the amount of liquid it absorbs. If there is liquid left in the pot after the rice is tender, simply drain it off and return the rice to the pot, cover it, and allow it to steam and "dry out" in the residual heat. If all of the liquid has been absorbed and the rice is not yet tender, stir in 2 to 4 tablespoons of boiling water, cover, and continue to simmer until done.

If all of these details raise your anxiety level, skip right along to the recipe for Timid Cook's Casserole Brown Rice (page 127) and your worries will be over.

To Salt or Not to Salt

When cooking rice, some people (I'm one of them) like to add a short strip of the sea vegetable called kombu, thought to aid digestibility. I can't prove that it does, but since kombu provides a boost of minerals, I always throw some in. The kombu also adds a touch of saltiness; once it is cooked, chop the kombu (it will have expanded dramatically) and toss it with the rice or—if you share my love of sea vegetables—consider it the cook's reward and eat it out of hand.

I find that adding salt takes away from the natural sweetness of plain brown rice, so I rarely do.

If you think you can, or if you think you can't—you're right.

Basic Brown Rice

Makes 2¼ cups

Use 1¾ cups liquid for a chewier rice with more separate grains. Use 2 cups for a softer, slightly sticky SUSHI BROWN RICE that is excellent for making sushi rolls (page 270).

Cooking the rice 15 minutes under pressure will result in a very chewy product; increasing the cooking time (and liquid) makes the rice softer and more digestible. Experiment to discover your preference. Once you have, use that timing for all of the recipes that follow.

Pressure cooker: 15 to 40 minutes high pressure, 10-minute natural pressure release
Standard stovetop: 45 minutes plus 10 minutes standing

1 cup short- or long-grain brown rice, picked over, rinsed, and drained
1 tablespoon oil (optional except for jiggle-top cookers; see Cook's Notes)
1¾ to 2 cups boiling water or vegetable stock
Seasoning Options (see box, page 120)
½ teaspoon sea salt, or to taste (optional)

1. Place the rice in the cooker. Stir oil (if using) into the rice. Sauté the rice until lightly browned, stirring frequently, about 1 to 2 minutes. Turn off the heat and stir in the boiling water (watch for sputtering oil!), seasoning options, and salt (if using).

2. Lock the lid in place and over high heat bring to high pressure. Lower the heat just enough to maintain high pressure and cook for 15 to 40 minutes, as desired. Allow the pressure to come down naturally for 10 minutes. Remove the lid, tilting it away from you to allow any excess steam to escape. If the rice is not sufficiently tender, replace the lid and allow it to steam in the residual heat for another few minutes.

Standard Stovetop: In a heavy 2-quart saucepan, bring 2¼ cups water and the salt to the boil over high heat. Stir in the rice. Return to the boil, then reduce the heat and simmer, covered, for 45 minutes. Turn off the heat and let stand, covered, for 10 minutes.

Cook's Notes: Browning the rice in oil adds a pleasing toasted flavor but can be considered optional (*except for owners of jiggle-top cookers who should add 1 tablespoon of oil per cup of dry rice to control foaming*). If you want to skip this step, bring the water to boil directly in the cooker, add the rice, and proceed.

If you experience sticking or scorching on the bottom of the pressure cooker, set it on a heated flame tamer once high pressure has been reached.

Variations

- Add any of the Seasoning Options shown in the box.
- Replace ¼ cup uncooked brown rice with ¼ cup any whole grain berry (rye, wheat, or triticale) that has been soaked overnight and drained.
- Stir 2 to 3 tablespoons toasted sesame seeds into the cooked rice.

Seasoning Options

When preparing plain brown or white rice to serve with Italian, French, Spanish, or American Southern food, consider adding 1 or more of the following seasonings to the pot per 1 cup of dry rice:

1 large clove garlic, peeled and sliced in two or minced
1 bay leaf
½ teaspoon dried oregano, basil, or thyme
Dash cayenne (ground red) pepper
½ teaspoon sweet Hungarian paprika

Or after cooking, stir in any of the following:

1 tablespoon finely minced or grated orange or lemon peel (colored part only, organic if possible)
¼ cup toasted pine nuts, coarsely chopped walnuts, hazelnuts, or pecans
1 to 2 teaspoons poppy seeds
¼ cup finely chopped fresh herbs, such as basil, parsley, dill, or coriander

When serving rice with Indian, Moroccan, or Middle Eastern food, you can substitute orange or apple juice for half of the water and add 1 or more of the following to the pot per 1 cup of dry rice:

One 3-inch stick cinnamon, broken in two
2 to 3 crushed cardamom pods or ¼ teaspoon ground cardamom
1 teaspoon ground coriander
3 to 4 teaspoons mild curry powder
2 to 3 whole cloves or ⅛ teaspoon ground cloves
⅛ teaspoon ground allspice
2 to 3 quarter-sized slices fresh ginger or ¼ teaspoon ground ginger
¼ cup toasted pine nuts
⅓ cup raisins, dried currants, chopped apricots, or prunes

Pressure Cooker*
Brown Rice Cooking Chart

For a dry rice, use the smaller amount of liquid.
For a moist rice, use the maximum.

Brown Rice	Cups Boiling Liquid	Optional Salt	Optional Oil†	Approximate Yield in Cups
1 cup	1¾–2	½ teaspoon	1 tablespoon	2¼
1½ cups	2½–2¾	¾ teaspoon	1 tablespoon	3½
2 cups	3½–4	1 teaspoon	1½ tablespoons	5
3 cups	5–5½	1½ teaspoons	2 tablespoons	7

Do not fill the cooker beyond the halfway mark.
*See instructions, page 119.
†Required in jiggle-top cookers.

Standard Stovetop*
Brown Rice Cooking Chart

Brown Rice	Cups Liquid	Optional Salt	Approximate Yield in Cups
1 cup	2¼	½ teaspoon	3–3½
1½ cups	3	¾ teaspoon	4½
2 cups	3¾	1 teaspoon	6
3 cups	5½	1½ teaspoons	8½

*See instructions, page 119.

Herbed Mediterranean Rice
with Chick-peas

Serves 5 to 6

It's easy to keep the ingredients for this dish on hand. It's always been one of my favorite grain and bean dishes.

Pressure cooker: 25 minutes high pressure, 10-minute natural pressure release
Standard stovetop: 60 to 90 minutes (chick-peas); 45 minutes plus 10 minutes standing (Mediterranean Rice)

¾ cup dried chick-peas, picked over and rinsed, soaked overnight in ample water to cover
1 tablespoon olive oil
1 large leek (white and green parts), thinly sliced and thoroughly rinsed, or 1 large onion, peeled and coarsely chopped
2½ cups water
1½ cups long-grain or basmati brown rice
1 teaspoon dried summer savory or marjoram
¾ teaspoon dried rosemary leaves
½ teaspoon dried leaf oregano
½ teaspoon dried chervil (optional)
1 large bay leaf
⅓ cup finely chopped sun-dried tomatoes packed in oil, or pitted, oil-cured black olives
¼ cup tightly packed, finely minced fresh parsley
Sea salt and freshly ground pepper to taste

GARNISH
¼ cup toasted, coarsely chopped almonds

1. Drain and rinse the chick-peas and set aside.
2. Heat the oil in the cooker. Sauté the leek until soft, about 2 minutes. Add the water (watch for sputtering oil!) and bring to the boil over high heat.
3. Add the rice, reserved chick-peas, herbs, and bay leaf.
4. Lock the lid into place. Over high heat bring to high pressure. Transfer to a heated flame tamer. Lower the heat just enough to maintain high pressure and cook for 25 minutes. Allow the pressure to drop naturally for 10 minutes. Remove the lid, tilting it away from you to allow any excess steam to escape.
5. If the rice is not quite tender, set the lid back in place and allow it to steam in the residual heat for another few minutes.

6. Fluff up the rice as you stir in the sun-dried tomatoes (with a bit of the marinating oil, if you like) and parsley, and add salt and pepper to taste. Remove the bay leaf. Transfer to a serving bowl and garnish with almonds.

Standard Stovetop: Cook the soaked chick-peas in ample water to cover until tender, about 1 to 1½ hours. Drain and reserve in a warm place. In a heavy 3-quart saucepan, follow step 2, increasing the water to 3 cups. Add the rice, herbs, and bay leaf. Return to the boil, then reduce the heat and simmer, covered, until almost all of the liquid has been absorbed, about 45 minutes. Turn off the heat and let stand, covered, until all of the liquid has been absorbed, about 10 minutes. Follow step 6, adding the cooked chick-peas and remaining ingredients.

Cook's Notes: It's tricky to cook rice and beans together because of unpredictable variations in cooking times. Chick-peas work well in this regard, since they hold their shape nicely even if they are cooked slightly longer than necessary.

Variation: Instead of one type of rice, a blend of long- and short-grain brown rice with perhaps a few grains of wehani or wild rice makes a nice change.

Before eating we always gave thanks for our food. We had been told, "Your attitude when you eat anything should be one of joy and pleasure and thanksgiving. You are to be constantly aware that all these gifts are Mine."

—The Findhorn Community, *The Findhorn Garden*
(Forres, Scotland: The Findhorn Press, 1975).

Brown Basmati with Cashews and Currants

Serves 4 to 6

For nutty taste and aroma, basmati rice can't be beat. It's lighter than other varieties of brown rice and makes the ideal accompaniment to spicy Indian fare.

Pressure cooker: 25 minutes high pressure, 10-minute natural pressure release
Standard stovetop: 45 minutes plus 10 minutes standing

1 tablespoon oil
1 large onion, peeled and finely chopped
1½ cups brown basmati rice, picked over and rinsed
2½ cups boiling vegetable stock or water
⅓ cup dried currants or raisins (sweeter)
1½ teaspoons ground coriander seeds
½ teaspoon whole fennel seeds
¾ teaspoon sea salt, or to taste
½ cup coarsely chopped toasted cashews

1. Heat the oil in the cooker and sauté the onion for 2 minutes, stirring frequently.

2. Stir in the rice, taking care to coat the grains with oil. Add the stock (watch for sputtering oil!), currants, coriander, fennel, and salt.

3. Lock the lid into place. Over high heat bring to high pressure. Lower the heat just enough to maintain high pressure and cook for 25 minutes. Allow the pressure to come down naturally for 10 minutes. Remove the lid, tilting it away from you to let any excess steam to escape. If the rice is not quite tender, replace the lid and allow it to steam in the residual heat for another few minutes.

4. Stir in the cashews while fluffing up the rice with a fork. Serve.

Standard Stovetop: In a heavy 2-quart saucepan, follow steps 1 and 2, increasing the liquid to 3 cups. Bring to the boil over high heat, then reduce the heat and simmer, covered, until almost all of the liquid has been absorbed, about 45 minutes. Turn off the heat and let stand, covered, until all of the liquid has been absorbed, about 10 minutes. Follow step 4.

Variations
- Substitute ¼ to ½ cup wild rice for an equivalent amount of basmati.
- Serve any leftovers as a room-temperature salad, lightly coated with Herb Vinaigrette (page 294).

Pistachio Rice Curry

Serves 4

Curry and rice are a natural pair. This pilaf goes well with steamed vegetables or a stir-fry. Better yet, team it with Quick Chick-pea Curry (page 180).

Pressure cooker: 25 minutes high pressure, 10-minute natural pressure release
Standard stovetop: 45 minutes plus 10 minutes standing

1 tablespoon oil
2 teaspoons cumin seeds
1 small onion, peeled and finely chopped
1 large clove garlic, peeled and finely chopped
1¾ cups water or vegetable stock
1 cup brown basmati or long-grain brown rice, picked over and rinsed
1 tablespoon mild curry powder
½ teaspoon sea salt, or to taste
⅓ cup coarsely chopped pistachios

1. Heat the oil in the cooker. Sauté the cumin seeds for 5 seconds, then add the onion and garlic and sauté for 2 minutes, stirring frequently.

2. Add the water (watch for sputtering oil!) and bring to the boil. Add the rice, curry powder, and salt.

3. Lock the lid into place. Over high heat bring to high pressure. Lower the heat just enough to maintain high pressure and cook for 25 minutes. Allow the pressure to drop naturally for 10 minutes. Remove the lid, tilting it away from you to allow any excess steam to escape. If the rice is not quite tender, replace the cover and allow it to steam in the residual heat for a few minutes.

4. Stir in the nuts while fluffing up rice with a fork. Serve.

Standard Stovetop: In a heavy 2-quart saucepan, follow steps 1 and 2, increasing liquid to 2 cups. Return to the boil, then reduce the heat and simmer, covered, until almost all of the liquid has been absorbed, about 45 minutes. Turn off the heat and let stand, covered, until all of the liquid has been absorbed, about 10 minutes. Follow step 4.

Variations
- Use roasted peanuts instead of pistachios.
- Toss ½ cup cooked or frozen (defrosted) green peas into the cooked rice.
- Cook ¼ cup dried currants with the rice.

Coconut Rice with Lemongrass

Serves 3 to 4

Although the authentic Thai version is made with coconut milk, cooking shredded coconut with the rice eliminates the extra step of preparing the milk, and it creates a very pleasing texture.

Coconut rice goes well with Oriental baked tofu. Add a steamed green vegetable to the menu for color and crunch.

Pressure cooker: 25 minutes high pressure, 10-minute natural pressure release
Standard stovetop: 45 minutes plus 10 minutes standing

2¼ cups water
1 stalk fresh lemongrass, cut into 1-inch pieces, or 2 teaspoons dried
     lemongrass, placed in an aluminum tea ball
1 cup long-grain or basmati brown rice
½ cup dried, grated coconut (unsweetened; see Cook's Notes)
¾ teaspoon sea salt
⅛ to ¼ teaspoon crushed red pepper flakes
¼ cup minced fresh coriander (optional)

1. Bring the water and lemongrass to the boil in the cooker. Add the rice, coconut, salt, and red pepper flakes.

2. Lock the lid in place and over high heat bring to high pressure. Lower the heat just enough to maintain high pressure and cook for 25 minutes. Allow the pressure to come down naturally for 10 minutes. Remove the lid, tilting it away from you to allow any excess steam to escape.

3. Remove the tea ball or pieces of lemongrass. Stir in the coriander (if using) as you fluff up the rice and stir well to distribute the coconut.

Standard Stovetop: In a heavy 2-quart saucepan, follow step 1, increasing the water to 2½ cups. Return to the boil, then reduce the heat and simmer, covered, until almost all of the liquid has been absorbed, about 45 minutes. Turn off the heat and let stand, covered, until all of the liquid has been absorbed, about 10 minutes.

Cook's Notes: If you can only get flaked coconut rather than grated, simply spin it in a food processor, blender, or spice grinder until it's coarsely ground.

Timid Cook's Casserole Brown Rice

Makes 3½ cups

If cooking rice intimidates you, or if you find pressure-cooked rice too sticky, try this foolproof method. The rice is steamed to perfection in a 1½- or 2-quart soufflé dish or heatproof bowl placed on a rack over water in the pressure cooker. (There should be at least a half-inch of space between the bowl and the sides of the cooker.) With this method, the rice is initially mixed with less water than normal and the grains absorb just the amount of moisture they need from the steam inside the cooker. You can serve the rice right in the bowl: no risk to prepare and no pot to clean. Your rice troubles are over.

This recipe calls for 1½ cups of brown rice. The chart on page 128 gives the formulas for cooking other quantities and varieties of brown rice.

Please Note: Short-grain brown rice requires 25 minutes under high pressure to become tender. All other rice varieties—such as long-grain, basmati, and wehani—require only 20 minutes under high pressure. All require the additional 20-minute pressure-release time.

Pressure cooker: 20 to 25 minutes high pressure, 20-minute natural pressure release
Standard stovetop: not recommended

1½ cups long- or short-grain brown rice
1¾ cups water
¾ teaspoon sea salt (optional)
Seasoning Options (page 120)

1. In a 1½- to 2-quart casserole, combine the rice, 1¾ cups water, and optional salt and seasonings. Set the rack and 2 cups of water into the cooker. Lower the uncovered casserole into the cooker with the aid of a foil strip (page 10).

2. Lock the lid in place and over high heat bring to high pressure. Lower the heat just enough to maintain high pressure and cook for 20 minutes (for long-grain brown, wehani, and brown basmati, etc.) and 25 minutes for short-grain brown rice. Allow the pressure to come down naturally for 20 minutes. Remove the lid, tilting it away from you to allow any excess steam to escape. If the rice is not quite tender, replace the lid and allow it to steam in the residual heat for a few more minutes.

3. Lift the casserole from the cooker with the aid of the foil strip.

4. Fluff up the rice before serving. (If there is any extra water in the casserole, set a plate on top, and the water will quickly be absorbed as the rice stands.)

continued

Standard Stovetop: There is no advantage to using this technique with standard cooking equipment. Follow the basic stovetop brown rice recipe, page 119.

Cook's Notes: It is not advisable to cook more than 2 cups of dry rice by this method as larger quantities, when cooked, will overflow the 2-quart casserole.

Timid Cook's Casserole Cooking Chart

This chart can be used for all varieties of brown rice.
Remember that short-grain brown rice cooks an additional
5 minutes under high pressure (see the note on Cooking Times).

Brown Rice	Cups Liquid	Optional Salt	Approximate Yield in Cups	Minimum Casserole Size
1 cup	1½	½ teaspoon	2½	1 quart
1½ cups	1¾	¾ teaspoon	3½	1½ quarts
2 cups	2¼	1 teaspoon	5	2 quarts

Cooking Times: Cook long-grain brown or brown basmati rice for 20 minutes under high pressure plus a 20-minute natural pressure release.

Cook short-grain brown rice for 25 minutes under high pressure plus a 20-minute natural pressure release.

The average U.S. food is transported about 1,400 miles before it is eaten.

—*East West,* September 1990.

Chestnut Brown Rice Casserole

This extremely simple preparation is one of my standards when I'm in the mood for festive and luxurious. The chestnuts give the rice a slightly sweet and smoky character and provide an appealing textural contrast.

Chestnut Brown Rice makes a lovely stuffing for baked or steamed squash.

Pressure cooker: 25 minutes high pressure, 20-minute natural pressure release
Standard stovetop: 45 minutes plus 10 minutes standing

1 cup water or apple juice (for a sweeter version)
¾ cup water
¾ cup short-grain brown rice, picked over and rinsed
*¼ cup wild or wehani rice (for visual and textural contrast) or additional
    short-grain brown rice*
½ cup dried, peeled chestnuts
¾ teaspoon ground coriander seeds
½ teaspoon ground cinnamon
¼ teaspoon ground cardamom
*½ teaspoon sea salt, or to taste (use less salt than usual to allow the
    sweetness of the chestnuts to dominate)*
*1 tablespoon finely minced or grated orange peel (colored part only,
    preferably organic)*

1. In a 1½- to 2-quart casserole, combine all of the ingredients except the orange peel. Set the rack and 2 cups of water into the cooker. Lower the uncovered casserole into the cooker with the aid of a foil strip (page 10).

2. Lock the lid into place. Over high heat bring to high pressure. Lower the heat just enough to maintain high pressure and cook for 25 minutes. Allow the pressure to drop naturally for 20 minutes. Remove the lid, tilting it away from you to allow any excess steam to escape. If the rice is not quite tender, replace the lid and allow it to cook in the residual steam for a few more minutes.

3. Lift the casserole from the cooker with the aid of the foil strip.

4. Fluff up the rice while breaking up the chestnuts (if desired), and stirring in the orange peel. Serve immediately.

Standard Stovetop: Soak the chestnuts overnight in 3 cups of water. Remove any loose skins. Drain, reserving the soaking liquid. Coarsely chop the chestnuts. In a heavy 2-quart saucepan, bring the soaking liquid (plus additional water, if needed, to equal 2¼ cups) to the boil over high heat. Add the chestnuts and all of the remaining ingredients except the orange peel. Return to the boil, then reduce the heat and simmer, covered, until almost all of the liquid has been absorbed, about 45 minutes. Turn off the heat and let stand, covered, until all of the liquid has been absorbed, about 10 minutes. Follow step 4.

Variation: For a savory version, use water or vegetable stock instead of apple juice. Omit the spices and orange peel. Add 1 teaspoon of dried tarragon and a small handful of soaked dried mushrooms, using the strained soaking water to replace part of the liquid.

Hijicki Brown Rice Casserole   Serves 4 to 6

The sea vegetable known as hijicki (see Ingredients A to Z) is first soaked for 20 minutes and then cooked with the rice. It comes out looking like long black spaghetti and dyes the rice a rich rusty brown—quite a conversation piece. And tasty too!

Pressure cooker: 20 minutes high pressure, 20-minute natural pressure release
Standard stovetop: 45 minutes plus 10 minutes standing

*1 cup loosely packed (1¼ ounces) hijicki, rinsed, then soaked for 20
    minutes in ample water to cover*
1 small onion, peeled and coarsely chopped
4 large cloves garlic, peeled and finely chopped
1½ cups long-grain brown or brown basmati rice
1¾ cups water
1 to 2 tablespoons toasted (Oriental) sesame oil
2 tablespoons toasted sesame seeds
Tamari soy sauce to taste

GARNISH
Toasted pumpkin seeds

1. Drain and rinse the hijicki.

2. In a 2-quart casserole, combine the onion, garlic, rice, 1¾ cups water, and hijicki. Set the rack and 2 cups of water into the cooker. Lower the uncovered casserole into the cooker with the aid of a foil strip (page 10).

3. Lock the lid in place and over high heat bring to high pressure. Lower the heat just enough to maintain high pressure and cook for 20 minutes. Allow the pressure to come down naturally for 20 minutes. Remove the lid, tilting it away from you to allow any excess steam to escape. If the rice is not quite tender, replace the lid and allow it to steam in the residual heat for a few more minutes.

4. Remove the casserole from the cooker with the aid of the foil strip.

5. Stir in the sesame oil, sesame seeds, and tamari as you fluff up the rice and distribute the hijicki. Garnish with pumpkin seeds.

Standard Stovetop: Follow step 1. In a heavy 3-quart saucepan, sauté the onion and garlic in 1 tablespoon canola or light sesame oil. Add 3 cups of water (watch for sputtering oil!) and bring to the boil over high heat. Stir in the rice and hijicki. Return to the boil, then reduce the heat and simmer, covered, until almost all of the liquid has been absorbed, about 45 minutes. Turn off the heat and let stand, covered, until all of the liquid has been absorbed, about 10 minutes. Follow step 5.

Variations

- To create heat in this dish, stir in a few drops of hot chili sesame oil at the end of cooking, or add a generous pinch of crushed red pepper flakes to the rice as it cooks.
- For color, cook the rice with a coarsely chopped carrot or red pepper.
- For a more substantial dish, stir in ½ pound diced seitan (page 453) or pan-fried tempeh (page 228) with the sesame oil and steam until heated through.

Eating is an activity that joins me with all humanity. I recognize that to be an eater is to be accountable for the care of the earth and its resources. I acknowledge that despite our differences, we are all ultimately nourished by the same source. As such I agree to share.

—From "The Eater's Agreement," in
Marc David, *Nourishing Wisdom*
(New York: Bell Tower, 1991).

Creole Brown Rice Casserole

Serves 4 to 6

Please don't be put off by the long list of ingredients—they're mostly dried herbs and spices that you probably already have in the pantry. A pinch of this and a sprinkle of that add up to a complex blend of flavors that makes Creole, Creole.

This dish goes well with Black Soybeans (page 191) or with Beans and Greens Italiano (page 199).

Pressure cooker: 20 minutes high pressure, 20-minute natural pressure release
Standard stovetop: 45 minutes plus 10 minutes standing

1½ cups long-grain brown rice, picked over and rinsed
1½ cups water or vegetable stock (see Cook's Notes)
2 to 3 large cloves garlic, peeled and thinly sliced
4 large ribs celery, cut into ½-inch chunks
1 large carrot, coarsely chopped
1 large red or green bell pepper, seeded and diced
1 teaspoon dried leaf oregano
¾ teaspoon dried rosemary leaves
½ teaspoon dried thyme
Pinch crumbled sage leaves or ground sage
1 teaspoon dry mustard
¼ teaspoon ground cloves
1 large bay leaf
Large pinch crushed red pepper flakes or ½ dried chili pepper
1 teaspoon sea salt, or to taste
⅛ teaspoon freshly ground black pepper
1 to 2 tablespoons olive oil (optional)
¼ cup thinly sliced scallion greens
¼ cup tightly packed minced fresh parsley
Tabasco sauce and/or apple cider vinegar to taste

GARNISH
Pitted and chopped green olives

1. In a 2-quart heatproof casserole, combine all of the ingredients except the scallion greens, parsley, and Tabasco.

2. Set the rack and 2 cups of water into the cooker. Lower the uncovered casserole into the cooker with the aid of a foil strip (page 10).

3. Lock the lid in place and over high heat bring to high pressure. Lower the heat just enough to maintain high pressure and cook for 20 minutes. Allow the pressure to come down naturally for 20 minutes. Remove the lid, tilting it away from you to allow any excess steam to escape. If the rice is not quite tender, replace the lid and allow it to steam in the residual heat for a few more minutes.

4. Remove the casserole from the cooker with the aid of the foil strip.

5. Remove the bay leaf. Stir in the scallion greens and parsley. Taste and sprinkle on Tabasco and/or a few teaspoons of vinegar if the flavors need perking up. Garnish with chopped olives.

Standard Stovetop: In a heavy 3-quart saucepan, bring 2½ cups of water to the boil. Stir in the rice and remaining ingredients except for the scallion greens, parsley, and Tabasco. Bring to the boil, cover, and reduce heat. Simmer until the rice is tender and almost all of the liquid has been absorbed, about 45 minutes. Turn off the heat and let stand, covered, until all of the liquid has been absorbed, about 10 minutes. Follow step 5.

Cook's Notes: Because the celery gives off so much water during cooking, this recipe calls for less liquid than is normally required for 1½ cups of rice.

Variations

- If you have some sun-dried tomatoes on hand, add 4 to 5 tomato halves, broken into bits, to the rice as it cooks. They deepen the color of the finished dish and give a faint tart edge.
- For a more substantial (and very attractive) dish, stir cooked baby okra into the cooked rice. Garnish with strips of pan-fried tempeh (page 228) to create a jambalaya-like dish.

Put your energies into sustaining the system that sustains you.

—Alice Devine Loebel,
The Simmering Pot Cookbook
(New York: Macmillan, 1974).

Shiitake Brown Rice Casserole Serves 4 to 6

There have been many treatises written on the health-promoting properties of shiitake mushrooms, so it's nice to note that they taste delicious too!

I like to serve this with black soybeans and steamed broccoli on the side.

Pressure cooker: 25 minutes high pressure, 10-minute natural pressure release
Standard stovetop: 45 minutes plus 10 minutes standing

12 medium (about ½ ounce) dried shiitake mushrooms
2 cups boiling water, approximately
1 heaping tablespoon dark miso or ¾ teaspoon sea salt
1 large onion, peeled and finely chopped
1 clove garlic, peeled and minced, or 1 tablespoon freshly grated ginger
1½ cups short-grain brown rice, picked over and rinsed
1 to 2 tablespoons toasted (Oriental) sesame oil

1. Set the mushrooms in a 4-cup measure or bowl and pour the boiling water on top. Cover with a plate or pot lid and let sit until the mushrooms are soft, about 20 minutes.

2. Remove the mushrooms with a slotted spoon. Remove the stems and reserve them for stock. Cut the caps into slivers. Strain the mushroom water directly into a 2-cup measure. Add water, if needed, to equal 1¾ cups liquid.

3. Dissolve the miso in the mushroom stock. Alternatively, stir in the salt.

4. Place the miso-mushroom stock plus the reserved mushrooms, onion, garlic, and rice into a 2-quart casserole.

5. Set the rack and 2 cups of water into the cooker. Lower the uncovered casserole into the cooker with the aid of a foil strip (page 10).

6. Lock the lid in place and over high heat bring to high pressure. Lower the heat just enough to maintain high pressure and cook for 25 minutes. Allow the pressure to come down naturally for 10 minutes. Remove the lid, tilting it away from you to allow any excess steam to escape. If the rice is not quite tender, set the cover back in place and let steam a few more minutes in the residual heat.

7. When the rice is done, remove it from the cooker with the aid of the foil strip.

8. Fluff up the rice as you stir in toasted sesame oil to taste.

Standard Stovetop: Follow steps 1 and 2, adding enough water to the shiitake stock to equal 3 cups. Follow step 3. Place the miso liquid in a heavy 2-quart saucepan and bring to the boil over high heat. Add the reserved mushrooms, onions, garlic, and rice. Return to the boil, then reduce the heat and simmer, covered, until almost all of the liquid has been absorbed, about 45 minutes. Turn off the heat and let stand, covered, until all of the liquid has been absorbed, about 10 minutes. Follow step 8.

Chili-Hot Peanut Brown Rice

Serves 4 to 6

A simple rice preparation that will win fans among those who like it hot. Add ⅛ teaspoon of crushed red pepper for less adventurous palates. Go for ¼ teaspoon if members of the Fire-Alarm Chili Club are expected for dinner.

Pressure cooker: 25 minutes high pressure, 20-minute natural pressure release
Standard stovetop: 45 minutes plus 10 minutes standing

1 tablespoon olive oil (optional)
1 large onion, peeled and coarsely chopped
2 cloves garlic, peeled and finely chopped
1 small red bell pepper, seeded and chopped
2 tablespoons mild chili powder
⅛ to ¼ teaspoon crushed red pepper flakes
1½ cups short-grain brown rice
1¾ cups water
¾ to 1 teaspoon sea salt
2 to 3 teaspoons apple cider vinegar
½ cup toasted peanuts, coarsely chopped

GARNISH
Sliced avocado or a dollop per portion of Avocado Vinaigrette (page 297)

1. Heat the oil in the cooker. Sauté the onion, garlic, and bell pepper for 2 minutes, stirring frequently. (This step is optional: You can simply place the onion, garlic, and red bell pepper directly into the casserole and omit sautéing in oil.)

2. Transfer the mixture to a 2-quart heatproof casserole. Add the chili powder, crushed red pepper flakes, rice, water, and salt.

3. Set a rack or trivet and 2 cups of water into the cooker. Lower the uncovered casserole into the cooker with the aid of a foil strip (page 10).

4. Lock the lid in place and over high heat bring to high pressure. Lower the heat just enough to maintain high pressure and cook for 25 minutes. Allow the pressure to come down naturally for 20 minutes. Remove the lid, tilting it away from you to allow any excess steam to escape.

continued

5. Stir in enough cider vinegar and additional salt, if needed, to bring up the flavors. Mix in the peanuts as you fluff up the rice. Garnish with sliced avocado or avocado vinaigrette.

Standard Stovetop: In a heavy 3-quart saucepan, heat the oil and sauté the onion, garlic, and red bell pepper for 2 minutes, stirring frequently. Stir in the chili powder, crushed red pepper flakes, 3 cups of water, and salt. Bring to the boil over high heat and stir in the rice. Return to the boil, then reduce the heat and simmer, covered, for 45 minutes. Turn off the heat and let stand, covered, for 10 minutes. Follow step 5.

Variations
- Use pitted and coarsely chopped green olives instead of peanuts.
- Stir in ½ cup finely chopped parsley or cilantro as you fluff up the rice.

Spanish Casserole Rice

Serves 4 to 6

Fresh tomato puree is the primary liquid base in this spicy dish. For best results, use a thoroughly ripened large tomato (or two smaller ones) for making the puree.

Pressure cooker: 20 minutes high pressure, 20-minute natural pressure release
Standard stovetop: 45 minutes plus 10 minutes standing

1 tablespoon olive oil (optional)
1 large onion, peeled and finely chopped
1 large clove garlic, peeled and finely chopped
1 large green bell pepper, seeded and finely chopped
1 large (about 10 ounces) ripe tomato, pureed (about 1¼ cups)
1 tablespoon balsamic vinegar
1 teaspoon dried leaf oregano
1 teaspoon sweet paprika
½ teaspoon sea salt
⅛ to ¼ teaspoon crushed red pepper flakes
1½ cups long-grain brown rice
½ cup tightly packed minced fresh parsley or coriander
½ cup coarsely chopped, pitted green olives
Dash hot sauce (optional)

1. Heat the oil in the cooker. Sauté the onion, garlic, and green pepper for 2 minutes, stirring frequently. (This step is optional: Just place the onion, garlic, and green pepper directly into the casserole and omit the oil.)

2. Transfer the mixture to a 2-quart heatproof casserole.

3. Set the tomato puree in a measuring cup and add enough water to equal 1¾ cups. Add this liquid plus the vinegar, oregano, paprika, salt, crushed red pepper flakes, and rice to the casserole.

4. Set a rack or trivet and 2 cups of water into the cooker. Lower the uncovered casserole into the cooker with the aid of a foil strip (page 10).

5. Lock the lid in place and over high heat bring to high pressure. Lower the heat just enough to maintain high pressure and cook for 20 minutes. Allow the pressure to come down naturally for 20 minutes. Remove the lid, tilting it away from you to allow any excess steam to escape. If the rice is not quite tender, set the cover back in place and let steam a few more minutes in the residual heat.

6. When the rice is done, remove the casserole from the cooker with the aid of the foil strip.

7. Fluff up the rice as you stir in the parsley and olives. Add hot sauce to taste, if desired.

Standard Stovetop: In a heavy 3-quart casserole, heat the oil. Sauté the onion, garlic, and green pepper for 2 minutes, stirring frequently. Add the tomato puree plus enough water to equal 3 cups. Add the vinegar, oregano, paprika, crushed red pepper flakes, and salt and over high heat bring to the boil. Stir in the rice. Return to the boil, then reduce the heat and simmer, covered, until almost all of the liquid has been absorbed, about 45 minutes. Turn off the heat and let stand, covered, until all of the liquid has been absorbed, about 10 minutes. Follow step 7.

How they live reflects what they believe. Their life is their art.
—Sue Bender, *Plain and Simple*
(New York: Harper & Row, 1989).

Skillet-Fried Brown Rice

This is a fine way to recycle leftover cooked rice (and most other grains). It's such an appealing dish that you might want to prepare a double amount of rice with an eye toward serving it the next day. You can exercise enormous flexibility in the ingredients. The dish doesn't ever have to come out the same way twice.

Skillet or wok: 15 minutes

1 tablespoon oil
2 teaspoons freshly grated ginger
1 to 2 cloves garlic, peeled and finely chopped
1 small green or red bell pepper, seeded and chopped
2 ribs celery, cut into ¼-inch slices on the diagonal
¼ pound mushrooms, sliced
5 scallions, thinly sliced (keep white and green parts separate)
1½ cups shredded cabbage
1 cup cooked fresh or frozen (defrosted) green peas or chopped, cooked kale
3 cups cooked brown rice or other grain
2 to 3 teaspoons toasted (Oriental) sesame oil
1 to 2 tablespoons tamari soy sauce

OPTIONAL GARNISH
Chopped watercress or shredded nori sea vegetable

1. In a large skillet or wok, heat the oil. Sauté the ginger and garlic for 30 seconds. Add the pepper, celery, mushrooms, scallion whites, and cabbage. Sauté for 2 minutes, stirring frequently.

2. Stir in the green peas, rice, and optional variations (see below). Cook over medium heat until the ingredients are hot and most of the liquid has evaporated. (If the mixture becomes dry and begins to stick to the skillet, stir in 2 to 3 tablespoons of water or the marinating liquid from the seitan or tofu, if using; see Variations.)

3. Just before serving, stir in the scallion greens and season with sesame oil and soy sauce to taste. Garnish with watercress or nori, if desired.

Variations: Other tasty ingredients to toss into the rice include coarsely chopped, cooked broccoli, cooked corn kernels, toasted peanuts, pumpkin or sunflower seeds, ½ pound seitan (page 453), cut into ½-inch dice (reserve soaking liquid), ¼ pound pan-fried tempeh (page 228) in ½-inch dice, or ¼ pound marinated tofu (page 220) in ½-inch dice (reserve soaking liquid).

Basic Wild Rice

Because the time and amount of water needed to prepare wild rice vary, I pressure-cook it in ample liquid, then drain off any excess and let the rice steam in the covered pot for a minute or two. Most batches will be properly butterflied (split open) in 22 minutes. If not, just bring the pressure back up for another few minutes.

Use wild rice as the stuffing for baked squash or to dress up a grain salad.

Pressure cooker: 22 to 28 minutes high pressure, optional natural pressure release
Standard stovetop: 50 to 55 minutes plus 10 minutes standing

1 cup (about 6 ounces) wild rice, rinsed
2 teaspoons oil (needed in jiggle-top cookers to control foaming)
3 cups water or vegetable stock
¼ teaspoon sea salt, or to taste

1. Combine the rice, oil (if needed), stock, and salt in the cooker.

2. Lock the lid in place and over high heat bring to high pressure. Adjust the heat to maintain high pressure and cook for 22 minutes. Quick-release the pressure or allow it to come down naturally. Remove the lid, tilting it away from you to allow any excess steam to escape.

3. If more than half of the rice is not butterflied, return to high pressure for a few more minutes or simmer, covered, without pressure until done.

4. Drain (reserve the liquid for stock) and return to the pot. Cover and let steam over low heat for a few minutes to dry out. Fluff up and serve.

Standard Stovetop: In a heavy 2-quart saucepan, bring 2½ cups water and ¼ teaspoon salt to the boil. Stir in the rice, return to the boil, reduce heat and simmer, covered, until most of the grains have butterflied and most of the liquid has been absorbed, 50 to 55 minutes. Turn off the heat and let stand for an additional 10 minutes. Fluff up before serving.

Variations

- Add a rib of chopped celery, a chopped onion, a bay leaf, and a small handful of dried mushrooms.
- Cook the rice with a cinnamon stick, broken in two.
- Add a generous ¼ teaspoon of nutmeg, cloves, or allspice to the rice while cooking.

Wild Rice with Chestnuts

This is a lovely marriage of mellow, sweet chestnuts with crunchy wild rice. Serve it on its own or use it to stuff squash.

> **Pressure cooker:** 25 minutes high pressure
> **Standard stovetop:** 50 minutes plus 10 minutes standing

1 tablespoon oil
5 medium shallots, peeled and finely chopped
2 ribs celery, finely chopped
1 cup (about 6 ounces) wild rice, rinsed
⅓ cup dried, peeled chestnuts
¼ cup dried currants
2 teaspoons aniseed
¼ teaspoon sea salt, or to taste
4 cups water
1 teaspoon finely chopped or freshly grated orange peel (colored part only, organic if possible)

1. Heat the oil in the cooker. Add the shallots and celery and cook, stirring frequently, until softened slightly, about 1 minute. Stir in the rice, chestnuts, currants, aniseed, salt, and water.

2. Lock the lid in place and over high heat bring to high pressure. Lower the heat just enough to maintain high pressure and cook for 25 minutes. Allow the pressure to come down naturally or use a quick-release method. Remove the lid, tilting it away from you to allow any excess steam to escape. If the rice or chestnuts are not quite cooked, return to high pressure for another few minutes.

3. Drain (reserve the liquid for stock) and return to the pot. Cover and let steam over low heat for a few minutes to dry out. Fluff up as you stir in the orange peel. Break up chestnuts into 2 to 3 pieces with a fork, if desired.

Standard Stovetop: Soak the chestnuts overnight. Drain and reserve the water. In a heavy 2-quart saucepan, heat the oil. Add the shallots and celery and sauté for 1 minute. Add the chestnut soaking liquid plus enough water to equal 3 cups and bring to the boil. Stir in the rice, reserved chestnuts, currants, aniseed, and salt. Return to the boil, cover, reduce heat, and simmer until most of the grains have butterflied and almost all of the liquid has been absorbed, about 50 minutes. Let stand, covered, off heat for 10 minutes. If there is still liquid left in the bottom of the pot, lift out the rice with a slotted spoon.

White Rice and Risotto

Since my diet consists almost entirely of whole foods, I don't worry about eating white rice from time to time, either when I don't feel like chewing quite as much as brown rice requires, or when I need to have dinner on the table in 10 minutes flat.

My all-time favorite white rice is white basmati, whose slender grains have a wonderful nutty aroma and delicate texture. Authentic basmati is imported from India, and many rice connoisseurs find it far superior to domestic kinds. It's available in Indian groceries and some gourmet shops. Most health food stores sell domestic basmati, which is quite satisfactory.

I'm crazy about risotto and always keep on hand a good supply of the short-grained, starchy white rice called Arborio that is traditionally used to make this classic Italian rice dish. Risotto is ideal company food. Like pasta, it seems to have universal appeal and can be prepared in a flash with ingredients easily kept on hand.

Everywhere people ask, "What can I actually do?" The answer is as simple as it is disconcerting—we can, each of us, work to put our own inner house in order. The guidance we need for this work cannot be found in science or technology, the value of which utterly depends on the ends they serve; but it can still be found in the traditional wisdom of humankind.
—E. F. Schumacher, *Small Is Beautiful* (Harper & Row, 1989).

Basic White Basmati or
Extra-Long-Grain Rice

It's not necessary to rinse white rice before cooking, but I prefer to give it a quick rinse anyway, especially when I've purchased it from an open bin. For a moist rice, use 1¾ cups liquid. For a drier rice, use 1½ cups.

Pressure cooker: 3 minutes high pressure, 7-minute natural pressure release
Standard stovetop: 15 to 20 minutes plus 5 minutes standing

1 cup white basmati or extra-long-grain white rice
1½ to 1¾ cups water or vegetable stock
½ to ¾ teaspoon sea salt (less if using salted stock)

SEASONING OPTIONS
see page 120

1. Combine all ingredients in the cooker (including seasoning options). Turn the heat to high and stir a few times to blend.

2. Lock the lid in place and over high heat bring to high pressure. Lower the heat just enough to maintain high pressure and cook for 3 minutes. Allow the pressure to come down naturally for 7 minutes. Quick-release any remaining pressure. Remove the lid, tilting it away from you to allow excess steam to escape. If the rice is not quite tender, replace the lid and allow it to steam in the residual heat for a minute or two.

3. When the rice is done, fluff with a fork, adjust seasonings, and serve.

Standard Stovetop: In a heavy 2-quart saucepan, bring 2 cups of water and the salt to the boil over high heat. Stir in the rice and seasonings of your choice and return to the boil. Reduce the heat and simmer, covered, until almost all of the liquid has been absorbed, about 15 to 20 minutes. Turn off the heat and let stand, covered, for 5 minutes. Follow step 3.

Work is love made visible.
—Kahlil Gibran, *The Prophet*, 1923.

Pressure Cooker*
White Rice Cooking Chart

For a dry rice, use the smaller amount of liquid.
For a moist rice, use the maximum.

White Basmati or Extra Long-Grain White Rice	Cups Liquid	Optional Salt	Yield in Cups
1 cup	1½–1¾	½ teaspoon	3
1½ cups	2¼–2½	¾ teaspoon	4–4½
2 cups	3–3¼	1 teaspoon	5½–6
3 cups	4¼–4½	1½ teaspoons	7½–8

Do not cook more than 3 cups of dry white rice in a 6-quart cooker.
*See basic cooking instructions, page 142.

Standard Stovetop*
White Rice Cooking Chart

White Basmati or Extra Long-Grain White Rice	Cups Liquid	Optional Salt	Yield in Cups
1 cup	2	½ teaspoon	3
1½ cups	3	¾ teaspoon	4½
2 cups	4	1 teaspoon	6
3 cups	6	1½ teaspoons	8½

*See basic cooking instructions, page 142.

Basic Casserole-Steamed
White Rice

Pressure-steam white rice in a heatproof casserole, then bring it right to the table.

> **Pressure cooker:** 5 minutes high pressure, 7- to 10-minute natural pressure release
> **Standard stovetop:** 20 minutes plus 10 minutes standing

> *1 cup white basmati or extra-long-grain white rice*
> *1½ cups water*
> *½ teaspoon sea salt, or to taste*

> **SEASONING OPTIONS**
> *see page 120*

1. In a 1½- to 2-quart casserole, combine the rice, water, salt, and seasoning options.

2. Set a rack or trivet and 2 cups of water into the cooker. Lower the uncovered casserole into the cooker with the aid of a foil strip (page 10).

3. Lock the lid in place and over high heat bring to high pressure. Lower the heat just enough to maintain high pressure and cook for 5 minutes. Allow the pressure to come down naturally, about 7 to 10 minutes. Remove the lid, tilting it away from you to allow any excess steam to escape. If the rice is not quite tender, set the cover back in place and let steam a few more minutes in the residual heat.

4. When the rice is done, remove the casserole from the cooker with the aid of the foil strip.

5. Fluff up the rice and adjust seasonings before serving.

Standard Stovetop: Follow step 1. Using a large pot, follow step 2. Bring the water in the bottom of the pot to the boil, cover, and steam over medium heat for 20 minutes, replenishing water if needed. Let stand off heat for 10 minutes. Follow steps 4 and 5.

You have only failed when you have failed to try.

White Basmati Rice with Carrots and Broccoli

A chance to give broccoli stalks their own grand finale when you are using the florets for another dish (such as in Marinated Broccoli, page 243).

The stalks are sliced, then cooked with the rice; they become mellow and offer a nice contrast to the chewy rice. Perky orange bits of carrot add good cheer.

Pressure cooker: 3 minutes high pressure, 7-minute natural pressure release
Standard stovetop: 15 to 20 minutes plus 5 minutes standing

Stalks from 1 medium bunch of broccoli
1 tablespoon olive oil
1 small clove garlic, peeled and finely chopped
1 cup white basmati or extra-long-grain white rice
1½ cups vegetable stock or water
2 medium carrots, cut into matchsticks approximately ¼ inch × 1½ inches
¾ teaspoon dried rosemary leaves or ½ teaspoon dried leaf oregano
¾ teaspoon sea salt (less if using salted stock)

1. Peel the broccoli stalks, and cut the stalks into slices ¼-inch thick. Cut large slices into quarters and small slices in half. (You should have about 1¾ cups.) Set aside.

2. Heat the oil in the cooker and sauté the garlic for 30 seconds. Stir in the rice and coat well with the oil. Add the broccoli and remaining ingredients.

3. Lock the lid into place. Over high heat bring to high pressure. Lower the heat just enough to maintain high pressure and cook for 3 minutes. Allow the pressure to come down naturally for 7 minutes. Reduce any remaining pressure with a quick-release method. Remove the lid, tilting it away from you to allow any excess steam to escape.

4. Fluff up the rice by stirring with a fork. Adjust seasonings before serving.

Standard Stovetop: In a heavy 2-quart saucepan, follow steps 1 and 2, increasing the liquid to 2 cups. Bring to the boil over high heat, then reduce the heat and simmer, covered, until almost all of the liquid has been absorbed, about 15 to 20 minutes. Turn off the heat and let stand, covered, until all of the liquid has been absorbed, about 5 minutes. Follow step 4.

White Basmati Rice
with Celery and Aniseed

If you'd like the celery to have a soft and mellow texture, cut the slices ¼ inch thick. For crunchier celery, slice it a bit thicker and on the diagonal. Either way, the marriage of celery and anise tastes like happily ever after.

Pressure cooker: 3 minutes high pressure, 7-minute natural pressure release
Standard stovetop: 15 to 20 minutes plus 5 minutes standing

1 tablespoon oil
⅓ cup finely minced shallots or onions
1 cup white basmati or extra-long-grain white rice
4 ribs celery, cut into ¼-inch (or slightly larger) slices, on the diagonal
1 large carrot, cut into matchsticks approximately ¼ inch × 1 inch
1½ cups vegetable stock
1¼ teaspoons aniseed
¾ teaspoon sea salt (less if using salted stock)

1. Heat the oil in the cooker and sauté the shallots for 2 minutes. Stir in the rice and coat well with the oil. Add the remaining ingredients.
2. Lock the lid into place. Over high heat bring to high pressure. Lower the heat just enough to maintain high pressure and cook for 3 minutes. Allow the pressure to come down naturally for 7 minutes. Quick-release any remaining pressure. Remove the lid, tilting it away from you to allow any excess steam to escape.
3. Fluff up the rice by stirring with a fork.

Standard Stovetop: In a heavy 3-quart saucepan, heat the oil and sauté the shallots for 2 minutes. Add 1¾ cups stock and bring to the boil. Stir in the rice and other ingredients. Return to the boil, then reduce the heat and simmer, covered, until most of the liquid has been absorbed, about 15 to 20 minutes. Turn off the heat and let stand, covered, for 5 minutes. Follow step 3.

Nothing ventured, nothing gained.

Although plain white basmati rice is interesting enough to stand on its own, especially when it's the backdrop for a well-seasoned curry or vegetable stew, I sometimes like to dress it up with diced vegetables that cook in an equivalent amount of time. With little extra effort, this approach turns a mound of plain rice into a special occasion.

I've given three examples here, but the possibilities for creating your own recipes are endless:

1. Select any vegetable that cooks in 3 to 6 minutes (check the charts on pages 235–237).

2. Select an appropriate herb or spice to cook with the rice from Flavorprints, page 4.

3. For added color and to perk up flavor, stir in a few tablespoons of finely minced fresh herbs at the end of the cooking time.

White Basmati Rice with Squash and Pine Nuts

Serves 6

This dish is especially striking when made with a green-skinned squash such as buttercup or a member of the kabocha family. Left unpeeled, the squash retains its shape nicely, and the pressure cooker does a fine job of softening the skin. (Do peel the skin, however, if the squash has been waxed, is not organic, or has tough, leathery skin.)

Pressure cooker: 3 minutes high pressure, 7-minute natural pressure release
Standard stovetop: 15 to 20 minutes plus 5 minutes standing

1 tablespoon oil
⅓ cup pine nuts
1½ teaspoons fennel seeds
1½ cups white basmati or extra-long-grain white rice
2¼ cups vegetable stock or water
¾ teaspoon sea salt (less if using salted stock)
1 pound winter squash (such as butternut or kabocha), well scrubbed, seeded, and cut into 1-inch chunks
Tamari soy sauce or Bragg Liquid Aminos to taste (optional)

continued

1. Heat the oil in the cooker and brown the pine nuts over medium heat, stirring frequently. (Proceed with caution as the nuts turn from brown to burned in a flash.) Add the fennel seeds toward the end of browning.

2. Stir in the rice and coat well with the oil. Add the stock (watch for sputtering oil!), salt, and squash.

3. Lock the lid into place. Over high heat bring to high pressure. Lower the heat just enough to maintain high pressure and cook for 3 minutes. Allow the pressure to come down naturally for 7 minutes. Quick-release any remaining pressure. Remove the lid, tilting it away from you to allow any excess steam to escape. If the rice or squash is not quite cooked, replace the lid and allow it to continue steaming in the residual heat for another minute or two.

4. Fluff up the rice by stirring with a fork. Taste and add tamari or Liquid Aminos if the flavors need perking up.

Standard Stovetop: Peel the squash and set aside. In a heavy 3-quart saucepan, follow step 1. Add 2¾ cups stock (watch for sputtering oil!) and bring to the boil. Stir in the rice, salt, and *peeled* squash. Return to the boil, then reduce the heat and simmer, covered, until most of the liquid has been absorbed, about 15 to 20 minutes. Turn off the heat and let stand, covered, for 5 minutes. Follow step 4.

Variation: Use toasted pumpkin seeds instead of the pine nuts. Stir them in at the end.

> When our strategies are formed and informed by a larger context than our narrow ego selves, when we realize we are acting not just from our own opinions or beliefs, but on behalf of a larger Self—the Earth—with the authority of more than four billion years of our planet's evolution behind us, then we are filled with new determination, courage and perseverance, less limited by self-doubt, narrow self-interest and discouragement.
>
> —John Seed, Joanna Macy, Pat Fleming, and Arne Naess,
> *Thinking Like a Mountain*
> (Philadelphia: New Society Publishers, 1988).

Herbed Bulgur Rice

Serves 4

A lovely alternative to plain white rice, the bulgur adds flecks of brown, providing an earthy depth not commonly associated with white rice. Because bulgur needs a bit more cooking time, it is brought to boil with the water before the rice is added.

Pressure cooker: 3 minutes high pressure, 7-minute natural pressure release
Standard stovetop: 20 minutes plus 5 minutes standing

1¾ cups water or vegetable stock
¼ cup medium or coarse bulgur
1 cup white basmati or extra-long-grain rice
¾ to 1 teaspoon sea salt (or season with tamari soy sauce to taste after
    cooking)
½ cup tightly packed, finely chopped fresh parsley, dill, or basil, or a
    combination of 1 teaspoon each dried leaf oregano and basil, and
    ¼ teaspoon dried rosemary leaves

1. In the cooker, bring the water and bulgur to the boil over high heat. Stir in the rice, salt, and dried herbs (if using).

2. Lock the lid in place and over high heat bring to high pressure. Lower the heat just enough to maintain high pressure and cook for 3 minutes. Let the pressure come down naturally for 7 minutes. Quick-release any remaining pressure. If the rice or bulgur is not sufficiently tender, replace the lid and allow it to steam in the residual heat for a few more minutes.

3. Toss in the fresh herbs (if using) as you fluff up the rice. Adjust seasonings, adding tamari to taste, if desired.

Standard Stovetop: In a heavy 2-quart saucepan, follow step 1, increasing the liquid to 2¼ cups. Return to the boil, then reduce the heat and simmer, covered, until all of the liquid has been absorbed, about 20 minutes. Turn off the heat and let stand, covered, for 5 additional minutes. Follow step 3.

Variation: Stir in ¼ cup toasted chopped walnuts or 2 tablespoons toasted sunflower seeds after cooking.

Risotto

One of my happiest discoveries is that the pressure cooker can produce a wonderfully chewy risotto in about 5 minutes with hardly a stir. (Classic risotto normally takes about 30 minutes of continual stirring.) As a result, risotto has become standard company fare in my household: It's quick, easy, and enormously popular—a terrific alternative to pasta!

Risotto is made with Arborio, a starchy Italian short-grained rice, available from gourmet shops and by mail order. When it is cooked in a generous quantity of stock, the starch is released, creating a luscious thick sauce. This slightly chewy, soupy rice becomes the backdrop for a whole panoply of added ingredients.

Many classic risottos rely on lots of butter and Parmesan cheese for richness and flavoring. The trick to making a top-notch low-fat and dairy-free risotto is to include a variety of assertive flavors and textures and to season effectively.

In making risotto, the rice is generally not rinsed before cooking so the starches that contribute to its velvety sauce are not washed away. The pressure is always quick-released to avoid overcooking the rice. Ideally, the risotto should be prepared just before it is served. Leftover risotto can be shaped into patties and pan-fried or reheated on an oiled baking sheet.

I love risotto so much I had to discipline myself to stop creating new recipes after coming up with the six that follow. But I hope you won't stop at such a small number. Just use the basic formula of 3½ to 4 cups of liquid to 1½ cups of Arborio rice, and come up with your own irresistible versions.

Risotto with Corn and Roasted Peppers

**Serves 4 as a main course
or 6 as an appetizer**

A very colorful risotto, full of decidedly Southwestern flavors.

Pressure cooker: 5 minutes high pressure
Standard stovetop: 30 to 35 minutes

1 to 2 tablespoons olive oil
1 large clove garlic, peeled and finely chopped
1½ teaspoons whole cumin seeds
1 large onion, peeled, or 1 leek (white part only), finely chopped
1½ cups Arborio rice
1½ to 2 cups fresh corn kernels (from 2 large ears of corn)
3½ to 4 cups vegetable stock
1 teaspoon sea salt (less if using salted stock)
2 large roasted red or green bell peppers (page 451), seeded and cut into
    strips about ¼ inch × ½ inch
⅓ cup tightly packed, finely minced fresh coriander or parsley
Freshly ground black pepper

1. Heat the oil in the cooker and sauté the garlic, cumin, and onion for 1 minute, stirring frequently. Stir in the rice, making sure to coat it thoroughly with the oil.

2. Stir in the corn kernels, 3½ cups of stock (watch for sputtering oil!), and salt. Lock the lid in place and over high heat bring to high pressure. Lower the heat just enough to maintain high pressure and cook for 5 minutes. Reduce the pressure with a quick-release method. Remove the lid, tilting it away from you to allow any excess steam to escape.

3. The rice will continue to absorb liquid at this point and the risotto should end up being slightly soupy. If necessary, stir in a bit more stock as you stir in the peppers, coriander, and ground pepper. Cook over medium heat, stirring constantly, until the rice achieves the desired consistency (it should be tender but chewy) and the ingredients are thoroughly heated. Serve immediately in shallow soup bowls.

Standard Stovetop: In a 3-quart saucepan, follow step 1. Stir in the corn kernels and salt. Reduce the heat to medium and immediately begin adding the stock, about ⅓ cup at a time. Stir constantly. As the rice absorbs each batch of liquid and you can create an empty strip by drawing a spoon along the bottom of the pot, add an additional ⅓ cup stock. Continue in this fashion until the rice is almost done, about 30 minutes. Follow step 3.

Variation: Use ⅓ cup chopped sun-dried tomatoes instead of the roasted red peppers.

Lemon-Scented Asparagus Risotto

Serves 4 as a main course
or 6 as an appetizer

This is one of the best ways I know of to showcase asparagus, whose great green trumpets become plentiful and announce the arrival of spring. I love the contrasts in texture provided by the tender-crisp asparagus and the chewy rice.

Pressure cooker: 5 minutes high pressure
Standard stovetop: 30 to 35 minutes

1½ pounds medium-sized asparagus
1 cup water
¼ ounce (⅓ cup chopped) dried mushrooms
½ cup boiling water
3½ to 4 cups vegetable stock
1 tablespoon olive oil
1 medium onion, peeled and finely chopped or 1 medium leek (white part
    only), thinly sliced and thoroughly rinsed to remove sand
1½ cups Arborio rice
½ teaspoon fennel seeds
1¼ teaspoons sea salt (less if using salted stock)
1 tablespoon finely minced or grated lemon rind (colored part only, organic
    if possible)
2 to 3 tablespoons freshly squeezed lemon juice
3 tablespoons finely chopped fresh parsley

1. Break off the tough stems of the asparagus and set aside. (Save them for Spring Asparagus-Celery Stock, page 28.) Rinse the spears.
2. Set the cup of water to boil in the cooker and place the asparagus directly into the water. Cover and steam over medium-high heat until the asparagus are tender-crisp, about 3 to 6 minutes (depending upon age and thickness of the spears).
3. Remove the asparagus with a spatula and pour the cooking liquid into a 4-cup measure. Cut the asparagus into 1-inch slices and set aside.

4. Set the mushrooms in a small bowl and pour the ½ cup boiling water over them. Let sit, covered, for about 10 minutes. Remove the mushrooms. If they are whole, slice them. Set aside. Strain the mushroom water through a double layer of cheesecloth into the 4-cup measure containing the asparagus broth. (This step is taken because dried mushrooms are often very sandy; if the mushrooms are not sandy, you can quickly rinse them instead.) Add enough vegetable stock to the asparagus-mushroom liquid to equal 4 cups total.

5. Dry out the cooker and in it heat the oil. Sauté the onion until soft, about 2 minutes. Stir in the rice until it is well coated with the oil. Stir in the reserved mushrooms, fennel seeds, salt, and 3½ cups of stock. (Watch for sputtering oil!)

6. Lock the lid in place and over high heat bring to high pressure. Lower the heat just enough to maintain high pressure and cook for 5 minutes. Reduce the pressure with a quick-release method. Remove the lid, tilting it away from you to allow any excess steam to escape.

7. The risotto will continue to absorb liquid at this point and should end up being slightly soupy. If necessary, stir in a bit more stock as you add the cooked asparagus, lemon rind, lemon juice, and parsley. If the rice is not quite tender (it should be chewy but not crunchy), continue to cook, uncovered, over medium-high heat for another minute or so, stirring all the time. Adjust seasonings before serving in shallow soup bowls.

Standard Stovetop: In a 3-quart saucepan, follow steps 1 to 3 (cut asparagus in half if necessary). Proceed to step 4. Dry off the saucepan and complete step 5, omitting the stock. Reduce the heat to medium and immediately begin adding the stock, about ⅓ cup at a time, and stir constantly. Just as the rice absorbs each batch of liquid and you can create an empty strip by drawing your spoon along the bottom of the pot, add an additional ⅓ cup liquid. Continue adding liquid until the rice is almost done, about 30 minutes. Follow step 7.

Variation: Steam fiddlehead ferns until tender, about 12 to 15 minutes, and substitute them for the asparagus. However, don't use the fiddlehead steaming water.

The seminal signs of spring are fragile, tender and easily bruised. Cooks beware: the less done, the better. The impressionability of a life not yet weathered is the essential charm of spring ingredients. Sparing the rigors of long cooking and heavy or complicated seasoning will not spoil this sort of child.

—Molly O'Neill, *The New York Times*, March 27, 1991.

Risotto with Carrots, Peas, and Mint

When you have unexpected company, this is the dish to prepare. Use those peas in your freezer and just add extra parsley if there is no fresh mint within arm's reach.

Pressure cooker: 5 minutes high pressure
Standard stovetop: 30 to 35 minutes

1 tablespoon olive oil
1 small onion, peeled and finely chopped
1½ cups Arborio rice
2 medium carrots, halved lengthwise and cut into ¼-inch half-moons
3½ to 4 cups vegetable stock
1 teaspoon sea salt (or less if using salted stock)
1 cup fresh cooked or frozen (defrosted) green peas
⅓ cup tightly packed minced fresh mint
¼ cup tightly packed minced fresh parsley

1. Heat the oil in the cooker and sauté the onion for 1 minute, stirring frequently. Stir in the rice, making sure to coat it thoroughly with the oil.

2. Stir in the carrots, 3½ cups of the stock (watch for sputtering oil!), and the salt.

3. Lock the lid in place and over high heat bring to high pressure. Lower the heat just enough to maintain high pressure and cook for 5 minutes. Reduce the pressure with a quick-release method. Remove the lid, tilting it away from you to allow any excess steam to escape.

4. The risotto will continue to absorb liquid at this point and should end up being slightly soupy. If necessary, stir in a bit more stock as you stir in the peas, mint, and parsley. Cook over medium heat, stirring constantly, until the rice achieves the desired consistency (it should be tender but chewy) and the peas are thoroughly heated. Serve immediately in shallow soup bowls.

Standard Stovetop: In a 3-quart saucepan, follow step 1. Reduce the heat to medium and stir in the carrots and salt. Immediately begin adding the stock, about ⅓ cup at a time, and stir constantly. As the rice absorbs each batch of liquid and you can create an empty strip by drawing a spoon along the bottom of the pot, add an additional ⅓ cup stock. Continue in this fashion until the rice is almost done, about 30 minutes. Follow step 4.

Crimson Risotto with Pine Nuts and Currants

An eye-arresting risotto, dyed a brilliant crimson by beets.

Pressure cooker: 5 minutes high pressure
Standard stovetop: 30 minutes

1 tablespoon olive or canola oil
1 cup thinly sliced leeks (white and green parts)
1½ cups Arborio rice
1 medium (6 ounces) unpeeled beet, coarsely chopped or cut into ¼-inch
     dice (see Cook's Notes)
3½ to 4 cups vegetable stock
¼ cup dried currants
½ teaspoon ground cinnamon
¼ teaspoon ground cloves
1 teaspoon sea salt (less if using salted stock)
5 to 6 large (about 3 ounces) beet greens, thick ribs removed, finely
     chopped, or an equivalent amount of trimmed and chopped spinach
     (optional)
⅓ cup toasted pine nuts
Umeboshi plum vinegar to taste (optional)

1. Heat the oil in the cooker and sauté the leeks for 1 minute, stirring frequently. Stir in the rice, making sure to coat it thoroughly with the oil.

2. Stir in the chopped beet, and 3½ cups of the stock (watch for sputtering oil!), currants, spices, and salt.

3. Lock the lid in place and over high heat bring to high pressure. Lower the heat just enough to maintain high pressure and cook for 5 minutes. Reduce pressure with a quick-release method. Remove the lid, tilting it away from you to allow any excess steam to escape.

4. The risotto will continue to absorb liquid at this point and should end up being slightly soupy. If necessary, stir in a bit more stock with the optional beet greens and pine nuts. Add salt or a few drops of umeboshi plum vinegar if the flavors need perking up. Cook over medium heat, stirring constantly, until the rice achieves the desired consistency (it should be tender but chewy) and the beet greens are tender, about 2 to 3 minutes. Serve immediately in shallow soup bowls.

continued

Standard Stovetop: In a 3-quart saucepan, follow step 1. Reduce the heat to medium and stir in the chopped beet, currants, spices, and salt. Immediately begin adding the stock, about ⅓ cup at a time, and stir constantly. Just as the rice absorbs each batch of liquid and you can create an empty strip by drawing a spoon along the bottom of the pot, add an additional ⅓ cup stock. Continue in this fashion until the rice is almost done, about 30 minutes. Stir in the beet greens (if using), pine nuts, and extra salt, if needed. Continue stirring until the greens are cooked and the rice tender but chewy.

Cook's Notes: The finished risotto looks prettier if the beet is diced rather than chopped, although this requires a bit more effort. A friend of mine removes the cooked beet, purees it, and stirs it back into the cooked risotto. She raves about the results.

Risotto with Spinach, Chick-peas, and Sun-Dried Tomatoes

Serves 4 as a
main course or
6 as an appetizer

A risotto rich in some of the most distinctive flavors of the Mediterranean— sun-drenched tomatoes, basil, and rosemary. The chick-peas and greens add an unexpected twist.

Pressure cooker: 5 minutes high pressure, 2 minutes simmering
Standard stovetop: 30 to 35 minutes

1 to 2 tablespoons oil from sun-dried tomatoes
1 cup coarsely chopped leeks (white and green parts) or onions
2 large cloves garlic, peeled and finely chopped
1½ cups Arborio rice
3½ to 4 cups vegetable stock
1 teaspoon dried basil or leaf oregano
½ teaspoon dried rosemary leaves (optional)
1 teaspoon sea salt (less if using salted stock)
½ cup sun-dried tomatoes packed in oil, drained and coarsely chopped
1 to 1½ cups tightly packed chopped spinach, beet greens, or chard
1 cup cooked chick-peas
Lots of freshly ground black pepper to taste

1. Heat the oil in the cooker. Sauté the leeks and garlic until soft but not brown, about 2 minutes. Stir in the rice, making sure to coat it thoroughly with the oil.

2. Stir in 3½ cups of the stock (watch for sputtering oil!), basil, rosemary (if using), and salt. Lock the lid in place and over high heat bring to high pressure. Lower the heat just enough to maintain high pressure and cook for 5 minutes. Reduce pressure with a quick-release method. Remove the lid, tilting it away from you to allow any excess steam to escape.

3. The risotto will continue to absorb liquid at this point and should end up being slightly soupy. If necessary, stir in a bit more stock as you stir in the sun-dried tomatoes, spinach, chick-peas, and pepper. Cook over medium heat, stirring constantly, until the rice achieves the desired consistency (it should be tender but chewy) and the spinach is cooked, about 2 more minutes. Serve immediately in shallow soup bowls.

Standard Stovetop: In a 3-quart saucepan, follow step 1. Stir in the basil, rosemary, and salt. Reduce the heat to medium and immediately begin adding the stock, about ⅓ cup at a time, and stir constantly. Just as the rice absorbs each batch of liquid and you can create an empty strip by drawing your spoon along the bottom of the pot, add an additional ⅓ cup stock. Continue in this fashion until the rice is almost done, about 30 minutes. Follow step 3.

Variation: Use chopped, *cooked* escarole or kale instead of the raw spinach. Simmer just until warmed throughout, about 1 to 2 minutes.

Tarragon Risotto with Mushrooms and Leeks

Serves 4 as a main course or 6 as an appetizer

If you're looking for a simple risotto, with no need to cook any of the ingredients in advance, this is it. The rice is an ideal setting for that irresistible union of mushrooms and leeks.

Pressure cooker: 5 minutes high pressure
Standard stovetop: 30 to 35 minutes

1 to 2 tablespoons olive oil
1½ cups thinly sliced leeks (white and green parts), carefully rinsed
1½ cups Arborio rice
3½ to 4 cups vegetable stock
½ pound small mushrooms, sliced
1 teaspoon dried tarragon
1 teaspoon sea salt (less if using salted stock)
⅓ cup coarsely chopped, pitted black olives, preferably oil-cured

1. Heat the oil in the cooker and sauté the leeks for 1 minute, stirring frequently. Stir in the rice, making sure to coat it thoroughly with the oil.

2. Stir in 3½ cups of the stock (watch for sputtering oil!), the mushrooms, tarragon, and salt. Lock the lid in place and over high heat bring to high pressure. Lower the heat just enough to maintain high pressure and cook for 5 minutes. Reduce pressure with a quick-release method. Remove the lid, tilting it away from you to allow any excess steam to escape.

3. The risotto will continue to absorb liquid at this point and should end up being slightly soupy. If necessary, stir in a bit more stock as you stir in the olives and additional salt (if needed). Cook over medium heat, stirring constantly, until the rice achieves the desired consistency (it should be tender but chewy). Serve immediately in shallow soup bowls.

Standard Stovetop: In a 3-quart saucepan, follow step 1. Stir in the mushrooms, tarragon, and salt. Reduce the heat to medium and begin adding the stock, about ⅓ cup at a time. Stir constantly. Just as the rice absorbs each batch of liquid and you can create an empty strip by drawing your spoon along the bottom of the pot, add an additional ⅓ cup stock. Continue in this fashion until the rice is almost done, about 30 minutes. Follow step 3.

Pasta

Getting to Know Whole Grain Pasta

Once maligned as a fattening food (a reputation largely due to the rich sauces it was doused in), pasta has now been recognized as the fine source of complex carbohydrates that it is.

One of the most exciting new developments in the world of pasta is the range of non-wheat–based and Oriental pastas now readily available in well-stocked health food stores. An array of organic Italian-style pastas in familiar sizes and shapes has also appeared.

The main challenge is to find varieties that have satisfying texture. All too often, pastas made of healthful, high-protein grains such as quinoa or amaranth break into a million tiny pieces and become meltingly soft when cooked. As a result, although they often have an appealing taste, they don't have that nice resistance to the tooth called *al dente*. In addition, whole grain pastas often have a gritty texture (due to the bran content) that won't win fans among pasta connoisseurs.

While Italian and domestic pastas are generally made from very hard durum wheat, most of the wheat flour in the best Japanese pasta is milled from varieties of soft white wheat. Because of their lower gluten content, these pastas tend to have a softer texture than we are generally accustomed to. To cook them properly and avoid stickiness, follow the package instructions: Add cold water each time the water comes to a boil, until the noodles are cooked.

The good news is that the taste and texture of most whole grain pastas have improved enormously over the last few years. This is partly due to the increased availability of well-made Oriental varieties and partly to increasingly sophisticated American manufacturing practices. Among the best domestic brands is Eden, which produces (and also imports) a wide variety of Oriental-style and Western-style noodles of all sizes and shapes. Westbrae Soba Shop Udon and Mitoku noodles are also excellent. I like the noodles made from whole wheat and brown rice flours. (*Note*: While most American products labeled noodles contain eggs, Oriental noodles traditionally do not; if this is a consideration for you, always check the label.)

If you try these brands and still favor more traditional Western-style pasta, go for it. If there are plenty of whole grains in your daily diet, eating noodles made of refined flour from time to time is just fine.

For descriptions of specific types of noodles, check Ingredients A to Z under Pasta and individual listings.

ECO-TIP: Most Italian cookbooks tell you to boil pasta in oodles of water—a technique that is inefficient and costly in terms of time, water, and fuel. My Italian friend Pietro Frassica—a superb cook—once prepared pasta for 4 (1 pound's worth!) in a tiny 1½-quart pot. When I expressed amazement, he told me that this was how his mother and sister always did it. I've been doing it that way ever since.

Warning: When cooking pasta in a small pot, just be sure to stir it from time to time and make certain that all of the pasta is submerged in the water. Add a tablespoon of oil to prevent the noodles from sticking together.

Oriental Ways with Pasta

China and Japan have ancient traditions of noodle-making. If you've ever eaten Chinese wontons or lo mein, you've already participated in that tradition.

I know an American whose life was changed by a bowl of Oriental noodles. One day, while living and working in Japan, James Udesky tasted handmade buckwheat noodles for the first time. The difference between them and machine-produced buckwheat noodles was so startling that Udesky decided on the spot to dedicate the next chapter of his life to making noodles.

Noodle-making in Japan is a craft taken very seriously, and it took Udesky more than three years to become skilled at it. His *Book of Soba* (Kodansha, 1988) contains recipes and detailed, illustrated instructions for making buckwheat (soba) noodles at home.

For centuries the Japanese have recognized the healthful properties of whole grain noodles, which are not only high in complex carbohydrates and dietary fiber, but contain little to no fat. Japanese noodles are often eaten plain or with a lightly seasoned dipping sauce on the side or in a bowl of hot broth.

Buckwheat noodles have an especially impressive nutritional profile, with a high percentage of usable protein. Their distinctive flavor is quite assertive. When combined with wheat and/or soy flours (as in soy-soba noodles), the taste of the buckwheat is modified and the pasta becomes almost as complete a protein as eggs, with none of the fat or cholesterol.

To derive the full nutritional benefit of buckwheat, without losing any of the water-soluble vitamins and minerals, you should also eat the noodle cooking broth. For this reason, according to Udesky, soba-shop customers are always offered a bowl of the cooking water near the end of their meal. Try it and if you don't like it, the broth can always go in the stockpot.

Never doubt that a small group of thoughtful, committed citizens can change the world. Indeed, it's the only thing that ever has.

—Margaret Mead

Whole Wheat Udon
with Squash and Toasted Nori

I enjoyed this creation so much that I prepared it three nights in a row. If you can find a green-skinned, unwaxed squash, cook it with the skin on, which adds extra color contrast.

Standard stovetop: 5 to 6 minutes (squash); 8 to 12 minutes (pasta)

1 pound winter squash, such as butternut or kabocha, peeled if necessary
1 tablespoon freshly grated ginger
8 ounces whole wheat udon or buckwheat soba
2 to 3 tablespoons (toasted) Oriental sesame oil
2 sheets toasted nori sea vegetable, shredded (see Cook's Notes)
Tamari soy sauce or Bragg Liquid Aminos to taste

GARNISH
Sesame seasoning salt (page 454) or toasted pumpkin seeds

1. Remove the seeds and cut the squash into 1-inch chunks. Place the squash in a saucepan, skin side down, in 1 inch of water. Add the ginger. Bring to the boil, cover, then lower the heat to medium, and cook the squash over medium heat until tender (but still firm), about 5 to 6 minutes. Check from time to time and replenish water as needed.

2. Meanwhile, cook the pasta in boiling salted water until al dente (tender with a bit of chewiness), following package directions, about 8 to 12 minutes.

3. Drain and toss immediately with sesame oil, nori, cooked squash, and any remaining squash cooking liquid.

4. Add tamari soy sauce to taste.

5. Sprinkle with sesame salt or toasted pumpkin seeds. Serve warm or at room temperature.

Cook's Notes: To shred the nori, tear each sheet into quarters, then eighths. Continue tearing until you have tiny pieces. When adding the nori, sprinkle it while stirring. If you add it all at once, it has a tendency to clump together.

ECO-TIP: When draining whole grain pasta, reserve the cooking liquid to use as the base for stock or soup.

Udon with Broccoli and Ginger Peanut Sauce

Serves 4

Peanut Sauce transforms noodles and broccoli into company fare. Toss just before serving to avoid soggy noodles.

Standard stovetop: 2 to 3 minutes (broccoli); 8 to 12 minutes (noodles)

1 large bunch broccoli (about 2 pounds)
8 ounces whole wheat or whole wheat brown rice udon
¼ to ⅓ cup Peanut Sauce (page 302)
Tamari soy sauce or Bragg Liquid Aminos to taste
Toasted (Oriental) sesame oil or hot-chili toasted sesame oil (optional)

GARNISHES
2 tablespoons chopped, roasted peanuts
Greens of 3 scallions, thinly sliced

1. Cut off the broccoli stalks and set aside for another use (such as in a vegetable stir-fry). Cut the florets into small pieces and steam them until tender-crisp, about 2 to 3 minutes. Refresh florets under cold running water and drain. Set aside.

2. Cook the udon until tender but still chewy, 8 to 12 minutes. Drain and rinse under cold water to halt the cooking process. Drain thoroughly.

3. Immediately place the noodles in a bowl or storage container and toss with ¼ cup of the peanut sauce. Add the broccoli.

4. Toss in more dressing if needed. (The noodles and broccoli should be generously coated with dressing.)

5. Taste and sprinkle with tamari and toasted sesame oil, if desired.

6. Garnish with peanuts and scallion greens. Serve at room temperature.

Cook's Notes: It's important to toss the noodles in the sauce as soon as they are cooked or they will stick together. This dish is best eaten when just cooked as the noodles become soggy after refrigeration. Leftovers will probably need moistening with additional dressing.

Variation: Substitute 1 pound of steamed asparagus, cut into 1-inch lengths, for the broccoli.

Cold Sesame Noodles

Serves 2 to 3

A spicy version of a Chinese take-out favorite thanks to cayenne or hot pepper sesame oil. You can make the noodles and sauce in advance, but don't toss them together until right before serving; otherwise the noodles absorb the sauce and get soggy.

Standard stovetop: 10 to 12 minutes

¼ *pound snow peas, trimmed*
½ *pound whole wheat or whole wheat/brown rice udon*
1 *tablespoon toasted (Oriental) sesame oil*
3 *tablespoons sesame tahini, (toasted sesame tahini is especially flavorful)*
1 *large clove roasted garlic (page 425), peeled, or ½ to 1 small clove raw*
    garlic, peeled and minced
1½ *to 2 tablespoons tamari soy sauce*
¼ *to ½ teaspoon ground Szechuan peppercorns or ⅛ teaspoon freshly*
    ground black pepper
2 *teaspoons brown rice vinegar*
½ *teaspoon maple syrup*
¼ *cup pasta cooking water, approximately*
Pinch cayenne (ground red) pepper or a few drops of hot pepper sesame oil
    (to taste)

GARNISHES
1 *large cucumber, peeled, seeded, and diced, or 2 to 3 small Kirbies*
    (preferable), diced
1 *scallion (green part only), thinly sliced*
Sesame seasoning salt (page 454)

1. Bring about 6 cups of water to the boil. Blanch the snow peas in the water for 1 minute. Remove them with a slotted spoon, place in a strainer, and refresh immediately under cold running water. Cut into thirds and set aside.

2. In the same boiling water used for the snow peas, cook the pasta until tender but still chewy. Drain well and reserve about ½ cup of the cooking water.

3. In a serving bowl, immediately toss the hot pasta in the sesame oil to prevent it from clumping together.

4. In a blender or food processor, combine the remaining ingredients, starting with 1½ tablespoons tamari and ¼ teaspoon Szechuan peppercorns, with just enough of the pasta cooking liquid to create a medium-thick sauce (the consistency should be like pancake batter).

5. Toss the sauce and reserved snow peas with the pasta. Taste and add more tamari and pepper if desired.

6. Garnish with the cucumber and scallion, and sprinkle with sesame seasoning salt before serving.

7. Serve warm or at room temperature.

Ten-Ingredient Lo Mein
Serves 4

Lo mein is a great dish for using up odd bits of vegetables, both cooked and raw. This recipe is just a general guide, not a strict formula. Feel free to add as many ingredients as you like—who's counting? But include at least one strong-flavored ingredient. Baked tofu (page 223), small cubes of quick-marinated tofu (see Cook's Notes), or pan-fried tempeh (page 228) all work well.

Use a large wok or a 12-inch skillet for this dish. If you have neither, cook the vegetables in your largest skillet, and mix them with the cooked noodles in a large bowl.

Wok or large skillet: 6 to 8 minutes

1 tablespoon peanut or safflower oil

2 large cloves garlic, peeled and finely chopped

6 scallions, thinly sliced (keep white and green parts separate)

2 cups broccoli stalks, peeled and thinly sliced

2 ribs celery, thinly sliced on the diagonal

1 large carrot, cut into matchsticks

*½ pound baked tofu (page 223) or pan-fried tempeh (page 228), cut into
   ½-inch cubes (see Cook's Notes)*

2 tablespoons tamari soy sauce mixed with 2 tablespoons water

1 medium red pepper, seeded and diced

1 large zucchini, trimmed, halved, and cut into ¼-inch slices

2 ounces snow peas, trimmed and cut into thirds

1 cup fresh, cooked, or frozen (defrosted) green peas

¼ pound mushrooms, sliced

*8 ounces whole wheat udon (cooked until tender but still chewy, then
   "run" under cold water to prevent further cooking, drained
   thoroughly, and tossed immediately in 2 teaspoons toasted (Oriental)
   sesame oil to prevent sticking)*

Additional tamari soy sauce to taste

continued

1. Heat the oil in the wok and sauté the garlic and scallion whites for 30 seconds. Stir in the broccoli, celery, carrot, tofu, and soy sauce mixture. Cover and cook over medium-high heat for 3 minutes.

2. Add the pepper, zucchini, snow peas, green peas, and mushrooms, and stir-fry until tender-crisp, about 2 more minutes.

3. Add the udon and stir-fry all ingredients until heated through, about 1 to 2 minutes.

4. Add more tamari, if needed, before serving.

Cook's Notes: If you have only plain tofu, do a quick marination. Shake cubed tofu with 1 tablespoon soy sauce in a small covered container. One-quarter teaspoon of ground star anise added to the soy sauce lends a hint of licorice flavor.

Pasta with Stir-fried Greens and White Beans
Serves 4

You can make this versatile recipe with any cooked white beans and greens on hand. An especially good—and rather classic Italian—duo is escarole and cannellini. Keep in mind, however, that some greens have a slightly bitter taste, so choose your combinations carefully. You can always play it safe with spinach or Swiss chard.

The hearty sauce is great with organic fettuccine (such as Eden Foods' parsley garlic ribbons), buckwheat soba, or whole wheat udon. Double the amount of sauce and serve it on its own as a vegetable side dish the following day.

Wok or large skillet: 3 to 10 minutes (greens); 8 to 12 minutes (pasta)

*¾ pound escarole, broccoli rabe, or kale, or 1 pound spinach
    or Swiss chard*
1 to 2 tablespoons olive oil
1 large onion, peeled and coarsely chopped
3 large cloves garlic, peeled and finely chopped
½ teaspoon dried leaf oregano
½ teaspoon gently crushed fennel seeds
Generous pinch crushed red pepper flakes (optional)
1½ cups bean cooking liquid or vegetable stock
*1½ cups cooked small or medium white beans, such as navy, cannellini,
    or Great Northern*
Freshly grated nutmeg
Salt and freshly ground black pepper to taste
8 ounces uncooked pasta

1. Trim the greens, cut off the stems, and reserve them for stock. Chop the leaves into ¾-inch strips.

2. In a wok or a large skillet, heat the oil. Add the onion, garlic, oregano, fennel seeds, and crushed red pepper flakes (if using), and sauté for 1 minute, stirring constantly.

3. Add the greens and 1 cup of the bean cooking liquid. Cover (you may have to stuff the greens under the lid; they will quickly shrink dramatically), bring to the boil, then reduce heat slightly to medium-high and steam the greens until tender, about 8 minutes for escarole and kale, 5 to 6 minutes for broccoli rabe, and 2 to 3 minutes for spinach or chard. Stir occasionally.

4. Puree ½ cup of the beans with the remaining ½ cup of liquid and stir into the mixture along with the remaining beans, nutmeg, and salt and pepper to taste.

5. Cook the pasta until just tender but still chewy. Drain thoroughly.

6. To serve, place a mound of pasta on each plate and spoon the sauce on top. Alternatively, stir the pasta into the sauce and serve the mixture family style in a large bowl.

Shipping is a terrible thing to do to vegetables. They probably get jet-lagged, just like people.

—Elizabeth Berry, organic specialty produce gardener,
Abique, New Mexico

Stir-fry Noodles with Seitan, Ginger, and Scallions

Serves 3 to 4

I rely on this simple stir-fry when there's little on hand but basic ingredients. It's one of the few uses I make of seitan, a chewy "wheat-meat," which works very nicely in this context. (Check Ingredients A to Z for further details.)

Wok or large skillet: 5 minutes

8 ounces whole wheat udon or other noodles
2 tablespoons toasted (Oriental) sesame oil
1 tablespoon light sesame or safflower oil
1½ tablespoons freshly grated ginger
2 to 3 teaspoons finely chopped garlic
½ pound seitan, drained and cut into ½-inch dice (reserve marinating liquid; see Cook's Notes)
5 scallions, thinly sliced
1 to 2 tablespoons tamari soy sauce
A few drops chili oil or hot pepper sesame oil (optional)

OPTIONAL GARNISH
Sesame seasoning salt (page 454)

1. Cook the pasta al dente according to package instructions. Rinse under cold running water, drain thoroughly, and stir in 1 tablespoon of the toasted sesame oil to prevent pasta from sticking. Set aside.

2. Remove the seitan from its marinating liquid (reserve the liquid) and coarsely chop. Set aside.

3. In a wok, heat the light sesame oil and sauté the ginger and garlic for 1 minute. Add the diced seitan, marinating liquid, scallions, and 1 tablespoon of soy sauce, and stir-fry for another minute.

4. Stir in the reserved noodles and stir-fry until they are heated throughout. Stir in the remaining tablespoon of toasted sesame oil, tamari, and chili oil (if using) to taste. Serve hot or at room temperature, sprinkled with sesame seasoning salt (if using).

Cook's Notes: If there is little or no seitan marinating liquid, substitute 1 teaspoon of tamari soy sauce mixed with 2 tablespoons of water.

Variations
  • Stir in steamed broccoli florets or other cooked vegetables of your choice when you add the noodles.

- Stir-fry quick-cooking vegetables (such as shredded cabbage, snow peas, or green peas) in the wok before adding the seitan.
- Substitute pan-fried tempeh (page 228) for the seitan.

Pasta–Kidney Bean Salad with Roasted Shallot Vinaigrette

Serves 4 to 6

A dish combining beans and pasta works best when the components are about the same size. Dress the salad just before serving to avoid limp, soggy pasta.

4 cups small whole wheat pasta, such as spirals, elbows, or shells
2 cups firm-cooked red kidney beans, drained
1½ cups finely chopped cooked kale or other greens
1 large red bell pepper, seeded and chopped
⅓ to ½ cup Roasted Shallot Vinaigrette (page 300)
Juice of 1 large lemon
Sea salt and lots of freshly ground black pepper to taste

1. Cook the pasta in boiling water according to package directions until tender but still chewy. Drain and run under cold water to halt the cooking process. Drain thoroughly and set in a large bowl. (If not serving immediately, toss the pasta in a few tablespoons of the vinaigrette dressing to prevent it from sticking.)

2. Toss in the cooked beans, kale, and chopped pepper.

3. Pour on enough dressing to moisten. Bring out the flavors with lots of fresh lemon juice and salt and pepper to taste.

Cook's Notes: If there are any leftovers the day after, you may need to perk up the flavors with additional lemon juice.

Variations
- Instead of Roasted Shallot Vinaigrette (page 300), try Herb Vinaigrette (page 294) or Moroccan Vinaigrette (page 295).
- Anasazis or scarlet runner beans are good substitutes for the red kidney beans.

ECO-TIP: Imported pastas have to be transported thousands of fuel-costly miles before they reach your dinner plate. If you have a choice, go for domestically produced varieties.

Summer Harvest Pasta Salad for a Crowd

Serves 8

Some of the most abundant warm-weather vegetables are tossed together in this cooling basil-flecked salad. Toss with the dressing just before serving to keep the pasta from becoming limp.

1 pound whole wheat spirals, elbows, or shells
1½ pounds small zucchini
3 cups cooked corn kernels (from 3 large ears)
2 cups small cherry tomatoes
1½ cups tightly packed minced fresh basil
¼ cup minced fresh chives (optional)
1 cup small mushrooms (or quartered large mushrooms)
½ cup oil-cured black olives, pitted (if you have the patience; I usually just
*   warn guests about the pits)*
½ cup fruity olive oil
3 tablespoons balsamic vinegar
2 small cloves roasted garlic (page 425), peeled and mashed, or 1 small
*   clove raw garlic, peeled and minced*
1 tablespoon Dijon mustard
1 teaspoon sea salt, or to taste
2 to 3 tablespoons fresh lemon juice, if needed

1. Cook the pasta in boiling water according to package directions until tender but still chewy. Run under cold water to halt the cooking process. Drain thoroughly and set into a large serving bowl. (If not dressing and serving immediately, toss the pasta in a tablespoon of olive oil to prevent sticking.)

2. Steam the zucchini until tender-crisp, about 3 to 5 minutes. (The zucchini retains its flavor if it is steamed whole.) When it is cool enough to handle, halve the zucchini and cut into ¼-inch thick slices.

3. Toss the zucchini, corn, tomatoes, basil, chives (if using), mushrooms, and olives into the pasta.

4. With a whisk and a bowl, or in a food processor, prepare the dressing by combining the olive oil, vinegar, garlic, mustard, and salt.

5. Just before serving, pour the dressing over the pasta salad and toss well. Add lemon juice, if needed, to perk up the flavors. Serve at room temperature.

Full of Beans

Bean Basics

Beans are twice as rich in protein as grains. They are high in iron, B vitamins, and fiber. And besides all this good news, they also happen to be delicious.

My enthusiasm for beans seems to know no bounds. I read everything about them I can get my hands on, and I shamelessly collect them. How could I not be totally fascinated by the endless variety of sizes, shapes, and colors that Mother Nature brings forth? Indeed, my cupboard bulges with Black Valentines, Tongues of Fire, Scarlet Runners, Christmas Limas, and Calypsos. Clearly, whoever named these beans was as taken with them as I am.

Yet despite this infatuation with boutique beans, I still have an ongoing love affair with the plain old chick-pea, lentil, black bean, and baby lima. Their very familiarity is what is so appealing. If you're now wondering if I've really lost it, I suspect that you have never tasted organically grown, recently harvested varieties. The difference between them and supermarket beans "of unknown origin" is equivalent to the difference between fresh and canned asparagus.

Because dried beans can keep a long time, we tend to underestimate the value of freshness. "Fresh" dried beans—those harvested within the last twelve months—not only cook relatively quickly, but have a vibrant and more complex taste than those that have been languishing in storage and on supermarket shelves over the last few years.

Shopping for Beans

I recommend two mail-order sources for recently harvested beans: Bean Bag in California and Dean & DeLuca in New York City. Both will send you catalogs upon request (see page 476). Beans are heavy (2 to 3 cups weigh about 1 pound) and therefore relatively expensive to ship, but this is offset by their low price per pound.

In addition to basic beans (see Stocking the Ecological Pantry, page 2), here is my current list of favorite boutique beans, with some tasting notes. Their unusual look, taste, and texture make these beans an exciting addition to any meal, served on their own, tossed perhaps with a little olive or walnut oil and a dash of herb vinegar.

Black Runner: large black bean that turns chocolate brown after cooking; exquisite chestnutlike taste.

Black Valentine: elegant ebony-colored bean that retains its shape beautifully during cooking and has a potatolike flavor and texture.

Christmas Lima: large, flat lima-shaped bean with dramatic splashes of maroon and a very creamy texture.

Madeira: large, plump, reddish-brown bean with dark striations; full flavored, with an appealing nuttiness.

Rattlesnack: earthy bean with a creamy texture and a faintly nutty taste that suggests pistachios.

Steuben Yellow Eye: small cream-colored bean with brownish splotches; a very satisfying mild bean with a slightly sweet flavor and mellow texture.

Tolosana: small, reddish bean that fades to pink after cooking; an unusually full-flavored bean that tastes similar to the red kidney.

White Runner: large cream-colored bean with a taste and texture reminiscent of potatoes.

If your local health food store is well stocked, you will find an excellent assortment of packaged organic beans. Buying from a bulk bin requires more vigorous attention. Avoid a batch that contains many split or broken beans, indicating rough handling or delayed harvesting. Once a bean loses the protection of its skin, its flavor and the quality of its proteins and fats gradually diminish. Look for beans of uniform color and size (for even cooking), and for those that are rich in hue; a faded color indicates that they have been around for a while. Don't be shy about asking the store owner the source and age of the batch.

Beans from bulk bins are generally less expensive than packaged beans, but it always pays to compare price and quality.

Storing Beans

Beans can be so pretty and decorative that you may be tempted to line them up in glass jars and show them off in your kitchen. Resist this temptation: They stay fresher longer when stored in a dark place. The ideal spot is a cupboard or drawer as far as possible from the oven—the coolest, driest place in the kitchen. Store them in glass bottles (preferable) or recycled plastic bags and mark the date of purchase. Try to use the beans within six months—the older the bean, the drier and harder it becomes. "Aged" beans absorb more water and take longer to become tender. For this reason, avoid cooking different batches of beans together.

Cleaning Beans

Most packaged and bulk beans are quite clean, but it's always a good idea to inspect for stones and grit. Rinse the beans in a strainer, twirling them around with your fingers as you dunk them up and down in a bowl of water. Then give the beans a quick rinse under cold running water.

Soaking Beans

Soaking decreases cooking time dramatically, allows for more even cooking, and improves taste. It also permits the gas-producing sugars in beans to be released into the soaking water, thereby reducing or eliminating the nasty problem of postprandial flatulence.

Although it is common to soak beans overnight, small and medium-sized beans are usually sufficiently softened in 4 hours. Large beans will often take a few hours longer. My colleague Carol Gelles taught me a trick to determine whether beans are ready for the pot: Slice a soaked bean in half with a sharp paring knife. If there is an opaque spot in the center, the bean requires more soaking. If the inside of the bean is all one color, get the water boiling.

If you've forgotten to presoak the beans, you can bring them up to high pressure for 1 minute in the cooker, using 3 cups of water per 1 cup of dried beans. Let the pressure come down naturally for 10 minutes. (When you open the lid, tilt it away from you to allow any excess steam to escape.) Drain and rinse. Or, using the stovetop method, bring the beans to the boil in ample water to cover. Turn off the heat, cover the pot, and let stand for 1 hour. Drain and rinse. Always discard any loose bean skins before cooking.

In a pinch you can cook beans without any presoaking. Check the bean cooking charts (pages 175 and 177) for approximate cooking times.

Pressure-Cooking Beans

Beans cooked in the pressure cooker are done in one quarter or less the usual cooking time, making this method incredibly fuel- and time-efficient.

To pressure cook soaked beans:

1. Use approximately 3 cups of water per cup of dried beans that have been soaked; use 4 cups of water for unsoaked beans. The beans must be covered with water to cook evenly, but don't fill the cooker more than halfway.
2. *Add 1 tablespoon of oil per cup of dried beans.* The oil prevents foaming, which might catapult a bean skin into the vent. (This is more critical for old-fashioned, jiggle-top cookers; see Fat-Free Bean Cooking, page 178.)

3. Add optional flavorings, such as 1 clove garlic, peeled and smashed or sliced; 1 bay leaf; ½ teaspoon dried herbs, such as thyme or oregano; 1 three-inch strip of kombu sea vegetable (adds minerals; and is thought to make the beans more digestible; has a very slightly salty flavor). *Do not add salt* until you read the section on page 176.
4. Lock the lid into place and bring up to high pressure.
5. Cook for the time indicated on the bean cooking chart (page 175), preferably using natural pressure release rather than quick-release as the latter can wreak havoc on bean skins. (If you need to quick-release, place the cooker under cold running water to avoid foaming or sputtering at the vent.)
6. If the beans require considerably more cooking, return to high pressure for a few more minutes. If they need just a bit more, cover the pot and simmer over low heat until done.
7. Drain. If you like the taste of the cooking liquid, set it aside for soup-making or for cooking grains. Alternatively, let the beans cool in the cooking liquid—which is likely to thicken—and serve them in their own "sauce."
8. Clean the lid thoroughly.

Note to users of jiggle-top pressure cookers: If you hear loud sputtering, it means that a bean skin has gotten caught in the vent. Immediately turn off the heat, and place the cooker under cold running water to bring down the pressure. Remove and clean the lid, vent, and rubber gasket. Remove any free-floating bean skins. Lock the lid back in place and proceed with cooking.

A Note on Determining Timing for Boutique Beans

Boutique beans (page 172) are so various in number that it's impractical to provide a chart for them. When dealing with an unfamiliar bean, first soak it overnight, rinse, and set in a pot with water to cover. With standard stovetop cooking, just bring to the boil, reduce to a simmer and cook, covered, until tender.

In the pressure cooker, cook the beans in water to cover for 4 minutes under high pressure for small and medium-sized beans and 6 minutes for large beans. Then let the pressure come down naturally. Test the beans, for doneness. If the beans are almost tender, finish them by simmering, covered, until done. If they are still quite hard, return to high pressure for a few more minutes and again let the pressure come down naturally.

ECO-TIP: When cooking plain beans, make a double or triple batch and freeze in tightly sealed 1- or 2-cup containers. Beans freeze well for up to 4 months, with surprisingly little loss of taste and texture. Defrost as needed to add to soups or to make spreads or bean salads.
Cooked beans last for 3 to 4 days in the refrigerator.

Pressure Cooker Bean Cooking Times at a Glance

For instructions on cooking beans, see pages 173–175.

Beans (1 Cup Dry)	Approximate Minutes Under High Pressure*		Yield in Cups
	Soaked 4–8 hours	Unsoaked	
Aduki	5–9	14–20	2
Anasazi	4–7	20–22	2¼
Black (turtle)	9–11	20–25	2
Black-eyed (cow) peas	—	9–11	2¼
Cannellini	9–12	22–25	2
Chick-peas (garbanzos)	10–12	30–40	2½
Christmas lima	8–10	16–18	1¼
Cranberry	9–12	30–35	2¼
Fava[†]	12–18	22–28	2
Flageolets	10–14	17–22	2
Great Northern	8–12	25–30	2¼
Lentils	—	7–10	2
Lima (large)[‡]	4–7[§]	12–16	2
Lima (baby)	5–7	12–15	2½
Peas (split, green)	—	8–10	2
Peas (whole, green)	—	16–18	2
Pigeon peas (gandules)	6–9	20–25	3
Pinto	4–6	22–25	2¼
Navy (pea)	6–8	16–25	2
Red kidney	10–12	20–25	2
Scarlet runner	12–14	17–20	1¼
Soybeans (beige)[‡]	9–12	28–35	2¼
Soybeans (black)[‡]	20–22[§]	35–40	2½

NOTE: Do not fill the pressure cooker more than halfway. Owners of jiggle-top cookers should add 1 tablespoon of oil per cup of dried beans to control foaming.

*The timings on this chart are calculated for quick-releasing pressure. If time permits, let the pressure come down naturally, and reduce the cooking time under high pressure by 4 minutes.

[†]Skins remain leathery after cooking and must be removed before serving unless the beans are pureed.

[‡]Requires 2 tablespoons of oil for each cup of dried beans. For special instructions on soaking and cooking limas and black soybeans, see pages 206 and 191.

[§]Be sure to remove loose skins before cooking.

Cooking Beans: Standard Stovetop Method

The problem with cooking beans by the standard stovetop method is that it is neither time- nor fuel-efficient. After a few bouts of cooking beans "forever," I hope you'll feel inspired to try making them in a pressure cooker.

Meanwhile, here's how to cook beans in a standard pot:

1. In a heavy saucepan, use 3 cups of water per cup of dried beans that have been soaked; use 4 cups of water for unsoaked beans. Don't fill the pot more than three quarters full. Except for limas and black soybeans, *do not add salt.*

2. Add any of the flavoring options suggested under Pressure-Cooking Beans, item 3.

3. Bring to the boil, reduce the heat and simmer, covered, until tender. Replace water as needed so that the beans are always covered with liquid. Check the chart on page 177 for approximate timing and begin checking for doneness shortly before the minimum recommended time has elapsed.

4. Drain. If you like, set aside the cooking liquid to make soup or for cooking grains. Alternatively, let the beans cool in the cooking liquid, which in most cases will thicken into a nice sauce.

To Salt or Not to Salt

Adding salt or any acid (like tomatoes or vinegar) to beans hardens their skins and prevents them from cooking properly. Therefore, in most instances it's best to add salt after the beans are almost entirely cooked.

There are two exceptions to this rule:

1. When cooking beans with exceptionally delicate skins—such as limas and black soybeans—the salt should be added to keep the bean skins intact. (See Black Soybeans, page 191, for details.)

2. When pressure-cooking soups, adding a small amount of tomatoes or using a lightly salted stock may lengthen cooking time slightly, but does not prevent the beans from softening.

Determining Cooking Time

Since no two batches of beans have been grown or stored under the same conditions, timings are approximate at best. When I pressure-cook beans, I try to cook them just short of tenderness under pressure, then finish them off by simmering with the cover on but not locked in place. This method speeds up cooking time dramatically and diminishes any risk of overcooking the beans. When cooking beans by the standard method, allow plenty of extra time: You can end up with a batch of beans that will go right off the charts before they become tender.

Beans are properly cooked when you can smash one fairly easily between your tongue and hard palate. For *firm-cooked* beans to be used in salads, check for doneness after the minimum time indicated on the chart. For *soft-cooked* beans that will be pureed, a longer cooking time is advisable.

Standard Stovetop Bean Cooking Times at a Glance

For instructions on cooking beans, see page 176.

Beans (1 cup dry)	Approximate Hours Standard Cooking Time‡		Yield in Cups
	Soaked	Unsoaked	
Anasazi	1½–2	2–3	2¼
Aduki	1–1½	2–3	2
Black (turtle)	1½–2	2–3	2
Black-eyed (cow) peas	½	¾–1	2¼
Cannellini	1–1½	1½–2	2
Chick-peas (garbanzos)	1½–2	3–4	2½
Christmas lima	1–1½	1½–2	1¼
Cranberry	1½–2	2–3	2¼
Fava*	1½–2	2–3	2
Flageolets	1–1½	1½–2	2
Great Northern	1–1½	2–3	2¼
Lentils	—	½–¾	2
Lima (large)†	¾–1	1½–1¾	2
Lima (baby)	¾–1	1½–1¾	2½
Peas (split, green)	—	¾	2
Peas (whole, green)	1–1½	1½–2	2
Pigeon peas (gandules)	¾–1	1½–2	3
Pinto	1½–2	2–3	2¼
Navy (pea)	1½–2	2½–3	2
Red kidney	1½–2	2–3	2
Scarlet runner	1½–2	2–3	1¼
Soybeans (beige)	2–3	3–4	2¼
Soybeans (black)†	1½	2½–3	2½

*Skins remain leathery after cooking and must be removed before serving unless the beans are pureed.
†See special soaking and cooking instructions on pages 191 and 206.
‡Bean cooking times vary widely. Always begin checking for doneness about ½ hour before the minimum recommended time.

ECO-TIP: Soak beans 4 to 8 hours to reduce cooking time dramatically.

Fat-Free Bean Cooking

This interesting technique for cooking beans in the pressure cooker without needing oil to control foaming is based on a suggestion made in *Recipes for a Small Planet* by Ellen Buchman Ewald.

Pour 2 cups of water into the cooker. In a 1½- to 2-quart stainless-steel bowl, place the beans and enough water to cover them by 2 inches. Lower the bowl into the cooker with the aid of a foil strip (page 10) and set the bowl directly on the bottom of the cooker. Lock the lid in place. Over high heat, bring to high pressure, then lower the heat just enough to maintain high pressure.

The trade-off is time: It takes approximately three times longer to cook the beans this way. For example, if it normally takes 8 minutes for a soaked bean with the standard pressure cooking technique, it will take about 24 minutes for a soaked bean to become tender when cooked in the bowl.

Pat's Spicy Black-eyed Peas
Serves 6

For dinner, I often serve this dish with Creole Brown Rice Casserole (page 132) and a tossed salad. For lunch, roll them up in a warm corn tortilla or stuff them into a pita pocket.

Pressure cooker: 10 to 12 minutes high pressure
Standard stovetop: 45 to 60 minutes

2 tablespoons olive oil (see Cook's Notes)
3 large cloves garlic, peeled and finely chopped
1 large onion, peeled and coarsely chopped
2 large ribs celery, coarsely chopped
1 large red or green bell pepper, seeded and diced
1 to 2 large fresh jalapeño peppers, stemmed and finely chopped (wear
    rubber gloves when handling)
2 cups dried black-eyed peas, picked over and rinsed
3 cups water
1 bay leaf
1 teaspoon dried thyme or leaf oregano
¼ teaspoon freshly grated nutmeg
⅛ teaspoon crushed red pepper flakes
⅛ teaspoon freshly ground black pepper
1 to 2 tablespoons balsamic vinegar
1 teaspoon sea salt, or to taste
Hot sauce (optional)

1. Heat the oil in the cooker. Add the garlic, onion, celery, bell and jalapeño peppers, and cook over high heat until the onion begins to brown, stirring frequently, about 4 to 6 minutes.

2. Stir in the peas, water, bay leaf, thyme, nutmeg, and the red and black pepper.

3. Lock the lid in place and over high heat bring to high pressure. Lower the heat just enough to maintain high pressure and cook for 10 minutes. Reduce the pressure by putting the cooker under cold running water. Remove the lid, tilting it away from you to allow any excess steam to escape. If the beans are undercooked, add more liquid if needed and return to high pressure for 2 to 3 more minutes. If the beans are almost soft, replace the lid and allow them to steam in the residual heat for a few more minutes, adding extra liquid if necessary.

4. Remove the bay leaf. Stir in the vinegar, salt, and hot sauce (if using) to taste.

Standard Stovetop: In a heavy 3-quart saucepan, follow steps 1 and 2, reducing oil to 1 tablespoon if desired. Bring to the boil, reduce heat, and simmer, covered, until the peas are tender, about 45 to 60 minutes. Stir occasionally and add more water if mixture becomes dry. Follow step 4.

Cook's Notes: The use of 2 tablespoons of oil is necessary to control foaming in the pressure cooker. This dish thickens considerably on standing. I like the consistency, but you may want to thin it slightly with water or stock before serving or when reheating.

Variations
- Stir in ⅓ to ½ cup finely chopped fresh herbs after the beans are cooked. Coriander, parsley, and basil are especially nice.
- Use ½ cup of the peas as a "stuffing" for Curried Brown Rice Muffins (page 334).
- Toss the drained peas with macaroni or spiral pasta and add a vinaigrette dressing for a pasta-bean salad (page 169).

Waste not, want not.

Quick Chick-pea Curry

Chick-peas are quick to absorb the delicious flavors of the homemade curry blend. You can serve them "dry" by lifting them from the sauce with a slotted spoon (and use the broth for cooking rice). I prefer to puree some of the chick-peas to thicken the sauce and serve the fragrant curry over brown basmati rice. Add a salad or a steamed vegetable for a memorable meal.

> **Pressure cooker:** 10 minutes high pressure plus a 10-minute natural pressure release or 14 minutes high pressure
>
> **Standard stovetop:** 90 to 120 minutes

1½ cups dried chick-peas, picked over and rinsed, soaked 8 to 12 hours in ample water to cover
1 tablespoon oil
1 tablespoon whole cumin seeds
1 teaspoon black mustard seeds (optional but very tasty)
½ teaspoon fenugreek or fennel seeds
1 teaspoon ground coriander
¾ teaspoon ground turmeric
¾ teaspoon ground cinnamon
1 bay leaf
⅛ to ¼ teaspoon cayenne (ground red) pepper or crushed red pepper flakes
1 large onion, peeled and coarsely chopped
1 tablespoon freshly grated ginger (preferable) or ¾ teaspoon ground ginger
2 to 3 cups water or vegetable broth (unsalted or lightly salted)
Sea salt or tamari soy sauce to taste
10 ounces chopped fresh or frozen (defrosted) spinach (squeeze out excess moisture if defrosted) or 3 cups loosely packed chopped greens, such as Swiss chard, beet greens, watercress, or arugula
2 large plum tomatoes (preferable) or 1 large beefsteak tomato, coarsely chopped

1. Drain the soaked chick-peas and rinse. Set aside.

2. Over a medium flame, heat the oil in the cooker. Toast the cumin, mustard, and fenugreek seeds, stirring constantly, until they begin to pop and emit a fragrant aroma, about 20 to 30 seconds. (Pay close attention as the spices can burn easily; if they begin to darken as soon as you put them in the oil, turn off the heat and toast them in the residual heat of the oil while stirring continuously.)

3. Stir in the remaining spices, then the onion and ginger and cook, stirring, until the onion begins to soften, about 1 to 2 minutes. Stir in the reserved chick-peas and just enough water to cover them.

4. Lock the lid into place and over high heat bring to high pressure. Reduce the heat to maintain high pressure and cook for 10 minutes, plus a 10-minute natural pressure release (preferred), or 14 minutes with a quick-release method.

5. Remove the lid, tilting it away from you to allow any excess steam to escape. Test for doneness and return to high pressure for a few more minutes if chick-peas are not cooked.

6. To thicken the curry, remove about 1 cup of chick-peas with a slotted spoon and mash them well with a fork or puree them in a food processor. Stir them back into the pot. Remove the bay leaf.

7. Stir in salt to taste and the spinach and tomato. Simmer until the spinach is cooked, about 2 to 3 minutes.

Standard Stovetop: In a heavy 3-quart saucepan, follow steps 1, 2, and 3. Bring to the boil, then reduce the heat and simmer, covered, until the chick-peas are tender, about 90 to 120 minutes. Replenish liquid as needed to keep the chick-peas just covered. Follow steps 6 and 7.

Variations

- Use 2 tablespoons curry powder (make sure it's fresh and doesn't taste bitter) instead of the black mustard seeds, fenugreek, coriander, and turmeric.
- Use ½ teaspoon dried leaf oregano instead of the cinnamon.

I believe that we are summoned now to awaken from a spell. The spell we must shake off is a case of mistaken identity, a millennia-long amnesia as to who we really are. We have imagined that we are separate and competitive beings. . . . For our own sakes and the sake of all beings, we are called to rediscover our true nature, coextensive with all life on this planet. . . . This is happening. An ecological selfhood is emerging. I feel it in myself; I see it in my sisters and my brothers as, out of deep concern over what is happening to our world, they begin to speak and act on its behalf.

— Joanna Macy, "Awakening to the Ecological Self,"
in *Healing the Wounds*, Judith Plant, ed.
(Philadelphia: New Society Publishers, 1989).

Chick-pea Vegetable Medley

Serves 4 to 6

The requirements for this luscious fat-free stew are pretty uncomplicated: a few cups of cooked chick-peas, squash, and carrots and celery from the vegetable bin. Serve it over fluffy millet or bulgur.

Pressure cooker: 4 minutes high pressure
Standard stovetop: 20 to 25 minutes

1 tablespoon oil
2 cups coarsely chopped onion
2 large cloves garlic, peeled and finely chopped
1½ teaspoons dried basil
4 large ribs celery, cut into 1-inch slices
3 large carrots, cut into 2½-inch slices
1 pound winter squash, peeled, seeded, and cut into ½-inch chunks
1 cup chick-pea cooking liquid or water
¾ teaspoon sea salt, or to taste
2 cups cooked chick-peas

1. Heat oil in the cooker and sauté onion and garlic for 2 minutes. Stir in the basil and then the celery, carrots, squash, water, and salt.

2. Lock the lid into place. Over high heat bring to high pressure. Lower the heat just enough to maintain high pressure and cook for 4 minutes. Reduce the pressure with a quick-release method. Remove the lid, tilting it away from you to allow any excess steam to escape.

3. Stir in the chick-peas and simmer, covered, just long enough for the chick-peas to be heated through. Adjust the seasonings before serving.

Standard Stovetop: In a heavy 3-quart saucepan, follow step 1. Bring to the boil, then reduce the heat and simmer, covered, until the vegetables are tender, about 20 to 25 minutes. Stir every 10 minutes and add a bit of extra water if the mixture becomes dry. Follow step 3.

Variations
- Substitute any other cooked beans for the chick-peas.
- Add ½ pound marinated tofu (page 221), cut into ½-inch dice, when you add the vegetables.

Lima Beans à la Grecque

Serves 4

The foods of Greece focus on ingredients that almost vibrate with the sun's energy. The predominant flavors—olive oil, oregano, lemon, parsley, and tomatoes—turn a bean stew into the kind of simple feast that Odysseus must have hungered for when he was far from Penelope's hearth. Your yen can be more easily satisfied—in about 15 minutes. The limas are especially heavenly, with a slight hint of sweetness and a texture reminiscent of creamy potatoes.

Unlike other beans, large limas *must be soaked and cooked with salt* or their thin skins will float off and the beans will turn to mush. Also they *must be pressure-cooked with oil* to subdue foaming.

Pressure cooker: 1 minute high pressure, 10- to 12-minute natural pressure release
Standard stovetop: 45 to 60 minutes

1½ cups large limas, soaked for 8 to 12 hours in ample water to cover
    plus ¾ teaspoon sea salt
2 tablespoons olive oil, divided
1 large onion, peeled and coarsely chopped
1 large clove garlic, peeled and finely chopped
½ teaspoon dried leaf oregano
2 bay leaves
½ teaspoon sea salt
1½ to 2 cups water or vegetable stock
2 large plum tomatoes (preferable) or 1 large beefsteak tomato, finely
    chopped
Juice of ½ to 1 lemon
¼ cup tightly packed, finely minced fresh parsley
A few grinds of fresh black pepper

1. Drain and rinse the beans. Discard any loose skins and set the beans aside.

2. Heat 1 tablespoon of the oil in the cooker and sauté the onion and garlic for 2 minutes, stirring frequently. Add the oregano, bay leaves, salt, reserved beans, and just enough water to cover (watch for sputtering oil!).

3. Lock the lid in place and over high heat bring to high pressure. Lower the heat just enough to maintain high pressure and cook for 1 minute. Allow the pressure to come down naturally, about 10 to 12 minutes. Remove the lid, tilting it away from you to allow any excess steam to escape. If the beans are not quite tender, set the lid back in place and allow them to steam in the residual heat for a few more minutes or simmer them for a few additional minutes.

continued

4. When the beans are done, remove the bay leaves. Puree about ½ cup of beans and stir the puree back into the pot to thicken the sauce.

5. Stir in the additional tablespoon of olive oil, tomatoes, lemon juice, parsley, and pepper to taste. Serve warm or at room temperature in small bowls.

Standard Stovetop: In a heavy 2-quart saucepan, proceed as directed in steps 1 and 2. Bring to the boil, reduce heat and simmer, covered, until limas are tender, about 45 to 60 minutes. Stir in more water if the mixture becomes dry. Follow steps 4 and 5.

Variations

- Instead of pureeing some of the beans to create a sauce, strain them all before serving, and save the broth for another use—it's delicious to drink as is, or used instead of stock or water for cooking grains.
- Use cranberry or Great Northern beans instead of limas. Soak the beans overnight, drain, and follow steps 1 to 5. Check the chart (page 175) for cooking times. *Do not soak or cook these beans with salt.*

White Beans with Parsley Pesto

Serves 4 to 6

In this recipe, white runner beans or large limas make a very dramatic presentation. But the taste is equally delicious if you use Great Northern, navy, or cannellini beans.

For best results, use beans that are tender but still maintain their shape, and add them to the sauce when they're still warm; they quickly absorb much of the flavor and color of the pesto. If you're not serving immediately, save some of the pesto and toss it on just before eating for a more vibrant taste.

Serve small portions as part of a Mediterranean meal, with Eggplant Caponata (page 250) and a pasta salad.

4 cups loosely packed parsley leaves (2 large bunches, preferably flat-leaf), trimmed of all but the slenderest stems

¼ cup olive oil

3 large cloves roasted garlic (page 425), peeled, or 1 to 2 small cloves raw garlic, peeled

¼ cup coarsely chopped walnuts

1 to 3 tablespoons freshly squeezed lemon juice, approximately

2 to 3 teaspoons grated or very finely minced lemon peel (colored part only, preferably organic)

1 to 2 teaspoons balsamic vinegar

½ to ¾ teaspoon sea salt or 1 teaspoon blond miso, or to taste

3 cups firm-cooked white beans, such as white runners, Great Northerns, large limas, or French navies, just-cooked, drained, and still warm

GARNISH

4 to 6 large leaves of radicchio or red-leaf lettuce

1. Place the parsley leaves, olive oil, garlic, walnuts, 1 tablespoon lemon juice, 2 teaspoons lemon peel, 1 teaspoon balsamic vinegar, and ½ teaspoon salt in the bowl of a food processor or blender (for a creamier consistency).

2. Process until smooth, scraping down bowl once or twice. The volume will reduce drastically to about ½ cup!

3. Taste and add more lemon juice, lemon peel, vinegar, and salt as desired. The predominant taste of the pesto should be parsley and lemon. It should also be assertively salty, since it will be tossed with unsalted beans.

4. Toss about ¼ cup of the pesto with the beans. A few minutes later, or just before serving, toss in almost all of the remaining pesto. Taste. If the flavor is not distinctly lemony, add more lemon juice and toss again. Add more salt, if needed.

5. Serve nestled in a large leaf of radicchio or lettuce.

Variation: Substitute an equivalent amount of fresh basil or coriander for the parsley.

Triple Bean Maybe It's Chili

Serves 6 to 8

I was prepared to call this dish chili until my neighbor and loyal taster Bobby Troka sampled it, called it delicious, asked for the recipe, and insisted that "under no circumstances can this be considered chili."

See for yourself. Whatever you decide to call it, this combination is very soul-satisfying. Cooking all of the ingredients together creates a stew with very soft vegetables that suggests a thick sauce. By the way, the third bean is soy, in the form of tofu.

I enjoy this chili with Quinoa with Corn (page 98).

Pressure cooker: 12 minutes high pressure
Standard stovetop: 90 minutes

*1 cup pinto beans, picked over and rinsed, soaked 4 to 8 hours in ample
    water to cover*
*1 cup red kidney beans, picked over and rinsed, soaked 4 to 8 hours in
    ample water to cover*
1 tablespoon olive oil
1 large onion, peeled and coarsely chopped
2 to 4 large cloves garlic, peeled and finely chopped
2 teaspoons whole cumin seeds
1½ to 2 tablespoons mild chili powder
1 teaspoon dried leaf oregano
1 teaspoon dried basil
½ teaspoon ground cinnamon
3 whole cloves
2 bay leaves
*1 jalapeño pepper, thinly sliced (wear rubber gloves when handling), or a
    generous pinch of crushed red pepper flakes (optional)*
1 large red bell pepper, seeded and diced
2 ribs celery, cut into 1-inch chunks
1 large carrot, coarsely chopped
½ pound firm or extra-firm tofu, cut into 1-inch cubes
2 cups water, approximately
*1 cup tightly packed, finely chopped coriander or ½ cup tightly packed,
    finely chopped parsley*
Sea salt or soy sauce to taste

1. Drain and rinse the pintos and red kidney beans and set aside.

2. Heat the oil in the cooker. Sauté the onion and garlic for 2 minutes. Add the cumin and continue to sauté for 10 seconds. Add the remaining spices and herbs, the jalapeño pepper (if using), reserved beans, red bell pepper, celery, carrots, tofu, and just enough water to cover.

3. Lock the lid into place. Over high heat bring to high pressure. Lower the heat just enough to maintain high pressure and cook for 12 minutes. Reduce pressure with a quick-release method. Remove the lid, tilting it away from you to allow any excess steam to escape. If the beans are not tender, replace the lid and simmer until done.

4. If the chili is too soupy, lift about a cupful of the beans and vegetables out of the pot with a slotted spoon. Puree them and stir back into the pot.

5. Remove the bay leaves and stir in the coriander and salt to taste.

Standard Stovetop: In a heavy 3-quart saucepan, follow steps 1 and 2. Bring to the boil, then reduce the heat and simmer, covered, until the beans are done, about 90 minutes. Add water, if needed, to keep the beans submerged. Follow steps 4 and 5.

Can we lead our lives in ways that:
- are deeply satisfying, fulfilling, and appealing, and at the same time
- are environmentally benign, so that everyone else could live in similar ways without damaging the Earth?

—Robert Gilman, "Economics, Ecology, and Us,"
In Context, A Quarterly of Humane Sustainable Culture,
No. 26, Summer 1990.

Nosmo King's Moroccan Chili

New York City's Nosmo King is one of the new breed of American restaurants devoted to serving regional organic foods. Chef Alan Harding has developed a loyal following for his artfully prepared dairy-free vegetarian dishes. This is a superb chili—though there's not a chili pepper to be found in the recipe.

Serve this with plain whole wheat couscous, barley, or Job's Tears.

Pressure cooker: 11 minutes high pressure
Standard stovetop: 40 to 50 minutes

1 juice orange, preferably organic, thoroughly scrubbed
12 cloves
2 tablespoons olive oil
2 cloves garlic, peeled and finely chopped
2 medium onions, peeled and coarsely chopped
2 medium leeks, cleaned and chopped (white part only), about 2 cups
1 cup medium-sized mushrooms, cut into quarters
3 large carrots, chopped into ½-inch pieces
1 rib celery, finely chopped
1 large red bell pepper, seeded and diced
½ cup raisins
2 cups chopped tomatoes (preferably plum tomatoes)
1½ cups brown lentils, picked over and rinsed
3 cups vegetable stock or water
2 teaspoons ground coriander seeds
½ to ¾ teaspoon ground cardamom
Two 2-inch cinnamon sticks, broken in half
Sea salt and freshly ground pepper to taste

1. Cut the orange in half. Squeeze out and reserve the juice. Stick the cloves into the peels of both orange halves. (This task is eased by making small slits with the tip of a paring knife.) Set aside.

2. Heat the oil in the bottom of the cooker. Add the garlic, onions, and leeks, and sauté until the leeks begin to soften, about 2 minutes. Add the mushrooms, carrots, celery, and red bell pepper, and cook another minute over medium-high heat, stirring frequently.

3. Add the raisins, tomatoes, lentils, stock, spices, reserved orange juice, and clove-studded peels. Make sure that the orange peels are submerged in the liquid.

4. Lock the lid into place and over high heat bring to high pressure. Lower the heat just enough to maintain high pressure and cook for 11 minutes. Reduce the pressure with a quick-release method. Remove the lid, tilting it away from you to allow any excess steam to escape. If the lentils are not quite cooked, replace the cover and steam them for a minute or two in the residual heat.

5. Remove the clove-studded orange peels. Stir well, and add salt and pepper to taste before serving.

Standard Stovetop: Follow step 1. Using a heavy 3-quart saucepan, follow steps 2 and 3. Bring to the boil, then reduce the heat and simmer, covered, until the lentils are tender, about 40 to 50 minutes. Follow step 5.

He prayeth best, who loveth best
All things both great and small;
For the dear God who loveth us,
He made and loveth all.
—Samuel Taylor Coleridge,
The Ancient Mariner, 1798.

Black Bean Skillet Casserole with Cornbread Topping

Serves 6

Served right in the skillet, this one-pot meal makes a dramatic presentation and gets rave reviews every time. You can prepare the dish with any leftover beans, or even with a bean soup that has thickened considerably on standing.

Oven: 20 to 25 minutes at 375°

1 tablespoon olive oil
1 large onion, peeled and coarsely chopped
2 large cloves garlic, peeled and finely chopped
2½ cups firm-cooked black beans
¼ cup bean cooking liquid or water
1 small red or green bell pepper, seeded and diced
1 large carrot, finely chopped
1 large rib celery, finely chopped
½ cup tightly packed, finely chopped fresh coriander or parsley
¼ cup coarsely chopped, pitted green olives
½ jalapeño pepper, thinly sliced (wear rubber gloves when handling), or
  generous pinch crushed red pepper flakes (optional)
¾ teaspoon dried leaf oregano
Sea salt to taste

FOR THE CORNBREAD TOPPING
1¼ cups yellow cornmeal
¾ cup whole wheat pastry flour
⅓ cup soy milk powder (also known as soy powder)
1 tablespoon baking powder
½ teaspoon sea salt, or to taste
1 cup fresh or frozen (defrosted) corn kernels
1 tablespoon maple or barley malt syrup, measured from an oiled spoon
1 cup water
⅓ cup corn oil

GARNISH
2 tablespoons pumpkin or black sesame seeds

1. In an 8- or 10-inch cast-iron skillet, heat the oil. Sauté the onions and garlic for 1 minute. Stir in the beans, bean cooking liquid, pepper, carrot, celery, coriander, olives, jalapeño (if using), oregano, and salt. Sauté another minute. Turn off the heat and set aside.

2. To prepare the topping, in a bowl combine the cornmeal, whole wheat flour, soy powder, baking powder, and salt. Stir in the corn kernels.

3. In a small bowl, whisk together the maple syrup, water, and corn oil. Pour the wet ingredients into the dry and stir until just blended. Pour the batter over the beans. Sprinkle the seeds on top.

4. Bake on the middle rack of a preheated 375° oven until the sides begin to pull away from the skillet and a skewer inserted into the center of the cornbread topping comes out clean, about 20 to 25 minutes.

5. Cut into wedges and lift out with a large serving spoon.

Black Soybeans

Makes 2½ cups cooked beans

If soybeans bring to mind all the worst of what you think of as "health food," take heart. It turns out that most of the soybeans we purchase in health food stores have been bred for further processing (such as the production of tofu or tempeh) and are not intended to be eaten straight out of the pot. That's why they don't taste that terrific and are usually a challenge to the digestive system.

Enter the black soybean, king of the 2,000 or so varieties of soybean and utterly elegant. It is a roundish, ebony black bean (it turns a mahogany color during cooking) with a sweet and nutty taste so good and a texture so silken that no embellishments are required except perhaps a squirt of soy sauce or a sprinkling of scallion greens for color. The cooking liquid is so rich and delicious that I often drink a cupful straight, like bouillon, and use the rest for cooking rice.

Black soybeans are nationally distributed and usually available in health food stores. A good mail-order source is Gold Mine (see page 475).

While most beans are tough-skinned, the black soybean has a delicate, paper-thin covering. The challenge is to keep that skin on, thereby keeping the bean intact. To do so requires breaking a cardinal rule of bean cooking: Add salt!

Usually adding salt to beans toughens the skins, preventing them from cooking properly. Here you add salt to the cooking and soaking water to toughen their skins on purpose.

Pressure cooker: 20 to 22 minutes high pressure, 10- to 12-minute natural pressure release

Standard stovetop: about 90 minutes

continued

1 cup dry black soybeans, soaked 8 to 12 hours in 4 cups of water and ½ teaspoon sea salt

3 cups water, approximately

½ teaspoon sea salt

1 large clove garlic, peeled and thinly sliced

One 2-inch strip kombu sea vegetable (optional)

1 tablespoon oil (see Cook's Notes)

Bragg Liquid Aminos (especially delicious) or tamari soy sauce to taste

GARNISH

2 tablespoons finely chopped scallion greens

1. Carefully drain and rinse the beans, discarding any loose skins. Place the beans in the cooker with water to cover and salt.

2. Over medium-high heat, bring to the boil uncovered. Reduce the heat to simmer and skim off the whitish-gray bubbly foam on top. Bring to the boil again, reduce to a simmer, and skim off most of the foam. Rinse any beans that come out of the pot with the skimmer and return them to the pot. Add the garlic, kombu (if using), and oil.

3. Lock the lid in place and over high heat bring to high pressure. Lower the heat just enough to maintain high pressure and cook for 20 to 22 minutes. Allow the pressure to come down naturally, about 10 to 12 minutes. (Do not use a quick-release method as this would dislodge the bean skins.) Remove the lid, tilting it away from you to allow any excess steam to escape.

4. Season the beans, if desired, with Bragg Liquid Aminos or tamari. Serve the beans in small bowls with the cooking liquid, or strain them (reserve the broth to drink or for stock) and serve as a vegetable side dish, garnished with scallions.

Standard Stovetop: In a heavy 2-quart saucepan, follow steps 1 and 2. Return to the boil, then reduce the heat and simmer, covered, until tender, about 90 minutes. Replenish water as needed. Follow step 4.

Cook's Notes: This recipe can be doubled or tripled. For soaking, figure on 4 cups of water and ½ teaspoon of salt per cup of dry beans. For cooking, use 3 cups of water, 1 tablespoon oil, and ½ teaspoon salt per cup of dry beans.

It is necessary to use oil to control the foaming produced during cooking. Since soybean skins have a tendency to fall off, they could be catapulted into the vent and clog it. Owners of the newly designed pressure cookers have little cause for concern; however, if you use an old-fashioned jiggle-top cooker, stay in the kitchen while the beans are cooking and let down the pressure under cold running water if the cooker begins to hiss loudly.

Ful Medames

Ful medames is a simple bean dish so earthy in taste and texture, it's easy to understand how it has sustained the Egyptians since the time of the Pharaohs. Redolent of parsley, olive oil, and lemon juice, it is prepared with small dried fava beans (large ones have tough skins that have to be peeled off). Small favas are readily available in Middle Eastern groceries. However, black-eyed peas make a fine substitute (see Cook's Notes).

For a great meal, serve Ful Medames as part of a Middle Eastern medley, including Tabbouleh (page 107) and Hummus (page 312), with oil-cured black olives and lots of warm pita bread.

Pressure cooker: 4 minutes high pressure, 10-minute natural pressure release
Standard stovetop: 75 to 90 minutes

1½ cups small dried fava beans, picked over and rinsed, soaked 8 to 12
*   hours in ample water to cover*
2 cups water, approximately
2 large cloves garlic, peeled and thinly sliced
2 to 3 tablespoons fruity olive oil
½ cup tightly packed minced fresh parsley
2 to 3 tablespoons lemon juice
1¼ teaspoons sea salt, or to taste

1. Drain and rinse the soaked favas. Place them in the cooker with water to cover, garlic, and 1 tablespoon of oil.

2. Lock the lid in place and over high heat bring to high pressure. Lower the heat just enough to maintain high pressure and cook for 4 minutes. Allow the pressure to come down naturally for 10 minutes. Quick-release any remaining pressure. Remove the lid, tilting it away from you to allow any excess steam to escape. If the favas are not quite tender, replace the lid and cook them in the residual heat for a few more minutes. (The skins, even on the small favas, tend to be slightly tough no matter how long you cook them.)

3. While the favas are still warm, stir in the parsley, the remaining olive oil, lemon juice, and salt to taste. (There should be a nice balance between oil and lemon juice, with the lemon prevailing slightly.) Serve in small bowls, warm or at room temperature.

Standard Stovetop: In a heavy 2-quart saucepan, follow step 1. Bring to the boil, then reduce the heat and simmer, covered, until the beans are tender, about 75 to 90 minutes. Replenish water to keep the beans barely covered. Follow step 3.

continued

Cook's Notes: Ful Medames is usually slightly soupy, but if the beans sit in the cooker for more than a few minutes, they absorb all of the cooking liquid. You can either eat them as is or stir in a bit more water and reheat.

If you make this dish with black-eyed peas, you don't need to soak them overnight. Simply place 1½ cups of peas in the cooker with water to just cover and the garlic and olive oil. Cook under high pressure for 4 minutes plus a 10-minute natural pressure release, and proceed as directed in step 3.

Red Beans and Chicos *Serves 4 to 6*

I first tasted this wonderful combination of beans and oven-dried sweet corn in the Rocky Mountain home of natural food specialist Rebecca Wood. Never have beans tasted so good! In contrast to the soft, creamy beans, the faintly sweet chicos retain just a bit of chewiness. I just couldn't get enough of them and one morning even had a small portion for breakfast.

When I asked Rebecca for the recipe, she casually responded, "Just throw the beans in the pressure cooker with a handful of chicos and some garlic." I've added a bit of oregano and crushed pepper for good measure.

You can mail-order chicos (also called *hornos chicos*) if they aren't available locally (see page 476). Dried sweet corn cracked into bits is nationally distributed in health food stores and makes a pleasing substitute for chicos.

These red beans are great with Spanish Casserole Rice (page 136), or wrapped up in a warmed corn tortilla slathered with mustard.

Pressure cooker: 5 minutes high pressure, 10-minute natural pressure release
Standard stovetop: 90 minutes

1 cup red kidney beans, picked over and rinsed, soaked overnight in a
   bowl in ample water to cover
½ cup chicos or sweet dried corn, soaked overnight in the cooker in 2 cups
   water
3 large cloves garlic, peeled and thinly sliced
1 teaspoon dried leaf oregano
¼ to ½ teaspoon crushed red pepper flakes (optional)
1 teaspoon sea salt and/or Bragg Liquid Aminos to taste

OPTIONAL GARNISH
¼ cup tightly packed, finely chopped fresh coriander or parsley

1. Drain and rinse the kidney beans. Bring the chicos in their soaking water to the boil. Add the kidney beans, garlic, oregano, red pepper (if using), and a bit more water, if needed, to just cover the beans and chicos.

2. Lock the lid into place. Over high heat bring to high pressure. Lower the heat just enough to maintain high pressure and cook for 5 minutes. Allow the pressure to come down naturally for 10 minutes, then quick-release any remaining pressure. Remove the lid, tilting it away from you to allow any excess steam to escape.

3. Stir in salt and/or Bragg Liquid Aminos to taste. If the beans or chicos are not quite tender, replace the lid and simmer an additional few minutes.

4. When done, lift out the beans and chicos from the cooker with a slotted spoon, reserving the liquid for soup or stock. Alternatively, serve the beans with the liquid in small bowls. (The cooking liquid will thicken considerably upon standing or refrigeration.) Garnish with coriander, if desired.

Standard Stovetop: In a heavy 2-quart saucepan, follow step 1. Return to the boil, then reduce the heat and simmer, covered, until the beans and chicos are almost tender (the chicos may remain slightly chewy but should not be hard), about 90 minutes. Add water as needed to keep the beans covered. Follow steps 3 and 4.

Variations

- Instead of chicos or dried sweet corn, stir in some fresh, uncooked corn kernels or 1-inch chunks of corn on the cob at the end of cooking; continue simmering the beans until the corn is cooked, about 3 to 5 minutes.
- Dress up reheated leftovers by stirring in a handful of green olives.

Let your food be your medicine, and your medicine be your food.
—Hippocrates

Bean Burritos

A great way to use leftover beans for an informal lunch. I tried this recipe with organic red kidney beans that I had cooked previously, had frozen, and then defrosted overnight in the refrigerator. It was a great success, and the flavor and texture of the beans were not in any way marred by their detour in the freezer.

Depending upon what else is on the menu and the appetites of those present, figure on 1 or 2 burritos per person. You can assemble them before serving as directed below, or put all the makings on the table and have diners create their own.

A large green salad and some raw carrot sticks are just the right accompaniments.

Skillet or wok: 8 minutes

1 tablespoon olive oil
2 large cloves garlic, peeled and finely chopped
1 large onion, peeled and coarsely chopped
1 jalapeño pepper, stemmed and thinly sliced (wear rubber gloves when
    handling), or generous pinch crushed red pepper flakes
2 teaspoons mild chili powder
1½ teaspoons dried leaf oregano
1½ teaspoons whole cumin seeds
2½ to 3 cups cooked beans (red kidneys, black beans, or pintos)
½ to 1 cup bean cooking liquid or water
1½ cups tightly packed minced fresh coriander or 1 cup tightly packed
    minced fresh parsley
¼ cup pitted, chopped green olives
Sea salt and/or hot sauce to taste
6 large flour tortillas, warmed just before serving

OPTIONAL GARNISHES
Chopped tomato, chopped onions or scallion greens, chopped avocado,
    shredded lettuce

1. Heat the oil in a large skillet or wok and sauté the garlic, onion, jalapeño, chili powder, oregano, and cumin, stirring frequently, until the onions are soft, about 2 to 3 minutes.

2. Stir in the beans, ½ cup liquid, coriander, and olives. Cover and simmer until the flavors are mingled and the beans are well heated, about 3 to 5 minutes. Add more liquid during this time if the mixture becomes dry. (It should be so thick that a spoon could stand up in it.)

3. Add salt and/or hot sauce to taste.

4. Place about ½ cup of the mixture in the center of each tortilla. Place a small spoonful of one or more of the garnishes on top (if using) and fold up the bottom and sides of the tortilla into a small packet. Proceed with the remainder of the mixture. Serve immediately.

Variation: Rolling up the tortillas rather than folding them turns them into enchiladas.

We must begin to allow our connections and live our wholeness. Our world will blossom. We must give up our separateness to experience wholeness. When we "move our hand" we must know that it affects the entire planet. Just knowing this will make decisions for us.

—Michael E. Reynolds, *A Coming of Wizards*
(Taos, New Mexico: The High Mesa Foundation, 1989).

Chinese-Style Beans and Greens

Here's a 1-2-3 way to prepare a surprisingly tasty and pretty dish by stir-frying fresh greens and Chinese seasonings with cooked beans. I like to keep the greens on the crunchy side, to provide a contrast to the mellow beans.

Stirring in a small handful of salty fermented black beans gives the dish punch and a strong Chinese character. Available in some supermarkets, most Oriental groceries, and by mail order, they last a long time, and since a little of them goes a long way, it's worthwhile to keep a small jar in the refrigerator.

Serve with plain-cooked white or brown rice.

Skillet or wok: 3 to 5 minutes

1 tablespoon light sesame or peanut oil
1 tablespoon freshly grated ginger
1 large clove garlic, peeled and finely chopped
1 to 2 tablespoons fermented black beans (optional but tasty), coarsely
  chopped
1½ pounds bok choy or Napa cabbage, cut into ½-inch slices
1 cup cooked beans (small or medium-sized preferred), such as red
  kidneys, pintos, or black-eyed peas
Tamari soy sauce and hot pepper sesame oil to taste

1. In a large skillet or wok, heat the oil. Sauté the ginger and garlic for 5 seconds.

2. Stir in the black beans (if using) and then the bok choy. Stir-fry for 1 minute and add the beans.

3. Cook covered until the greens shrink in volume, about 1 to 2 minutes. (The bok choy will shrink down to about one quarter of the original volume.) Then continue to stir-fry over medium-high heat until the greens are crisp-tender and the beans are heated through.

4. Season with tamari and hot pepper sesame oil to taste.

Cook's Notes: If you've used fermented black beans, be sure to taste the dish before adding tamari: It's unlikely that you'll need much, since the black beans are so flavorful and salty.

Variation: Instead of hot pepper sesame oil, throw in a pinch of crushed red pepper flakes during cooking. Then season with plain toasted sesame oil at the end.

Beans and Greens Italiano

Serves 3 to 4

This basic recipe offers endless possibilities for combining cooked beans and fresh, chopped greens. Especially good combinations include kale and limas, escarole and cannellinis, mustard greens and adukis, and Swiss chard and navy beans.

Minced sun-dried tomatoes or olives add a dramatic touch of taste and color to these down-home ingredients.

Skillet or wok: 3 to 8 minutes

1 tablespoon olive oil (try using the oil from the sun-dried tomatoes)
3 large cloves garlic, peeled and thinly sliced
½ teaspoon dried rosemary leaves
¾ pound greens, such as Swiss chard, spinach, or kale, trimmed (thick
    stems reserved for stock), rinsed, and finely chopped
2 to 4 tablespoons bean cooking liquid or water (optional)
1½ cups firm-cooked beans
⅓ cup finely chopped sun-dried tomatoes or coarsely chopped, pitted black
    olives
Sea salt and freshly ground pepper to taste

1. In a large skillet or wok, heat the oil. Sauté the garlic over medium-high heat, stirring frequently until lightly browned, about 1 minute. (Take care as garlic burns easily.) Add the rosemary and let sizzle for 5 seconds.

2. Add the greens (along with any rinse water still clinging to the leaves) and cover the pot (you may have to squash the greens under the cover). Cook over medium-high heat until the greens are almost tender, about 2 to 3 minutes for spinach, chard, or beet greens and 5 to 8 minutes for kale or escarole. Stir every few minutes and add a bit of liquid, if needed, for the longer-cooking greens.

3. Stir in the beans and sun-dried tomatoes a minute or so before the greens are done.

4. Season with salt and pepper to taste.

Variations
- Toss with 3 to 4 cups of cooked, small pasta, such as spirals or elbows. Drizzle on a bit of olive oil and balsamic vinegar. Serve warm or at room temperature.
- Use pan-fried tempeh (page 228) instead of beans.
- Heat any leftovers in vegetable stock for a quick soup.

Chili "Barbecued" Beans

Prepared in under half an hour, these beans taste as if they've been hanging out at the back of the stove all day. The liquid thickens considerably upon standing and the flavors deepen as the dish sits at room temperature. For optimum taste, prepare the beans the day before or a few hours in advance of dinner, and then reheat them just before serving.

Serve with brown rice and a steamed vegetable.

Pressure cooker: 10 to 12 minutes high pressure, 7 to 10 minutes simmering
Standard stovetop: 60 to 90 minutes

*2 cups navy beans, picked over and rinsed, soaked 8 to 12 hours in ample
  water to cover*
1 to 2 tablespoons olive oil
2 large onions, peeled and coarsely chopped
3 large cloves garlic, peeled and finely chopped
¾ teaspoon dried rosemary leaves
½ teaspoon dried thyme
2 tablespoons mild chili powder
2 cups water, approximately
2 carrots, thinly sliced
⅓ cup barley malt syrup, measured from an oiled cup
2 tablespoons prepared mustard, preferably coarse-grained
1 tablespoon apple cider vinegar, approximately
Sea salt or tamari soy sauce to taste

1. Drain and rinse the beans. Set aside.

2. Heat the oil in the cooker and sauté the onions and garlic, stirring frequently, until the onions are lightly browned, about 3 to 4 minutes. Add the drained beans, rosemary, thyme, chili powder, water to cover, and carrots. Be sure to scrape up any onions sticking to the bottom of the cooker.

3. Lock the lid in place and over high heat bring to high pressure. Lower the heat just enough to maintain high pressure and cook for 10 minutes. Allow the pressure to come down naturally or reduce the pressure with a quick-release method. Remove the lid, tilting it away from you to allow any excess steam to escape. If the beans are not tender (they should easily be squashed when pressed against the roof of the mouth), return to high pressure for another few minutes.

4. Stir in the barley malt syrup, mustard, cider vinegar, and salt, simmer, covered, until the flavors mingle, an additional 7 to 10 minutes.

Standard Stovetop: Follow step 1. In a heavy 3-quart saucepan, follow step 2. Bring to the boil, then reduce the heat and simmer, covered, until the beans are almost tender, about 45 to 60 minutes. Follow step 4 and simmer, uncovered, stirring occasionally, until the beans are infused with flavor and very tender, about 15 more minutes.

Pepper-Flecked Potato-Lentil Medley   Serves 4

A comforting dish that's bound to become a favorite. A bit of mustard stirred in at the end makes the flavors pop.

> **Pressure cooker:** 9 minutes high pressure, 3 minutes simmering
> **Standard stovetop:** 35 to 40 minutes

1 to 2 tablespoons olive oil
1 large red bell pepper, seeded and diced
2 large cloves garlic, peeled and finely chopped
1½ teaspoons dried oregano
Generous pinch crushed red pepper flakes
1½ cups brown lentils, picked over and rinsed
2¾ to 3 cups water (use larger amount for jiggle-top cookers)
12 small (about 1¼ pounds) new red potatoes, well scrubbed
2 large carrots, thickly sliced on the diagonal
1 to 2 tablespoons Dijon mustard, preferably coarse-grained
½ teaspoon sea salt, or to taste
Freshly ground black pepper
¾ pound quick-cooking greens, such as spinach, Swiss chard, beet greens,
*   or watercress, trimmed and finely chopped*

1. Heat the oil in the cooker. Sauté the red bell pepper and garlic for 1 minute, stirring frequently. Stir in the oregano, crushed red pepper, and lentils. Add the water (watch for sputtering oil!), potatoes, and carrots.

2. Lock the lid in place and over high heat bring to high pressure. Lower the heat just enough to maintain high pressure and cook for 9 minutes. Reduce the pressure with a quick-release method. Remove the lid, tilting it away from you to allow any excess steam to escape.

3. Stir in the mustard, salt (as much as 1 teaspoon), pepper, and greens, and simmer until the greens are cooked, about 3 minutes.

continued

Standard Stovetop: In a heavy 3-quart saucepan, follow step 1, using 3 cups of water. Bring to the boil, then reduce the heat and simmer, covered, until the lentils and potatoes are tender, about 35 to 40 minutes. Follow step 3.

Cook's Notes: If only large potatoes are available, cut them in quarters; for best taste and texture use the thin-skinned varieties.

Beans and Not Dogs

Serves 4

I usually don't try to make vegetarian imitations of hallowed dishes like franks and beans, but this one—using tofu pups instead of hot dogs—is fun for Sunday night suppers. Serve it with Reliably Fluffy Millet (page 89) or Spanish Casserole Rice (page 136).

Pressure cooker: 10 to 12 minutes high pressure, 10 to 15 minutes simmering
Standard stovetop: 90 minutes

1½ cups red kidney or pinto beans, picked over and rinsed, soaked 4 to 8
    hours in ample water to cover
1 tablespoon oil (to control foaming)
1 large onion, peeled and coarsely chopped
2 large cloves garlic, peeled and minced
2 large carrots, chunked
4 whole cloves
1 tablespoon freshly grated ginger
½ teaspoon ground cumin
2 cups water, approximately
8 tofu pups (12 ounces), each cut into 5 to 6 pieces
2 tablespoons tomato paste
2 tablespoons Dijon mustard
2 tablespoons barley malt or maple syrup, measured from an oiled spoon
2 teaspoons cider vinegar
Sea salt to taste

1. Drain the soaked beans and rinse. In the cooker, place the beans, oil, onion, garlic, carrots, cloves, ginger, cumin, and water to barely cover.
2. Lock lid into place and over high heat bring to high pressure. Lower the heat just enough to maintain high pressure and cook for 10 minutes.
3. Reduce the pressure with a quick-release method (or release pressure under cold running water if quick-release causes sputtering). Remove the lid, tilting

it away from you to allow any excess steam to escape. Test the beans for tenderness and return to high pressure for a few more minutes if they aren't sufficiently cooked.

4. When the beans are tender, drain off any liquid in excess of 1 cup. (Reserve this liquid for soup or to thin any leftovers, which will thicken after overnight refrigeration.) Stir in the remaining ingredients and simmer until flavors mingle, about 10 to 15 minutes. Adjust seasonings before serving.

Standard Stovetop: In a heavy 3-quart saucepan, follow step 1, omitting the oil if you wish. Bring to the boil, then reduce the heat and simmer, covered, until the beans are tender, about 90 minutes. Add water toward the end of cooking if the mixture seems dry. Follow step 4.

Variation: If tofu pups are not your thing, you can cook cubed marinated tofu, tempeh, or seitan with the beans, or just serve the zesty beans on their own.

One thing is certain: nothing will happen if we all wait for others to do it first. . . . The still, small voice whispering to me in the depths of my consciousness is saying exactly the same thing as the voice whispering to you: "I want an Earth that is healthy, a world at peace, and a heart filled with love."

—Eknath Easwaran, "The Lesson of the Hummingbird,"
In Context, A Quarterly of Humane Sustainable Culture,
No. 26, Summer 1990.

Lentils with Chestnuts

Serves 4

Dried chestnuts are expensive, but so few go such a long way in adding luscious taste and texture that they end up being a bargain. Dried chestnuts are readily available in health food stores and by mail order, and are carried in many gourmet shops.

I discovered the sensational combination of lentils and chestnuts in an ancient Roman cookbook. The lentil-chestnut soup on page 53 is a variation on this time-tested duo.

Serve these lentils as a side dish or use them to top couscous, barley, or brown rice.

Pressure cooker: 7 minutes high pressure, 2 to 3 minutes simmering
Standard stovetop: 40 minutes

½ cup dried, peeled chestnuts, soaked overnight in the cooker in 4 cups water
2 cups brown lentils, picked over and rinsed
½ teaspoon ground cardamom
⅓ cup raisins (optional)
2 to 3 teaspoons apple cider vinegar
1 to 2 tablespoons light miso, sea salt, or tamari soy sauce

1. After the chestnuts have soaked overnight, remove any dark brown skins floating on top of the water.

2. Lift the chestnuts out of the water with a slotted spoon. Rub off any dark skins still clinging to the soaked chestnuts, and discard them. (If any cling tenaciously, let them.) With a large chef's knife, cut the chestnuts in quarters. (For any hard ones, pound on the top edge of the knife with your fist.)

3. Return the chestnuts to the liquid in the cooker and add the lentils, cardamom, and raisins (if using).

4. Lock the lid into place. Over high heat bring to high pressure. Lower the heat just enough to maintain high pressure and cook for 7 minutes. Let the pressure come down naturally or use a quick-release method. Remove the lid, tilting it away from you to allow any excess steam to escape.

5. Stir in vinegar to taste. If using miso, dissolve it in a cupful of the lentil mixture and then stir it back into the pot. Otherwise, stir salt or tamari directly into the mixture and simmer, uncovered, for 2 to 3 minutes more.

Standard Stovetop: Using a heavy 3-quart saucepan, follow steps 1 to 3. Bring to the boil, then reduce the heat and simmer, covered, until the lentils and chestnuts are tender, about 40 minutes. Follow step 5.

Tarragon-Scented Succotash

This is a contemporary interpretation of the Native American dish based on the sacred three sisters: corn, beans, and squash. Ideally the squash will remain in firm chunks with only 2 minutes under pressure, but once I overcooked it to mush and the dish was delicious anyway.

When fresh corn is available, I love to chop the raw ears into chunks (by pounding my fist on the wide end of a heavy chef's knife) rather than use kernels. This makes a beautiful presentation, and the corncobs add a touch of sweetness to the dish.

Pressure cooker: 2 minutes high pressure
Standard stovetop: 12 to 15 minutes

1 cup water
1 large onion, peeled and coarsely chopped
2 ribs celery, finely chopped
2½ teaspoons dried tarragon
2 pounds peeled winter squash (butternut and kabocha are nice), seeded
     and cut into 1½-inch chunks (about 7 cups)
3 ears corn, husks and silk removed, cut into 1-inch chunks, or 2 cups
     fresh or frozen (defrosted) corn kernels
½ teaspoon sea salt, or to taste
3 cups firm-cooked large limas
¼ cup tightly packed, finely chopped fresh parsley

1. Over high heat, bring the water to the boil in the cooker as you add the onion, celery, tarragon, squash, corn, and salt.

2. Lock the lid into place. Over high heat bring to high pressure. Lower the heat just enough to maintain high pressure and cook for 2 minutes. Reduce the pressure with a quick-release method. Remove the lid, tilting it away from you to allow any excess steam to escape. If the squash is not quite cooked, replace the lid and allow it to steam in the residual heat for another 1 to 2 minutes.

3. Stir in the limas and parsley and cook just until the limas are heated through.

Standard Stovetop: In a 3-quart saucepan, follow step 1. Bring to the boil, cover, reduce the heat, and simmer until the squash is tender, about 12 to 15 minutes. Follow step 3.

Cook's Notes: Like black soybeans, thin-skinned large limas require special treatment:

continued

To pressure-cook limas: For 3 cups, soak 1¼ cups of dried limas overnight in ample water to cover with ¼ teaspoon salt. (The skins of the limas tend to loosen and the salt helps retain them.) After soaking the limas, remove any loose or free-floating skins. Place the limas in the cooker with 2 tablespoons of oil (to control foaming) and ⅛ teaspoon salt. Bring up to high pressure, then let the pressure come down naturally for 10 minutes. Remove the lid, tilting it away from you to allow any excess steam to escape. If the limas are not sufficiently cooked, cover and simmer until done. Drain, reserving the cooking liquid for soup, stock, or cooking grains.

For standard stovetop follow instructions above and cook covered until the limas are tender, about 45 to 60 minutes. You may omit the oil.

Bean Empanadas

Makes 8 to 10 large turnovers

Making savory turnovers is a great way to transform small amounts of leftover beans (or grains) into an appealing appetizer or entrée. The labor involved is very much reduced when the filling is recycled from another day's cooking. Good possibilities include Pat's Spicy Black-eyed Peas (page 178), Lentil-Quinoa Salad with Curry Vinaigrette (page 214), and Quick Chick-pea Curry (page 180). Whatever you use, make sure it's highly seasoned.

I learned this simple technique for making the dough from Lissa De Angelis at the Natural Gourmet Institute for Food and Health in New York. You can make the dough well in advance and refrigerate or freeze it; then bring it to room temperature before rolling it out. The filled turnovers can also be frozen, baked or unbaked.

This is a nice opportunity to enjoy the added flavor of amaranth; the little seeds are transformed into flour quickly and easily in a coffee grinder. But the dough is just fine when made with all whole wheat flour.

Oven: 30 to 35 minutes at 375°

¼ cup canola oil plus extra for greasing a cookie sheet
¼ cup olive oil
1 cup water
1 teaspoon dried leaf oregano
½ teaspoon sea salt
Pinch cayenne (ground red) pepper (optional)
1⅔ to 2 cups whole wheat flour plus additional for sprinkling
⅓ cup amaranth or quinoa flour or additional whole wheat flour

FOR THE FILLING
2 cups cooked, well-seasoned beans, thoroughly drained
Mustard

1. Lightly brush a cookie sheet with oil and set aside.

2. In a 2-quart saucepan, heat the oils, water, oregano, salt, and cayenne (if using) until bubbles just begin to appear (do not boil). Slowly whisk in 1⅔ cups whole wheat flour and the amaranth flour (or additional ⅓ cup whole wheat flour). Use a spoon to stir when dough becomes thick. Transfer to a small bowl, cover with a kitchen towel, and refrigerate for 30 to 45 minutes.

3. Sprinkle a smooth surface (such as a cutting board or a pastry board) with whole wheat flour and rub flour onto the roller. Roll out the dough to ⅛-inch thickness. (If the dough is too sticky, knead in additional flour until it develops a good rolling consistency.)

4. Press a small bowl with a 5-inch diameter firmly into the dough to make rounds. Transfer the dough rounds to the cookie sheet. Spread a thin layer of mustard on each, then set 2 generous tablespoons of filling onto the lower half of each round, leaving about a 1-inch border along the edge. (If the dough tears at any point, press it together firmly with your fingers.)

5. Carefully fold over the dough and press the edges together firmly with the tines of a fork. Arrange the filled turnovers about 1 inch apart and proceed to reroll the dough, cut, and fill the turnovers until the dough and filling are used up (see Cook's Notes).

6. Bake on the middle rack of a preheated 375° oven until the bottoms are golden and the edges are browned and crispy, about 30 to 35 minutes. Serve warm.

Cook's Notes: If you run out of filling before you run out of dough, try rolling out the extra dough and making crackers. Press some sesame seeds or pumpkin seeds and dried herbs or ground spices into the dough and cut into cracker-sized rounds or squares. Bake on a cookie sheet (along with the turnovers) until crisp, about 12 to 15 minutes. Cool on a rack.

Variations
- To make appetizers, cut the dough into rounds about 2½ inches in diameter and fill with about 1 tablespoon of filling. Proceed as above and bake for about 20 minutes.
- Use any well-seasoned grains or a combination of grains and beans for the filling.

Bean Salads

Because beans are densely textured, they are often better appreciated when they appear in small doses, dotted here and there among other companionable ingredients.

There are a few aspects to consider when you are creating bean salads:

Taste: Since most beans and grains are mildly flavored, include at least one ingredient that has intense flavor—such as olives, capers, or chopped sun-dried tomatoes.

Appearance: The majority of beans and all grains come in earth tones, so for color accents add some chopped carrots, red peppers, minced herbs, or thinly sliced scallion greens. It's also a good idea to keep the other ingredients similar in size and shape to the beans you're using.

Texture: To contrast with the mellow, often creamy texture of beans and the chewiness of grains, add an ingredient with crunch. Nuts and seeds are ideal choices, as are finely chopped raw vegetables.

The first recipe will help you create your own salads from what's on hand. The recipes that follow will give you some more specific ideas. But remember, the only limits to bean salads are the limits of your imagination.

We return thanks—first to our mother, the earth, which sustains us, then on to the rivers and streams, to the herbs, to the corn and beans and squashes, to bushes and trees, to the wind, to the moon and stars, to the sun, and finally to the Great Spirit who directs all things.

—From an Iroquois Thanksgiving ritual, in
Thomas Berry, *The Dream of the Earth*
(San Francisco: Sierra Club Books, 1990).

What's Available
Bean-and-Grain Salad

Here's the basic formula for creating an endless variety of wholesome, tasty, and colorful salads based on what you find in the refrigerator and pantry. Just choose one or more ingredients from each category.

THE BASICS

2 to 3 cups cooked beans

2 to 3 cups cooked grains (including already seasoned grains or pilafs and pasta)

1 to 2 cups carrots, celery, or red bell pepper—or a combination, thinly sliced or coarsely chopped (for color and crunch)

⅓ cup oil-cured black olives, capers, or chopped sun-dried tomatoes (for flavor punch)

OPTIONAL INGREDIENTS

1 to 2 cups diced or coarsely chopped (nonstarchy) cooked vegetables, such as beets, cauliflower, green beans, or broccoli (for color and texture variation)

1 to 2 cups cooked corn (for crunch, sweetness, and color; almost always a good choice)

¼ cup thinly sliced scallion greens or finely chopped red onion (for color and assertive taste)

½ to 1 cup tightly packed minced fresh herbs, such as parsley, dill, or coriander (for vibrant color and taste)

⅓ cup coarsely chopped, pitted olives (for assertive taste)

¼ cup toasted sunflower or pumpkin seeds or 1 to 2 tablespoons toasted black or white sesame seeds (for crunch)

1. Put the beans, grains, crunchy vegetables, and ingredients with punch in a large bowl or storage container.

2. Stir in any of the optional ingredients.

3. Toss with the Impromptu Vinaigrette below or your choice of dressing—about ⅓ to ½ cup should do—and serve.

continued

IMPROMPTU VINAIGRETTE

Drizzle the smaller amount of each of the three types of ingredients (oil, acid, flavor enhancer) directly onto the salad. Toss and taste, adding a bit more of each as required to coat the ingredients and to achieve a balance.

Choose One Oil
3 to 4 tablespoons olive oil
2 tablespoons light sesame oil plus 3 to 4 teaspoons Oriental (toasted) sesame oil

Choose One Acid
2 to 3 tablespoons lemon juice
2 to 3 tablespoons wine vinegar
2 to 3 teaspoons umeboshi plum vinegar (umeboshi is quite salty, so you will probably not need tamari or salt)

Choose One Flavor Enhancer
Tamari soy sauce
Bragg Liquid Aminos
Sea salt and freshly ground pepper to taste

Cook's Notes: If the beans or grains have already been seasoned, add more of the same seasonings to the whole salad.

Refrigerated bean and grain salads usually need to be perked up with extra dressing, a generous squeeze of lemon juice, or a few sprinklings of umeboshi plum vinegar (my personal favorite).

People eat with their minds, not their bodies. . . . When people rejected natural food and took up refined food instead, society set out on a path toward its own destruction. This is because such food is not the product of true culture. Food is life, and life must *not* step away from nature.

—Masanobu Fukuoka, "The One-Straw Revolution,"
cited in Gretel Ehrlich, "Growing Lean, Clean Beef," in Robert Clark, ed.,
Our Sustainable Table (Berkeley: North Point Press, 1990).

Southwest Bean Salad

A great hit among vegetarians and nonvegetarians alike, this is an ideal salad to serve to a "mixed" crowd. Try to prepare it while the beans are still warm, so that they can absorb the dressing more fully. Serve on a bed of greens.

2 cups cooked anasazi or pinto beans

2 cups cooked corn kernels

2 ribs celery, cut into ¼-inch slices

1 large carrot, cut into matchsticks

½ cup tightly packed minced fresh coriander or 3 tablespoons dried coriander

¼ cup coarsely chopped, pitted green olives

¼ cup olive oil

2 to 3 tablespoons freshly squeezed lime or lemon juice

1 tablespoon whole cumin seeds

2 teaspoons mild chili powder

1 teaspoon sea salt, or to taste

1 small fresh jalapeño pepper (wear rubber gloves when handling), chopped, or generous pinch crushed red pepper flakes (optional)

1 clove roasted garlic (page 425), mashed, or 1 clove raw garlic, peeled and minced

1. In a large serving bowl, combine the beans, corn, celery, carrots, coriander, and olives.

2. In a small jar, prepare the dressing by shaking together the oil, lime juice, cumin, chili powder, salt, jalapeño (if using), and garlic.

3. Pour the dressing over the beans and toss to blend thoroughly. Taste and add more salt or lemon juice, if needed, to perk up the flavors.

Aduki Watercress Salad
with Horseradish Dressing

Phil Teveraux, of Dean & DeLuca in New York City, gave me the idea for this recipe. He's the only person I know whose passion for beans exceeds my own.

The adukis' earthy flavor and creamy texture make a nice backdrop for spicy, crunchy watercress. Toss in the dressing while the beans are still warm for maximum flavor. If time permits, marinate the beans in the dressing for a few hours at room temperature, then toss in a bit more dressing along with the watercress just before serving.

Serve a vegetable soup with this pretty salad and accompany it with a crusty loaf for the makings of a very nice lunch.

1 large bunch watercress, rinsed and dried in a salad spinner
3 cups firm-cooked aduki beans
1½ cups cooked corn kernels
⅓ cup thinly sliced scallion greens (save the white part for another use,
*   such as sautéing with onions)*
⅓ to ½ cup Horseradish Dressing (page 299)
Soy sauce or brown rice vinegar to taste

1. Separate the watercress leaves from the stems. Discard any tough and fibrous stems or reserve them for stock. Coarsely chop the leaves and finely chop the stems. Set aside.

2. In a large bowl or storage container, combine the beans, corn, and scallion greens.

3. Pour ¼ to ⅓ cup of dressing over the beans, toss, and let sit for a few hours, if time permits.

4. Just before serving, toss in the watercress and extra dressing. Adjust the seasonings and sprinkle on soy sauce or vinegar, or stir in a bit more horseradish, if needed, to give the salad a bold, vibrant taste.

Cook's Notes: The amount of horseradish needed to flavor the salad will depend upon its freshness and your tolerance for hot stuff. If the horseradish has been in the refrigerator for a month or so, you may need 2 to 3 tablespoons in addition to the dressing to give this salad its proper due.

The watercress is tossed in just before serving so that it will maintain its crunch.

Variation: Instead of tossing the beans in the watercress, make a bed of the greens and mound the adukis on top. The salad also looks gorgeous on a bed of radicchio.

Black Bean Salad
with Coriander Pesto

A must for those who love fresh coriander and black beans.

4 cups cooked black beans
3 large carrots, coarsely grated
1 roasted red pepper, seeded and diced (page 451)
2 cups cooked corn kernels
½ to ⅔ cup Coriander Pesto (page 298)
1 to 4 tablespoons freshly squeezed lime juice
Sea salt to taste

1. In a large serving bowl, combine the beans, carrots, pepper, and corn.
2. Toss in enough coriander pesto to coat mixture thoroughly.
3. Add lime juice and salt, as needed, to perk up the flavors.

Let nature have her way. She knows her business better than we do.

—Montaigne

Lentil-Quinoa Salad
with Curry Vinaigrette

Any combination of beans and grains will do nicely, but the curry flavor marries especially well with the peppery flavor of lentils.

2½ cups firm-cooked brown lentils
1½ cups cooked quinoa
⅓ cup finely chopped scallion greens
¼ to ⅓ cup Lime-Curry Vinaigrette (page 292)
Lemon juice and/or sea salt to taste

1. In a large bowl or serving container, combine the lentils, quinoa, and scallions.
2. Add enough vinaigrette to just moisten.
3. Add enough lemon juice and/or salt to make the flavors pop.
4. Serve immediately or refrigerate for up to 3 days.

Cook's Notes: After refrigeration, the salad will need extra dressing and lemon juice.

Variations
• Add 1 cup cooked or sprouted green peas (page 289).
• Add 1 to 2 cups cooked corn.

If our kids are going to continue to see green growing things on this earth, we're going to have to start taking care of it now.

—Ernie New, organic quinoa farmer,
Mosca, Colorado

Red Bean Salad Olé

A bean and roasted pepper salad with a Spanish accent and great charm. The flavor is at its best after the beans have marinated awhile, so plan to prepare the dish a few hours before serving.

2½ cups firm-cooked red kidneys

¼ cup finely chopped red (Spanish) onion or thinly sliced scallion greens

2 large red peppers, roasted (page 451), seeded, and cut into thin strips (about 1 cup)

1 cup thinly sliced celery

½ cup tightly packed minced fresh parsley

¼ cup tightly packed minced fresh coriander or 1 tablespoon dried coriander (if any coriander haters are coming to town, just substitute an extra ¼ cup of fresh parsley)

FOR THE DRESSING

2 tablespoons olive oil

Juice of 2 limes (about ⅓ cup)

3 to 5 tablespoons sherry wine (very yummy) or balsamic vinegar

1 teaspoon coarsely ground juniper berries (you may be tempted to skip this ingredient: don't!)

½ teaspoon sweet paprika

½ teaspoon sea salt, or to taste

Pinch cayenne (ground red) pepper

1. In a salad bowl or storage container, combine the beans, onion, red peppers, celery, parsley, and coriander.

2. In a jar, combine the oil, lime juice, 3 tablespoons vinegar, juniper berries, paprika, salt, and cayenne. Shake well to blend. Pour over the beans and mix well to coat.

3. Add more salt, if needed, and sprinkle on enough additional vinegar to give the salad a distinctly pickled flavor. (The amount of vinegar will depend upon your preference and the strength of the vinegar.)

4. Let marinate for 2 to 3 hours at room temperature before serving.

Variations

- If you have a half cup or so of plain-cooked grains, toss it in about an hour before serving to absorb the liquid released as the salad marinates.
- Try using some of the pretty and less common beans, such as Christmas Limas, Dixie Speckled Butter Beans, Black Valentines, or black turtle beans.

Hoppin' John Salad

Hoppin' John—a combination of black-eyed peas and rice—is a dish Southerners eat for good luck on New Year's. This Yankee finds the tradition too tasty to reserve for eating just once a year.

Although Hoppin' John is generally served hot, this recipe is for a cold salad with an herb vinaigrette—a convenient addition to a New Year's buffet table.

For best flavor, dress the salad at least an hour before serving.

2 cups cooked brown rice, cooled to room temperature
4 cups firm-cooked black-eyed peas, cooled to room temperature
4 large ribs celery, thinly sliced
3 large carrots, coarsely chopped
1 cup coarsely chopped, pitted green olives
1 large red bell pepper, seeded and diced
1 to 2 jalapeño peppers (wear rubber gloves when handling), seeded and
*   minced, or generous dash cayenne (ground red) pepper (optional)*
1 to 1¼ cups Herb Vinaigrette (page 294)
Lemon juice and/or sea salt to taste

1. In a large bowl, toss the rice, peas, celery, carrots, olives, and red and jalapeño peppers (if using) together.

2. Pour on enough dressing to thoroughly season the salad.

3. Add lemon juice and/or salt as required to bring up the flavors.

Cook's Notes: After overnight refrigeration, the salad will need perking up with additional lemon juice.

Tofu and Tempeh

Tofu

Having a block of tofu at arm's reach guarantees that a tasty meal is only 15 minutes away. Sometimes referred to as "meat without the bone," tofu is remarkably nutritious, easy to digest, and a bargain to boot—under two dollars a pound and often on sale for much less. An 8-ounce serving of tofu is approximately 147 calories and contains about 8 percent protein; it is relatively high in fat, but cholesterol free and a fine source of calcium, vitamins, and minerals.

Tofu is made in a process analogous to cheese-making. Soaked and ground soybeans are combined with water and a coagulant to create curds. These curds are pressed into blocks—hence the alternative name "bean curd."

The coagulating agent is of interest to some tofu connoisseurs. The traditional coagulant is nigari, a mineral derived from sea salt. In the United States, many tofu manufacturers use a refined form of nigari called magnesium chloride along with either calcium sulfate or calcium chloride, both of which add significantly to the calcium content of tofu.

For many people the blandness of tofu is a turnoff, but to me that is its greatest virtue: It's incredibly versatile and goes well with an enormous variety of flavors.

Selecting Tofu

Years ago I used to purchase small cakes of tofu from a local Korean market, but once I made the decision to give my body the best-quality fuel available, I switched to the tofu sold in health food stores. Unpackaged tofu, while probably more ecologically sound (it creates little to no garbage), is nevertheless of uncertain origin and age.

Nowadays, I buy tofu made of organically grown soybeans and well water. And I reach to the back of the refrigerator case to get the freshest tofu, with the most advanced expiration date. When there's a sale on tofu about to "expire," I purchase it and use it the same day or put it immediately in the freezer (see Freezing Tofu below).

There is a mind-boggling range of tofu available, categorized according to water content: extra-firm, firm, regular, soft, and silken. The firmer the tofu, the less water it contains, and the better it holds its shape in cooking. If you really get into tofu cookery, you might want to make your selections on a recipe-by-recipe basis. For me, being so exacting about cooking is no fun, so I just keep firm or extra-firm tofu on hand. These styles work best in stir-frying and baking; I simply add a bit of liquid if I'm making a tofu-based spread. I occasionally buy silken tofu to make Tofu Whip (page 398) or for an especially creamy dip.

One other form of tofu that bears mentioning is freeze-dried. These light little dehydrated cakes are handy to have in the cupboard or to take on camping trips. They weigh next to nothing and last indefinitely. Pour boiling water on them to rehydrate, then squeeze out excess water and proceed with the recipe. Freeze-dried tofu has a very chewy-spongy texture.

Storing Tofu

Tofu purchased in a sealed container will stay fresh at least until the expiration date on the package; often it remains fresh even a week beyond. Once opened, the tofu should be used quickly, but it will last 3 to 4 days in the refrigerator in a well-sealed container if the water is changed daily.

Fresh tofu has little to no smell. Once it starts to become rancid it develops a mildly sour aroma and taste, and a slippery surface. I usually toss it at this point, but I've read that you can cut away the yellowing edges and cook it for a few minutes in boiling water to resuscitate. (This plan is commendable for its thriftiness but not very aesthetically appealing; I prefer to keep on my toes about the expiration date.)

Freezing Tofu

You can freeze tofu for up to 3 months covered with water in a well-sealed container or right in the tub it comes in. It develops a chewy meatlike texture that works nicely in stews and stir-fries.

Either defrost the tofu at room temperature or, to speed up the process, immerse it in a pot of just-boiled water. Place the tofu between two plates and squeeze out excess moisture before cooking.

Preparing Tofu for Cooking

Although tofu can be drained, sliced or cubed, and cooked as is, I like to vary flavor and texture by using the following techniques:

Marinating: Soaking cubes in a marinade, such as tamari soy sauce or barbecue sauce enhances the flavor of the final dish. See pages 220–221 for some possibilities. Tofu marinated in a vinaigrette dressing is good on its own or tossed in a salad.

Freezing and defrosting: Creates a much chewier tofu (see page 218).

Expressing extra liquid: This helps the tofu absorb liquids or flavoring agents. To quick-press tofu, set the block between two plates and squeeze over the sink, tipping out the liquid as it is released. If time permits, place the tofu in a shallow bowl and set a plate on top. Place a heavy object or some bags of dried beans on the plate. Let tofu sit for 15 to 30 minutes, tipping out liquid as it accumulates.

Cutting into slices or cubes: Drain the tofu and squeeze out liquid, if desired. Set tofu on a cutting board. Using a serrated knife, cut slices to the thickness called for in the recipe.

For cubed tofu, first cut slices of the desired width without separating them from the block. Then cut slices vertically in the opposite direction. Finally, make horizontal slices.

The following recipes put tofu in the limelight. A few others in which tofu plays a major role are Sun-Dried Tomato Dip (page 318), Arame Zucchini Stir-fry (page 269), and Roasted Shallot Cream (page 303).

Either I will find a way or I will make one.
—Sir Philip Sidney

Marinated Tofu: Method One

Here's your chance to give that wallflower tofu some assertiveness training. Let it marinate for at least 2 hours, or overnight in the refrigerator. I usually prepare a 1-pound batch to use as needed throughout the week.

If you're caught at the last minute without any marinated tofu (perish the thought), see the Last-Minute version that follows.

1 pound firm or extra-firm tofu, drained
2 tablespoons tamari soy sauce
1 tablespoon plus 1 teaspoon barley malt syrup, measured from an oiled
  spoon
2 teaspoons apple cider or brown rice vinegar
2 cloves garlic, peeled and minced
1 tablespoon freshly grated ginger
1 tablespoon toasted (Oriental) sesame oil

1. Set the block of tofu between 2 plates and place a heavy weight on the top plate (I use a bag or two of dried beans). Let sit for 15 to 30 minutes to release excess liquid. Drain off the liquid and cut the tofu block into 1-inch cubes or into the size requested in individual recipes.

2. In a medium-sized jar or other storage container, combine the tamari, barley malt syrup, vinegar, garlic, ginger, and sesame oil. Shake well.

3. Add the tofu cubes and shake again. Refrigerate and marinate for a minimum of 2 hours and preferably overnight, shaking every now and then.

4. To use, lift the tofu out with a slotted spoon.

Cook's Notes: If the flavorings are compatible, you can use any leftover marinade as part of the liquid ingredient in the dish you are making.

My cooking buddy Judy Bloom likes to pressure-cook marinated tofu with Timid Cook's Casserole Brown Rice (page 127). She sets the tofu and any unabsorbed marinating liquid on top of the raw rice and water in the casserole and proceeds as directed in the recipe. When done, she stirs it all together, perhaps adding ¼ cup finely chopped parsley or coriander. The tofu comes out delightfully chewy, with a punchy saltiness that contrasts nicely with the rice.

Variation: Add a pinch of cayenne or crushed red pepper flakes to the marinade, if you can take the heat.

Last-Minute Marinated Tofu: Method Two

This fast marinade is quite effective if you suddenly need some well-seasoned tofu. In 10 minutes or so, the tofu absorbs a mild tamari taste. Double the recipe if necessary.

½ pound tofu, drained
3 teaspoons tamari soy sauce

1. Press the tofu between two plates to squeeze out as much liquid as possible. Slice the tofu into ½- or 1-inch cubes, according to the directions in any given recipe.

2. In a small container, set half of the tofu. Drizzle on 2 teaspoons of tamari. Add the remaining tofu to the container and drizzle with the remaining teaspoon of tamari.

3. Cover securely and shake to distribute the tamari. Shake occasionally over the next 10 minutes, or until needed.

Within the last year, I've made big changes. I have found the greatest epicurean pleasure in eating mostly fresh, organically grown fruits and vegetables, whole grains, nuts, tofu, and hardly any sweets. I feel better and have more energy than I ever had.

What inspired me to change the way I eat was the simple realization that we literally are what we eat. Food is both the fuel and the raw building material that keep our body structures sound and functioning. Food, healthful food comes directly from the plants of the Earth, which get their nutrients from the soil and air, their water from the rain, and their energy from the sun. Would you rather have a body built from pesticide-contaminated, processed, artificially flavored, and preserved fried potato chips, or luscious, vine-ripened, organically grown vegetables and fruits?

—Debra Lynn Dadd, *Nontoxic, Natural, & Earthwise* (Los Angeles: Tarcher, 1990).

"Barbecued" Tofu

Baking tofu with barbecue sauce brings lots of good flavor and personality to it. Serve it with any plain-cooked grain and a tossed green salad.

Oven: 30 minutes at 375°

⅔ to 1 cup Barbecue Sauce (page 305)
2 large onions, peeled, halved, and thinly sliced
1 pound firm tofu, drained, cut across the short end into ¼-inch
*   thick slices*

1. Pour about ⅓ cup of the barbecue sauce into a large bowl and add the onions. With your hands, toss the onions to coat them well with the sauce. Transfer them to a medium-sized Pyrex baking dish.

2. Place the tofu slices in the bowl and pour ⅓ cup of the barbecue sauce on top. Gently toss the sliced tofu until it is well coated, adding a bit more sauce if needed.

3. Transfer the tofu slices to the baking dish and arrange them on top of the onions.

4. Bake at 375° (preheating not necessary) for 20 minutes. Using a spatula, flip the tofu and onions over so that most of the onions are on top, and bake until the onions are tender but still a bit crunchy, about 10 additional minutes.

5. Heat the remaining sauce and spoon it on top before serving, if desired.

Variation: Slather thick slices of tofu with barbecue sauce and grill or broil them.

Oriental Baked Tofu

Here is a way to give tofu a memorable Oriental personality: Serve it baked as is—accompanied by grains and a vegetable—or cut it into cubes and add it to a stir-fry or to a grain or bean salad. It makes a fine pita filling, topped with shredded lettuce, cabbage, carrots, or sprouts.

Oven: 25 minutes at 375°

1 pound firm tofu, drained
2 tablespoons tamari soy sauce
2 tablespoons toasted (Oriental) sesame oil
1 tablespoon water
1 tablespoon freshly grated ginger
2 teaspoons finely minced garlic
1 tablespoon sesame seeds
¼ teaspoon ground star anise or aniseed (optional but highly
    recommended)

1. Cut the tofu across the short end into slices ¼-inch thick. Leave the slices as is or cut them into triangles.

2. In a large cast-iron skillet or Pyrex baking dish, combine the remaining ingredients. Place the tofu in one layer along the bottom (cut some pieces in half to fit), turning each piece over once or twice in the marinade.

3. Bake uncovered in a 375° oven (preheating not necessary) for 15 minutes. Turn with a spatula and bake until all of the liquid is absorbed, about 10 minutes more. When serving, scrape up any sesame seeds that have stuck to the bottom of the pan and set them on top of the baked tofu.

Scrambled Tofu

Serves 2 to 3

Great for brunch or a light supper dish, this recipe can easily be doubled to serve 4 to 6. Silken tofu results in a very soft-cooked texture, while soft tofu will be slightly firmer.

Skillet or wok: 10 minutes

1 tablespoon olive or canola oil
1 large onion, peeled and coarsely chopped
2 large cloves garlic, peeled and finely chopped
6 scallions, thinly sliced (keep white and green parts separate)
¼ pound mushrooms, thinly sliced
1 small red bell pepper, seeded and diced
1 pound silken or soft tofu, drained and mashed or crumbled
½ teaspoon dried leaf oregano
¼ teaspoon turmeric (optional; see Cook's Notes)
¼ cup finely chopped, pitted green olives
1 sheet toasted nori sea vegetable, finely shredded (optional)
Tamari soy sauce or sea salt to taste
Lots of freshly ground black pepper
Hot sauce (optional)

1. In a large skillet or wok, heat the oil and sauté the onion, garlic, and whites of scallions until the onions turn light brown, about 4 to 5 minutes.

2. Add the mushrooms, red pepper, tofu, oregano, and turmeric (if using), and continue to sauté over medium-high heat for another 3 minutes, stirring frequently.

3. Stir in the scallion greens, olives, nori (if using), soy sauce and pepper to taste. Pass optional hot sauce.

Cook's Notes: Turmeric will give a faint yellow color to the mixture, but will not contribute significantly to the taste.

Mom's Tofu Curry in a Hurry

Serves 3 to 4

My mother, Eleanor, who sets an inspiring example in the kitchen, makes this Sunday-night supper dish any night of the week she doesn't have much time to cook. She prefers to press the tofu between two plates for about 10 to 15 minutes to release any excess liquid (and thereby absorb more seasoning). This can be done while you are preparing the other ingredients, but if you don't have time to be bothered with this step, no great harm done.

Serve this curry with brown rice and a green salad or steamed vegetable, with some chutney on the side.

Skillet or wok: 10 minutes

1 cup frozen peas
1 pound firm or extra-firm tofu, drained
1 tablespoon canola oil
2 teaspoons whole cumin seeds
1½ tablespoons freshly grated ginger
1 small hot red chili pepper or pinch cayenne (ground red) pepper
    (optional)
3 medium (¾ pound) tomatoes, cored and finely chopped (about 2 cups)
2 to 3 teaspoons mild curry powder
½ teaspoon ground turmeric
3 tablespoons finely chopped fresh coriander or parsley (optional)
Tamari soy sauce

1. Remove the peas from the freezer to thaw.

2. Set the block of tofu between 2 plates and place a heavy weight on the top plate. (I usually use a bag or two of dried beans.) Let sit for 10 to 15 minutes to release excess liquid. Drain off the liquid and cut the tofu into ½-inch cubes (page 219).

3. Heat the oil in a large skillet or wok. Stir the cumin seeds into the oil and let them sizzle for a second or two; then stir in the ginger and chili pepper and sauté for another few seconds.

4. Add the tofu and cook over medium-high heat, stirring frequently, until the tofu cubes are lightly browned on most sides, about 5 minutes.

5. Stir in the tomatoes, 2 teaspoons of the curry powder, and the turmeric. Cook for 3 minutes, stirring frequently. Taste, and add more curry powder if the curry taste is not sufficiently pronounced.

6. Stir in the peas, breaking up any frozen clumps, coriander (if using), and tamari to taste. Continue to cook, stirring frequently, until most of the liquid released by the tomatoes has evaporated and the peas are thoroughly defrosted and warmed throughout, another 1 to 2 minutes. (Do not overcook the peas or they will lose their bright green color.)

Variations

- Add 1 to 2 cups shredded raw cabbage with the tomatoes.
- Sauté 1 large thinly sliced onion before adding the tofu.
- Use 2 large cloves of minced garlic instead of, or in addition to, the ginger.

Tofu Italiano

This alternative to Mom's Tofu Curry in a Hurry (page 224) uses the same basic principle, but infuses the tofu with Italian seasonings rather than Indian ones.

Skillet or wok: 10 minutes

1 cup frozen or fresh corn kernels
1 pound firm or extra-firm tofu, drained
1 tablespoon olive oil
1 medium onion, peeled and finely chopped
1 to 2 large cloves garlic, peeled and chopped
½ teaspoon dried basil
½ teaspoon dried leaf oregano
Pinch crushed red pepper flakes (optional)
3 medium (¾ pound) tomatoes, cored and finely chopped
¼ cup tightly packed, finely minced fresh parsley
Sea salt and freshly ground pepper to taste

1. If using frozen corn, remove it from the freezer to thaw.

2. Set the block of tofu between 2 plates and place a heavy weight (I use a bag or two of dried beans) on the top plate. Let sit for 15 to 30 minutes to release excess liquid. Drain off the liquid and cut the tofu block into ½-inch cubes (page 219).

3. Heat the oil in a large skillet or wok. Sauté the onion and garlic for 2 minutes, stirring almost continuously. Stir in the basil, oregano, and red pepper flakes (if using).

4. Add the tofu and cook over medium-high heat, stirring frequently, until the tofu cubes are lightly browned on most sides, about 5 minutes.

5. Stir in the tomatoes and corn (fresh or partially defrosted) and continue to cook, stirring frequently, until most of the liquid given off by the tomatoes has evaporated and the corn is cooked, about 3 to 5 additional minutes.

6. Stir in the parsley, salt, and pepper to taste.

Variations

- Omit the dried basil and stir in ¼ cup finely minced fresh basil instead of parsley at the end.
- Use 1 cup chopped leek (white part only) instead of the onion.

Tempeh

Like its soy-based relative tofu, tempeh (TEM-pay) is an awesome example of human ingenuity. Developed centuries ago by Indonesian villagers, tempeh-making involves a multistep process in which hulled and partially cooked soybeans are injected with a culture and then incubated until the beans become bound together by a cottony white filament called *mycelium*. During this fermentation process, the tempeh develops flavor and the soy protein becomes considerably more digestible, making tempeh a very rich source of usable protein.

Selecting and Storing Tempeh

Most health food stores offer a variety of tempehs, including plain soy, brown rice, millet, barley, and quinoa. I have also seen multigrain tempeh. There is a dramatic variation in taste and texture among the brands, so keep switching around until you find your favorites. (I prefer quinoa tempeh for its mild taste.)

Tempeh is sold either refrigerated or frozen in 8-ounce rectangular cakes. Always check the expiration date marked on the package and buy the freshest available. Tempeh can be refrigerated until the expiration date or frozen for up to 4 months. Defrost it overnight in the refrigerator or at room temperature a few hours before using, but refrigerate or use it immediately once it is defrosted.

A live, fermenting food, tempeh occasionally develops a grayish or black mold, which is safe to eat. But discard the tempeh if it has developed mold of any other color. Fresh tempeh should have a mild mushroomlike aroma; a strong ammoniac odor indicates that it's time to throw it out.

Although most package labels consider 4 ounces a single serving, because tempeh is such a dense food, I find that an 8-ounce cake is sufficient to serve 3 to 4—particularly when the tempeh is just one of the ingredients in a larger dish.

Cooking with Tempeh

Slice tempeh when it is partially frozen or chilled. Use a sharp chef's knife to slice it into "fingers" about 2 inches long and ¾ inch wide, or cut it into squares or triangles.

Unlike tofu—which stays moist and delectable when baked—tempeh easily becomes dried out in the oven unless it is heavily sauced. Poaching or brief pressure cooking is a better technique to use because it results in juiciness and enhanced flavor.

Because it has a dense, slightly meaty texture, tempeh stands up well to assertive seasonings and provides a distinctive heartiness to vegetable dishes. Cook minced tempeh, for example, with Tomato Sauce (page 304) or simmer it in a robust Barbecue Sauce (page 305). Tempeh holds its shape nicely when poached or briefly pressure-cooked in a vegetable stew.

Marinated/Pan-fried Tempeh

Serves 3 to 4

Marinated, pan-fried tempeh is delicious on its own or added at the last minute to boiled grains or tossed into a pasta dish. It also makes a great sandwich filling with mustard and sauerkraut or coleslaw.

If time permits, pan-fry tempeh before combining it with other foods to give it a more appealing color and slightly crispy exterior. Because tempeh is so concentrated, most people find a small portion (4 to 6 "fingers") quite filling. I usually marinate and pan-fry the entire amount and then reheat it as needed.

Cut into ½-inch dice, pan-fried tempeh works nicely as "croutons" in bean, grain, and green salads.

Skillet or wok: 3 to 4 minutes

1 tablespoon lemon juice
1 tablespoon water or apple juice
1 tablespoon tamari soy sauce
¼ teaspoon dry mustard
1 tablespoon freshly grated ginger
1 large clove garlic, peeled and finely chopped
8 ounces tempeh, cut into ½-inch × 2-inch "fingers"
1 to 2 tablespoons olive oil

GARNISHES
Lemon wedges
2 tablespoons finely chopped parsley

1. Combine the lemon juice, water, soy sauce, dry mustard, ginger, and garlic in a small storage container and blend well.

2. Add the tempeh "fingers," cover the container, and gently shake it to coat tempeh with the marinade. Refrigerate for 3 to 4 hours, shaking once or twice to distribute the marinade.

3. Brush a thin film of oil on a large skillet or wok and fry half of the tempeh over medium-high heat until browned, about 2 minutes on the first side and 1 minute on the second side. Brush the skillet with extra olive oil, if needed, to fry the second batch.

4. Serve hot or at room temperature with lemon wedges and parsley.

Variation: PAN-FRIED TEMPEH: Eliminate the marinating step and follow steps 3 and 4.

Tempeh Chili

Tempeh for chili lovers. Serve over Reliably Fluffy Millet (page 89) or brown rice.

Pressure cooker: 3 minutes high pressure plus 2 to 3 minutes simmering
Standard stovetop: 20 to 25 minutes

2 tablespoons oil, divided
8 ounces tempeh, cut into 1-inch × 2-inch "fingers"
1 large onion, peeled and coarsely chopped
2 large cloves garlic, peeled and chopped
2 cups water or vegetable broth
2 large carrots, cut into ½-inch slices
2 ribs celery, cut into ½-inch slices
¼ cup old-fashioned oatmeal (rolled oats)
3 tablespoons Tomato Paste (page 306)
1 tablespoon mild chili powder
1 teaspoon whole cumin seeds
¼ teaspoon ground cinnamon
Pinch cayenne
Sea salt to taste

1. Heat 1 tablespoon of oil in a heavy skillet. Brown the tempeh on both sides. Set aside.

2. Heat the remaining oil in the cooker. Sauté the onion and garlic for 3 minutes. Add the tempeh and all remaining ingredients (watch for sputtering oil!).

3. Lock the lid into place. Over high heat bring to high pressure. Lower the heat just enough to maintain high pressure and cook for 3 minutes. Reduce pressure with a quick-release method. Remove the lid, tilting it away from you to allow any excess steam to escape.

4. Adjust the seasonings before serving.

Standard Stovetop: Follow step 1. In a 2-quart saucepan, follow step 2. Bring to the boil, reduce heat, cover, and simmer, stirring occasionally, until the tempeh is infused with the chili flavor, about 20 to 25 minutes. Follow step 4.

Variation: Stir 2 cups cooked, chopped spinach or kale into the cooked chili.

Deli-Style Tempeh with Sauerkraut

This recipe is the creation of Irwin Burnstein, as told to me by his wife Sheryl. I had some bottled organic sauerkraut on hand and was intrigued enough to try it out. What a winner! It's great served plain on a bed of grains and heavenly on a sandwich, slathered with additional mustard.

Skillet or wok: 6 to 7 minutes

1 tablespoon peanut or olive oil
1 large onion, peeled and thinly sliced
1 small red pepper, seeded and diced
2 to 3 large cloves garlic, peeled and finely chopped
½ pound firm tofu, cut into 1-inch cubes, marinated if desired (page 221)
½ pound tempeh, cut into 1-inch × 2-inch "fingers" and pan-fried (page 228)
3 cups sauerkraut (rinse if too salty), thoroughly drained
¼ cup water
1 to 2 tablespoons prepared mustard

1. In a large skillet or wok, heat the oil and sauté the onion, red pepper, garlic, and tofu until the onion is lightly browned, about 4 to 6 minutes.

2. Stir in the tempeh, sauerkraut, and the water blended with 1 tablespoon of mustard. Continue to cook over medium-high heat, stirring continuously, until heated through.

3. Stir in additional mustard, if desired.

Variations
- Add ½ teaspoon caraway seeds during step 1.
- Use sliced seitan instead of tofu.

Barbecue-Style Tempeh Sauce

Makes about 3 cups

Tempeh cooked in barbecue sauce is delicious served over any pressure-cooked grain and is especially nice over pasta. The tempeh becomes infused with good flavor and develops a pleasantly puffed-up appearance. This recipe makes enough sauce to top 8 ounces of cooked pasta or 4 moderate portions of cooked grain.

Pressure cooker: 1 minute high pressure, 10-minute natural pressure release
Standard stovetop: 15 to 20 minutes

1 tablespoon olive oil
1 large onion, peeled and coarsely chopped
1 rib celery, thinly sliced
1 large red or green bell pepper, seeded and diced
2 cups Barbecue Sauce (double the recipe on page 305, omitting
    the mesquite and Tabasco)
½ to ¾ cup vegetable stock
8 ounces tempeh (quinoa tempeh is especially tasty), cut into 1-inch cubes
    or 1-inch × 2-inch "fingers"
Liquid mesquite and Tabasco sauce to taste (optional)

1. Heat the oil in the cooker and sauté the onion, celery, and pepper for 2 minutes.

2. Add the barbecue sauce and stir in the stock to thin it to the consistency of a medium-thick sauce. Stir in the tempeh.

3. Lock the lid in place and over high heat bring to high pressure. Lower the heat just enough to maintain high pressure and cook for 1 minute. Allow the pressure to come down naturally for 10 minutes. Remove the lid, tilting it away from you to allow any excess steam to escape.

4. Adjust the seasonings, adding mesquite and Tabasco (if using) to taste. Serve over pasta or grain.

Standard Stovetop: (If time permits, marinate the tempeh overnight in the barbecue sauce.) In a 2-quart saucepan, follow steps 1 and 2. Bring to the boil, then reduce the heat and simmer, covered, until the tempeh is slightly puffy and well infused with flavor, about 15 to 20 minutes. Follow step 4.

Variation: Before adding the tempeh, you can brown it on both sides in a cast-iron skillet brushed lightly with olive oil. This extra step adds a crisp texture and deepens the color of the tempeh.

Land and Sea Vegetables

Land Vegetables

What an exciting time to be a lover of vegetables! Farmers' markets are springing up all over the country, making available once again the fresh regional produce that had all but disappeared. And who among us, once we've experienced the sweetness of a just-picked, unsprayed ear of corn, would willingly go back to opening a can of Niblets?

The growing organic food movement not only brings more robust and flavorful vegetables to our table, it enables farmers to bring their soil back to life. We all know that vegetables provide vitamins and minerals, but many of us don't realize that they contain protein as well. Although any single vegetable may not supply all of the essential amino acids, if you eat a wide variety of vegetables your body will receive a fine boost of valuable nutrients. (Specific nutritional strengths of many vegetables are given in Ingredients A to Z.)

Once your larder is stocked with the basic beans, grains, and condiments (see pages 2–4), you need only supplement these by adding some fresh vegetables to round out a meal. You can participate in the change of the seasons by focusing on root vegetables in the winter, asparagus in the spring, corn in the summer, and squash in the fall.

I had an opportunity to plug into this natural rhythm recently when I participated in a community-supported agriculture project. Along with about one hundred other New Yorkers, I purchased shares in a farmer's harvest, thereby providing the financial backing he needed to grow organic vegetables on a small upstate farm. Each week we picked up our nine pounds of produce from Jean-Paul's stand at the farmers' market in Greenwich Village and learned about the challenges he had in getting that produce to us (one week we lost all of our lettuce to the raccoons!). Knowing that I was eating just-picked produce, after meeting with the man who grew it, gave me a deep sense of satisfaction. (For more on community-supported agriculture, see Further Reading and Resources, page 469.)

In the summer, when the finest and freshest produce is available, sometimes the best thing to do is the simplest: Eat it raw or steam it. But what about the other nine months of the year? Ingredients A to Z gives you basic cooking instructions under the entry for each vegetable. For other suggestions, take a look at the following selection of recipes and check the Index under individual listings.

My single most important goal is to get the cook to feel connected to the earth by growing something. I've seen the transformation so many times. It gives the cook a totally new dimension. We have a whole nation of farmers who haven't tasted a thing they've grown, and a whole nation of cooks who haven't grown a thing they've eaten. It's social schizophrenia and we're so disconnected that we've gotten ourselves into real trouble. Part of the healing process is to get cooks into the garden. They get addicted to how much better food tastes and then become connected to the soil.

—Rosalind Creasy, organic gardener, author, Los Altos, California

Pressure Cooker
Vegetable Cooking Times at a Glance

For pressure steaming <u>quick-cooking vegetables</u> on a rack above boiling water

	Approximate Minutes Total Cooking Time*
Asparagus	
Average—fat	1½–2
Slender	1–1½
Beans, green	
Whole	2–3
Halved or frenched	2–3
Broccoli	
Large florets	2–3
Stalks, peeled, ¼-inch slices	3–4
Stalks, peeled, ⅛-inch slices	2–3
Brussels sprouts	
Large, 2 inches long	4–5
Small, 1½ inches long	3–4
Cabbage	
White or Savoy, quartered	3–4
Coarsely shredded	1½
Cauliflower	
Large florets	2–3
Celeriac	
½-inch dice	3–4
Celery	
1-inch slices	3–4
Corn on the cob	
Large, old	3–4
Young, fresh	2–3
Eggplant	
1½-inch chunks	2–3

continued

	Approximate Minutes Total Cooking Time*
Leeks	
Whole, large (white part only)	3–4
Whole, small (white part only)	2–3
Okra	
Small pods	2–3
Zucchini	
½-inch slices	2–3

*Timing begins as soon as the lid is locked into place.

Pressure Cooker
Vegetable Cooking Times
at a Glance

For pressure steaming slower-cooking vegetables on a rack above boiling water

	Approximate Minutes Under High Pressure
Artichokes	
Whole, large (9–10 ounces)	9–11
Whole, medium (6–8 ounces)	6–8
Baby (1 ounce each)	3–4
Beets	
Whole, large (5–6 ounces)	20–22
Whole, small (3–4 ounces)	11–13
¼-inch slices	3–5
Carrots	
Large, 2-inch chunks	4–5
Large, ¼-inch slices	1

	Approximate Minutes Under High Pressure
Chestnuts	
Fresh, unshelled	5–6
Dried, peeled, unsoaked	20–22
Collard greens	
Young, coarsely chopped	1–2
Old, coarsely chopped	5–6
Kale	
Coarsely chopped	1–2
Onions	
Small, white (2 ounces)	4–5
Small, white (½ ounce)	2–3
Parsnips	
1-inch chunks	2–3
¼-inch slices	1
Potatoes, new red	
Whole, medium (2 ounces)	7–8
Whole, small (1 ounce)	5–6
Potatoes, sweet	
Large (7–8 ounces) quartered	5–7
¼-inch slices	2–3
Rutabaga	
½-inch dice	5–6
Squash	
Acorn, halved	6–7
Butternut, ½-inch slices	3–4
Pattypan, whole (2 pounds)	10–12
Winter, 1½-inch chunks	3–4
Turnips	
Medium (4 ounces), quartered	3–4
Small (1½ ounces), whole	7
¼-inch slices	1–2

Standard Stovetop
Vegetable Steaming Times
at a Glance

For steaming vegetables on a rack above boiling water

	Minutes Standard Cooking Time
Artichokes	
Whole, large (9–10 ounces)	35–40
Whole, medium (6–8 ounces)	25
Baby (1 ounce each)	15
Asparagus	
Average–fat	3–6
Slender	1–2
Beans, green	
Young, tender	6–8
Old, tough	10–12
Broccoli	
Medium florets	5–8
Stalks, peeled, ½-inch slices	6–8
Brussels sprouts	
Large, 2 inches long	10–12
Small, 1½ inches long	6–8
Cabbage	
White or Savoy, quartered	6–8
Carrots	
Large, ¼-inch slices	5–8
Cauliflower	
Large florets	6–10
Celeriac	
½-inch dice	4–6
Corn on the cob	
Large, old	7–10
Young, fresh	4–5

	Minutes Standard Cooking Time
Eggplant	
1½-inch chunks (peeled)	5–7
Green beans	
Young, tender, whole	6–8
Old, tough, whole	10–12
Leeks	
Whole, small (white part only)	5–6
Okra	
Small pods	12–16
Onions	
Medium (2 ounces) small, white peeled	10–12
Potatoes, new red	
Whole, medium (2 ounces)	30–35
Whole, small (1 ounce)	15–20
Rutabaga	
½-inch dice	8–10
Squash	
Winter, 1½-inch chunks, peeled	15–18
Turnips	
Small (1½ ounces), whole	20–22
¼-inch slices	3–5
Zucchini	
Whole, small	9–10
½-inch slices	5–7

Gingered Acorn Squash

I tend to overlook acorn squash except when I'm thinking of serving it baked and stuffed. However, with this quick little recipe, it's become more of a regular on my table.

Pressure cooking tenderizes the skin, so it's unnecessary to peel the squash—an arduous task because of its undulating shape. Here, the squash is cooked and served in its own gondola-shaped crescents, and its bright green skin is very striking.

Pressure cooker: 2 minutes high pressure
Standard stovetop: 6 to 12 minutes

1 small to medium acorn squash (1 to 1½ pounds)
½ to 1 cup apple or orange juice (use pressure cooker manufacturer's
recommended liquid minimum)
½ teaspoon ground ginger
⅛ teaspoon ground cinnamon
Pinch sea salt
Maple syrup (optional)

1. Trim both ends of the squash and cut it in half from stem to base. Scoop out the seeds with a spoon and slice each half into gondola-shaped wedges measuring about ½ inch at the widest part.

2. In the cooker, combine the juice, spices, and salt. Bring to the boil. Gently toss the squash slices in the sauce.

3. Lock the lid in place and over high heat bring to high pressure. Lower the heat just enough to maintain high pressure and cook for 2 minutes. Reduce the pressure with a quick-release method. Remove the lid, tilting it away from you to allow any excess steam to escape. If the squash is not quite done, replace the lid and allow it to continue to cook in the residual steam.

4. Lift out the squash with a slotted spoon and arrange the crescents in overlapping semicircles on each plate. Drizzle a hint of maple syrup, if desired.

Standard Stovetop: Pierce the squash skin all around with the tip of a paring knife. Follow step 1. In a 2-quart saucepan, follow step 2, reducing the juice to ¼ cup. Return to the boil, then lower the heat and simmer, covered, until the squash is tender but still firm, 6 to 12 minutes. Add a few more tablespoons of juice about halfway through cooking, if all of the liquid has evaporated. Follow step 4.

Variations

- Use other varieties of winter squash, such as Sweet Dumpling, Golden Acorn, delicata, or banana. Cut the squash into ½-inch cubes.
- Substitute 1 tablespoon freshly grated ginger for the ground ginger.
- Add ¼ cup raisins in step 2.
- For a savory version, briefly sauté a small chopped onion in 1 tablespoon of oil. Use vegetable stock instead of the juice; add a pinch of sage or thyme instead of the spices.

Quick Pickled Beets

Serves 6

I love pickled beets for both their wakeup taste and their gorgeous scarlet color. I was delighted to discover that when cooked under pressure with vinegar, they become instantly infused with a distinctly pickled flavor. (This quick pickling method doesn't work with standard stovetop cooking.) Apple juice accentuates the sweetness of the beets. An added bonus to cooking beets under pressure is that it's not necessary to peel them.

Serve the beets warm, right from the pot, or you can store them in the refrigerator for up to 2 weeks and serve them chilled or at room temperature.

Pressure cooker: 4 minutes high pressure
Standard stovetop: not recommended

4 medium beets (about 1½ pounds), scrubbed, trimmed, halved, and cut into ¼-inch slices
1 small onion, peeled and thinly sliced (optional)
¾ cup apple juice or water
¼ cup apple cider vinegar
⅛ teaspoon ground allspice
Pinch sea salt (optional)

1. Combine all ingredients in the cooker.

2. Lock the lid in place and over high heat bring to high pressure. Lower the heat just enough to maintain high pressure and cook for 4 minutes. Reduce the pressure with a quick-release method. Remove the lid, tilting it away from you to allow any excess steam to escape. If the beet slices are not quite tender, replace the lid and allow them to steam in the residual heat for another minute or two.

3. To serve, lift the beets out of the liquid with a slotted spoon. Or, transfer the beets and liquid to a container, cool, and refrigerate up to 2 weeks.

Variation: Use 1 tablespoon of freshly grated ginger instead of the allspice.

Puree of Beets and Parsnips

Parsnips and beets are a winning pair: The parsnips provide a rich texture, and the beets offer brilliant color. Each contributes its own sweetness to the dish, and a touch of mild vinegar at the end really makes the flavors soar.

Great news: It's not necessary to peel either vegetable if they are organic— just scrub them well.

Pressure cooker: 5 minutes high pressure
Standard stovetop: 20 to 30 minutes

1 tablespoon oil
1 large onion, peeled and coarsely chopped
1 tablespoon freshly grated ginger
3 medium (1 pound) beets, scrubbed and cut into ¼-inch slices
3 slender parsnips (6 ounces), scrubbed and cut into ½-inch slices
½ to 1 cup water (use pressure cooker manufacturer's recommended liquid
    minimum)
½ teaspoon sea salt, or to taste
2 to 3 teaspoons apple cider, raspberry, or tarragon vinegar

1. Heat the oil in the cooker. Sauté the onion and ginger until the onion is lightly browned, about 4 minutes. Add the beets, parsnips (cut any large top slices in half), water, and salt.

2. Lock the lid into place. Over high heat bring to high pressure. Lower the heat just enough to maintain high pressure and cook for 5 minutes. Reduce pressure with a quick-release method. Remove the lid, tilting it away from you to allow any excess steam to escape. If the beets or parsnips are not tender, replace the lid and continue to cook in the residual steam.

3. With a slotted spoon, transfer the beets, parsnips, and onions to the bowl of a food processor or blender and puree until smooth. (Use the pulsing action of the processor to avoid overprocessing.) Add enough cooking liquid to achieve a medium-thick puree.

4. Return the puree to the pot to reheat. Stir in just enough vinegar to perk up the flavors and serve.

Standard Stovetop: In a heavy 3-quart saucepan, follow step 1 using ½ cup water. Bring to the boil, cover, and simmer until the beets and parsnips are very tender, about 20 to 30 minutes. Add a few more tablespoons of water, if needed, after 15 to 20 minutes. Follow steps 3 and 4.

Marinated Broccoli

This is a particularly nice way to serve broccoli during warm weather. The vinegar wakes up sleepy taste buds and adds a zesty edge to the meal.

For best results, prepare at least 3 hours in advance of serving.

Standard stovetop: 4 to 5 minutes

1 medium bunch (about 1½ pounds) broccoli
1 large clove roasted garlic (page 425), mashed, or 1 small clove raw
   garlic, peeled and minced
½ cup tightly packed minced fresh dill or 2 tablespoons dried dillweed
2½ to 3 tablespoons olive oil
2 tablespoons apple cider vinegar or lemon juice
¼ teaspoon sea salt, or to taste

1. Cut the broccoli into small florets. (See Cook's Notes regarding the stalks.)

2. Steam the broccoli until tender-crisp, about 4 to 5 minutes. Transfer to a strainer, and refresh under cold water to stop the cooking process and to retain greenness. Drain thoroughly.

3. Transfer the broccoli to a large storage container. Combine the remaining ingredients for the marinade in a small jar and shake well. (This may not seem like enough marinade, but it is!) Pour the marinade over the broccoli, cover the container, and shake well.

4. Place in the refrigerator, shaking occasionally to distribute marinade, for at least 3 hours. For optimum taste, bring to room temperature before serving.

Cook's Notes: You can reserve the stalks to use in another recipe, such as White Basmati with Carrots and Broccoli (page 145), or you can peel them and cut them into quarter-sized slices to use in this dish: Steam them for a minute before adding the florets as stalks take longer to cook. Season with a bit more oil, vinegar, and salt, if needed, to allow for the larger amount of broccoli.

Variation: Use steamed cauliflower florets instead of broccoli.

My vegetables don't speak to me in words, but we are in communication. Before I harvest them to take them to the market, I always say, "Thank you so much, you sweeties."

—Elizabeth Berry, organic specialty produce gardener, Abique, New Mexico

Hot Thai-Style Broccoli

Serves 4

In this dish, the broccoli is stir-fried with characteristic Thai seasonings: chili pepper, lemongrass, and coriander. Recommended for those who can take the heat.

Skillet or wok: 6 to 8 minutes

½ cup boiling vegetable stock or water
1 tablespoon finely chopped fresh lemongrass or 1 teaspoon dried
    lemongrass
1 large bunch (about 2 pounds) broccoli
1 to 2 tablespoons peanut oil
2 large cloves garlic, peeled and finely chopped
½ jalapeño or serrano chili pepper, finely chopped (wear rubber gloves
    when handling), or generous pinch crushed red pepper flakes
¼ pound firm tofu, drained and cut into ½-inch cubes
1 small red bell pepper, seeded and cut into ¼-inch × 1-inch strips
½ cup tightly packed minced fresh coriander or 2 to 3 tablespoons dried
    coriander
4 scallions, cut into 1-inch slices
1 to 2 tablespoons lime juice
Tamari soy sauce to taste

1. In a small heatproof bowl, pour the stock over the lemongrass to steep while you are preparing the broccoli.
2. Cut the broccoli into small florets. Peel the stalks and cut them into slices ½ inch thick. Set aside.
3. Heat the oil in a heavy skillet or wok. Add the garlic, jalapeño pepper, and tofu, and stir-fry for 1 minute. Add the broccoli, red bell pepper, lemongrass-stock mixture (watch for sputtering oil!), and coriander (if using dried). Cover and cook over medium-high heat for 3 minutes.
4. Stir in the coriander (if using fresh) and scallions, cover, and cook until the broccoli is tender-crisp, about 1 to 2 additional minutes.
5. Sprinkle with lime juice and season to taste with tamari before serving.

Vinaigrette-Wokked Brussels Sprouts   Serves 3 to 4

This simple but delightful dish was inspired by a recipe in the late Jane Grigson's lovely *Vegetable Book*. It's likely to win over even those who think they don't like Brussels sprouts.

The sprouts are thyme-scented and infused with vinegar. The secret is to avoid overcooking: Pay close attention and stop the cooking when the sprouts are still bright green. Because of the acid in the vinegar, don't prepare this recipe using a cast-iron wok or skillet; use stainless steel or enameled porcelain instead.

Skillet or wok: 2 to 4 minutes

1 to 2 tablespoons olive oil
Scant ½ teaspoon dried thyme
1 pint (10 ounces) medium-sized Brussels sprouts, trimmed and halved
*   (leave very small sprouts whole)*
3 tablespoons balsamic or other red wine vinegar
2 to 4 tablespoons water or vegetable stock
Sea salt to taste

1. In a heavy skillet or wok, heat the oil. Add the thyme and sprouts and stir-fry for 30 seconds. Add the vinegar and 2 tablespoons of water (watch for sputtering oil!), stirring all the while.

2. Cover immediately, lower the heat slightly, and steam over medium-high heat until sprouts are tender-crisp, about 2 to 4 minutes (depending upon size). Check every minute for doneness and give a quick stir. Season with salt and replenish the water if the mixture seems dry or is beginning to scorch the bottom of the pan.

Variations: Substitute canola oil for olive oil and use dried tarragon or marjoram instead of thyme.

> . . . Every time you relate to an insect you are relating with the whole system of life, and . . . if you choose to dominate the insect world system of life, rather than work in harmony with it, part of the system dies. . . . When we choose dominating, death-oriented control, the scope and depth of our life become narrower and smaller.
>
> —John Jeavons, *How to Grow More Vegetables*
> (Berkeley: Ten Speed Press, 1982).

Moroccan Carrots

One of my favorite dishes, and one of the easiest to prepare. The paprika in the vinaigrette gives the carrots a reddish hue, and the spices accentuate their sweetness. Prepare this dish 2 hours in advance so the carrots become infused with the flavors. Serve warm or at room temperature.

Pressure cooker: 1 minute high pressure
Standard stovetop: 5 to 10 minutes

½ to 1 cup water (use pressure cooker manufacturer's recommended
    liquid minimum)
2 pounds carrots, scrubbed and cut into ½-inch slices
⅓ to ½ cup Moroccan Vinaigrette (page 295)
Fresh lemon juice (optional)
Sea salt to taste

1. Set the steaming rack into the cooker and pour in the water. Bring to the boil. Place the carrot slices on the rack.

2. Lock the lid in place and over high heat bring to high pressure. Adjust the heat to maintain high pressure and cook for 1 minute. Reduce the pressure with a quick-release method. Remove the lid, tilting it away from you to allow any excess steam to escape. If the carrots are not quite tender, replace the lid and allow them to steam for a few more minutes in the residual heat.

3. While the carrots are still warm, set them into a serving bowl or storage container and moisten them generously with the vinaigrette. Let the mixture sit at room temperature for at least 2 hours, tossing occasionally.

4. Just before serving, perk up the flavors with lemon juice and salt, if needed.

Standard Stovetop: In a saucepan large enough to accommodate a steaming rack, follow step 1. Cover, reduce the heat to medium, and steam the carrots until they are tender but still firm, about 5 to 10 minutes. Follow steps 3 and 4.

Carrots with Olives
and Twenty Cloves of Garlic

You may be surprised to see this combination of carrots and such a magnanimous quantity of garlic, but once you've experienced how sweet and mild whole garlic cloves are when cooked, you're bound to be pleased. The onions also add their own unique sweetness to this unusual dish.

Pressure cooker: 3 minutes high pressure
Standard stovetop: 8 to 12 minutes

1 tablespoon olive oil or canola oil
1 large onion, peeled and coarsely chopped
20 small or 10 large cloves garlic, peeled (leave whole)
1 cup vegetable stock
1 pound carrots, cut into 1-inch chunks
½ teaspoon dried rosemary leaves
¼ cup pitted, coarsely chopped black olives, preferably oil-cured
¼ teaspoon sea salt, or to taste

1. Heat the oil in the cooker and sauté the onions and garlic until the onions are soft, about 2 minutes.

2. Add the stock (watch for sputtering oil!) and bring to the boil. Add the carrots, rosemary, olives, and salt.

3. Lock the lid in place and over high heat bring to high pressure. Lower the heat just enough to maintain high pressure and cook for 3 minutes. Reduce the pressure with a quick-release method. Remove the lid, tilting it away from you to allow any excess steam to escape. If the carrots are not quite done, set the lid back into place and let them cook in the residual steam for another minute or two.

4. Serve the mixture in small bowls or lift out the solid ingredients with a slotted spoon and serve them on a plate, reserving any leftover liquid for cooking grains or adding to the soup pot, or see the last variation below.

Standard Stovetop: In a heavy 3-quart saucepan, follow steps 1 and 2. Bring to the boil, then reduce the heat and simmer, covered, until the carrots are tender, about 8 to 12 minutes. Follow step 4.

Variations
- POTATOES WITH TWENTY CLOVES OF GARLIC: Replace the carrots with small new potatoes about 1 ounce each, or larger thin-skinned potatoes cut into chunks. Cook them for 5 minutes under high pressure, or 12 to 15 minutes standard stovetop method.

continued

- CARROTS WITH HIJICKI AND TWENTY CLOVES OF GARLIC: In this striking alternative, long black strands of hijicki replace the olives.

  Rinse and then soak ½ cup of loosely packed (½ ounce) of hijicki in ample water to cover for 30 minutes. Drain. Add the hijicki instead of olives in step 2.
- To create an instant sauce, lift out about ½ cup of cooked carrots with a slotted spoon and puree them. Stir the puree into any leftover cooking liquid to thicken it for a sauce.

The following are quotes on gardening from kindergarten students:

A squash does not really look like its name sounds.

Some trees give us berries or cherries or plums. Others just stand around and add rings.

Cabbages look like Brussels sprouts only more so.

A hybrid is a thing that is not its real self.

Many of our weeds need some form of birth control.
                    —"Kinder in the Garten," by Bob Williams, *East West*, May 1990.

Curried Cauliflower Stir-fry

Serves 4

Indian seasoning meets Chinese technique. Cauliflower is a popular vegetable in Indian cooking, and it goes especially well with curry. Instead of slow-cooking it, I've stir-fried it just until tender-crisp. Serve it over rice, couscous, or bulgur wheat.

Skillet or wok: 9 to 11 minutes

1 tablespoon peanut oil
1 large onion, peeled and coarsely chopped
1 large clove garlic, peeled and finely chopped
1 pound firm tofu, drained and cut into 1-inch cubes (marinated is nice,
*   page 221)*
2 to 3 cups tightly packed, coarsely chopped kale leaves (ribs and stems
*   removed and reserved for stock)*
1½ tablespoons mild curry powder
¼ teaspoon ground cinnamon
1 to 1½ cups water or vegetable stock
1 large head (about 2 pounds) cauliflower, cut into small florets
1 large red bell pepper, seeded and diced
Sea salt or tamari soy sauce to taste
¼ cup tightly packed minced fresh coriander or parsley

1. In a large skillet or wok, heat the oil. Sauté the onion, garlic, and tofu, stirring frequently, until the tofu begins to brown, about 4 minutes.

2. Stir in the kale. Sprinkle on the curry powder and cinnamon and stir in ¼ cup water (watch for sputtering oil!). Cover and cook over medium-high heat for 2 minutes.

3. Add the cauliflower and red pepper and sprinkle on some salt or tamari. Add about ½ cup more water, cover, and continue to cook, stirring every minute or so, until the kale is tender and the cauliflower is tender-crisp, about 3 to 5 minutes. Add more water as needed to prevent scorching.

4. Stir in the coriander and additional salt or soy sauce if needed.

Variations
* For chewier tofu, try freezing it first (page 218).
* Use pureed tomatoes for all or part of the water.
* Add a small hot red pepper or a generous pinch of crushed red pepper flakes.

Eggplant Caponata

In this intriguing dish, a sweet-sour balance is achieved by using both vinegar and raisins.

The caponata tastes best after it has sat at room temperature for a few hours, or you can refrigerate it overnight and bring it to room temperature about an hour before serving.

Pressure cooker: 2 minutes high pressure
Standard stovetop: 30 to 40 minutes

1 small eggplant (about 1 pound), peeled and cut into ½-inch cubes
½ teaspoon sea salt
1 to 2 tablespoons olive oil (or the marinating oil from sun-dried tomatoes)
2 cloves garlic, peeled and finely chopped
1 medium onion, peeled and coarsely chopped
3 ribs celery, cut into ¼-inch slices
1 large red bell pepper, seeded and diced
½ cup pitted, oil-cured olives
⅓ cup raisins
1 tablespoon capers
4 large plum tomatoes (preferred) or 2 large beefsteak tomatoes, pureed
¼ cup balsamic vinegar
¼ teaspoon ground cinnamon
Sea salt and freshly ground black pepper to taste

GARNISH
¼ cup finely minced fresh parsley or 2 tablespoons toasted pine nuts

1. Sprinkle the eggplant cubes with the salt and set them in a colander. Place a clean kitchen towel on top of the eggplant and a weight on top of the towel, and let sit at room temperature for 1 hour, setting a plate underneath to catch drips. Squeeze the eggplant gently in the kitchen towel to release additional moisture.

2. Heat the olive oil in the cooker and sauté the garlic and onion for 1 minute, stirring frequently. Stir in the eggplant, celery, red pepper, olives, raisins, and capers.

3. In a small measuring cup, combine the pureed tomatoes, vinegar, and cinnamon. Pour this mixture over the vegetables, and add salt and pepper to taste.

4. Lock the lid in place and over high heat bring to high pressure. Lower the heat just enough to maintain high pressure and cook for 2 minutes. Reduce the pressure with a quick-release method. Remove the lid, tilting it away from you to allow any excess steam to escape. If the eggplant is not quite tender, replace the cover and allow it to steam in the residual heat until done.

5. Adjust the seasonings and transfer to a serving dish or storage container.

6. Before serving, garnish with fresh parsley.

Standard stovetop: Follow step 1. In a heavy 3-quart saucepan, follow step 2. Follow step 3. Bring to the boil, then reduce heat and simmer, covered, until the celery is easily pierced with a fork, about 30 to 40 minutes. Stir in a few tablespoons of water if the mixture begins to dry out. Follow steps 5 and 6.

As you watch plants grow, you watch yourself grow—mentally, physically, spiritually. As you pull away the weeds, it helps you clean yourself out. Keep out the bad and nourish the good.

—Inmate on a special gardening project run by
Catherine Sneed at San Francisco County Jail

Greens

That most cooks don't want to be bothered with greens—from Swiss chard to turnip and beet tops to dandelion, mustard, and collards—is a shame. These inexpensive and tasty vegetables are low in calories—an average size serving of 3½ ounces is less than 40 calories—and full of good nutrition. Most greens are high in potassium and beta-carotene, and are an excellent source of calcium. (This is especially important if your diet is dairy-free.) Some, such as chard, collards, and dandelion, contain impressive amounts of vitamin A. (Those on low-salt diets should be aware that greens are relatively high in sodium.)

I think most cooks don't get around to cooking greens because they've never really been part of standard American fare, except perhaps in the South. So here are some basic techniques, plus a handful of recipes that feature a few different varieties. You'll find others by checking the Index under specific greens.

Green Basics

Selection: Look for greens that are crisp; pass up those that are yellowed or limp. Small young greens are the tenderest and have the mildest flavor, while older specimens can be tough and have a detectable bitter edge. (Escarole and dandelion greens are slightly bitter no matter how youthful they look.) Greens wilt quickly, even under refrigeration, so cook them within a few days of purchase.

Serving Size: Allow about ½ pound per person when serving them plain, boiled, or sautéed as a side dish. During cooking, greens shrink dramatically to approximately one quarter or less of their original volume. One-half pound of raw greens yields 1 to 2 cups cooked, depending on the type of green.

Cleaning Greens: It's essential to wash greens thoroughly, since they are often quite sandy. First, discard any yellowed or very limp leaves. Then cut off and discard roots and any thick, tough stems. Soak the leaves and remaining stems in water to cover for a few minutes, swooshing them around from time to time. Then set them in a colander to drain for a few minutes.

Preparing Greens for Cooking: Chop the leaves of tender, quick-cooking greens (such as spinach, beet greens, or chard) into 1-inch strips. Reserve thick, fibrous stems for stock. Slice slender (tender) stems into ½-inch pieces. You can also shred the leaves by hand rather than cut them.

With tougher, larger, or more mature greens (such as kale and collards), cut away the thick ribs and stems and reserve them for making stock. (They tend to remain tough and stringy, even after cooking.) Then chop or shred the leaves into ½-inch strips, or finer for faster cooking.

Cooking Greens: There are three basic cooking techniques: boiling, steaming, and sautéing or stir-frying. I usually boil the tougher greens, such as collards or mature kale, because it's difficult to tenderize them otherwise. Delicate greens, such as spinach, chard, beet greens, or young (small) mustard greens, can either be steamed or sautéed. I don't advise pressure-cooking greens. They turn an ugly shade of olive and become bitter. For more details, see the recipes that follow, Ingredients A to Z under Greens, and individual listings.

Basic Boiled Greens

To preserve the clean, direct taste of greens, boiling is the best method. I also prefer boiling for old, tough, or large greens, such as collards or kale, which are difficult to tenderize by other techniques.

To boil greens, bring 1 quart of water to the boil for each ½ pound of trimmed and chopped greens. Add ¼ teaspoon sea salt, if desired. Add the chopped stalks first, followed about 30 seconds later by the greens, pressing them down into the water with the back of a large spoon. (If necessary, stuff them under the lid for a minute or so until they shrink down.) Boil, uncovered, until tender. Keep tasting periodically to avoid overcooking.

As soon as the greens are tender, quickly lift them out with a slotted spoon or pour them through a strainer set over a large bowl to catch the cooking liquid. Drain and serve, or refresh them immediately under cold running water to preserve the color and stop the cooking process. (Use the cooking liquid for soup stock or cooking rice, but taste it first for bitterness.)

To become tender, spinach and chard take only 1 to 2 minutes to cook, while kale and collards take 4 to 5 minutes (for young leaves) or 5 to 8 minutes (for older leaves).

Vegetables are my passion. They're my art, my food, my pleasure. I like to see them on plants, plates, and in the grocery store. I love consumable art.

—Ann Cutting, professional estate gardener,
St. Helena, California

Basic Sautéed Greens

Serves 3 to 4

This simple recipe requires no fuss or creativity but produces straightforward heartiness and appeal.

This approach works best for young, tender greens, such as broccoli rabe, turnip or beet tops, lamb's quarters, chard, or spinach. Use it for small, tender specimens of kale, collards, dandelion, or mustard greens. (Boil older, tough greens; see preceding method.)

As a general rule, beet greens and spinach take about 2 to 3 minutes; Swiss chard and broccoli rabe about 3 to 4 minutes; mustard, kale, and escarole about 5 to 8 minutes, and collards about 10 minutes. One pound produces modest servings for 2 to 3 people.

The greens can be served hot, right out of the pan. They're also delicious cold, with an extra drizzle of olive oil and lemon juice or vinegar. Chop up any leftovers and add them to bean, grain, or lettuce salads, or to mashed potatoes.

Skillet or wok: 4 to 8 minutes (depending upon type of green)

1 tablespoon olive oil
2 to 3 large cloves garlic, peeled and cut into thin slivers (optional)
1 large bunch (about 2 pounds) trimmed greens, leaves cut into 1-inch
strips, tough ribs and stems removed and chopped fine or reserved for
stock

SEASONINGS
Your choice of sea salt, sesame seasoning salt (page 454), tamari soy
sauce, lemon juice, apple cider, or umeboshi plum vinegar to taste

OPTIONAL GARNISH
Toasted pumpkin seeds or sunflower seeds

1. In a large skillet or wok, heat the oil. Sauté the garlic until lightly browned, stirring frequently, about 1 to 2 minutes.

2. Add the greens, reduce the heat to medium, cover the pot, and cook until the greens are tender, stirring occasionally. Most greens will cook well in the water clinging to their leaves, but check every few minutes and add 1 to 3 tablespoons water if greens are beginning to scorch or stick to the bottom of the pot.

3. When the greens are done, stir in seasoning. If there is any liquid on the bottom of the pot, lift out the greens with a slotted spoon to serve. Garnish with toasted seeds, if desired.

254   Recipes from an Ecological Kitchen

Variations: This basic dish can be transformed by varying the oil and seasonings. See, for example, the recipes for Curried Mustard Greens with Tofu (below) and Chinese-Style Stir-fry of Kale, Onions, and Marinated Tofu (page 258).

Other seasoning options: Add a dash of cayenne or a pinch of crushed red pepper flakes at the beginning of cooking; stir in a few chopped tomatoes or chopped fresh herbs at the end.

Curried Mustard Greens with Tofu   Serves 4

Mustard greens have a distinctive spiciness, which makes them a worthy complement to the complex flavors of curry. This dish goes nicely with brown basmati rice.

Skillet or wok: 8 to 10 minutes

1 tablespoon oil
2 teaspoons whole cumin seeds
½ teaspoon black mustard seeds (optional)
1 large onion, peeled and coarsely chopped
1 pound firm tofu, drained and cut into 1-inch cubes
1½ tablespoons mild curry powder
Pinch cayenne (ground red) pepper to taste (optional)
1 large bunch (1½ to 2 pounds) mustard greens, stems removed and
    reserved for stock, leaves finely shredded or chopped
Water
Sea salt or Bragg Liquid Aminos to taste

1. In a large skillet or wok, heat the oil. Sizzle the cumin and mustard seeds (if using) for 5 seconds, then add the onion and tofu and sauté, stirring frequently, until the onion begins to brown, about 4 to 5 minutes.

2. Stir in the curry powder and cayenne (if using).

3. Add the greens, pressing them down into the pan with a lid. Cook covered over medium-high heat until tender, about 4 minutes, stirring occasionally, and adding a few tablespoons of water if the mixture seems dry. Stir in salt or Bragg Liquid Aminos (my favorite) to taste.

Variation: This recipe works well with Swiss chard or spinach. Cut the chard stems into ¼-inch slices and add them with the onion. Shred the leaves coarsely. Proceed as above, but reduce cooking time in step 3 to 2 to 3 minutes. Trim spinach greens and shred large leaves. Cook small leaves whole. Cook for 2 to 3 minutes.

Swiss Chard with Winter Squash

The sweet spices normally associated with squash work surprisingly well with Swiss chard, which has a taste reminiscent of spinach.

> **Pressure cooker:** 2 minutes high pressure, 2 to 3 minutes simmering
> **Standard stovetop:** 7 to 9 minutes

1 large bunch (1½ pounds) Swiss chard
1 large red onion, coarsely chopped
¾ pound butternut, delicata, or kabocha squash, seeded and cut into
*   1-inch dice*
½ to 1 cup water (use pressure cooker manufacturer's recommended
*   liquid minimum)*
½ teaspoon ground cinnamon
¼ teaspoon ground nutmeg
⅛ teaspoon ground allspice
¼ teaspoon sea salt, or to taste

1. Swoosh the chard vigorously in a large bowl of water to remove all of the sand. Drain. Cut the stems into ½-inch slices and set aside. Shred the larger leaves into 2 to 3 pieces and set aside in a separate pile.

2. In the cooker, combine the chard stems, onion, squash, water, spices, and salt.

3. Lock the lid into place. Over high heat bring to high pressure. Lower the heat just enough to maintain high pressure and cook for 2 minutes. Reduce pressure with a quick-release method. Remove the lid, tilting it away from you to allow any excess steam to escape.

4. Add the chard leaves. (If the cooker is almost full to the brim, just stuff the leaves in; the chard will shrink dramatically as it cooks.) Cover, bring to the boil, then reduce the heat to medium and cook until the chard and squash are tender, about 2 to 3 minutes.

5. Adjust the seasonings. To serve, lift the chard, squash, and onions from the cooker with a slotted spoon.

Standard Stovetop: Follow step 1. In a heavy 3-quart saucepan, follow step 2, using ½ cup of water. Bring to the boil, then reduce the heat and simmer, covered, until the squash is almost tender, about 7 to 9 minutes. Add a few extra tablespoons of water, if needed. Follow steps 4 and 5.

Cook's Notes: To make a sauce of the cooking liquid, puree or mash ½ cup of the squash and stir it back into the liquid remaining in the pot. Pour the sauce over the squash and chard and serve in small bowls.

Kale with Pine Nuts and Raisins

Serves 3 to 4

The pairing of pine nuts and raisins in a savory dish dates back to the Middle Ages, and shows up in old Sicilian and Arabic recipes. Adding its strong flavor and texture, kale rises brilliantly to the occasion in this recipe.

You can serve this trio as a vegetable side dish. However, my favorite way to eat it is mounded on top of some steaming whole grain noodles. The quantities here work nicely with a pound of pasta to create 4 entrées.

Skillet or wok: 5 to 8 minutes

1 large bunch (1½ to 2 pounds) kale
1 tablespoon olive oil
3 large cloves garlic, peeled and finely chopped
¼ cup water, approximately
¼ cup raisins
Pinch ground cinnamon
¼ cup toasted pine nuts
Sea salt, tamari soy sauce, or Bragg Liquid Aminos to taste

1. Rinse kale thoroughly and cut off stems. Cut or strip leaves away from any thick ribs. (Reserve stems and ribs for stock, or chop them to add to a vegetable soup.) Coarsely chop leaves. Set aside.

2. In a large skillet or wok, heat the olive oil. Over medium-high heat sauté the garlic for 30 seconds.

3. Add the kale, water (watch for sputtering oil!), raisins, cinnamon, and salt to taste. Cover and continue to cook over medium-high heat, uncovering and stirring every minute or so, until kale is tender, 5 to 8 minutes. Add a few more tablespoons of water if the mixture becomes dry or begins to scorch the bottom of the pot. Stir in the pine nuts and salt to taste before serving.

Variation: Substitute 1½ pounds trimmed, coarsely chopped Swiss chard or spinach for the kale. With either green, you probably won't need to add water as they cook in the water clinging to their leaves. Reduce cooking to 2 to 3 minutes.

Our bodies are our gardens, to which our wills are gardeners.

—William Shakespeare

Chinese-Style Stir-fry of Kale, Onions, and Marinated Tofu

Serves 4

Some prominent flavor ingredients of Chinese cooking—ginger, star anise, soy sauce, and garlic—stamp their signatures on this dish.

Skillet or wok: 6 to 10 minutes

1 tablespoon tamari soy sauce
1½ tablespoons freshly grated ginger
¾ teaspoon ground star anise
½ pound firm tofu, cut into 1-inch cubes
1 large bunch (about 1½ pounds) kale
1 tablespoon peanut oil
2 large onions, peeled and coarsely chopped
2 large cloves garlic, peeled and finely chopped
1 large red bell pepper, seeded and diced
¼ cup water, approximately
Additional tamari soy sauce

1. In a small plastic container or wide-mouthed jar, combine soy sauce, ginger, and star anise. Marinate the tofu in this mixture for 5 to 10 minutes (or longer), shaking occasionally.

2. Meanwhile, trim the leaves from the kale stems. Discard any thick and fibrous stems, and cut the remaining stems into ¼-inch pieces. Chop the kale leaves coarsely. Set aside.

3. In a large skillet or wok, heat the oil. Sauté the onions, garlic, and red pepper for 2 minutes, stirring frequently. Add the tofu with its marinade (scrape out all of the spices), kale, and water (watch for sputtering oil!).

4. Cover and cook over medium-high heat, stirring every minute or two, until the kale is tender, about 5 to 8 minutes. Add a few more tablespoons of water if the mixture becomes dry or begins to scorch the bottom of the pot. Season with additional soy sauce before serving, if desired.

Variations

- Substitute mustard greens, bok choy (Chinese cabbage), or Napa cabbage for the kale.
- Add 1 to 2 tablespoons chopped fermented black beans when you add the kale.

Chestnut-Studded Yams

Good yams are absolutely delicious when baked to mellow softness and eaten on their own. My favorites are garnet yams, with their bright orange flesh, rich flavor, and purple skins. At their best, they taste as sweet as candy. I probably shouldn't admit it, but I often carry a baked sweet potato in my purse for those moments when the craving hits.

It's hard to improve on perfection, but here's a simple and winning combination for a special occasion or when you feel like fussing a bit. It can be made for any number of people—count on 1 yam and about 5 chestnuts per person. I've suggested some additional seasonings in case you *really* feel like fussing.

Oven: 20 to 30 minutes at 375°

4 large (2 pounds) garnet yams or sweet potatoes
20 roasted fresh chestnuts or cooked dried chestnuts (page 415), coarsely
*   chopped*
Sea salt to taste
Maple syrup and freshly grated nutmeg (optional)

1. Bake the yams in a 375° oven until soft, about 20 to 30 minutes. Remove the flesh and mash.

2. Stir the chestnuts into the mashed yams.

3. Add seasonings to taste, if desired. Reheat before serving.

I yam what I yam and that's all what I yam.
                                    —Popeye

Louise's Potato Latkes

Makes twelve 2-inch pancakes

This recipe for crispy, egg-free latkes was developed by natural-foods teacher Louise Hoffman.

For best results, use Idaho potatoes. Follow tradition and serve the latkes with Applesauce (page 391) or try Roasted Shallot Cream (page 303) on the side.

Skillet: 12 to 15 minutes

2 medium (1¼ pounds) potatoes, peeled and grated (about 3 cups)
1 tablespoon canola or safflower oil
3½ tablespoons water
1 medium (8 ounces) onion, peeled and grated (about ½ cup)
½ teaspoon baking powder
½ teaspoon sea salt
¼ teaspoon freshly ground white or black pepper
Canola oil for shallow frying

1. Set the grated potatoes in a colander over a bowl to drain for about 15 minutes. (The potatoes will turn a reddish brown.) Drain off any rusty potato liquid, but reserve the thick potato starch that has settled on the bottom of the bowl.

2. Add the potatoes, oil, water, and grated onion to the potato starch. Stir in the baking powder, salt, and pepper. Let stand for 5 minutes.

3. Heat about ¼ inch of oil in a large, heavy skillet. Drop heaping tablespoonfuls of latke mixture into the skillet. Press gently with the back of the spoon to shape round disks about 2 inches in diameter. Fry over medium-high heat until golden brown on both sides. Drain on flat sheets of brown paper (see Eco-Tip).

4. Reserve in a warm place until all of the latkes are cooked. Serve warm with applesauce or roasted shallot cream.

ECO-TIP: Instead of using paper towels for draining fried foods, use sheets of brown paper cut from supermarket shopping bags.

Butternut Squash and Parsnip Puree Serves 4 to 6

Two subtly sweet vegetables are combined to create a soothing texture, the ultimate in comfort food. The sesame tahini blended in at the end adds a richly complex flavor that belies the ease of preparation.

For a pretty effect, put the puree in a pie plate or shallow ovenproof bowl and garnish with pecans. Reheat, if necessary.

Pressure cooker: 4 minutes high pressure
Standard stovetop: 15 to 20 minutes

1 butternut squash (1½ pounds)
1 pound medium parsnips, trimmed and cut into ½-inch slices
1 tablespoon sesame tahini
Sea salt and freshly grated nutmeg to taste

1. Halve the squash lengthwise and scoop out the seeds. Cut each half into quarters. Cut each quarter into ½-inch slices.
2. Set a steamer basket in the cooker. Add 1 cup of water and bring to the boil over high heat. Place the squash and parsnips in the steamer basket.
3. Lock the lid into place. Over high heat bring to high pressure. Lower the heat just enough to maintain high pressure and cook for 4 minutes. Reduce pressure with a quick-release method. Remove the lid, tilting it away from you to allow any excess steam to escape.
4. Transfer the vegetables to a food processor or blender. Add the tahini, salt, and nutmeg and puree until just smooth. Do not overprocess or the puree will become gummy. If the puree is not warm enough, return it to the cooker to reheat before serving.

Standard Stovetop: Follow step 1. In a 3-quart saucepan, follow step 2. Cover and steam until the vegetables are tender, about 15 to 20 minutes. Follow step 4.

Sea Vegetables

It is as though garments in scarlet are mirrored in the Okami River while young girls wade in the shallows plucking the nori strands.

—The Manyoshu, an eighth-century anthology of Japanese poems and songs

If you've ever eaten in a Japanese restaurant, chances are you've already experienced at least one sea vegetable. Flattened sheets of crispy dried nori are used as the outer casings of sushi rolls (page 270), and softened bits of wakame are sometimes floated in miso soup.

For some, eating sea vegetables is an acquired taste. Others feel an immediate affinity for them; after all, they come from the ocean and so did we.

You may be surprised to learn that sea vegetables (a.k.a. marine algae) contain ten to twenty times more minerals than land plants. They are excellent sources of iodine, calcium, chlorophyll, vitamins, and protein. Nori and wakame, for example, offer ten times more niacin than spinach and at least as much vitamin C as tomatoes. Dulse is extremely rich in iron.

A fascinating range of dried sea vegetables is now readily available in health food stores and Asian markets. Most are imported from Japan, but more and more varieties—such as dulse, alaria (similar to wakame), kelp, and nori—are being harvested off the coasts of Maine and the Pacific Northwest. I like to support the domestic harvesters whenever possible. Although most of them tend to have limited local distribution through health food stores, some do have a lively mail-order business (page 478).

Where Do Sea Vegetables Fit into a Meal?

Any of the dishes in this section can be served instead of or in addition to a vegetable side dish. Since the mineral content of sea vegetables is quite concentrated, many people tend to serve them in small quantities—almost like condiments. I'm not one of those people! Let your own affinity for sea vegetables be your guide.

See also Hijicki Brown Rice Casserole (page 130), Marinated Cucumber-Dill and Wakame Salad (page 278), and Dulse Oatmeal Muffins (page 339).

What follows is a brief description of the most commonly available sea vegetables. Details on selection, storage, and preparation for cooking are in Ingredients A to Z under Sea Vegetables and individual entries.

Nori: The flattened sheets are used for making sushi. Good for tearing into shreds and adding to hot pasta or to bean and grain salads.

Dulse: Second to nori, dulse probably appeals the most to North American palates, because of its intense, salty taste. Dulse is a deep red color and is sold in the form of wrinkled leaves. Try adding a few scissor-snipped leaves of dulse to soups and stews. Stir about ¼ cup of snipped dried dulse into your morning oatmeal, just like the Scots and Irish have done for centuries. Or grind dried dulse and mix it with toasted sesame seeds and sea salt (page 454) for a very tasty seasoning. You can also soak dulse in water until soft (2 to 3 minutes), drain, chop, and add to tossed salads.

Kombu and Kelp: Kelp is commonly sold in powdered form and makes a nutritious and tasty alternative to salt. Both kelp and kombu, its close relative, are available in wide, dark green dehydrated strips that quadruple in size when rehydrated. A strip of kombu adds a slightly salty taste to soups and stews, and many believe that rice and beans become more digestible when kombu is added to the cooking pot.

Wakame and Alaria: Frequently served in miso soup, wakame can also be softened in water for 2 to 3 minutes, cut into slivers, and added to green salads. Alaria, the American East Coast relative of Japanese wakame, has a considerably tougher texture and requires cooking. It also has a fibrous midrib, which can be cut away if it remains too chewy.

Arame and Hijicki: Both of these sea plants are sold in charcoal-black, spaghetti-thin strips. Since they are precooked, they require very little actual cooking time. Arame is considerably more delicate in texture than hijicki and requires less cooking.

Agar and Irish Moss (also known as carrageen): Both are valued as gelling agents. Agar creates a firmer gel and is the more readily available; recipes using agar are found in the dessert section.

Must be some memory of an earlier time that draws us to the sea and to its luxuriant green offerings. Wild and primitive, sea vegetables give us their grace, their resilience, their endurance, their supple flexibility. They are an antidote to our modern plastic world.

—Ann Bond, quoted in Larch Hanson,
Thoughts of a Seaweed Harvester
(privately published).

Basic Hijicki

Hijicki may well become your favorite sea vegetable, as it has become mine. The striking spaghettilike black strands are slightly chewy and have a delicate sweetness that offsets the briny taste of the sea.

If you have time to prepare ahead, here's good news: Hijicki can be soaked 8 to 12 hours in ample water to cover and it will become sufficiently tender to rinse, chop, and eat. For a milder taste, change the soaking water once after about 4 hours.

Hijicki tastes delicious when cooked with carrots, onions, and garlic. A drizzling of toasted sesame oil and sesame seeds added at the end has a marvelous effect.

I usually make this recipe as a vegetable side dish for one meal, and then incorporate leftovers into a grain, pasta, or green salad the next day.

Pressure cooker: 5 minutes high pressure
Standard stovetop: 30 to 40 minutes

*1½ cups (about 1¾ ounces) loosely packed hijicki, swooshed in a bowlful
    of cold water to clean, then drained*
1 large onion, peeled and thinly sliced
1 large carrot, thinly sliced on the diagonal
1 large clove garlic, peeled and thinly sliced
1½ cups water
2 to 3 teaspoons toasted (Oriental) sesame oil
Tamari soy sauce

GARNISH
2 tablespoons toasted sesame seeds

1. Soak the hijicki in fresh water to cover for 15 minutes. Drain.
2. Place the hijicki, onion, carrot, garlic, and fresh water in the cooker.
3. Lock the lid in place and over high heat bring to high pressure. Lower the heat just enough to maintain high pressure and cook for 5 minutes. Reduce the pressure with a quick-release method. Remove the lid, tilting it away from you to allow any excess steam to escape.
4. With a slotted spoon, transfer the vegetables to a serving bowl. Stir in sesame oil and tamari to taste and garnish with sesame seeds.

Standard Stovetop: Follow step 1. Using a 2-quart saucepan, follow step 2. Bring to the boil, then cover and reduce heat. Simmer until the hijicki is tender, about 30 to 40 minutes. Follow step 4.

Cook's Notes: Hijicki expands dramatically when soaked and cooked: 1 cup dried sea vegetable yields 4 to 5 cups cooked.

Variation: Stir ¼ cup finely minced parsley into the cooked hijicki for a splash of vibrant color.

I am a professional Northern California sea vegetable harvester, taking sea vegetables by hand from wild patches on the Mendocino County coast. Since I usually backpack fresh, wet sea vegetables up steep cliff trails, I have focused on selecting, rinsing and drying sea vegetables for maximum eating quality.

Sea vegetables are one of the few major undamaged native food sources where I live. My main concern is to harvest lightly within the natural flow, taking sparingly and using regeneration harvesting techniques. Sea vegetables have regenerated annually for millennia, and we must be careful not to disturb this cycle.

We must oppose the pollution of the oceans with all our spirits and energies. Ocean destruction is self-destruction. The sea vegetables have vital trace elements and toxin-eliminating properties which people need now as never before. Sea vegetable habitats must be guarded as sacred shrines of beauty and health.

—John and Eleanor Lewallen, *Sea Vegetable Gourmet Cookbook and Forager's Guide* (privately published).

Basic Arame

Prepare arame as you would hijicki (page 264), using 2½ cups (about 1¾ ounces) loosely packed dried arame. Arame is more delicate than hijicki and requires considerably less cooking time: 2 minutes under high pressure (unsoaked), 1 minute under high pressure (soaked), or 5 to 10 minutes standard stovetop. You can also eat arame uncooked after soaking it for an hour in boiling water to cover. Arame does not expand as dramatically as hijicki: 1 cup dried yields approximately 2 to 3 cups cooked.

Wakame (Alaria) with Browned Onions

Serves 4

In this dish the wakame remains slightly chewy and marries perfectly with the soft, sweet browned onions. Since alaria is tougher than wakame, it requires a longer cooking time. For more on both vegetables, see Ingredients A to Z.

> **Pressure cooker:** 2 minutes high pressure (wakame) or 7 minutes high pressure (alaria)
> **Standard stovetop:** 5 to 10 minutes (wakame) or 20 to 30 minutes (alaria)

1¾ to 2 ounces wakame, snipped into 1-inch bits, soaked in water to cover
*   for 10 minutes, rinsed, and drained*
2 small carrots, very thinly sliced
1 cup water
1 tablespoon olive oil
3 large (1½ pounds) onions, peeled, halved, and thinly sliced
2 large cloves garlic, peeled and finely chopped
2 to 3 teaspoons toasted (Oriental) sesame oil
Tamari soy sauce or Bragg Liquid Aminos to taste

1. Place the wakame or alaria, carrots, and water in the cooker.

2. Lock the lid in place and over high heat bring to high pressure. Lower the heat just enough to maintain high pressure and cook for 2 minutes (wakame) or 7 minutes (alaria).

3. While the wakame is cooking, heat the olive oil in a large, heavy skillet and sauté the onions and garlic until the onions are browned, stirring frequently, about 8 to 10 minutes.

4. When the timer for the wakame or alaria goes off, reduce the pressure with a quick-release method. Remove the lid, tilting it away from you to allow any excess steam to escape. If the sea vegetable is still tough, cover and simmer until tender.

5. Strain off the cooking liquid. Coarsely chop the sea vegetable, discarding any tough central ribs. Return to the pot and stir in the browned onions.

6. Season to taste with sesame oil and tamari.

Standard Stovetop: In a heavy 3-quart saucepan, follow step 1. Bring to the boil, reduce heat, cover, and simmer until the sea vegetable and carrots are tender, about 5 to 10 minutes (for the wakame) or 20 to 30 minutes (for the alaria). Follow steps 3, 5, and 6.

Cook's Notes: On occasion, a package of sea vegetable labeled wakame is actually alaria. You will know that this has happened if the sea vegetable takes longer than expected to become tender.

Take what's natural and combine it in the most delectable way. That's cooking.

—Heart Phoenix, vegan,
mother, earth steward

Hijicki with Winter Vegetables

Serves 4 to 6

A hearty stew with lots of flavorful sauce. It's suitable for a main dish when spooned over a grain—millet and bulgur are good choices. Otherwise you can use it as a side dish.

Pressure cooker: 5 minutes high pressure
Standard stovetop: 30 to 40 minutes

1 tablespoon oil
1 large onion, peeled and coarsely chopped
1 large clove garlic, peeled and finely chopped
1½ tablespoons freshly grated ginger
2 cups (about 2½ ounces) loosely packed hijicki, swooshed in cold water
    until clean, then drained
2½ cups boiling water
2 cups finely chopped kale
3 large carrots or parsnips, cut into 1-inch slices on the diagonal
3 ribs celery, cut into 1-inch slices on the diagonal
3 medium turnips, peeled and quartered
1 pound butternut or kabocha squash, cut into 1½-inch chunks
1 tablespoon tamari soy sauce, approximately
1 to 2 tablespoons toasted (Oriental) sesame oil or hot pepper toasted
    sesame oil

GARNISH
Toasted sesame seeds

1. Heat the oil in the cooker and sauté the onion, garlic, and ginger until the onion is lightly browned, about 4 minutes.

2. Stir in the hijicki, water (watch for sputtering oil!), vegetables, and tamari.

3. Lock the lid into place. Over high heat bring to high pressure. Lower the heat just enough to maintain high pressure and cook for 5 minutes. Reduce the pressure with a quick-release method. Remove the lid, tilting it away from you to allow any excess steam to escape. Stir well.

4. Transfer to a serving bowl. Stir in toasted sesame oil and additional soy sauce to taste. Garnish with sesame seeds.

Standard Stovetop: In a heavy 4-quart saucepan, follow steps 1 and 2. Bring to the boil, reduce heat and simmer, covered, until the hijicki and vegetables are tender, about 30 to 40 minutes. Add water, ¼ cup at a time, if the mixture becomes dry. Follow step 4.

Arame-Zucchini Stir-fry

The black, delicate strands of arame, half-moon slices of green zucchini, and dots of red sun-dried tomatoes look especially striking served over noodles or steamed basmati rice.

Wok or skillet: 15 minutes

1 pound firm or extra-firm tofu, drained and cut into ½-inch cubes
2 to 3 tablespoons tamari soy sauce, divided
1 cup (½ ounce) loosely packed arame, swooshed vigorously in cold water,
*   then drained*
1 cup boiling water
1 tablespoon olive oil
2 large cloves garlic, peeled and finely minced
1 pound zucchini, halved lengthwise and cut into ¼-inch slices (about 6
*   cups)*
⅓ cup finely chopped sun-dried tomatoes marinated in oil
¼ cup tightly packed minced fresh basil or parsley

1. Place the cubed tofu and 1 tablespoon of tamari into a medium-sized container with a tight-fitting lid. Set aside to marinate for 10 to 15 minutes, shaking occasionally. (This step can be done the night before, if desired.)

2. While the tofu marinates, place the arame in a bowl and pour over the boiling water. Let sit for 15 minutes, pressing the arame down into the water from time to time. Drain the arame through a sieve.

3. In a wok or large skillet, heat the oil. Sauté the garlic for 10 seconds, stirring constantly. Add the tofu, any unabsorbed tamari, and the soaked arame, and stir-fry for 1 minute.

4. Stir in the zucchini and 2 tablespoons of water.

5. Cover and cook over medium-high heat until the zucchini is tender-crisp, about 2 to 3 minutes.

6. Stir in the sun-dried tomatoes and basil, and additional tamari to taste. Serve hot or at room temperature.

Rice-Stuffed Nori Rolls

Nori is the flat sheet of toasted seaweed used for wrapping sushi. Stuffed with rice and vegetables, nori rolls make elegant hors d'oeuvres when served in bite-sized slices.

Nori rolls can be prepared a day in advance. The umeboshi plum paste spread along one end acts as a preservative, and the rolls last without refrigeration for at least 24 hours.

Plain rice-filled nori rolls are fine, but they are even better when the rice is flecked with tasty surprises, such as toasted sesame seeds or sliced scallions. My personal favorite alternates mellow bits of avocado with jolts of pickled ginger.

When the rolls are eaten as soon as they are prepared with room-temperature rice, the nori is crisp. When they are allowed to sit for an hour or more or are prepared with freshly cooked, still-hot rice, the nori becomes soft and chewy. Either way, they're delicious.

> 4 sheets toasted sushi nori (see Cook's Notes)
> 1 teaspoon umeboshi plum paste, wasabi, or prepared mustard, approximately
> 1⅓ cups cooked Sushi Brown Rice (see headnote under Basic Brown Rice, page 119)
> Generous sprinkling of sesame seasoning salt (page 454) or your favorite condiment

OPTIONAL ADDITIONS
> ½ ripe avocado, preferably Haas, cut into ½-inch cubes
> 4 tablespoons chopped scallion greens
> 8 to 12 thin slivers pickled ginger or daikon root (available in health food stores)
> ¼ cup chopped pan-fried tempeh (page 228) or baked tofu (page 223)
> 4 spears cooked asparagus
> ¼ cup grated raw carrots or beets

1. Cover the bottom third of each sheet of nori with a very thin layer of plum paste, wasabi, or mustard.

2. Spread about ⅓ cup rice on top of the plum paste, leaving about an inch along the bottom edge uncovered. Distribute any of the optional additions on top of the rice.

3. Wet your middle fingers in a small bowl of water and use them to moisten the top edge of the nori sheet.

4. Lift the bottom edge (nearest the filling) and press it gently into the rice, rolling the rice into the nori as you would a jelly roll until it is folded over to the top edge. Press gently to seal. (The moistened nori should adhere nicely.) Let the rolled nori sit for a minute or two, seam side down, while you are preparing the remainder.

5. Store in a cool place for up to 24 hours or refrigerate until needed, up to 3 days.

6. Eat whole, out of hand, or cut into 1-inch pieces with a serrated knife, and place decoratively on a platter, cut side up.

Cook's Notes: You can buy nori already toasted, but it is more expensive. To toast nori at home, simply pass each sheet—shiny side down—briskly over a gas flame or an electric burner: The color will appear greenish when held up to the light.

Variation: Try a variety of fillings besides rice: leftover steamed greens, well-drained and chopped, or seasoned noodles.

Come forth into the light of things,
Let Nature be your teacher.
—William Wordsworth

Salads, Slaws, and Sprouts

Salads

Green salads are a mainstay in my diet. Their raw, vital crunch provides a refreshing counterpart to the mellow texture of cooked foods. Eating a salad gives me a sense of well-being. I usually have at least one a day.

I try not to have too many preconceived notions about what I want in my salad before I head to the market. Once there, I select whatever looks freshest and most appealing, focusing on what's in season locally. (For selection, washing, and storage information, refer to Ingredients A to Z under individual listings.) You can use only one green, or combine different varieties and toss in some sliced raw mushrooms and radishes.

Here are a few combinations that I've found particularly successful.

Belgian endive—watercress—mushrooms
Boston lettuce—radicchio—arugula
Fennel—Boston lettuce
Spinach—red leaf lettuce—mushrooms
Watercress—Romaine

Apple-Arugula Salad

Serves 6

An unusual salad that's simple to make. It's best to prepare and dress this salad just before serving.

1 large bunch arugula
4 tart apples, such as Granny Smiths, cored, peeled, cut into chunks, and sprinkled immediately with 2 to 3 tablespoons lemon juice to prevent discoloration
¼ to ⅓ cup Maple–Poppy Seed Dressing (page 292)

1. Trim off the roots and any tough or fibrous stems from the arugula. Slosh the arugula leaves in a large bowl of cold water to release any sand. If the arugula seems very dirty, slosh it again in a fresh bowl of water.
2. Place the arugula in a strainer and rinse under cold running water.
3. Dry the arugula in a salad spinner or by gently rolling it in a clean kitchen towel.
4. Place the arugula in a salad bowl with the apples.
5. Toss in enough dressing to moisten.
6. Serve immediately.

Variations
- Watercress makes a nice substitute for arugula. To prepare, see Watercress in Ingredients A to Z.
- Try Lime-Curry Vinaigrette (page 292) instead of the Maple–Poppy Seed Dressing.

Everyone thinks he knows what a lettuce looks like. But start to draw one and you realize the anomaly of having lived with lettuces all your life but never having seen one, never having seen the semi-translucent leaves curling in their own lettuce way, never having noticed what makes a lettuce a lettuce rather than a curly kale.... What applies to lettuces applies equally to the all-too-familiar faces of husbands ... wives ...

—Frederick Franck, *The Zen of Seeing*
(New York: Vintage, 1973).

Orange and Fennel Salad with Walnuts

Serves 4

Arrange this salad on individual plates, alternating fennel slices with segments of orange and topping with chopped walnuts. Garnish with a few sprigs of watercress or arugula, or place it on a bed of blushing radicchio.

2 large bulbs fennel
2 large navel oranges
⅓ cup walnuts, coarsely chopped
3 tablespoons walnut or olive oil, approximately
1½ to 2 tablespoons balsamic vinegar or lemon juice
Sea salt to taste

OPTIONAL GARNISH
A few sprigs of watercress or arugula, or about 8 leaves of radicchio

1. Remove the stringy stalks of the fennel and reserve for stock.

2. Cut each of the bulbs in half and then thinly slice the halves to create half-moons.

3. Peel the oranges and remove any white pith. With a serrated knife, thinly slice the oranges. Remove and discard any pits.

4. If using radicchio, arrange it on 1 large platter or 4 small ones.

5. Set alternate layers of orange and fennel in an attractive pattern on top of the greens or directly on the platter (if not using radicchio).

6. Either drizzle the oil and vinegar and sprinkle the salt directly on top of the salad (holding your thumb over most of the bottle top prevents any serious dousings), or combine the oil, vinegar, and salt in a small jar, shake it, and drizzle the dressing on the salad. Taste and add more vinegar and salt, if needed.

7. Garnish with greens (if using) and serve.

Middle Eastern Pita Salad

Serves 6

This is a twist on a great tossed salad and a fun way to use up dried-out pita. Prepare it about 10 minutes in advance to give the pita a chance to absorb the dressing and soften.

Two 7-inch whole wheat pitas
2 cups peeled, diced cucumber
1 cup chopped tomatoes (halved cherry tomatoes are nice)
¾ cup tightly packed, finely chopped parsley
⅓ cup pitted black olives, preferably oil-cured, halved or coarsely chopped
¼ cup thinly sliced scallion greens

FOR THE DRESSING
¼ cup olive oil
3 to 4 tablespoons freshly squeezed lemon juice
½ teaspoon finely minced garlic
½ teaspoon sea salt, or to taste

1. If the pita is not dried out enough to break, bake it in a toaster oven at 350° until crisp, about 5 minutes. Break the pita into 1-inch bits.

2. In a medium-sized salad bowl, combine the pita, cucumber, tomatoes, parsley, olives, and scallion greens.

3. In a small jar, combine the olive oil, lemon juice, garlic, and salt, and shake until well blended. Pour over the salad and toss until thoroughly mixed.

4. Let sit for about 10 minutes before serving.

Sprout Salad with Toasted Sesame Vinaigrette

If you associate sprouts strictly with alfalfas, consider trying some other varieties. This salad works well with a mix of lentil, sunflower, green pea, and aduki bean sprouts—in other words, sprouts with short tails and lots of crunch. It's actually best not to use more than a small handful of alfalfas or other leggy sprouts, because they can be difficult to toss.

4 cups fresh mixed sprouts, homegrown (page 287) or store bought
1 red pepper, seeded and very thinly sliced or finely diced
2 tablespoons thinly sliced scallion greens
1 small carrot, finely chopped
⅓ cup Toasted Sesame Vinaigrette (page 299), approximately
Lemon juice and tamari soy sauce to taste

1. Combine the sprouts, red pepper, scallion greens, and carrots in a salad bowl.
2. Just before serving, toss in just enough dressing to moisten the salad.
3. Taste and add lemon juice and additional tamari, as needed, to make the flavors soar.

When I look at a dish made with my peppers, it gives me great pleasure to know that it took nine months for me to make that dish. After all, I had to create the environment in which they could grow.

—Ann Cutting, professional estate gardener, St. Helena, California

Marinated Cucumber-Dill and Wakame Salad

Serves 4 to 6

This salad can be a wonderfully simple and refreshing introduction to the mild-tasting sea vegetable called wakame. Floating in the familiar context of dill and paper-thin slices of cucumber, the wakame technically plays the supporting role—but don't be surprised if it steals the show.

Prepare this salad at least 4 hours in advance to allow enough time for the wakame to soften and marinate. It keeps well in the refrigerator for up to 3 days.

2 large cucumbers
One 12-inch-long piece of wakame (1 to 1½ ounces)
¼ cup white wine vinegar
2 tablespoons finely chopped scallion greens or sweet red onion (optional)
1½ to 2 teaspoons dried dillweed
Pinch sea salt

1. Peel the cucumbers (unless they are organic and have thin, sweet-tasting skins). Slice the cukes paper thin. (This task is most easily accomplished with the cutting disk of a food processor, a mandoline, or the shredding side of a box grater.) Set the cucumbers in a salad bowl or storage container.

2. With kitchen scissors, snip the wakame into pieces roughly ½ inch long by ½ inch wide. (The wakame will quadruple in size once it has absorbed the liquid given off by the cucumbers.) Set the wakame bits in a strainer and quickly pass running water over to rinse. Drain thoroughly.

3. Toss the wakame, vinegar, scallion greens (if using), 1½ teaspoons dillweed, and salt with the cucumbers. Cover and refrigerate until the wakame is tender, about 4 to 6 hours. Stir occasionally to make sure that the wakame is submerged in the juice. Taste, and if the dill flavor is not strong enough, add some more dillweed at least 1 hour before serving.

4. Serve slightly chilled or at room temperature.

Unless we change direction, we are likely to end up where we are headed.

—Chinese proverb

Vegetable Salads

Warm Kale and Potato Salad   Serves 4

Inspired by the warm German-style potato salads I often ate as a child, this recipe is a natural, since potatoes and kale are such an ideal pair. Made with waxy red potatoes, the dish takes on a rich taste with minimal use of oil.

Pressure cooker: 2 minutes high pressure
Standard stovetop: 15 to 20 minutes

1 small bunch (about ¾ pound) kale
2 to 3 tablespoons olive oil, divided
1 large onion or leek (white part only), coarsely chopped
3 cloves garlic, peeled and finely chopped
⅓ to 1 cup water or vegetable stock (use pressure cooker manufacturer's recommended liquid minimum)
1¼ pounds small thin-skinned potatoes, well scrubbed and cut into ⅛-inch slices
¼ teaspoon sea salt, or to taste
1 to 2 tablespoons apple cider vinegar
Freshly ground black pepper to taste

GARNISH
¼ cup tightly packed minced fresh parsley

1. Strip the kale leaves from the stems by holding the stem in one hand, folding each leaf together lengthwise, and pulling gently but firmly. Reserve the stems for stock. Chop the leaves into pieces roughly 2 inches square. (You should have about 3 to 4 cups.) Set aside.

2. Heat 1 tablespoon of oil in the cooker and sauté the onion and garlic for 1 minute, stirring frequently.

3. Add the water (watch for sputtering oil!), kale, potatoes, and salt.

4. Lock the lid in place and over high heat bring to high pressure. Lower the heat just enough to maintain high pressure and cook for 2 minutes. Reduce the pressure with a quick-release method. Remove the lid, tilting it away from you to allow any excess steam to escape.

continued

5. If the potatoes or kale are not quite cooked, set the lid back in place and allow them to steam in the residual heat for another minute or two. Drain the kale and potatoes, reserving the liquid for another use (such as stock or a grain-cooking liquid). Place the kale and potatoes into a serving bowl.

6. Stir in the remaining 1 to 2 tablespoons of olive oil, 1 tablespoon of vinegar, and pepper. Taste and adjust seasonings, adding more vinegar or salt, if desired.

7. Garnish with parsley. Serve warm or at room temperature.

Standard Stovetop: Bring a large pot of salted water to the boil. Follow step 1. Add the chopped kale and cook until it is tender, about 3 to 5 minutes. Remove with a slotted spoon, transfer to a strainer, and refresh under cold running water. Place in a serving bowl in a warm place.

Return the water to the boil and add the potatoes (cut them in half or into quarters if they are large). Reduce the heat to medium, cover, and cook until the potatoes are tender, about 5 to 8 minutes. Drain and, when cool enough to handle, cut the potatoes into slices ⅛-inch thick. Set the potatoes into the bowl with the kale.

In a large skillet, follow step 2, but increase the sauté time to 4 minutes. Add sautéed onions to potato-kale mixture. Follow steps 6 and 7.

Beet-Potato Salad   Serves 4

This gorgeous magenta salad is perfect for picnic fare or home entertaining. If the beets and potatoes aren't cooked yet and are approximately the same size, you can steam them together, either in the pressure cooker or in a saucepan.

Because the beets are boldly flavored, I like to dress the salad lightly right before serving. The following day, you may find that the flavors need perking up with a dash more oil, vinegar, and salt.

¾ pound cooked beets, peeled and diced
1 pound cooked thin-skinned potatoes, diced
2 ribs celery, coarsely chopped
2 to 3 tablespoons walnut, hazelnut, or olive oil
2 to 3 tablespoons apple cider vinegar or 1 to 2 teaspoons umeboshi plum
*   vinegar (fantastic!)*
Sea salt to taste

1. In a bowl, combine the beets, potatoes, and celery.

2. Drizzle on about 2 tablespoons each of oil and vinegar (if you use umeboshi plum vinegar, 8 drops are sufficient). Toss gently.

3. Taste and add salt as required.

Dilled Potato–Green Bean Salad

Whatever got us into the habit of peeling potatoes? Not only does much of the good nutrition lie just beneath the skin, but there's great flavor in the skin as well

I like to juxtapose the very different textures of potatoes and green beans. For best results, toss the potatoes in the dill-mustard dressing while they are still warm and can readily absorb the flavors. Then let the dish stand at room temperature for an hour to marinate before serving.

1 pound green beans, trimmed
1 pound just-cooked small new potatoes
⅓ cup coarsely chopped walnuts (optional)
¼ cup olive oil
¾ to 1 cup tightly packed minced fresh dill
1 to 3 teaspoons Dijon mustard
1½ to 2 tablespoons white wine vinegar
Sea salt and freshly ground pepper to taste

1. Steam the green beans until tender-crisp, about 3 to 5 minutes. Run under cold water and drain thoroughly. Cut into thirds lengthwise and place in a serving bowl.

2. Cut the cooked new potatoes into ¼-inch slices and add them and the walnuts (if using) to the beans.

3. In a food processor or blender, combine the oil, ¾ cup dill, 1 teaspoon mustard, 1½ tablespoons of vinegar, salt, and pepper. Blend to a thick, creamy dressing. Taste and add more mustard or vinegar if desired.

4. Toss the dill-mustard vinaigrette into the potato-bean mixture.

5. Let the mixture marinate at room temperature for at least 1 hour before serving. Adjust seasonings before serving, adding more dill if desired.

Slaws

Cabbage offers a terrific long-lasting alternative to green salads. You can keep cabbage on hand for 4 to 5 days without paying it any mind, and there are so many imaginative ways to make a slaw, to which the following recipes will attest.

Oriental Cilantro Slaw
Serves 6

The Thai trio of lime juice, fresh coriander, and chili peppers creates a most unusual cabbage salad. Unlike most slaws, this one tastes best when the cabbage retains its crunch, so try to finish it off within 24 hours of preparation. Somehow I don't think this will be too great a challenge.

> 1 medium (1½ pounds) cabbage
> 1 large carrot, finely chopped
> 1 cup tightly packed minced fresh coriander
> ¼ cup thinly sliced scallion greens (optional)
> 3 tablespoons peanut oil (see Cook's Notes)
> 3 tablespoons canola or safflower oil
> 3 to 4 tablespoons lime juice
> 2 to 3 tablespoons tamari soy sauce
> 1 to 2 jalapeño peppers (wear rubber gloves when handling), seeded and
>   finely chopped
> Sea salt to taste
> Dash hot chili oil (optional)

GARNISH
½ cup coarsely chopped, lightly salted roasted peanuts

1. Quarter the cabbage; remove and discard the tough central core. Shred the cabbage by cutting very thin slices along the length of each quarter. (You should have about 6 cups; reserve any extra for salad or for another dish.)

2. Place the shredded cabbage in a large serving bowl. Mix in the carrot, coriander, and scallion greens (if using).

3. In a jar, combine the oils, 3 tablespoons lime juice, 2 tablespoons tamari, jalapeños, and salt. Shake well to blend. Taste and add a few drops of hot chili oil if more heat is desired.

4. Pour dressing over the slaw and toss well. Add more lime juice and tamari as needed. Garnish with peanuts before serving.

Cook's Notes: If a fragrant peanut oil is unavailable, use all canola oil and blend 1 heaping teaspoon of peanut butter into the dressing.

Sweet and Sour Coleslaw

Serves 6 to 8

People always seem to come back for seconds, so don't be surprised when a large bowlful empties out quickly. Try to prepare this slaw a few hours before serving for the best taste.

1 medium (1½ pounds) cabbage
2 large carrots, coarsely grated
⅓ cup dried cherries or finely chopped dried apricots
⅓ cup canola or safflower oil
1 tablespoon maple syrup
2 to 3 tablespoons apple cider vinegar
¾ teaspoon sea salt, or to taste
⅛ to ¼ teaspoon ground allspice

1. Quarter the cabbage, remove and discard the central white core. Shred the cabbage by cutting very thin slices along the length of each quarter. You should have about 6 cups, tightly packed; reserve any extra for salad or for another dish. (You can also use the shredding disk of your food processor to prepare both the cabbage and the carrots.)

2. Place the shredded cabbage in a large bowl. Toss in the carrots and cherries. In a small jar, combine the oil, syrup, 2 tablespoons of cider vinegar, salt, and ⅛ teaspoon allspice. Shake vigorously to blend, and then pour over the cabbage. Taste and add more cider vinegar and allspice if desired.

3. Refrigerate for at least 1 hour before serving. For optimum taste, serve at room temperature.

Variation: For some extra pizzazz, add 1 teaspoon of caraway seeds to the whole batch, or a prorated amount to whatever is left over the day after.

Red Cabbage Slaw
with Maple-Mustard Dressing

Serves 6

The compliments will start pouring in for this tasty, gorgeous salad, which you've thrown together in about 5 minutes.

Don't be tempted to leave out the juniper berries: They are the secret ingredient that makes the whole greater than the sum of its parts.

If possible, prepare the dressing an hour or so before serving to allow its flavors to "ripen." Then toss the cabbage in the dressing about 10 minutes before serving.

1 teaspoon coarsely ground juniper berries
½ to ¾ cup Maple-Mustard Dressing (page 293)
1½ pounds red cabbage, finely shredded
1 large carrot, grated
⅓ cup tightly packed minced fresh parsley
Sea salt to taste (optional; you probably won't need it)

1. Stir the juniper berries into the maple-mustard dressing and, if time permits, let sit for an hour.

2. Just before serving, toss the cabbage, carrot, and parsley in a salad bowl.

3. Toss in just enough dressing to coat the salad. Add salt to taste if desired.

When you make a salad, as you handle each vegetable or herb, let your mind dwell on how each was made. You can feel the struggle that some of them have had to pull through, whereas with others, you can feel the ease and freedom in which they have been brought to fruition. All these thoughts and feelings are important. They bring the very life force into your body.

—The Findhorn Community, *The Findhorn Garden*
(Forres, Scotland: The Findhorn Press, 1975).

Chili Bean Slaw

Just after the slaw is prepared, the cabbage is still crunchy, offering an interesting contrast to the soft beans. The next day, after the cabbage has absorbed more of the dressing, its texture is mellower, and the salad is bursting with complex flavor. I like it both ways.

Should there be any leftovers, you can perk up the flavors with a bit of extra lemon or lime juice.

1 medium (1½ pounds) cabbage

1½ cups cooked red beans, such as red kidneys, small pinks, or Dixie
    Speckled Butter Beans

1 medium red bell pepper, cored, seeded, and diced

¼ cup thinly sliced scallion greens

1 teaspoon whole cumin seeds

1 teaspoon dried leaf oregano

1 tablespoon mild chili powder

Dash cayenne (ground red) pepper (optional)

½ cup soy mayonnaise

2 to 4 tablespoons lime juice (preferable) or lemon juice

Sea salt to taste, if desired

1. Quarter the cabbage and cut away any hard core. Shred the cabbage by cutting very thin slices along the length of each quarter. Place the shredded cabbage—there should be about 6 cups—in a large bowl or storage container.

2. Toss in the beans, red pepper, and scallion greens.

3. To prepare the dressing, heat a small, heavy skillet (preferably cast iron) for 30 seconds. Add the cumin seeds and stir constantly until they begin to brown and pop, about 10 to 20 seconds. Immediately turn off the heat and stir in the oregano, chili powder, and cayenne (if using). Cool slightly, then grind the mixture to a powder in a spice mill or with a mortar and pestle.

4. In a small bowl, combine the chili powder mix with the soy mayonnaise, then stir in 2 tablespoons of the lime juice.

5. Toss enough of the dressing into the salad to thoroughly coat the cabbage. (You will probably use most or all of the dressing.) Add extra lime juice and salt to taste.

Variations

- Mash a clove of roasted garlic (page 425) and blend it into the dressing.
- Use a roasted red pepper cut into thin strips in place of the raw pepper.

Celery Slaw

Celery is rarely given center stage. With its crisp texture and refreshing sweet-saltiness, it deserves better treatment. With those thoughts in mind, I created this simple, flavorful slaw. It tastes best after a few hours of refrigeration.

1 medium bunch celery (1 pound), very finely chopped (4 cups)
1 large carrot, finely chopped
¼ cup dried currants or raisins
⅓ cup soy mayonnaise
2 tablespoons apple cider vinegar
1 teaspoon Dijon mustard
Sea salt to taste

1. In a bowl, combine the celery, carrot, and currants.
2. In a food processor or with a whisk, blend the mayonnaise, vinegar, and mustard. Pour the dressing over the celery mixture and toss until thoroughly blended. Add salt to taste.
3. Refrigerate for at least 1 hour before serving.

We feed 800 elderly and homeless people with the produce from this garden. We're doing something good. It feels like you're giving back instead of taking.

—Inmate on a special gardening project run by
Catherine Sneed at San Francisco County Jail

Sprouting Dinner Under the Sink

If you find yourself eyeing your neighbor's vine-ripened zucchini and lamenting the lack of a garden, consider sprouting.

For year-round, rain-or-shine cultivation, nothing beats the indoor sprout farm. With a bottle, some cheesecloth, and a few rubber bands, you are all set to cast your seeds upon the waters. A few days later, it's harvest time—about the most instant gratification a gardener could ever dream of.

I find it very satisfying to control the process from start to finish: buying organic seeds, using filtered or spring water, and enjoying optimum freshness. I recently sprouted some mung beans and was amazed at how much crisper and more flavorful they were than those I've purchased at Oriental grocery stores—well worth the few moments it took to grow them.

More good news about sprouting is that as seeds and beans germinate, their fat and starch content decreases and there is an increase of protein, vitamin C, and B vitamins. Many sprouts also boast significant quantities of potassium, iron, calcium, and phosphorus.

And they're the best bargain in town! From start to finish, an 8-ounce crop of alfalfa sprouts takes about 5 minutes of labor and costs about 25 cents, roughly one fourth the purchase price of the commercially grown variety.

Beyond Alfalfas

Other sproutable seeds include mustard, radish, clover, and sunflower. If you want to get really adventurous, try sprouting beans and grains.

I've had great success with a combination of dried green peas, adukis, and lentils (see the recipe on page 288). You can make a potpourri of any beans that have similar sprouting times. They are ready when the "tails" are about one and a half times the length of the unsprouted bean. Soy beans and limas are not healthful to eat raw.

When sprouting grains, be sure to use the whole grain. Winter wheat berries, rye, barley, and oats are the easiest grains to sprout at home. I suggest that you read *Raw Energy* by Leslie and Susannah Kenton for more information on all aspects of sprouting.

Guidelines for Home Sprouting

Shop for organic seeds, beans, or grains in health food stores, or check the mail-order sources. Almost anything goes, but I suggest starting with alfalfas or red lentils (see the sprout chart on page 289) for guaranteed success if you are a novice.

As a general rule, start with 3 to 4 tablespoons of seeds, and about 1 cup of beans or grains. Tiny seeds like alfalfa and radish expand about six to eight times their original volume, while larger seeds (like sunflower), beans, and grains double in size.

continued

1. In a large, wide-mouthed jar, soak the seeds, beans, or grains in ample water to cover overnight.

2. The next morning, set a double layer of cheesecloth over the jar and secure it tightly with a rubber band. Drain the seeds, fill the jar with water, shake, and drain again *thoroughly*.

3. Leave the jar in a dark place (under the sink or in a cabinet). Prop the jar up so that the mouth tilts into its own lid, allowing the sprouts to continue draining.

4. Rinse and drain two to three times a day for 1 to 4 days, depending upon the type of sprout and the length desired (see chart, page 289). Sprouts are not fussy about growing. If you forget to rinse them one night, the chances are good that they will survive the drought.

5. Before refrigerating mature sprouts, you can "green" certain varieties (such as alfalfa, radish, clover, and wheat berries) by exposing them to sunlight for an hour or two. The chlorophyll produced by the greening process freshens the breath and is thought to aid in the regeneration of the blood.

6. Refrigerate the jars with the lids *loosely* in place (don't screw the lid on as the sprouts need to breathe) until you eat them—the sooner the better, but certainly within 3 days.

Green Pea, Aduki, and Lentil Mix

Makes about 3 cups

¼ *cup dried green peas*
¼ *cup dried adukis*
¼ *cup lentils*

Follow the directions for sprouting above. The mixture will be ready to harvest in 3 to 4 days.

Sprout Chart

Type	Rinses per Day	Days Until Harvest	Harvesting Length (root)	Yield	Taste and Texture	Uses
alfalfa	2	3–4 (24 hours for ⅛ inch)	1½ inches greened ⅛ inch for baking	¼ c → 2½ c greened	mild, vibrant, crisp, and crunchy	greened: salads, sandwiches ⅛ inch: baked goods, pancakes
chick-peas	2–3	2½–3	½ inch	1 c → 3 c	nutty, like water chestnuts, crunchy	steam 5 minutes before eating; add to salads, soups, breads
lentils, brown	2–3	3–4	1 inch greened ¾ inch for baking	1 c → 5–6 c	peppery, crisp	greened: salads, sandwiches ¾ inch: bake into vegetable loaves; add to pancakes or soups
lentils, red	2	1–2	⅛–½ inch	1 c → 4 c	peppery, crisp	salads; add to soup at the very last minute
mung beans	3–4	3–4	1½–2 inches	1 c → 4–5 c	faintly like raw string beans, crisp	salads, sandwiches; stir-fry in sesame oil for Chinese dishes
peas (whole green)	2–3	3	length of seed	1½ c → 2 c	like fresh peas, crunchy	add to salads and to stir-fries at the last minute
radish	2	3–4	1½–2 inches greened	1 tbs → 1½ c	like radishes, crisp	salads, sandwiches

Legend:

c = cup

→ = yield

continued

Type	Rinses per Day	Days Until Harvest	Harvesting Length (root)	Yield	Taste and Texture	Uses
sunflower seeds	2	1–1½	just softened or length of seed	1 c → 3 c	faintly like artichoke heart, crunchy	salads, snacks; bake into savory muffins
winter wheat berries	2–3	3–4	½ inch or ¾ inch (sweeter)	1 c → 3–4 c	sweet, chewy	salads, sandwiches; add to cereal, pancakes; bake into bread, muffins

Legend:

c = cup

→ = yield

Who cannot believe in the power of seeds. The power, the energy stored within the earth is so unimaginable that we can't conceive of it. It's like infinity. That kind of energy you can't grasp.

—Elizabeth Berry, organic specialty produce gardener, Abique, New Mexico

Dressings and Sauces

Dressings

While clothes may not really make the man, I do believe that dressings make the salad. And the nice thing about them is that so little effort brings such great rewards. Throw a few ingredients in a jar, shake them up, and voilà, even a tired lettuce leaf practically stands at attention.

The secret to producing an exciting repertoire of dressings is to stock a variety of good oils and vinegars (see Stocking the Ecological Pantry, page 3), a selection of vibrant herbs and spices, a high-quality unrefined sea salt, and a reliable pepper mill. Then just fill in with fresh herbs as needed.

Classic proportions of oil to vinegar are generally three to one, but I like my dressings more acidic, especially for use on bland bean or grain salads. If my proportions don't quite suit you, it's easy to experiment with them until you strike the perfect balance for your own taste buds. Keep in mind, though, that the impact of any dressing is somewhat subdued when it is tossed with other ingredients. On its own, therefore, it should be intensely flavored.

Although most dressings can be refrigerated for a week or two, they lose vibrancy after a few days and need to be perked up with extra herbs and lemon juice or vinegar. Here are some of my current favorites.

Lime-Curry Vinaigrette

This vinaigrette works extremely well on bean or grain salads, and is especially tasty with lentils (page 214).

Before attempting this recipe, taste your curry powder and make sure it's absolutely fresh. A bitter taste indicates that it's time to replace it.

⅔ cup canola oil
3 to 4 tablespoons lime or lemon juice
2 tablespoons mild curry powder
2 tablespoons freshly grated ginger
1 teaspoon ground coriander seeds
1 teaspoon sea salt, or to taste

1. In a jar, combine all ingredients, using 3 tablespoons of the lime juice. Shake well.

2. Taste and add extra lime juice and salt as needed.

3. Use immediately or refrigerate in a tightly sealed container for up to 10 days. Shake well before each use.

Maple–Poppy Seed Dressing

A quick dressing to whip up with ingredients on hand. Nice tossed with shredded cabbage or greens, and especially good on Apple-Arugula Salad (page 274).

1 cup soy mayonnaise
1½ tablespoons apple cider vinegar or lemon juice
1 tablespoon maple syrup
2 tablespoons poppy seeds
¼ cup water, approximately

1. In a food processor or blender, combine all of the ingredients, adding sufficient water to achieve a thick but pourable consistency.

2. Use immediately or refrigerate in a tightly sealed container for up to 10 days. Blend well before each use.

Creamy Green Garlic Dressing

Makes 1 cup

The mild and tantalizing flavor of roasted garlic complements the refreshing taste and color of parsley. The dressing can be used as a flavorful topping for plain-cooked beans or grains and is equally good poured over boiled greens.

8 large cloves roasted garlic (page 425), peeled
½ cup tightly packed minced fresh parsley
2 tablespoons finely chopped shallots
½ cup olive oil
⅓ cup (2 ounces) mashed silken tofu
2 to 3 tablespoons white wine vinegar
½ teaspoon sea salt, or to taste
2 to 3 tablespoons water

1. In a blender or food processor, combine all of the ingredients and process until smooth, adding water as required to create a slightly thick consistency.

2. Use immediately or refrigerate in a tightly sealed container for up to 1 week. Bring to room temperature before using and reblend, if necessary.

Maple-Mustard Dressing

Makes ¾ cup

A sassy dressing that adds zing to a salad of spinach and sliced mushrooms. Or, for a spectacular presentation, try it on Red Cabbage Slaw (page 284).

It also makes a fine sauce for pan-fried tempeh or a grain salad.

½ cup safflower or canola oil
2 tablespoons apple cider vinegar
1 tablespoon maple syrup
2 tablespoons Dijon mustard
¼ teaspoon dry mustard
Pinch sea salt

1. In a small jar, combine all of the ingredients and shake well.

2. Use immediately or refrigerate in a tightly sealed container for up to 2 weeks.

Peanut-Lime Dressing

Makes about 1 cup

Make this recipe when you have some fragrant peanut oil on hand (or see Cook's Notes). This dressing is used for Oriental Cilantro Slaw (page 282), and is also delectable on grain and pasta salads.

⅓ cup peanut oil
⅓ cup canola or safflower oil
4 to 6 tablespoons freshly squeezed lime juice
4 to 6 tablespoons tamari soy sauce
Generous pinch cayenne (ground red) pepper (optional)
½ cup coarsely chopped roasted peanuts

1. In a jar, combine all the ingredients, using 4 tablespoons each lime juice and soy sauce. Shake well to blend.

2. Taste and add extra lime juice and soy sauce, if desired.

3. Use immediately or refrigerate in a tightly sealed container for up to 10 days.

Cook's Notes: If you have no peanut oil, use ⅔ cup canola oil and blend in 2 heaping teaspoons of peanut butter.

Herb Vinaigrette

Makes about 1 cup

You can vary this basic recipe by your choice of fresh herbs. Use ¼ cup of minced herbs if the dressing is for a green salad. Increase the amount of herbs to ½ cup for a grain or bean salad.

¾ cup olive oil
¼ cup white, red, or sherry wine vinegar
¼ to ½ cup tightly packed minced fresh basil, parsley, dill, or coriander
1 to 2 teaspoons finely minced shallots (optional)
1 teaspoon sea salt, or to taste

1. In a jar, combine all of the ingredients and shake well.

2. Taste and adjust seasonings. Refrigerate in a tightly sealed container for up to 2 weeks. (The herbs will turn brown, but the taste will still be delicious.)

Moroccan Vinaigrette

I've used this lively dressing on just about everything. It works especially well as a marinade for cooked chick-peas tossed with thinly sliced celery and a diced green pepper.

It can dress up bean, grain, and lettuce salads, and is delicious tossed with carrots (see Moroccan Carrots, page 246).

⅔ cup fruity olive oil
2 tablespoons freshly squeezed lemon juice, approximately
2 tablespoons red wine vinegar, approximately
1½ teaspoons sweet paprika
1 teaspoon ground cumin seeds
1 large clove roasted garlic (page 425), peeled and mashed, or 1 small
*   clove raw garlic, peeled and finely minced*
Generous pinch cayenne (ground red) pepper
⅓ cup tightly packed minced fresh parsley or coriander
1 teaspoon sea salt, or to taste
Lots of freshly ground black pepper

1. In a jar, combine all of the ingredients and shake well.

2. Taste and adjust seasonings, adding more lemon juice or vinegar if required.

3. Use immediately or refrigerate in a tightly sealed container for up to 2 weeks.

Cook's Notes: The flavor of this dressing is most vivid when just prepared. After a day or two, it needs extra lemon juice, ground cumin, and fresh herbs to pick it up.

Patience and the mulberry leaf become a silk robe.
> —Chinese proverb

Sweet Potato Vinaigrette

Inspired by chef Alan Harding of Nosmo King, a Manhattan restaurant featuring organic food, this vinaigrette has the creaminess of a classic French dressing and sufficient color, texture, and flavor to do justice to the most sophisticated greens. In summer, when I spot mâche, lamb's quarters, purslane, and edible flowers in the farmers' market, that's when I think about Sweet Potato Vinaigrette.

Since the flavor improves after overnight refrigeration, try to prepare some the day before you buy your greens.

1 medium (8 ounces) sweet potato or garnet yam, baked until very soft
½ cup plus 2 tablespoons canola or safflower oil
2 to 3 tablespoons apple cider vinegar
Large pinch ground cloves
Large pinch sea salt
¼ cup water, approximately

1. Peel and mash the baked sweet potato. (You should have about ½ to ¾ cup.)

2. In a blender (preferably) or food processor, combine the sweet potato, oil, 2 tablespoons vinegar, cloves, salt, and enough water to create a thick but pourable dressing.

3. Taste and add more vinegar and salt as required. Use immediately or refrigerate in a tightly sealed container for up to 5 days.

Cook's Notes: I love to use garnet yams in this dressing. They're very sweet and creamy and have gorgeous orange flesh.

If the dressing thickens in the refrigerator, thin it with a tablespoon or two of water.

Variation: Add a luscious richness and complexity to the dressing by substituting ¼ cup of hazelnut or walnut oil for ¼ cup of canola oil.

ECO-TIP: This is a great way to use a leftover baked yam or sweet potato.

Avocado Vinaigrette

A great way to make use of an overripe avocado. The dressing uses relatively little oil, since the avocado provides much of its own, as well as rich flavor and texture. I like it on rice and pasta salads, both hot and cold, and especially over Creole Brown Rice Casserole (page 132).

1 ripe Haas avocado
2 tablespoons minced shallot or onion
2 tablespoons safflower or canola oil
2 to 3 tablespoons tarragon vinegar or 2 to 3 tablespoons white wine
*   vinegar plus ⅛ teaspoon dried leaf tarragon*
⅓ to ½ cup water or vegetable stock
¼ to ½ teaspoon sea salt
Freshly ground black pepper to taste

1. Cut the avocado in half, discard the pit, and scoop out the flesh with a spoon.

2. In a blender (preferably) or food processor, puree the shallot, avocado, oil, and 2 tablespoons vinegar.

3. Thin with enough liquid to create a thick but pourable dressing.

4. Add additional vinegar, if desired, salt, and pepper to taste.

5. Use immediately or refrigerate in a tightly sealed container for up to 5 days. Reblend before serving, if necessary.

Coriander Pesto

Great served over plain boiled beans or grains, or on bean and grain salads, this pesto is delicious brushed lightly onto corn on the cob or tossed with cooked corn kernels.

> ⅓ cup olive oil
> 3 tablespoons freshly squeezed lime juice, approximately
> 1 cup tightly packed minced fresh coriander
> ¼ cup pine nuts (pignoli) or walnuts, finely chopped
> 2 large cloves roasted garlic (page 425), peeled and mashed, or 1 small
>   clove raw garlic, peeled and minced
> 1 teaspoon mild chili powder
> ½ teaspoon whole cumin seeds
> ⅛ teaspoon ground cinnamon
> ¾ teaspoon sea salt, or to taste

1. In a food processor or jar, combine all of the ingredients.

2. Use immediately or store in a well-sealed container in the refrigerator for up to 4 days.

Once our personal connection to what is wrong becomes clear, then we have to choose: we can go on as before, recognizing our dishonesty and living with the best we can, or we can begin the effort to change the way we think and live.

—Wendell Berry, *The Unsettling of America*
(San Francisco: Sierra Books, 1986).

Horseradish Dressing

Horseradish is one of those clean, terrific flavors that is all too often overlooked. I love using this dressing with beans, which really come alive when horseradish is near.

4 tablespoons light sesame or safflower oil
1½ to 2 tablespoons tamari soy sauce
4 to 5 teaspoons brown rice vinegar
1 to 4 tablespoons prepared horseradish (see Cook's Notes)

1. In a small jar, combine the oil, 1½ tablespoons tamari, 4 teaspoons vinegar, and 1 tablespoon horseradish.

2. Shake well to blend, then taste and keep adding small amounts of tamari, vinegar, and horseradish to achieve a good balance of flavors.

3. Use immediately or refrigerate in a well-sealed container for up to 3 weeks.

Cook's Notes: The amount of prepared horseradish you need depends upon both how fresh it is and how great your tolerance is for heat. Add the horseradish slowly until the desired effect is reached—you can add a bit more once the dressing has been tossed with the salad.

Toasted Sesame Vinaigrette

Makes about ½ cup

A delicious quick sauce for whole wheat udon or steamed broccoli, Brussels sprouts, green beans, or green and grain salads. Just toss on enough dressing (room temperature) to barely coat the pasta or vegetables while they are just cooked. Serve warm or at room temperature.

2 tablespoons toasted (Oriental) sesame oil
4 tablespoons untoasted sesame, safflower, or canola oil
2 tablespoons brown rice vinegar
1 to 2 tablespoons tamari soy sauce
2 tablespoons toasted sesame seeds

1. In a small jar, combine all of the ingredients and shake well. Taste and adjust the seasonings.

2. Use immediately or refrigerate in a well-sealed container for up to 3 weeks.

Roasted Shallot Vinaigrette

Roasting shallots brings out their natural sweetness. Combining them with the subtle flavor of roasted garlic in a dressing makes this a memorable blend.

Oven: 15 to 20 minutes at 375°

4 large (¼ pound) shallots
¼ teaspoon olive oil
2 cloves roasted garlic (see Cook's Notes)
⅓ cup safflower or canola oil
Additional ⅓ cup olive oil
4 to 6 tablespoons lemon juice or white wine vinegar
¾ to 1 teaspoon sea salt
Generous ⅛ teaspoon dry mustard

1. Brush the unpeeled shallots with ¼ teaspoon oil and set them on a pie plate. Roast them in an oven set at 375° until very soft, about 15 to 20 minutes.

2. When the shallots are cool enough to handle, peel them.

3. In a blender or food processor, combine the shallots, garlic, oils, 4 tablespoons lemon juice, salt, and mustard until thoroughly blended. Taste and add more lemon juice and salt as desired.

4. Use immediately or refrigerate in a tightly sealed container for up to 10 days.

Cook's Notes: If you don't have roasted garlic on hand, you can roast the garlic along with the shallots; see page 425 for instructions.

Roasted Red Pepper Sauce

This sauce has a haunting, delicate flavor that is sensational for pasta and grains. This recipe provides enough for 2 to 3 portions; double the amount if you require more.

2 roasted red bell peppers (page 451)
3 large cloves roasted garlic (page 425), peeled
3 tablespoons olive oil
1 tablespoon red wine vinegar, preferably balsamic
2 tablespoons toasted pine nuts (pignoli)
¼ teaspoon sea salt
Pinch ground cinnamon
1 to 2 tablespoons chopped fresh basil or coriander (optional)

1. In a blender or food processor, puree all of the ingredients until smooth.

2. Serve warm or at room temperature, or refrigerate in a tightly sealed container for up to 48 hours.

Cook's Notes: If the sauce is too thick, thin it slightly with 1 to 2 tablespoons of vegetable stock, tomato juice, or water.

Variation: Toss some shredded nori with hot grains or pasta before adding the sauce.

Organic should be a religion. I don't want to pollute my food source or do anything to hurt the earth. Yet the public wants perfect produce: you can't have it both ways.

—Rosalind Creasy, organic gardener, author,
Los Altos, California

Peanut Sauce

This velvety sauce is superb atop noodles, plain grains, or steamed greens.

½ cup unsalted peanut butter
2½ tablespoons freshly grated ginger
2 large cloves roasted garlic (page 425), peeled, or 2 small cloves raw
garlic, peeled and minced
½ to ⅔ cup water
2 tablespoons tamari soy sauce
1 teaspoon brown rice vinegar
1 teaspoon maple or barley malt syrup (less sweet), measured from an
oiled spoon
Dash cayenne (ground red) pepper (optional)

1. In a blender or food processor, blend all of the ingredients together until smooth, using just enough water to create a medium-thick consistency.

2. Taste and adjust seasonings. (The dressing may seem a bit salty, but keep in mind that it will be served over bland foods.) Use immediately or refrigerate in a tightly sealed container for up to 1 week.

Cook's Notes: The sauce thickens upon refrigeration. To thin it, vigorously stir in a bit of warm water with a fork.

Creamy White Bean Sauce

This quick-and-easy, silky-smooth sauce for steamed greens or grains is surprisingly creamy considering that it's so low in fat. Serve it warm or at room temperature.

1½ cups cooked white beans, such as navy or cannellini
2 large cloves roasted garlic (page 425), peeled, or 1 small clove raw
garlic, peeled and minced
1 to 2 tablespoons olive oil
1½ teaspoons Dijon mustard, preferably coarse-grained
2 tablespoons white wine vinegar
½ teaspoon dried rosemary leaves
½ teaspoon sea salt
⅓ to ½ cup bean cooking liquid, stock, or water
Freshly ground white or black pepper to taste

1. In a blender (preferably) or food processor, combine all of the ingredients and puree until very smooth while gradually adding enough liquid to create a thick sauce.

2. Serve warm or at room temperature or refrigerate until needed in a tightly sealed container for up to 3 days. (After refrigeration, thin it with water or stock.) Alternatively, freeze for up to 3 months.

Roasted Shallot Cream

Makes 1 cup

Thanks to chef Alan Harding of New York City's organic food restaurant Nosmo King for this elegant recipe. It makes a superb substitute for sour cream, and I like using it as a topping for Louise's Potato Latkes (page 260) and Creamy Sorrel Soup (page 59). With a little luck, there'll be some left over to use as a dip for raw vegetables.

Oven: 15 to 20 minutes at 375°

¼ pound shallots of approximately equal size and shape
1¼ teaspoons olive or safflower oil, divided
¾ cup (6 ounces) mashed silken or firm tofu (see Cook's Notes)
2 to 3 teaspoons brown rice vinegar
1 teaspoon maple syrup
½ teaspoon sea salt

1. Brush the shallots with ¼ teaspoon oil and set them in a pie plate. Roast them in a 375° oven until very soft, about 15 to 20 minutes.

2. When they are cool enough to handle, peel the shallots.

3. In a blender or food processor, combine the shallots with the remaining oil, tofu, 2 teaspoons vinegar, syrup, and salt. Process until smooth.

4. Taste and adjust the seasonings, adding a bit more vinegar, syrup, or salt, if needed, to achieve a slightly sweet taste with just a hint of acid.

5. Use immediately or refrigerate in a tightly sealed container for up to 3 days. Reblend before using, if necessary.

Cook's Notes: Silken tofu produces a soft and creamy product; firm tofu creates a slightly thicker topping with a bit more texture.

10-Minute Tomato Sauce

Makes about 5 cups
(enough for 4 medium-sized
portions of pasta)

Make this when vine-ripened tomatoes are in season. Plum tomatoes are your best choice—they're denser and less seedy than beefsteaks and produce a thicker, more flavor-packed sauce.

> **Pressure cooker:** 3 minutes high pressure, 7- to 10-minute natural pressure release plus optional simmering
> **Standard stovetop:** 30 to 40 minutes

1 tablespoon olive oil
2 large cloves garlic, peeled and thinly sliced
2 cups coarsely chopped onions
1 teaspoon dried leaf oregano
½ teaspoon dried rosemary leaves
2½ to 3 pounds very ripe plum tomatoes, cored and coarsely chopped
1 teaspoon sea salt, or to taste
¼ cup tightly packed, finely chopped fresh parsley or basil
1 to 3 teaspoons balsamic or other red wine vinegar

1. Heat the oil in the cooker. Sauté the garlic, onion, oregano, and rosemary until the onion is soft, about 3 minutes.

2. In a food processor or blender, puree half of the tomatoes. Coarsely chop the other half. Stir the tomatoes and salt into the onion mixture.

3. Lock the lid in place and over high heat bring to high pressure. Lower the heat just enough to maintain high pressure and cook for 3 minutes. Allow the pressure to come down naturally, about 7 to 10 minutes. Remove the lid, tilting it away from you to allow any excess steam to escape.

4. Stir in the parsley and some vinegar or salt, if needed, to bring up the flavors. If you prefer a thicker sauce, cook at a medium boil, uncovered, until it reaches the desired consistency.

5. Use immediately or store in a well-sealed container for up to 4 days in the refrigerator or up to 4 months in the freezer.

Standard Stovetop: In a heavy 3-quart saucepan, follow steps 1 and 2. Bring to the boil, then reduce heat and simmer with the lid partially ajar until thick, about 30 to 40 minutes. Follow steps 4 and 5.

Cook's Notes: Don't be tempted to prepare this sauce in anything smaller than a 4-quart cooker or there will be considerable sputtering at the vent. If the liquid minimum of your cooker is 1 cup or more and you have any trouble bringing up the pressure, add a bit of water to the sauce. In my experience, the liquid provided by the tomatoes and onions is sufficient.

Variations
- Use thinly sliced leeks (white part only) instead of onion for a subtle flavor enhancement.
- Add a generous pinch of crushed red pepper flakes to give the sauce some heat.
- Add 2 tablespoons of capers.
- Cook 1 cup or so of finely chopped tempeh with the sauce to achieve a heartier flavor and texture.

Barbecue Sauce

Makes about 1 cup

This versatile sauce is simple to prepare with ingredients easily kept on hand. Try it on barbecued tofu or tempeh (pages 222 and 231), or thin it slightly with water or bean cooking liquid and toss it into beans, grains, or pasta.

¼ cup apple cider vinegar
¼ cup tamari soy sauce
¼ cup Tomato Paste (page 306)
¼ cup maple syrup
1 to 2 tablespoons olive oil
3 teaspoons dry mustard
2 large cloves garlic, peeled and finely minced
½ teaspoon freshly ground black pepper
Tabasco sauce or crushed red pepper flakes to taste
2 to 3 drops liquid mesquite smoke (optional)

1. In a blender or with a whisk, mix all of the ingredients together.
2. Adjust the seasonings to your taste.
3. Use immediately or refrigerate until needed in a tightly sealed container for up to 1 week.

Tomato Paste

A good way to avoid buying tomato paste in a can or tube is to make your own—and enjoy a superior product to boot.

Standard stovetop: 3 to 10 minutes

½ cup water
3 ounces sun-dried tomatoes (dry pack)

1. Bring the water to the boil in a small pot.

2. Add the tomatoes, cover, and simmer until the tomatoes are very soft, about 3 to 10 minutes (depending upon how dry they are).

3. Lift out the tomato pieces with a slotted spoon and puree in a blender, adding a bit of the cooking liquid if the paste becomes too thick.

4. Use immediately or transfer to a storage container and cool to room temperature. Pour a thin layer of olive oil on top and refrigerate for up to 2 weeks. Alternatively, freeze in quantities of 2 tablespoons in individual ice-cube molds and store, tightly covered, for up to 4 months.

Dips and Spreads

The main difference between dips and spreads is the amount of liquid they contain: Dips are more runny than spreads. This fact invites the cook to perform some quick kitchen wizardry. For example, you can thin a spread by adding a little tomato juice, water, or vegetable stock and you have a dip. Thinning it just a little more makes an instant soup or a wonderful sauce for pasta and grains.

Spreads and dips are ideal vehicles for any cooked ingredients that are screaming for attention. The majority of my recipes for spreads are based on cooked beans, low in fat and high on flavor. People are always surprised at what wonders can be done with just a cupful or two of leftover beans as inspiration. For example, take cooked chick-peas: By pureeing the chick-peas with a little sesame tahini, parsley, and garlic, you've created a delicious Hummus (page 312). Cooked, pureed beans of any kind can be mixed with coarsely chopped nuts or seeds, a bit of olive oil and vinegar, and a sprinkling of fresh or dried herbs to create an irresistible spread—or packed into a small loaf pan and refrigerated for a coarse country-style pâté.

Spreads with cooked vegetables as the base, such as Sweet Potato Butter (page 309) or Carrot-Almond Butter (page 309) become delicious sandwich fillings or toppings for crackers.

It's very easy to invent your own dips and spreads, since they all follow a basic formula. Choose one or more ingredients from any of the following categories and use the recipes in this section as examples:

Base: tofu, soft-cooked beans, starchy vegetables such as sweet potatoes
Savory Seasonings: roasted or raw garlic, herbs and spices—fresh or dried
Piquancy: mustard, grated fresh ginger, chopped onion, lemon juice, vinegar
Salt: sea salt, miso, tamari, Bragg Liquid Aminos, umeboshi plum paste
Richness: nut butter, toasted sesame oil, olive oil, toasted ground nuts or seeds
Hint of Sweetness: maple, rice or barley malt syrup, pureed sweet vegetables
Liquid for Thinning: water, vegetable stock, fruit or vegetable juice

Ideally, the blending is done when the ingredients are at room temperature, when their flavors are closest to what they'll be when you serve the final product. Just add seasonings as you go, tasting along the way, until you achieve the balance of flavors you're looking for. For the smoothest possible spread, use a blender rather than a food processor.

And there's no need to get fancy. Try pulsing some organic pinto or black beans in the blender with grated carrot and celery, a chili pepper, and just enough salt or tamari soy sauce to bring out the flavors. Sometimes the simplest preparations are the most delicious, particularly when the ingredients are high quality and prepared with love.

I love to grow things, to get my hands in the earth. It's the only thing that keeps you sane in this world.

—Lou Tenenbaum, organic home gardener,
Boulder, Colorado

Carrot-Almond Butter

This heavenly spread, created by Meredith McCarty, is nice to serve for breakfast, brunch, or as a snack on crackers or whole grain bread.

2 cups sliced carrots, steamed until fork-tender, then cooled
2 tablespoons almond butter
1½ teaspoons tamari soy sauce
¼ teaspoon sea salt

1. Place the carrots in a blender (preferable for a smoother spread) or food processor and puree with the almond butter, tamari, and salt, gradually adding a bit of water or carrot cooking liquid, if needed, to create a spreadable consistency. Adjust seasonings to taste.

2. Use immediately or refrigerate in a tightly sealed container for up to 5 days.

Sweet Potato Butter

A simple variation of Carrot-Almond Butter (above) resulting in a distinctly sweeter spread.

1½ cups mashed sweet potato
2 tablespoons peanut or almond butter
1 to 2 tablespoons maple syrup
⅛ teaspoon freshly grated nutmeg
Pinch sea salt

1. By hand or in a blender, combine all of the ingredients, adding maple syrup to taste.

2. Use immediately or refrigerate in a well-sealed container for up to 3 days.

3. Serve at room temperature.

Mushroom Spread

I discovered the sublime pairing of mushrooms with leeks while writing my first cookbook, *To the King's Taste*, which was based on fourteenth-century English recipes. Back then I was fond of saying that this was a match made in heaven, but now I know better: It's a match made in our good earth.

The same recipe makes an elegant vegetable side dish when you slice the mushrooms and leeks. To make a spread, the mushrooms and leeks are finely chopped and then cooked down to a coarse puree.

The amounts given here produce 2 to 3 small servings, but you can always double the quantities. Serve the spread warm or at room temperature on whole grain crackers or warm pita bread cut into small triangles.

Standard stovetop: 5 to 10 minutes

1 to 2 tablespoons olive oil
1 cup coarsely chopped leeks (white part only)
1 large clove garlic, peeled and finely chopped
¾ pound mushrooms, wiped clean and coarsely chopped
½ teaspoon dried leaf oregano
½ teaspoon sea salt
Plenty of freshly ground black pepper
1 to 2 tablespoons freshly squeezed lemon juice
¼ teaspoon prepared horseradish or ½ teaspoon prepared mustard

1. In a large skillet, heat the oil. Sauté the leeks and garlic for 2 minutes, stirring frequently.

2. Add the mushrooms, oregano, salt, and black pepper. Reduce the heat slightly and continue to cook, stirring occasionally, until the mushrooms are cooked and their liquid has evaporated, about 5 to 10 minutes.

3. Puree in a blender or food processor and stir in lemon juice and horseradish to taste.

Variation: Before pureeing, this combination makes a fine filling for turnovers (page 206); if necessary, you can stretch the amount by blending in some mashed tofu and additional seasonings.

White Bean–Horseradish Spread

Makes 1¼ cups

The tantalizing idea of blending cooked pureed beans with horseradish comes from Elizabeth Schneider's classic *Uncommon Fruits and Vegetables: A Common Sense Guide*.

I can't think of a better way to transform a batch of forlorn-looking cooked beans into a sophisticated and complex taste treat. White beans, with their delicate taste and sweetness, work best.

Serve the spread on mild-tasting crackers or bread. It's also nice to use the spread as a stuffing for celery or seeded cucumber boats cut into 2-inch lengths.

> *2 cups soft-cooked beans, such as navy, cannellini, or Great Northern*
> *2 tablespoons olive oil*
> *2 teaspoons prepared horseradish, approximately (see Cook's Notes)*
> *½ to ¾ teaspoon dried rosemary leaves*
> *Scant ½ teaspoon sea salt (if beans are unsalted)*
> *Bean cooking liquid or water*

1. Combine ingredients (using ½ teaspoon rosemary) in a blender or food processor and pulse until well blended, scraping down the sides once or twice. Add a few teaspoons of bean cooking liquid or water, if necessary, to achieve a spreading consistency.

2. Taste the mixture and add more rosemary, if desired (the rosemary flavor will intensify on standing).

3. Transfer to a small bowl and serve, or refrigerate in a tightly sealed container until needed, up to 4 days. Bring to room temperature and add more horseradish, if necessary, before serving.

Cook's Notes: The amount of horseradish will depend on the flavor of the beans, the freshness of the horseradish, and your personal taste. Two teaspoons worked well for the mild navy beans I used when working out this recipe.

Variations

- For a different taste sensation, omit the rosemary and substitute mustard for the horseradish. Start with 1 teaspoon of mustard and add more as needed.
- To make an unusual dip, thin the spread slightly with additional bean cooking liquid or water.

Hummus

Toasted sesame tahini gives this traditional Middle Eastern preparation an espe-cially rich flavor. Serve it with raw vegetables as a dip, or on rice cakes or crackers as a spread.

For lunch or a light warm-weather dinner, stuff hummus into warmed pita-bread halves with grated carrots, shredded lettuce, or fresh alfalfa sprouts on top.

3 cups soft-cooked chick-peas, drained (reserve cooking liquid)
2 to 3 large cloves roasted garlic (page 425), peeled, or 2 to 3 small cloves
*   raw garlic, peeled and finely chopped*
3 tablespoons sesame tahini, preferably toasted
1 tablespoon fruity olive oil
3 to 4 tablespoons fresh lemon juice
½ teaspoon ground cumin
½ teaspoon ground coriander
Dash cayenne (ground red) pepper
1 teaspoon sea salt, or ½ teaspoon sea salt and ½ teaspoon umeboshi plum
*   vinegar (very yummy!)*
¼ to ⅔ cup chick-pea cooking liquid, vegetable stock, or water

GARNISHES
½ teaspoon sweet paprika
2 tablespoons minced fresh parsley
6 to 8 oil-cured black olives

1. Remove and discard any loose chick-pea skins.

2. In a food processor or blender, puree the chick-peas with the garlic, tahini, olive oil, 3 tablespoons lemon juice, spices, and salt.

3. Thin to a spreadable consistency by blending in the chick-pea cooking liquid.

4. Taste and add more lemon juice, if desired.

5. Transfer hummus to a serving bowl and sprinkle on paprika. Strew the parsley around the edges and garnish with the olives.

Cook's Notes: Hummus can be refrigerated for up to 3 days in a tightly sealed container. Perk it up with additional lemon juice, if needed, before serving.

Variations
- Instead of using the olives as a garnish, pit and chop them and stir them into the hummus after it is pureed.
- Stir in ⅓ cup finely chopped, oil-marinated sun-dried tomatoes.

Sunny Lentil Spread

A spread that is reminiscent of a French country pâté. My favorite way to serve it is on ¼-inch thick slices of crunchy white daikon radish or peeled cucumber instead of on crackers or whole grain bread. It also makes a great sandwich filling combined with lettuce or sprouts and a dab of mustard.

Make the pâté when the lentils are still warm and will more readily absorb flavors. For a coarse puree, pulse the mixture in the food processor; for a smooth puree, use the blender.

2 cups cooked lentils, preferably still warm
¼ cup toasted sunflower seeds
¼ to ½ teaspoon dried leaf oregano
½ to 2 teaspoons Dijon mustard, to taste
3 to 4 teaspoons white or red wine vinegar
2 to 4 tablespoons water or lentil cooking liquid (optional)
Umeboshi plum vinegar or sea salt to taste

1. In a food processor or blender, combine the lentils, sunflower seeds, and the smaller quantities of oregano, mustard, and vinegar, adding liquid, if needed, to achieve a spreadable consistency.

2. Add umeboshi vinegar or salt to taste and additional seasonings until you achieve the desired balance of flavors.

3. Use immediately or refrigerate in an airtight container for up to 4 days.

Southwest Pinto Spread

Makes about 2 cups

My sister Marian, who lives in Seattle, sent me this recipe—just one example of how much the flavors of the Southwest are beloved beyond their borders. She doesn't toast the spices first. She just tosses them into the blender with the beans and uses raw garlic instead of roasted. (I find raw garlic overpowering.)

Marian often doubles this recipe to use the spread as a filling for rolled-up tortillas or chapatis a few days in a row. Some chunks of avocado, sprouts, chopped scallions, or black olives can be added as the spirit moves you. This spread can be served on small rectangles of bread or as a dip for tortilla chips.

¾ teaspoon whole cumin seeds (see Cook's Notes)
¾ teaspoon coriander seeds (see Cook's Notes)
1 teaspoon dried leaf oregano
¾ teaspoon sweet paprika
2½ cups soft-cooked pinto or red kidney beans
4 large cloves roasted garlic (page 425), peeled, or 1 to 2 small cloves raw
  garlic, peeled
2 to 3 tablespoons lime or lemon juice
¼ to ½ cup bean cooking liquid or water
Sea salt or tamari soy sauce to taste
Hot sauce (optional)

GARNISH
Paprika and pumpkin seeds or spicy pepitas (if serving as a spread)

1. Heat a small, heavy skillet, preferably cast iron. Toast the cumin and coriander over medium-high heat, stirring constantly, until the cumin begins to turn brown, about 5 seconds. Turn off the heat and add the oregano and paprika, stirring constantly until the paprika turns brown. (This will happen almost instantly.)

2. Immediately transfer the spices to a grinder or a mortar and pestle. Cool slightly, then grind into a powder.

3. Put the ground spices, beans, garlic, 2 tablespoons lime juice, and ¼ cup cooking liquid into a blender or food processor and process to a smooth puree. (You can also mash the beans and the remaining ingredients with a fork to create a coarse puree.)

4. Taste and add more lime juice, liquid, and salt as needed to create vibrant flavor and a spreadable consistency. Sprinkle in some hot sauce, if desired.

5. If serving as a spread, transfer to a small bowl and sprinkle lightly with paprika and some pumpkin seeds.

Cook's Notes: If you do not want to toast the whole spices first, you can use ½ teaspoon each ground cumin and coriander.

Tahini-Miso Spread

Makes ½ cup

This simple spread is one of the most delicious and long-lasting. Miso's salty and assertive taste makes the spread terrific to serve on hearty whole grain bread. The flavors have immediate appeal—even to newcomers to whole foods cuisine. A thin layer is all you need as a little goes a long way.

I also like to thin this spread with a little water to make a sauce for just-cooked brown rice and pasta.

½ cup sesame tahini (toasted tahini is nice), at room temperature
1 to 2 tablespoons miso, at room temperature

1. In a small storage container with a tight-fitting lid, blend the tahini and enough miso to create a flavorful, lightly salted spread.

2. Refrigerate, well sealed, for up to 1 month.

Cook's Notes: For information on miso, see Ingredients A to Z.

Variations
- Combine two different types of miso, perhaps blond and dark.
- Add 1 to 3 teaspoons freshly grated ginger.

There is no limit to what can be accomplished so long as it does not matter who gets the credit.

—Miguel de Cervantes

Skordalia

A rich and sophisticated version of a Greek spread and dip. Walnuts are the secret ingredient, adding luscious flavor and texture. The dip tastes even better the second day after the flavors have had a chance to converse. You may find that it takes on a slightly pinkish hue (for reasons that remain mysterious—to me, at least).

Skordalia makes a lovely sandwich spread or tortilla filling as well as a great dip for raw vegetables. Put a dollop on a mound of cooked greens for a perfect finishing touch.

> *2 cups soft-cooked small white beans, such as baby limas, cannellini, or French navies*
> *4 to 6 large cloves roasted garlic (page 425), peeled, or 1 to 2 large cloves raw garlic, pushed through a press*
> *2 tablespoons olive oil*
> *2 to 3 tablespoons lemon juice*
> *¼ to ½ teaspoon sea salt*
> *4 to 6 tablespoons bean cooking liquid, vegetable stock, or water*
> *¼ cup finely chopped walnuts*

GARNISHES
Additional olive oil (optional)
2 tablespoons finely chopped fresh parsley
6 to 8 olives, preferably Greek Kalamatas

1. Mash the beans together with 4 cloves of roasted garlic (or 1 to 2 cloves raw garlic), olive oil, 2 tablespoons lemon juice, ¼ teaspoon salt, and enough liquid to achieve a coarse puree (see Cook's Notes).

2. Blend in the walnuts and additional garlic, lemon juice, and salt to taste.

3. Transfer to a shallow serving bowl. Drizzle with a bit more olive oil, if desired, and garnish with parsley and olives. Serve warm or at room temperature.

Cook's Notes: You can pulse the ingredients in a food processor, but avoid over-processing or the skordalia becomes gummy. I find the mixture is too thick to puree effectively in a blender.

Babaghanoush (Eggplant Dip)

Makes 1½ to 2 cups

Traditionally, a delightfully smoky-tasting babaghanoush is made by first roasting the eggplant whole, then peeling and pureeing it. My neighbor Judy Bloom, uses steamed eggplant for a tasty version of the traditional dip. Her method is fast, and the results are delicious.

Standard stovetop: 3 to 5 minutes

1½ pounds white or purple eggplant, peeled and cut into 1½-inch chunks
¼ cup sesame tahini
¼ cup freshly squeezed lemon juice
⅓ cup tightly packed minced fresh parsley
2 large cloves roasted garlic (page 425), peeled, or 1 to 2 small cloves raw garlic, peeled and finely chopped
Tamari soy sauce to taste

GARNISHES
6 oil-cured olives
Whole wheat breadsticks or pita triangles
2 tablespoons finely minced fresh parsley

1. Set a steaming basket into a 2-quart saucepan or place a rack in the pressure cooker. Add 1 cup of water. Bring the water to the boil and set the eggplant in the basket.

2. Cover the pot (but don't lock the lid if using a pressure cooker) and steam until the eggplant is fork-tender, about 3 to 5 minutes.

3. Transfer the eggplant to a food processor or blender. Add the remaining ingredients and puree.

4. Serve in a bowl, warm or at room temperature, garnished with olives, breadsticks, and parsley.

Sun-Dried Tomato Dip

Judy Bloom also gets credit for this recipe—and rave reviews every time.

Silken tofu, with its creamy texture and bland taste, makes an ideal base. The intense flavor of the sun-dried tomatoes and the tartness of the lemon juice create a striking balance.

This dip tastes best when made with fresh basil, but parsley and coriander are fine alternatives.

½ pound silken tofu
¼ cup minced sun-dried tomatoes, marinated in olive oil
1 large clove roasted garlic (page 425), peeled, or 1 small clove raw garlic,
  peeled and finely minced
1 tablespoon olive oil (use the oil from the sun-dried tomatoes)
¼ cup tightly packed minced fresh basil, parsley, or coriander
1 to 3 tablespoons fresh lemon juice
Sea salt to taste

GARNISH
1 to 2 tablespoons finely minced basil, parsley, or coriander

1. Puree all of the ingredients (using 1 tablespoon lemon juice) in a blender or food processor. Add more lemon juice, if desired.

2. Transfer to a bowl. Garnish with fresh herbs.

3. Serve immediately or refrigerate in a tightly sealed container for up to 4 days. After the first day, taste before serving and add more fresh lemon juice, if needed, to perk up the flavors.

Brilliant Beet Dip

My friend and talented colleague Pat Baird created this dip. It is made in a flash, dramatic to behold, and very tasty. Serve it with lightly steamed broccoli and cauliflower florets or raw mushrooms and green or yellow squash slices.

4 small (1 pound) beets, soft-cooked, peeled, and cut into chunks
4 ounces soft tofu, drained
1 to 2 tablespoons apple cider vinegar
2 tablespoons minced shallots
½ teaspoon dry mustard
½ teaspoon dried thyme
½ teaspoon dried tarragon
Sea salt to taste

1. Puree the ingredients (using 1 tablespoon vinegar) in a food processor or blender until smooth.
2. Adjust the seasonings, adding more vinegar and salt to taste.
3. Serve immediately or refrigerate in a tightly sealed container for up to 3 days.

Variation: Heat the dip and thin it slightly with vegetable stock to create a tasty pasta sauce or a topping for cooked grains.

There may be some grand, sacrificial, heroic answer, but the best answers I know are almost trivial. Environmental problems are caused by billions of small, unthinking actions. They'll be cured by billions of small, sensible actions, simple substitutions of environmentally conscious habits for thoughtless and wasteful ones.

—*Annals of Earth*, Vol. VII, No. 1, 1989.

Quick Aioli

Makes about 1 cup

Aioli is a homemade garlic mayonnaise that is a specialty of the South of France. I felt slightly sacrilegious using soy mayonnaise to create this version, but repentance leaped out the window as soon as I had a taste. (Commercial soy mayonnaise is not as delicious as a made-from-scratch, egg-based version, but adding lots of roasted garlic to it will make most people quite happy—especially cholesterol watchers.)

Aioli is traditionally served with a large bowl of raw and cooked vegetables in season—try zucchini, broccoli, fennel, or cherry tomatoes in summer, serve it with boiled potatoes, turnips, or beets in winter.

1 cup prepared soy mayonnaise
6 large cloves roasted garlic (page 425), peeled and mashed, or 3 small
cloves raw garlic, peeled and minced (these must be absolutely
fresh and unblemished)
1 to 2 tablespoons lemon juice
2 to 3 teaspoons Dijon mustard, preferably coarse-grained

GARNISHES
A few sprinklings of sweet paprika
Cooked and raw vegetables in season

1. Blend the ingredients thoroughly and place in a small bowl.
2. Sprinkle with paprika, and surround with raw and cooked vegetables in season.

Variation: Thinned with water or tomato juice, aioli makes a tasty garlicky dressing for greens and grain salads.

Quick Breads, Biscuits, Muffins, and Scones

Leavened by baking powder rather than yeast, quick breads can be prepared from start to finish in well under an hour. When made with whole grain flours, they become healthful snacks and welcome additions to any meal. Since they freeze very well, I'm rarely without a muffin or scone at arm's reach—a great boon for me and unexpected guests.

For those of us accustomed to eating muffins made with eggs, butter, and white flour, dairy-free whole grain baked goods take a bit of getting used to. For one thing, they are tannish-brown rather than white. For another, they might be described as hearty rather than light.

To this day, the first bite of a barley muffin occasionally surprises me with its intense flavor and dense texture. But once beyond that first bite, I settle down to a very happy eating experience. I've discovered that since I've become accustomed to the wholesome flavors and textures of whole grain flours, more refined baked goods are no longer satisfying. In addition to seeming too sweet and rich, they now have a noticeable chemical aftertaste. Commercial baked goods no longer taste like real food.

If you're just getting used to the texture of whole grain baked goods, feel free to substitute 25 to 50 percent of unbleached white flour for any of the whole grain flours called for in these recipes. The result will be both a milder taste and a lighter texture. As time goes on, gradually decrease the amount of unbleached flour.

Purchasing and Storing Whole Grain Flour

Most of us are in the habit of storing refined white flour on our pantry shelves indefinitely, but whole grain flours require different treatment.

Once whole grains are ground into flour (thereby exposing the endosperm and oil-rich germ to the air), the nutrients slowly begin to diminish and the flour itself begins to get rancid. In the best of all possible worlds, we would all own home food mills and grind flour fresh each time we bake. In reality, few of us have the time or inclination to be millers. (However, a mail-order source called Gold Mine will grind whole wheat flour by request; see page 475.)

The next best thing is to keep the following in mind:

1. If possible, buy whole grain flours from stores that refrigerate them. Failing that, shop where there is a steady turnover, or use reliable mail-order sources.
2. At home, store whole grain flours in the freezer, where they will last approximately 4 months.
3. Grind small grains or grain flakes into flour at home as needed in a spice or coffee grinder. Whole millet, quinoa, buckwheat, rolled oats, kamut, soy, and barley flakes are good candidates.

What follows is a brief description of some of the flours now distributed nationally:

Whole Wheat Pastry Flour: Finely ground, it's closest in taste and texture to unbleached white flour, but because it contains some of the bran and germ, it creates a heavier texture. (Don't confuse whole wheat *pastry* flour with whole wheat flour, which is made from a different type of wheat and contains more gluten and bran. It is also more coarsely milled.)

Triticale, Kamut, and Spelt Flour: Similar in taste and texture to whole wheat flour, kamut and spelt have proven to be excellent alternatives for people who have sensitivities to wheat. All three flours can be used interchangeably with whole wheat pastry flour, but result in a slightly denser product.

Barley Flour: Next best in terms of light flavor and texture, barley is a good substitute for any of the unusual flours called for in the recipes.

Blue Cornmeal: A blue-gray flour with a delicate sweet taste; it creates a much more finely textured product than yellow cornmeal.

Yellow Cornmeal: This has a full-flavored corn taste, adds coarse and dense texture, and drinks up more liquid than most other flours.

Oat Flour: It has a sweet and pleasing flavor, creates a slightly denser and moister product.

Brown Rice Flour: It has a faintly nutty flavor and a sandy texture.

Soy Flour: Heavy but, used in small quantities, this flour adds a sweet taste and hearty texture and boosts the protein value of baked goods.

Onion Upside-Down Cornbread

Serves 6 to 8

Lots of onions are browned with slivered red pepper in a large cast-iron skillet, then the cornbread batter is poured on top and baked. Flip over the pie wedges as you serve them to reveal the flavorful topping.

Oven: 20 to 25 minutes at 375°

1 tablespoon corn or canola oil
2 large onions, peeled and thinly sliced
¼ teaspoon dried thyme or dried leaf oregano
1 small red bell pepper, seeded and cut into thin strips
1 cup uncooked corn kernels
1½ cups yellow cornmeal
1½ cups whole wheat pastry flour
1 tablespoon double-acting nonaluminum baking powder, such as
    Rumford
1 teaspoon baking soda
½ to ¾ teaspoon sea salt
¾ teaspoon cracked pepper (see Cook's Notes)
Dash cayenne (ground red) pepper (optional)
1¼ cups vegetable stock or water
⅔ cup (4 ounces) mashed soft tofu
Additional ⅓ cup corn or canola oil
2 tablespoons barley malt syrup, measured from an oiled spoon
1 tablespoon apple cider vinegar

   1. In an 8- or 10-inch skillet, heat the oil. Sauté the onions until they are deeply browned, stirring frequently over medium-high heat, about 8 to 10 minutes. Stir in the thyme, red pepper, and corn kernels. Set aside.

   2. In a large bowl, combine the cornmeal, flour, baking powder, baking soda, salt, cracked pepper, and cayenne (if using).

   3. In a food processor, combine the stock, tofu, oil, barley malt syrup, and vinegar, and spin until the liquid is frothy, about 2 minutes.

continued

4. Stir this liquid into the dry ingredients, just until all of the flour is absorbed.

5. Pour the batter over the onions and bake on the middle shelf of an oven preheated to 375° until the top springs back to a gentle touch and a skewer inserted into the center comes out without crumbs attached, about 20 to 25 minutes.

Cook's Notes: To crack pepper, place whole peppercorns into a spice grinder and pulse until the pepper is very coarsely ground. Freeze extra tofu for future use, or use it to make a dip such as Sun-Dried Tomato Dip (page 318).

Variations
- Add ⅓ cup pitted, chopped green olives to the browned onions.
- Stir a cup of cooked, chopped kale or collards into the browned onions.
- Add 1 cup grated carrot to the batter to create a slightly moister cornbread with pretty flecks of orange.

Crunchy Rye-Barley Flatbread

Makes about sixteen
1½-inch squares

In less than an hour from start to finish you can have savory flatbread to use as a base for the spreads on pages 309–316. It's also great on its own with soups and stews. Serve warm or at room temperature.

Oven: 16 to 20 minutes at 375°

¼ teaspoon oil for greasing a cookie sheet
1½ cups rye flour, plus about 2 to 3 tablespoons
¾ cup barley flour
2 teaspoons double-acting, nonaluminum baking powder, such as
*   Rumford*
2 teaspoons poppy seeds
2 teaspoons toasted sesame seeds
¾ teaspoon sea salt
2 teaspoons finely minced garlic
½ cup finely chopped red onion (see Cook's Notes)
3 tablespoons olive oil
⅓ to ⅔ cup water

1. Lightly brush the oil onto a cookie sheet.

2. Combine rye flour with the barley flour, baking powder, poppy and sesame seeds, and salt. Stir in the garlic, onion, oil, and enough water to create a dough that will hold the shape of a ball when firmly pressed.

3. Knead the dough 5 times and form it into a roughly rectangular shape. (If you've added too much water and the dough sticks to your fingers, knead in a bit more rye flour, but take care not to overwork the dough.)

4. On a lightly floured board, roll out the dough into a rectangle about ¼ inch thick. If the dough is too sticky to roll, sprinkle flour on the top and rub some onto the rolling pin.

5. Using a spatula, lift up the dough and transfer it to the cookie sheet.

6. Bake in an oven preheated to 375° until the bottom is lightly browned, about 16 to 20 minutes. (Do not overbake or the flatbread will dry out.)

7. Cool on the cookie sheet on a rack for 10 minutes. With a serrated knife, cut flatbread into 1½-inch squares. Serve warm or at room temperature.

Cook's Notes: To keep the onions from getting mushy, chop them by hand or use the pulsing action of a food processor.

Variation: Add ½ teaspoon of dried herbs, such as rosemary or oregano.

Biscuits

If you have never made biscuits, you're going to be amazed at how quick and simple it is to turn out these wholesome treats.

There's only one way in which biscuits are standoffish: They don't like receiving excessive attention—too much kneading activates the gluten in the flour, making the biscuits tough. Knead the dough just until it holds together enough to be rolled. Then, if you don't mind unconventionally shaped biscuits, cut the rolled dough into squares rather than circles. This eliminates the need to press together and reroll scraps.

Biscuits are in top form when they are freshly baked, but they can be refrigerated for up to 3 days or frozen for up to 3 months. I usually serve them plain when they're fresh. Reheated leftover biscuits are best when served with spreads or turned into mini-sandwiches.

Sesame Biscuits

Makes about eighteen
2½-inch biscuits

For an unusual treat, split these savory biscuits open and slather with White Bean–Horseradish Spread (page 311).

Oven: 14 to 16 minutes at 425°

Oil for greasing a cookie sheet
2¼ to 2½ cups whole wheat pastry flour
½ cup soy flour or unbleached white flour (for a lighter biscuit)
3 tablespoons toasted sesame seeds
¾ teaspoon sea salt
1 tablespoon double-acting, nonaluminum baking powder, such as
*   Rumford*
½ cup plus 2 tablespoons water
⅓ cup light (untoasted) sesame or canola oil
2 tablespoons barley malt syrup, measured from an oiled spoon

1. Brush the oil on a cookie sheet and set aside.

2. In a large bowl, combine 2¼ cups whole wheat flour with the soy flour, sesame seeds, salt, and baking powder.

3. In a food processor or blender, combine the water, oil, and barley malt. Pour the liquid into the dry ingredients and stir to create a soft dough.

4. Sprinkle some of the remaining flour onto a flat surface and rub some onto your palms and onto a rolling pin. Knead the dough to a consistency that can easily be rolled, working in additional flour if required until dough is no longer sticky. (Kneading about 12 to 15 times should do it. Try not to overwork the dough; the less handling, the lighter the biscuit.)

5. At this point you can choose to lightly roll out the dough to the thickness of ½ inch and cut biscuits with a 2½-inch biscuit cutter or glass. Lightly press scraps together (like the pieces of a jigsaw puzzle) or reroll them and cut additional biscuits. You can also shape the dough into a square or rectangle that is ½-inch thick. With a serrated knife, cut the dough into 2½-inch squares. (The advantage of the latter method is that you don't have to keep rerolling the dough scraps, which tends to make the biscuits tough.)

6. Place the biscuits on the greased cookie sheet, either touching (for a soft-sided biscuit) or about ½ inch apart (for a biscuit with lightly browned sides), and bake in an oven preheated to 425° until lightly browned, about 14 to 16 minutes. Serve warm or transfer to a rack to cool for storage.

To the man who is truly ethical all life is sacred, including that which from the human point of view seems lower in the scale.

—Albert Schweitzer

Yam Biscuits

These biscuits are delicately sweet and pale orange—an unrecognizable transformation of a lonely leftover baked yam. Try this recipe only if you can use a garnet yam. Results with sweet potatoes and other varieties of yam are unpredictable.

Oven: 12 to 14 minutes at 425°

*Oil for greasing a cookie sheet
2 to 2¼ cups whole wheat pastry flour
½ cup soy flour or unbleached white flour (for a lighter biscuit)
1 tablespoon double-acting, nonaluminum baking powder, such as
    Rumford
¼ teaspoon sea salt
1 cup mashed garnet yam, at room temperature
⅓ cup canola oil
1 tablespoon maple syrup
Water if needed*

1. Brush the oil on a cookie sheet and set aside.

2. In a large bowl, combine 2 cups of whole wheat flour with the soy flour, baking powder, and salt.

3. In another bowl, thoroughly blend the mashed yam, oil, and maple syrup. Pour into the dry ingredients and stir until about ¾ of the flour is absorbed.

4. Transfer the mixture to a lightly floured board and knead about 15 to 20 times to create a soft dough, adding a few tablespoons of water, if the dough seems dry, or additional flour, if the dough seems sticky. (Whether you need to add extra water or flour depends upon the moisture content of the yam; the dough should be moist and pliable but not sticky. Try, however, not to overwork the dough; the less handling, the lighter the biscuit.)

5. Sprinkle a bit more flour onto the pastry board and rub some onto a rolling pin. At this point you can choose to lightly roll out the dough to a thickness of ½ inch and cut biscuits with a 2½-inch cutter or glass. Lightly press scraps together (like the pieces of a jigsaw puzzle) or reroll them to make additional biscuits.

Alternatively, you can shape the dough into a square or rectangle that is ½-inch thick. With a serrated knife, cut the dough into 2½-inch squares. (The advantage of the latter method is that you don't have to keep rerolling the dough scraps, which tends to make the muffins tough.)

6. Place the biscuits on the greased cookie sheet, either touching (for a soft-sided biscuit) or about ½ inch apart (for a biscuit lightly browned on the sides), and bake in an oven preheated to 425° until lightly browned, about 12 to 14 minutes. Serve warm or transfer to a rack to cool for storage.

Chive Biscuits

Flecked with bright green chives, these biscuits are great on their own or with Tahini-Miso Spread (page 315).

Oven: 12 to 14 minutes at 425°

Oil for greasing a cookie sheet
2¼ to 2½ cups whole wheat pastry flour
½ cup chick-pea flour, soy flour, or unbleached white flour (for a
*   lighter biscuit)*
1 tablespoon double-acting, nonaluminum baking powder, such as
*   Rumford*
1 teaspoon sea salt
½ teaspoon coarsely cracked pepper
¼ cup freeze-dried minced chives
⅓ cup olive oil
2 tablespoons barley malt syrup, measured from an oiled spoon
½ cup plus 2 tablespoons water, approximately

1. Brush oil on a cookie sheet and set aside.

2. In a large bowl, combine 2¼ cups whole wheat flour with the chick-pea flour, baking powder, salt, pepper, and chives.

3. In another bowl, thoroughly blend the oil, barley malt, and water. Pour this mixture into the dry ingredients and stir until about ¾ of the flour is absorbed. Transfer the mixture to a lightly floured board and knead about 15 to 20 times to create a soft dough, adding a few tablespoons water or additional flour if needed. (Whether you need to add extra water or flour is dependent upon the moisture content of the flour; the dough should be moist and pliable but not sticky. Do not overwork the dough; the less handling, the lighter the biscuit.)

4. Sprinkle a bit more flour onto the pastry board and rub some onto a rolling pin. At this point you can choose to lightly roll out the dough to a thickness of ½ inch and cut biscuits with a 2½-inch cutter or glass. Lightly press scraps together (like the pieces of a jigsaw puzzle) or reroll them to make additional biscuits.

Alternatively, you can shape the dough into a square or rectangle that is ½-inch thick. With a serrated knife, cut the dough into 2½-inch squares. (The advantage of the latter method is that you don't have to keep rerolling the dough scraps, which tends to make the muffins tough.)

5. Place the biscuits on the greased cookie sheet, either touching (for a soft-sided biscuit) or about ½ inch apart (for a biscuit with lightly browned sides), and bake in an oven preheated to 425° until lightly browned, about 12 to 14 minutes. Serve warm or transfer to a rack to cool for storage.

Muffins and Scones

In recent years, we have been experiencing a serious case of muffin mania. Many people eat a muffin for breakfast and think they're having something healthful, but in truth most commercial and bakery varieties are no more nutritious than a piece of cake.

My defense against muffin mania is to make my own. This way, when the irresistible urge strikes, I can satisfy it with whole grain treats that have a limited amount of oil and contain only natural sweeteners.

In this chapter you'll find both sweet and savory muffins. The sweet resemble the type you're probably accustomed to having for breakfast or a midmorning snack. Savory muffins are meant to be served with soup or as a substitute for bread. They also make a wholesome snack and, since they contain very little sweetener, will keep you off the sugar roller-coaster.

Although the texture of these muffins and scones is very pleasing, it is somewhat more crumbly than that of a commercial muffin. To transport them, use a firm-sided container rather than a bag.

Most of the recipes here take only about 20 minutes to prepare (not including baking time). You can speed up the process by mixing two or three batches of the dry ingredients at once and freezing them in separate containers. Then just add the liquid ingredients before you are ready to bake.

Muffins Versus Scones

During the course of developing recipes for this book, I often ended up with leftover batter and no available muffin tins. As an experiment, I plopped a few tablespoons of the batter on cookie sheets and baked drop scones along with the muffins. To my surprise, the scones often had a much better texture than the muffins. And their rustic shape was very appealing.

You can use any of the muffin batters to make scones, or you can split a batch of batter and make half scones and half muffins. Keep in mind, though, that scones require 3 to 4 minutes less baking time. Also, when baking two cookie sheets of scones at the same time, place them next to each other, or switch shelf positions after 10 minutes to assure that both batches bake evenly.

Tips on Muffin Making

- When mixing the dry ingredients, break up any small lumps of baking powder or soda, which will taste bitter if eaten in concentrated form.
- Mix the liquid and dry ingredients just until there are no visible lumps of dry flour; overmixing makes the muffins tough.
- For added lightness, spin the liquid ingredients in a food processor until foamy before adding to the dry ingredients. Preheat the oven and bake the

muffins as soon as you combine the liquid and dry ingredients and fill the muffin cups. (The baking powder starts acting as soon as it makes contact with a liquid.)

- Fill the muffin cups almost to the top with batter, but don't mound the batter beyond the top.
- If you have any leftover batter, make drop scones by dropping about ⅓ cup of batter for each scone on a greased cookie sheet. Bake until the bottoms are golden and the tops spring back to a gentle touch, about 14 to 16 minutes.
- These recipes were tested in muffin cups measuring 1 inch deep and 2¾ inches wide across the top. For smaller muffin cups, check for doneness 2 to 3 minutes before the recommended baking time. The yield will be slightly larger than indicated.
- Set the muffins on the *middle* shelf of the oven for even baking. If using two muffin tins, set them both on the same shelf, if possible.
- Cool the muffins on a rack in their tins for the time directed in each recipe, then unmold by running a knife around the edge and tipping them out. Muffins continue to cook and steam while in the tins. This improves the texture of some muffins, but makes others too moist. If the muffins are too doughy, try splitting them open and toasting them.
- Most muffins taste best warm. Reheat any that are left over.
- Cool muffins completely before refrigerating them in a well-sealed container (up to 1 week) or freezing them (up to 4 months).

Sweeten to Taste

The recipes that follow are fairly sweet, but not quite as sweet as commercial baked goods. If you prefer them sweeter, simply reduce the liquid by the number of tablespoons of sweetener you've added. For example, if you add 2 tablespoons of maple syrup, deduct 2 tablespoons of liquid. On the other hand, if you want to reduce the amount of sweetener, increase the liquid accordingly.

The Flax Seed Story

All of the muffin and scone recipes in this chapter call for an unusual ingredient—flax seeds. Here's how it came about:

Many recipes for eggless baked goods call for tofu as a binding agent. (Eggs both bind and aerate batter, which creates a light and pleasing texture.) However, I found that tofu made a very dense and heavy product with a recognizably "health food" taste.

I had read about using flax seeds as an egg substitute in an imaginative whole grain baking book called *Uprisings*. At first the idea seemed very strange, but after a series of tofu-based muffins that could have doubled for hockey pucks, I was desperate enough to try.

Meanwhile, I had learned that flax seeds' healing properties were well known to the ancients. In fact in Europe, prior to World War II, freshly pressed flax seed oil was delivered weekly to many homes and used regularly for its culinary and medicinal values. (Check Ingredients A to Z for details.)

In addition to lending a luscious richness to baked goods, when flax seeds are ground (in a spice mill or blender) and combined with water, the mixture develops a texture akin to egg whites. As a result, they bind the ingredients in the batter and provide a modest amount of leavening.

Please note: Because the oil in flax seeds easily goes rancid, it is *essential* to store the seeds in the freezer and grind them only as needed.

The Native American agricultural legacy is more than a few hardy, tasty cultigens waiting to be "cleaned up" genetically for consumers, and then commercialized as novelty foods. . . . These nutritious crops deserve to be revived as mainstays of human diets, and not treated as passing curiosities.

—Gary Naban, "Enduring Seeds," in Robert Clark, ed.,
Our Sustainable Table (Berkeley: North Point Press, 1990).

Savory Blue Corn Muffins
Makes 12 to 16 muffins

If you've never used blue cornmeal before, you're in for a color surprise: The muffins turn out a characteristic blue-gray. But the lightness of the cornmeal and its great taste will make you look forward to seeing this color in your muffins again and again. Serve with bean soups or chili.

Oven: 16 to 20 minutes at 375°

Canola or safflower oil for greasing muffin tins
3 tablespoons flax seeds
½ cup water
2 cups whole wheat pastry flour
1½ cups finely ground blue cornmeal
1 tablespoon double-acting, nonaluminum baking powder, such as
*   Rumford*
¾ teaspoon sea salt
⅔ cup very finely minced onion
1 large clove garlic, peeled and very finely chopped
⅛ teaspoon cayenne (ground red) pepper (optional)
1 cup vegetable stock or water
⅓ cup corn or canola oil
2 tablespoons barley malt syrup, measured from an oiled spoon

1. Brush the oil onto the bottom and sides of the muffin cups. Set aside.

2. In a blender, grind the flax seeds. Add the water and process until you achieve a slightly gummy mixture, about 30 seconds. Set aside. (This process does not work quite as well with a food processor, but it can be done. First, grind the flax seeds in a spice or coffee grinder. Combine ground seeds with water in the bowl of the processor and spin until slightly thickened, about 60 to 90 seconds.) A third alternative is to whisk the mixture vigorously by hand about 100 times.

3. In a large bowl, combine the flours, baking powder, salt, onion, garlic, and cayenne (if using).

continued

4. Add the stock, oil, and barley malt to the flax seed mixture and process until well blended and frothy, about 1 minute.

5. Stir this mixture into the dry ingredients, just until all of the flour is absorbed. (Do not overwork the batter or the muffins will be tough.)

6. Spoon the batter almost to the top of each oiled muffin cup. (If there is any leftover batter, see Tips on Muffin Making, page 331.) Bake the muffins on the middle shelf of an oven preheated to 375° until the tops are lightly browned and bounce back to a gentle touch, and a skewer inserted in the center comes out clean, about 16 to 20 minutes.

7. Run a knife along the edge of each muffin and pop it out of the tin onto a cooling rack. Serve warm or cool completely before storing for future use.

Curried Brown Rice Muffins   Makes 12 to 16 muffins

This recipe creates moist, slightly chewy, savory muffins with an intriguing mustard color. The muffins can be served instead of bread for lunch or dinner, and are a great accompaniment for soups.

Oven: 18 to 20 minutes at 375°

Canola or safflower oil for greasing muffin tins
½ cup sunflower seeds
3 tablespoons flax seeds
½ cup water
2 cups brown rice flour
1 cup whole wheat pastry flour
2 tablespoons double-acting, nonaluminum baking powder, such as
    Rumford
1 teaspoon baking soda
2 tablespoons mild curry powder (see Cook's Notes)
1 teaspoon freshly grated ginger or ¼ teaspoon ground ginger
¼ teaspoon turmeric
1 teaspoon whole cumin seeds (to release flavor, rub the seeds between your
    fingers into the bowl)
½ teaspoon sea salt
1 cup cooked brown rice (see Cook's Notes)
¾ cup vegetable stock or water
⅓ cup canola oil
3 tablespoons barley malt syrup, measured from an oiled spoon

1. Brush oil onto the bottom and sides of the muffin cups and set aside.

2. While the oven is preheating, toast the sunflower seeds in a pie plate in the oven until they are lightly browned, about 12 minutes. Stir the seeds and check every few minutes to avoid burning them. When done, transfer the seeds to a small bowl to halt the toasting process.

3. In a blender, grind the flax seeds. Add the water and process until you achieve a slightly gummy mixture, about 30 seconds. Set aside. (This process does not work quite as well with a food processor, but it can be done. First, grind the flax seeds in a spice or coffee grinder. Combine with water in the bowl of the processor and spin until slightly thickened, about 60 to 90 seconds.) A third alternative is to whisk the mixture vigorously by hand about 100 times.

4. In a bowl, combine the flours, toasted sunflower seeds, baking powder, baking soda, spices, and salt. Stir in the brown rice, making sure that the grains are coated with flour and do not lump together.

5. To the flax seed mixture, add the stock, canola oil, and barley malt, and process until the liquid is frothy, about 2 minutes. Stir the liquid into the dry ingredients, just until all of the flour is absorbed.

6. Fill each muffin cup almost to the brim with batter.

7. Bake on the middle shelf of an oven preheated to 375° until the tops are lightly browned and bounce back to a gentle touch, and a skewer inserted in the center comes out clean, about 18 to 20 minutes.

8. Let the muffins cool for about 2 minutes in the tins, then run a knife along the edges and carefully unmold them. Allow the muffins to cool slightly on a rack before serving, or cool thoroughly before storing for later use.

Cook's Notes: Fresh curry powder is critical to the success of this recipe. Sprinkle a bit on your finger and taste: If you detect any bitterness or if it is a very hot-and-spicy blend, buy a high-quality mild curry powder before making the muffins.

If your rice is moist and sticky, reduce the vegetable stock by 2 tablespoons to avoid an overly moist muffin.

Variation: For a delightful surprise inside, consider "stuffing" the muffins with a heaping teaspoon of well-seasoned beans such as Pat's Spicy Black-eyed Peas (page 178): Spoon a heaping tablespoon of batter into each muffin cup. Place a heaping teaspoon of beans on top, then cover the beans with enough additional batter to fill each muffin cup almost to the top. When checking the muffins for doneness, don't be tricked by the skewer coming out moist if it's been stuck into the beans.

The idea for "stuffing" muffins comes from my friend and muffin mentor Elizabeth Alston, author of a classic little volume appropriately named *Muffins*.

Chive-Flecked Barley Muffins   Makes 12 to 14 muffins

Freeze-dried chives are a convenient and winning addition to savory muffins—
they're full-flavored and team well with the robust taste of whole grain flours.

Oven: 18 to 20 minutes at 375°

Canola or safflower oil for greasing muffin tins
3 tablespoons flax seeds
½ cup water
2 cups whole wheat pastry flour
1 cup barley flour
1 tablespoon plus 1 teaspoon double-acting, nonaluminum baking powder,
*   such as Rumford*
1 teaspoon baking soda
¼ cup freeze-dried chives or finely chopped scallion greens
1½ teaspoons dried summer savory
¾ teaspoon sea salt
1 cup vegetable stock or water
¼ cup canola or safflower oil
2 tablespoons olive oil
2 tablespoons barley malt syrup, measured from an oiled spoon
1 tablespoon apple cider vinegar

1. Brush the oil onto the bottom and sides of the muffin cups and set aside.

2. In a blender, grind the flax seeds. Add the water and process until you
achieve a slightly gummy mixture, about 30 seconds. Set aside. (This process does
not work quite as well with a food processor, but it can be done. First, grind the
flax seeds in a spice or coffee grinder. Combine with water in the bowl of the
processor and spin until slightly thickened, about 60 to 90 seconds.) A third alternative is to whisk the mixture vigorously by hand about 100 times.

3. In a bowl, combine the flours, baking powder, baking soda, chives, savory,
and salt.

4. To the flax seed mixture, add the stock, canola and olive oils, barley malt,
and vinegar, and process until the liquid is frothy, about 2 minutes.

5. Stir this liquid into the dry ingredients, just until all of the flour is absorbed.

6. Spoon the batter almost to the top of each oiled muffin cup and bake on the
middle shelf of an oven preheated to 375° until the tops are lightly browned and
bounce back to a gentle touch, and a skewer inserted in the center comes out clean,
about 18 to 20 minutes.

7. Immediately unmold the muffins by running a knife along the edges and popping them out. Cool them on a rack briefly and eat them warm, or cool them thoroughly before storing for later use.

Crunchy 4-Grain Muffins   Makes 12 to 16 muffins

An especially delicious muffin to enjoy with soup or salad. The delightful crunch comes from toasted pumpkin seeds.

Oven: 16 to 18 minutes at 375°

Canola or safflower oil for greasing muffin tins
⅓ cup unsalted pumpkin or sunflower seeds
3 tablespoons flax seeds
½ cup water
2 cups whole wheat pastry flour
½ cup millet flour (see Cook's Notes)
½ cup brown rice flour
½ cup barley flour
1 tablespoon double-acting, nonaluminum baking powder, such as
*   Rumford*
1 teaspoon dried thyme or oregano
1 teaspoon sea salt
1 to 1¼ cups vegetable stock or water
¼ cup olive oil
¼ cup canola or safflower oil
2 tablespoons barley malt syrup, measured from an oiled spoon

1. Brush the oil lightly onto the bottom and sides of the muffin cups. Set aside.

2. While the oven is preheating, toast the pumpkin seeds in a pie plate in the oven until they are lightly browned, about 12 minutes. Stir the seeds and check every few minutes to avoid burning them. When done, transfer them to a small bowl to halt the toasting process.

3. In a blender, grind the flax seeds. Add the water and process until you achieve a slightly gummy mixture, about 30 seconds. Set aside. (This process does not work quite as well with a food processor, but it can be done. First, grind the flax seeds in a spice or coffee grinder. Combine with water in the bowl of the processor and spin until slightly thickened, about 60 to 90 seconds.) A third alternative is to whisk the mixture vigorously by hand about 100 times.

continued

4. In a large bowl, combine the four flours, toasted pumpkin seeds, baking powder, thyme, and salt.

5. To the flax seed mixture, add 1 cup stock, the oils, and barley malt, and process until well blended and frothy, about 2 minutes. Stir this mixture into the dry ingredients, just until all of the flour is absorbed, adding an extra ¼ cup of stock if the mixture seems very dry. (Do not overwork the batter or the muffins will be tough.)

6. Spoon the batter almost to the top of each oiled muffin cup. (If you have any extra batter, see Tips on Muffin Making, page 331.) Bake on the middle shelf of an oven preheated to 375° until a skewer inserted in the center comes out clean and the tops bounce back to a gentle touch, about 16 to 18 minutes.

7. Set the muffin tins on a rack and allow to cool for 2 to 3 minutes. Run a knife along the edge of each muffin and pop it out. Serve warm or cool completely before storing for future use.

Cook's Notes: It's a good idea to grind millet flour fresh, as it goes rancid quickly. Spin a heaping ½ cup whole grain millet in a spice or coffee grinder. If time permits, toast the millet first (page 89) to bring out a full-bodied flavor.

My grandmother used to say: Forget about that white bread. The life's been bleached out of it.

—Louise Frazier, biodynamic farmer and cook,
Housatonic, Massachusetts

Dulse Oatmeal Muffins

If you love the unique briny taste of dulse and enjoy a savory muffin, you'll love this recipe.

Oven: 18 to 22 minutes at 375°

Canola or safflower oil for greasing muffin tins
1 ounce dried dulse
¼ cup sesame seeds
3 tablespoons flax seeds
½ cup water
2½ cups whole wheat pastry flour
1 cup old-fashioned oatmeal (rolled oats)
1 tablespoon double-acting, nonaluminum baking powder, such as
*   Rumford*
1 teaspoon baking soda
2½ teaspoons freshly grated ginger
½ teaspoon sea salt
1 cup vegetable stock or water
⅓ cup canola or safflower oil
1 tablespoon barley malt syrup, measured from an oiled spoon
1 tablespoon apple cider vinegar

1. Brush oil onto the bottom and sides of the muffin cups. Set aside.

2. Snip the dulse with scissors into irregularly shaped 1-inch pieces. You should have about 2 cups of loosely packed dulse. Set the dulse in a fine-meshed strainer and quickly run water through it while stirring it with your fingers—just enough to remove any surface salt or sand and soften the dulse slightly, but not enough to make the dulse completely soggy. Set aside.

3. While the oven is preheating, toast the sesame seeds in a pie plate in the oven, until they turn a few shades darker in color and emit a toasted aroma, about 10 minutes. Stir and check for doneness every few minutes to avoid burning them. When seeds are done, transfer them to a bowl to halt the toasting process.

4. In a blender, grind the flax seeds. Add the water and process until you achieve a slightly gummy mixture, about 30 seconds. Set aside. (This process does not work quite as well with a food processor, but it can be done. First, grind the flax seeds in a spice or coffee grinder. Combine with water in the bowl of the processor and spin until slightly thickened, about 60 to 90 seconds.) A third alternative is to whisk the mixture vigorously by hand about 100 times.

continued

5. In a large bowl, combine the flour, oatmeal, toasted sesame seeds, baking powder, baking soda, ginger, and salt. Stir in the dulse.

6. To the flax seed mixture, add the stock, oil, barley malt, and vinegar, and process until well blended and frothy, about 2 minutes.

7. Stir this mixture into the dry ingredients, just until all of the flour is absorbed. (Do not overwork the batter or the muffins will be tough.)

8. Spoon the batter almost to the top of each oiled muffin cup. (If you have any extra batter, see Tips on Muffin Making, page 330.) Bake on the middle shelf of an oven preheated to 375° until the tops are lightly browned and bounce back to a gentle touch, about 18 to 22 minutes.

9. Set the muffin tins on a rack and allow the muffins to cool for 10 minutes. Run a knife along the edge of each muffin and pop it out. Serve warm or cool completely before storing for future use.

Food is not merely something sweet. It is a ceaseless reminder that we are mortal, earthbound, hungry, and in need. We are bound by a biological imperative that forever keeps us returning to the soil, plants, animals, and running water for replenishment. Eating is life. Each time we eat, the soul continues its earthly journey. With every morsel of food swallowed a voice within says, "I choose life. I choose to eat, for I yearn for something more."

—Marc David, *Nourishing Wisdom*
(New York: Bell Tower, 1991).

Zucchini Muffins

Makes 12 to 16 muffins

Children seem to adore these muffins. If you like yours spicy, go for the maximum amount of cinnamon and ginger.

Oven: 18 to 22 minutes at 375°

Canola or safflower oil for greasing muffin tins
1½ cups tightly packed, coarsely grated zucchini
3 tablespoons flax seeds
½ cup water
1½ cups whole wheat pastry flour
1 cup barley flour
1 tablespoon double-acting, nonaluminum baking powder, such as
 Rumford
1½ to 2 teaspoons ground cinnamon
¾ to 1 teaspoon ground ginger
¼ teaspoon ground cloves
Scant ½ teaspoon sea salt (see Cook's Notes)
½ cup dried currants or raisins
½ cup apple juice
⅓ cup maple syrup
⅓ cup canola or safflower oil
1 teaspoon vanilla

1. Brush the oil lightly onto the bottom and sides of the muffin cups. Set aside.
2. Set the zucchini in a colander over a plate to drain.
3. In a blender, grind the flax seeds. Add the water and process until a slightly gummy mixture is achieved, about 30 seconds. Set aside. (This process does not work quite as well with a food processor, but it can be done. First, grind the flax seeds in a spice or coffee grinder. Combine with water in the bowl of the processor and spin until slightly thickened, about 60 to 90 seconds.) A third alternative is to whisk the mixture vigorously by hand about 100 times.
4. In a large bowl, combine the flours, baking powder, spices, salt, and currants.

continued

5. To the flax seed mixture, add the apple juice, maple syrup, oil, and vanilla, and process until foamy, about 1 minute.

6. Press small amounts of the zucchini tightly in your fist to squeeze out excess moisture.

7. Blend the liquid mixture and the grated zucchini into the flour mixture, just until all of the flour is absorbed. (Do not overmix or the muffins will be tough.)

8. Fill the oiled muffin cups almost to the top with the batter and bake on the center shelf of an oven preheated to 375° until a skewer inserted in the center comes out clean and the tops bounce back to a gentle touch, about 18 to 22 minutes.

9. Set the muffin tins on a rack and cool for 5 minutes. Run a knife along the edges of each muffin and pop it out. Serve muffins warm or cool completely before storing for future use.

Cook's Notes: Adding just a pinch of salt is fine for most sweet muffins, but I found that these needed about ½ teaspoon for the flavors to emerge. If you're accustomed to using little to no salt, by all means reduce the amount.

Date-Nut Bran Muffins

Whatever ancient sage first thought of the happy combination of dates and nuts has my thanks. And whoever thought of combining them in a muffin was a genius.

For a special treat, use plump moist medjool dates. The more commonly available dates, deglet noors, tend to be dried out and leathery.

Oven: 16 to 20 minutes at 375°

Canola or safflower oil for greasing muffin tins
3 tablespoons flax seeds
½ cup water
1¾ cups whole wheat pastry flour
1¼ cups oat bran
1 tablespoon grain coffee, such as Cafix or Yannoh (optional)
1 tablespoon double-acting, nonaluminum baking powder,
*   such as Rumford*
1 teaspoon baking soda
1 teaspoon ground cinnamon
½ teaspoon ground allspice
⅛ teaspoon sea salt
½ cup coarsely chopped walnuts
10 to 12 dates, pitted and rolled in whole wheat pastry flour, coarsely
*   chopped (about ½ cup, tightly packed; see Cook's Notes)*
⅓ cup maple syrup
⅓ cup canola or safflower oil
1 cup apple juice

1. Brush the oil lightly onto the bottom and sides of the muffin cups and set aside.

2. In a blender, grind the flax seeds. Add the water and process until you achieve a slightly gummy mixture, about 30 seconds. Set aside. (This process does not work quite as well with a food processor, but it can be done. First, grind the flax seeds in a spice or coffee grinder. Combine with water in the bowl of the processor and spin until slightly thickened, about 60 to 90 seconds.) A third alternative is to whisk the mixture vigorously by hand about 100 times.

3. In a bowl, combine the flour, bran, grain coffee (if using), baking powder, baking soda, cinnamon, allspice, and salt. Stir in the walnuts and dates, making sure that the date pieces are coated with flour and do not stick together.

4. To the flax seed mixture, add the maple syrup, canola oil, and apple juice, and process until the liquid is frothy.

continued

5. Stir this liquid into the dry ingredients, just until all of the flour is absorbed.

6. Spoon the batter almost to the top of each oiled muffin cup and bake on the middle shelf of an oven preheated to 375° until the tops are lightly browned and bounce back to a gentle touch, and a skewer inserted in the center comes out clean, about 16 to 20 minutes.

7. Cool muffin tins on a rack for 10 minutes. Unmold the muffins (run a knife along the edges, if necessary) and eat them warm or set them on the rack to cool thoroughly before storing for later use.

Cook's Notes: Your health food store probably sells dates already cut up and dredged in oat bran. It's more expensive to buy them this way, but you may consider it a welcome time saver.

Variations

- For a wheat-free muffin, my friend Joanne Zitko substitutes barley flour for the whole wheat pastry flour and oatmeal for the oat bran. This produces a denser muffin that has even more flavor.
- Use chopped figs instead of dates.

Orange Marmalade Muffins   Makes 12 to 14 muffins

I like to make these muffins with a surprise pocket of orange marmalade inside, but my friend Beth Johnson blends the marmalade right into the batter. This recipe follows her method; mine is in the raspberry jam variation on page 345.

Oven: 20 to 22 minutes at 375°

Canola or safflower oil for greasing muffin tins
3 tablespoons flax seeds
½ cup water
3 cups whole wheat pastry flour
1 tablespoon double-acting, nonaluminum baking powder, such as
    Rumford
1 teaspoon baking soda
1 teaspoon ground cloves
¼ teaspoon sea salt
1 cup freshly squeezed orange juice
⅓ cup maple syrup
⅓ cup canola oil
1 teaspoon vanilla
½ cup fruit-sweetened orange marmalade

1. Brush oil onto the bottom and sides of the muffin cups and set aside.

2. In a blender, grind the flax seeds. Add the water and process until slightly gummy mixture is achieved, about 30 seconds. Set aside. (This process does not work quite as well with a food processor, but it can be done. First, grind the flax seeds in a spice or coffee grinder. Combine with water in the bowl of the processor and spin until slightly thickened, about 60 to 90 seconds.) A third alternative is to whisk the mixture vigorously by hand about 100 times.

3. In a large bowl, combine the flour, baking powder, baking soda, cloves, and salt.

4. To the flax seed mixture, add the orange juice, maple syrup, canola oil, vanilla, and orange marmalade, and spin until well blended and the liquid is frothy, about 2 minutes.

5. Stir this liquid into the dry ingredients, just until all of the flour is absorbed.

6. Fill each oiled muffin cup almost to the top. Bake on the middle shelf of an oven preheated to 375° until the tops are lightly browned and bounce back to a gentle touch, and a skewer inserted in the center comes out without crumbs, about 20 to 22 minutes.

7. Cool muffin tins on a rack for 2 minutes. Run a knife along the edges and carefully unmold the muffins. (If the muffins do not come out easily, wait another minute or two. However, the muffins become slightly doughy if they steam too long, so transfer them to a cooling rack as soon as they are easily unmolded.)

8. Eat the muffins warm or set them on the rack to cool thoroughly before storing them for later use.

Variation: RASPBERRY JAM-FILLED MUFFINS: Instead of mixing the jam into the liquid ingredients, hold it aside to create a surprise filling for each muffin as follows:

Spoon 1 heaping tablespoon of batter into each oiled muffin cup, making sure that the bottom of each cup is thoroughly covered with batter. Make a small well with the back of a moistened teaspoon and add a heaping teaspoon of raspberry jam. (Make sure that there is a solid layer of batter underneath the jam; otherwise, the jam seeps through to the bottom of the muffin cups, which makes it hard to unmold the muffins.)

Cover the jam with enough batter to almost fill each of the muffin cups and bake in an oven preheated to 375° until the tops are lightly browned and bounce back to a gentle touch and a skewer inserted in the center comes out without crumbs (it may look slightly moist from the jam), about 20 to 22 minutes.

For an even more interesting result, add 2 teaspoons of finely grated lemon peel to the batter in this version. To enhance the lemon flavor, substitute ¼ cup freshly squeezed lemon juice for an equivalent amount of orange juice.

Gingered Prune Drop Scones with Pine Nuts

These irregularly shaped scones have a homemade look and taste delicious. Beth Johnson deserves credit for coming up with the definitive version. Best when served warm.

Oven: 18 to 20 minutes at 375°

Canola or safflower oil for greasing cookie sheets
3 tablespoons flax seeds
½ cup water
1¼ cups whole wheat pastry flour
1¼ cups unbleached white flour
½ cup old-fashioned oatmeal (rolled oats)
2 teaspoons ground ginger
1 teaspoon ground cinnamon
½ teaspoon ground cardamom
¼ teaspoon sea salt
1 tablespoon double-acting, nonaluminum baking powder, such as
    Rumford
1 teaspoon baking soda
1½ cups tightly packed pitted prunes, snipped into 4 to 5 pieces
⅓ cup toasted pine nuts (pignoli)
2 teaspoons grated lemon peel (colored part only, organic if possible)
⅔ cup prune or apple juice
⅓ cup maple syrup
½ cup canola oil
2 tablespoons lemon juice
1 teaspoon vanilla

1. Brush the oil lightly onto two cookie sheets. Set aside.

2. In a blender, grind the flax seeds. Add the water and process until you achieve a slightly gummy mixture, about 30 seconds. Set aside. (This does not work quite as well with a food processor, but it can be done. First, grind the flax seeds in a spice or coffee grinder. Combine with water in the bowl of the processor and spin until slightly gummy, about 60 to 90 seconds.) A third alternative is to whisk the mixture vigorously by hand about 100 times.

3. In a large bowl, combine the flours, oatmeal, spices, salt, baking powder, and baking soda. Stir in the prunes, pine nuts, and lemon peel, making sure that the bits of fruit are coated with flour and do not stick together.

4. To the flax seed mixture add the juice, maple syrup, oil, lemon juice, and vanilla, and process until the liquid is frothy and well blended, about 1 minute.

5. Stir this mixture into the dry ingredients, just until all of the flour is absorbed. Do not overmix.

6. Using a ⅓-cup measure, drop the batter onto the cookie sheets, leaving about 2 inches between scones. (You may have to help the batter out of the measuring cup with a spoon or use your fingers.) Flatten the scones slightly with moistened fingers or the back of a wet spoon.

7. Bake on the middle rack of an oven preheated to 375° until the bottoms are nicely browned, the tops spring back at a delicate touch, and a skewer inserted into the center comes out clean, about 18 to 20 minutes. With a spatula, transfer scones to a cooling rack. Serve warm or at room temperature.

Variations

- Use 2 teaspoons freshly grated ginger instead of the ground ginger for a more vibrant taste.
- Use ¾ cup chopped prunes and ¾ cup chopped apricots instead of all prunes.
- Substitute ½ cup chopped walnuts or pecans for the pine nuts.

The longest journey starts with a single step.
—Chinese proverb

Pecan-Apple-Spice Drop Scones

Makes fourteen to sixteen
3-inch scones

These simple, odd-shaped, and delicious pastries remind me of large, soft cookies. Serve them at your next herbal tea party.

Oven: 16 to 18 minutes at 375°

Canola or safflower oil for greasing cookie sheets
3 tablespoons flax seeds
½ cup apple juice
1⅓ cups whole wheat pastry flour
1⅓ cups unbleached white flour
⅓ cup barley flour or additional unbleached white flour
1 tablespoon double-acting, nonaluminum baking powder, such as Rumford
2 teaspoons ground cinnamon
1½ teaspoons freshly grated ginger (preferable) or ground ginger
½ teaspoon ground allspice
¼ teaspoon ground cardamom
¼ teaspoon sea salt
1 large apple, peeled and coarsely chopped (1 to 1¼ cups)
¾ cup coarsely chopped toasted pecans or hazelnuts
⅓ cup raisins or dried currants
Additional 1 cup apple juice
½ cup maple syrup
½ cup canola oil
1 teaspoon vanilla

1. Brush the oil onto two large cookie sheets and set aside.

2. In a blender, grind the flax seeds. Add the ½ cup apple juice and process until you achieve a slightly gummy mixture, about 30 seconds. Set aside. (This does not work quite as well with a food processor, but it can be done. First, grind the flax seeds in a spice or coffee grinder. Combine with apple juice in the bowl of the processor and spin until slightly gummy, about 60 to 90 seconds.) Alternatively, whisk by hand about 100 times to form a thick and slightly gummy mixture.

3. In a large bowl, combine the flours, baking powder, spices, and salt. Stir in the chopped apple, pecans, and raisins, making sure that the apple pieces and raisins are coated with flour and do not stick together.

4. To the flax seed mixture, add the additional apple juice, maple syrup, oil, and vanilla, and process (or beat by hand) until the liquid is frothy, about 2 minutes.

5. Stir this mixture into the dry ingredients, just until all of the flour is absorbed. (The batter will be somewhat thick.)

6. Using a ⅓ cup measure, drop the batter onto the oiled cookie sheets, leaving about 2 inches between scones. (You may have to help the batter out of the measuring cup with a spoon or with your fingers.) With the back of a wet spoon, flatten the scones into irregular shapes measuring about 3 inches in diameter.

7. Bake on the middle shelf of an oven preheated to 375° until the bottoms are golden brown, the tops bounce back to a gentle touch, and a skewer inserted in the center comes out clean, about 16 to 18 minutes.

8. Transfer scones to a rack to cool. Serve warm or cool thoroughly and store for later use.

Variation: Use diced pears and pear juice instead of apples and apple juice.

Desserts

I suspect that I'm not alone in spending a disproportionate amount of time thinking about dessert. And although it's pretty much a foregone conclusion that I don't eat dessert for my physical health but rather for my psychological well-being, I do feel better when those desserts are relatively low in fat and based on whole foods instead of on highly refined ingredients. I can also usually avoid the energy seesaw when I use sweeteners such as barley malt or maple syrup in place of refined sugar. (The entries for these ingredients in Ingredients A to Z offer some explanations.)

Creating delicious recipes that fall within these guidelines is no easy task. Successful baking relies more on chemistry than on genius, and by eliminating butter and eggs from the ingredients mix, you are eliminating centuries of baking wisdom and the very foundation of good taste and texture.

So at the beginning of this enterprise, I found myself baking eggless whole grain cakes that might better have served as ballast for a transoceanic vessel than as delectable dishes to end a meal. But I'm stubborn, and I like challenges almost as much as I like desserts. I've also had the good fortune to study with colleagues who are wizards when it comes to whole foods, and who have the generosity of Santa Claus when it comes to sharing recipes. You'll find their names sprinkled throughout this chapter, these sugarplum fairies of the whole grain dessert world.

I think you'll be amazed at how very appealing wholesome desserts can be. Here's a way to have your cake and eat it too!

Lemon Poppy Seed Cake

Serves 8 to 10

This luscious cake is my personal favorite. I love the tart edge of lemon and the crunch of the poppy seeds.

The cake is baked in a 9-inch tube pan—the hollow tube that runs up the middle allows it to cook evenly in the center. Use a tube pan with a removable bottom so you can easily unmold the cake for a dramatic presentation. The results are so good-tasting and moist that I rarely add icing. But if you are feeling so inclined, try the lemon glaze below.

Oven: 35 to 40 minutes at 375°

About ½ teaspoon oil and 2 teaspoons flour to prepare a 9-inch tube pan
5 tablespoons flax seeds (see Cook's Notes)
1 cup apple juice
2 cups whole wheat pastry flour
1 cup unbleached white flour or barley flour
½ cup poppy seeds
4 teaspoons double-acting, nonaluminum baking powder, such as Rumford
2 tablespoons finely minced or grated lemon peel (colored part only, organic if possible)
½ teaspoon sea salt
½ cup canola or safflower oil
¾ cup maple syrup
½ cup freshly squeezed lemon juice

FOR THE GLAZE (OPTIONAL)
2 tablespoons maple syrup
3 tablespoons freshly squeezed lemon juice

1. Brush the oil onto the bottom, sides, and center of a 9-inch tube pan. Dust lightly with flour, tip out the extra, and set aside.

2. In a blender, grind the flax seeds. Add the apple juice and process until you achieve a slightly gummy mixture, about 30 seconds. Set aside. (This process does not work quite as well with a food processor, but it can be done. First, grind the flax seeds in a spice or coffee grinder. Combine with water in the bowl of the processor and spin until slightly thickened, about 60 to 90 seconds.) A third alternative is to whisk the mixture vigorously by hand about 100 times. Tip the mixture out into a measuring cup or small pitcher and set aside.

3. In a large bowl, combine the flours, poppy seeds, baking powder, lemon peel, and salt.

4. In a blender or processor, blend the oil and maple syrup for about 15 seconds. Add the lemon juice and then the flax seed mixture, processing for about 10 seconds between additions.

5. Stir the liquid ingredients into the dry ingredients, mixing just until all of the flour is absorbed. Transfer the batter to the prepared tube pan and gently smooth the top with a spatula.

6. Bake on the center shelf of an oven preheated to 375° until the top bounces back to a gentle touch and a skewer inserted into the center comes out clean, about 35 to 40 minutes.

7. Set on a rack to cool for 30 minutes. Then run a knife along the outside and center edges and unmold. Set the cake on the rack to cool completely.

8. If using the glaze, combine the maple syrup and lemon juice. Poke holes into the top of the cake with a toothpick, and brush the glaze onto the top of the cake. Brush the sides with any remaining glaze.

Cook's Notes: To learn more about flax seeds, see page 332 and the entry in Ingredients A to Z.

This cake stays moist for days if tightly wrapped and stored in a cool place. It can also be frozen for up to 3 months.

Variation: Baking buddy Beth Johnson came up with this variation for an orange poppy seed cake: Use 1 cup orange juice and ½ cup apple juice instead of 1 cup apple juice and ½ cup lemon juice. Substitute grated orange peel for the lemon peel, *or* add 1 teaspoon orange extract. Add ¼ teaspoon ground mace.

What we all need at this point in human evolution is to learn what it takes to learn what we should learn—and learn it.

—Aurelio Peccei, *No Limits to Learning,*
A Report to the Club of Rome, Rome 1979.

Carrot Cake

A dense, moist cake that seems much richer than the ingredients suggest. For best taste and texture, cool the cake thoroughly and then let it "age" at room temperature overnight, or at least half a day if you're pinched for time.

You can bake this cake in a tube pan, as described on page 352. However, if you want to serve it as a birthday cake, you can bake it in a 9 × 13 × 2-inch pan and get fine results.

Serve the cake plain or with Coconut Icing (page 396). If you're feeling really flamboyant, dot the icing with carob or chocolate chips.

Oven: 40 to 50 minutes at 375°

About ½ teaspoon oil and 2 teaspoons flour to prepare a 9-inch tube pan
5 tablespoons flax seeds (see Cook's Notes)
1 cup apple juice
2 cups whole wheat pastry flour
1 cup barley flour
4 teaspoons double-acting, nonaluminum baking powder, such as
  Rumford
2 teaspoons ground cinnamon
1 teaspoon ground allspice
¾ teaspoon ground nutmeg
¾ teaspoon ground cardamom
½ teaspoon sea salt
½ cup coarsely chopped walnuts or toasted hazelnuts
½ cup dried currants or raisins
⅔ cup safflower or canola oil
½ cup maple syrup
Additional ¼ cup apple juice
2 teaspoons vanilla
2½ cups tightly packed, finely grated carrots (4 to 5 large carrots)
¾ cup Coconut Icing (page 396 optional)

1. Brush the oil onto the bottom, sides, and center of a 9-inch tube pan. Dust lightly with flour, tip out the extra, and set aside.

2. In a blender, grind the flax seeds. Add the juice and process until you achieve a slightly gummy mixture, about 30 seconds. Set aside. (This process does not work quite as well with a food processor, but it can be done. First, grind the flax seeds in a spice or coffee grinder. Combine with juice in the bowl of the processor and spin until slightly thickened, about 60 to 90 seconds.) A third alternative is to whisk the mixture vigorously by hand about 100 times. Tip the mixture out into a measuring cup or small pitcher and set aside.

3. In a large bowl, combine the flours, baking powder, spices, salt, nuts, and currants.

4. In a blender or processor, blend the oil and maple syrup for about 15 seconds, then add the additional juice, vanilla, and flax seed mixture, processing for about 20 seconds after each addition.

5. Stir the liquid ingredients and grated carrots into the dry ingredients, mixing just until all of the flour in absorbed. (The batter will be quite thick.)

6. Transfer the batter to the prepared tube pan and gently smooth the top with a spatula. Bake on the center shelf of an oven preheated to 375° until the top bounces back to a gentle touch and a skewer inserted into the center comes out clean, about 40 to 50 minutes.

7. Set on a rack to cool for 30 minutes. Then run a knife along the outside and center edges and unmold. Set the cake on the rack to cool completely. Drape loosely with a kitchen towel for at least 4 hours, but preferably overnight.

8. Spread on the icing, if using, shortly before serving.

Cook's Notes: To learn more about flax seeds, see page 332 and the entry in Ingredients A to Z.

Devil's Food Carob Cake   Serves 8

I've tasted many a carob cake in my day, and most leave me longing for some real chocolate. This version, taught to me by pastry chef Laura Litterello at the Natural Gourmet Institute for Food and Health in Manhattan, is the only one that makes it.

Oven: 30 to 40 minutes at 350°

*About ½ teaspoon oil or ¼ teaspoon oil plus a 9-inch circle of baking
    parchment to line the bottom of a 9 × 2-inch round cake pan*
1⅔ cups whole wheat pastry flour
½ cup roasted carob powder, sifted (see Cook's Notes)
2 tablespoons grain coffee, preferably Cafix
1 teaspoon sea salt
2 teaspoons baking powder
⅔ cup maple syrup
½ cup canola oil
1 cup soy milk
2 teaspoons vanilla
1½ cups Carob Frosting (page 396)

continued

1. Brush the bottom and sides of the cake pan with ½ teaspoon oil, or brush only the sides with ¼ teaspoon oil, and set the parchment in place.

2. In a large bowl, combine the flour, sifted carob powder, grain coffee, salt, and baking powder.

3. In a small bowl, combine the maple syrup, oil, soy milk, and vanilla. Stir the wet ingredients into the dry, mixing just until the flour is absorbed and any lumps are dissolved.

4. Pour the batter into the prepared pan and bake in an oven preheated to 350° until a skewer inserted into the center comes out clean and the cake pulls away from the sides of the pan, about 30 to 40 minutes.

5. Set on a rack to cool for 30 minutes. Then run a knife along the outside and center edges and unmold. Set the cake on the rack to cool completely.

6. Spread on the icing shortly before serving.

Cook's Notes: I've had good results with Chattfield's carob powder, and Laura's favorite brand is Neshiminy.

Variations

- DOUBLE-LAYER DEVIL'S FOOD CAROB CAKE: Double the cake recipe and bake in two 9-inch pans. Use 2 cups of the carob frosting. Spread about one third of the frosting between the 2 layers, another third around the sides, and the remaining frosting on top.
- CAROB CUPCAKES: Bake the batter at 350° in half-filled, oiled muffin cups until a skewer inserted in the center comes out clean, about 18 to 20 minutes. Ice with carob frosting, if desired. Makes 15 to 16 cupcakes.

Holiday Fruitcake

Serves 12

Meredith McCarty, California-based whole foods cooking teacher and author of *FRESH from a Vegetarian Kitchen*, developed this party-worthy dessert, ideal for holiday celebrations. Don't be discouraged by the long list of ingredients; this recipe is very simple to prepare. Why not double the recipe and prepare two fruitcakes? They make wonderful holiday gifts and freeze very well.

Oven: 1½ to 2 hours at 350°

¼ cup (1 ounce) chopped, dried peach halves

¼ cup (1 ounce) chopped, dried pear halves

1½ cups (¼ pound) chopped, dried apples

2 cups apple juice

½ teaspoon sea salt

¼ teaspoon aniseed or fennel seeds

¼ orange (preferably organic), seeded and finely chopped (rind included)

1 tablespoon freshly grated ginger

¼ cup corn oil

6 tablespoons brandy or rum, plus an optional additional ¼ cup for
      soaking

1 teaspoon vanilla

1 cup whole wheat flour

¾ cup rye flour

¼ cup cornmeal

1 tablespoon double-acting, nonaluminum baking powder, such as
      Rumford

¾ cup tightly packed raisins or dried currants

½ cup fresh cranberries

1 cup toasted and chopped walnuts or pecans

FOR THE GLAZE

1 tablespoon brown rice syrup or barley malt syrup, measured from an
      oiled spoon

1 tablespoon apple juice

1. In a large pot, combine the dried fruits, apple juice, salt, and aniseed, and bring to the boil. Cover and simmer until the fruit is soft, about 10 minutes. Lift out the fruit with a slotted spoon (reserve liquid) and dice it small. Put diced fruit in a bowl and mix with the orange, ginger, oil, 2 tablespoons brandy, and vanilla. Stir in the reserved liquid.

continued

2. Blend the flours and baking powder. Stir in the raisins, cranberries, and walnuts. Add the diced fruit mixture to the flour mixture and stir well to distribute ingredients evenly. (The dough will be fairly stiff.)

3. Line a standard-size loaf pan (9 × 5 × 3 inches) with parchment paper: Place loaf pan on top of a piece of parchment and trace the shape of the bottom of the pan on the paper. Calculate enough paper for the side sections of the pan and cut to fit. Cut small squares out of the corners of the paper so that it will slip neatly into the pan.

4. Fill the pan with the batter. Press the batter down and create a smooth top surface with a spatula. Lay another piece of parchment (or aluminum foil) lightly on top to prevent browning.

5. Bake on the middle shelf of an oven preheated to 350° until a skewer inserted in the center comes out clean, about 1½ to 2 hours.

6. In a small bowl, mix the glaze ingredients. About 10 minutes before the cake is done, remove the parchment from the top of the cake. Brush on the glaze and return the cake to the oven for the last 10 minutes of baking.

7. When done, set the cake on a rack to cool for about 10 minutes. Remove the cake from the pan and cool for a half hour before removing the paper.

8. If desired, pierce the top of the cake in 6 to 8 places with a thin skewer. Drizzle ¼ cup of brandy over the top. When completely cool, refrigerate the cake wrapped in a piece of cheesecloth or linen soaked in additional brandy.

9. To serve, cut into thin slices and serve warm or at room temperature.

Variation: Bake the batter in miniature loaf pans for holiday gifts or freeze them and then defrost as needed. Since the small loaves bake faster, begin checking for doneness after 45 minutes.

Good things come in recycled packages.
—The Worldwatch Institute

Apple Pie

Serves 6

It takes only two simple steps to prepare this elegant open-faced apple pie. First, the sliced apples are baked on the pie shell and left to cool slightly. Then a glaze is poured on top and the pie is left to sit for about an hour at room temperature.

Oven: 20 to 30 minutes at 375° plus 4 to 5 minutes stovetop

3 to 4 medium apples (1¾ pounds), peeled, cored, and thinly sliced (see Cook's Notes)
1 unbaked 9-inch pie crust, preferably Nut Pie Pastry (page 367)

FOR THE GLAZE
1 cup apple juice
1½ tablespoons agar flakes
3 tablespoons freshly squeezed lemon juice
½ teaspoon ground cinnamon
2 teaspoons grated lemon peel (colored part only, preferably organic)
½ teaspoon vanilla

1. Place the apple slices decoratively on the crust (or just toss them in for a more rustic-looking pie). Bake in a 375° oven until apples are easily pierced with a fork but still firm, about 20 to 30 minutes. Remove the pie from the oven and set it on a rack to cool.

2. While the pie is baking, prepare the glaze: Combine the apple juice and agar flakes in a small saucepan. Heat, stirring frequently, and simmer (but do not boil) until the agar is completely dissolved. (This should only take 4 to 5 minutes.) Stir in the lemon juice, cinnamon, lemon peel, and vanilla, and transfer to a 2-cup measure or a small heatproof pitcher. Cool just until the mixture begins to set, about 15 to 20 minutes. (If the glaze becomes too set to pour, heat it slightly while stirring.)

3. Pour just enough glaze over the apples to reach the top of the pie plate. (Any extra glaze can be poured over fruit and served at another time.)

4. Let the pie sit at room temperature until the glaze gels, about 1 hour. (If you are in a hurry, set the pie in the refrigerator or freezer to firm up.)

5. Refrigerate if not needed within the next few hours, but for optimum taste, serve at room temperature.

continued

Cook's Notes: If the apple skins are thin and tender and the apples are organic, it isn't necessary to peel them; just scrub them well. Peel tough skins, since they become leathery when baked.

To create apple slices without coring the apple, cut into the apple toward the core twice at opposite angles to create the first slice. Pop that slice out and continue to cut slices on the diagonal with a small paring knife, twisting your wrist as you hit the core to pop out each slice. Discard the core.

Variation: PEAR PIE: Use 2 to 3 large, ripe Anjou pears instead of the apples. Substitute pear juice for apple juice.

Gorgeous-to-Behold, No-Bake, Quick-and-Easy Summer Fruit Pie

Serves 6

The expression "simple as pie" must have originated with a recipe just like this quick and foolproof one. It will bring out the artist in every cook and elicit oohs and aahs from appreciative guests. Even friends of mine who break out in a sweat at the very thought of baking have reported great success.

The reason that this pie is so easy is that Mother Nature has done all of the work by providing such magnificent summer fruit. Use the ripest and juiciest specimens you can find and arrange them decoratively on a simple, unbaked granola crust. Pour over a glaze and voilà!

When they hear that this pie is naturally sweetened and contains very little fat, most people want a big piece or come back for seconds.

FOR THE CRUST

¼ teaspoon canola oil
¾ cup granola (without dried fruit; maple walnut is nice)

FOR THE GLAZE

1 cup peach or apple juice
1½ tablespoons agar flakes
3 tablespoons freshly squeezed lemon juice
1 teaspoon vanilla

FOR THE FRUIT FILLING

2 to 3 large ripe peaches, cut into ¼-inch slices
1 to 2 ripe kiwis, peeled and cut into ¼-inch rounds
6 to 8 medium strawberries, halved
½ to 1 cup blueberries

1. Brush the bottom of a 9-inch pie plate lightly with the oil.

2. Using on-off pulses, buzz the granola in a food processor to break up any large lumps and create a fairly coarse flour. Spread the granola evenly on the bottom of the pie plate. Set aside.

3. To prepare the glaze: In a small saucepan, begin to heat the apple juice. Stir in the agar flakes and simmer until most of them are dissolved, about 1 to 2 minutes. Transfer to a liquid measuring cup and stir in the lemon juice and vanilla. Place in the refrigerator to cool.

4. Arrange a circle of peach slices around the outer rim of the pie plate so that about ⅓ of the slice covers the rim of the pie plate and the remaining ⅔ of the slice tilts down into the pie. Cover the remainder of the crust with a layer of sliced peaches. Arrange the kiwi slices on top of some of the peaches, partially overlapping each other, in a concentric circle. Arrange the strawberry halves in a circle inside of the kiwis. Mound blueberries in the center and dot them here and there between the kiwis and peaches. (The object is to fill the pie shell decoratively to the brim with fruit.)

5. Once the glaze is room temperature or cooler, pour it evenly over the fruit. The glaze should be thin enough to seep between the fruit. If the glaze becomes too thick to pour, return it to the pan and heat it slightly while stirring.

6. Allow the glaze to set at room temperature for about 1 hour. Chill the pie if it is not needed within the next few hours, but for optimum taste, serve it at room temperature.

Cook's Notes: This crust is different from a flaky pie crust. The granola becomes soft as it absorbs the fruit juices and glaze, and it creates a puddinglike base for the filling. However, you can slice the pie in the usual way.

Variations
- Instead of peaches, try sliced plums, apricots, or nectarines. Pitted cherries or grapes make a nice substitute for blueberries.
- For the glaze, either intensify or complement the fruit flavor by using juice to match. For example, use a peach juice glaze on a peach pie, or white grape juice on a plum pie.

I would rather lose my whole crop than spray apples with pesticides.

—Alan York, organic apple grower,
Anderson Valley, California

Pecan Pie

Serves 6 to 8

This recipe and the three that follow are generous gifts of cooking teacher and author Meredith McCarty.

This pie is stunning to behold, and just sweet and rich enough to satisfy without being cloying.

Oven: 15 to 20 minutes at 375° plus 5 minutes stovetop

1 unbaked 9-inch pie crust, preferably Oatmeal (page 369) or Granola
  (page 371)
1½ cups brown rice syrup (see Cook's Notes)
1½ cups water
¼ cup agar flakes
½ teaspoon ground cinnamon
½ teaspoon sea salt
2 tablespoons arrowroot or kuzu
Water to barely cover arrowroot or kuzu
2 cups toasted pecans
1 teaspoon vanilla

1. Set pie weights or beans into the pie crust and bake on the middle shelf of a 375° oven until lightly browned, about 15 to 20 minutes. Set on a rack to cool.

2. In a heavy saucepan, prepare the filling. Whisk together the rice syrup, water, agar flakes, cinnamon, and salt, and bring to the boil. Reduce heat and simmer over very low heat until the agar completely dissolves, stirring occasionally, about 5 minutes.

3. In a small bowl, dissolve the arrowroot in water to barely cover and add to the agar-rice syrup mixture. While cooking the mixture at a low simmer, whisk it until the chalky color becomes clear, taking care to distribute the pecans evenly.

4. Let the mixture cool for 15 minutes. Then stir in the pecans and vanilla and pour into the prepared pie crust.

5. Let the pie cool to room temperature and set, about 2 hours (or refrigerate pie about 1 hour to firm up more quickly). For optimum taste, bring to room temperature before serving.

Cook's Notes: For the filling, Meredith favors the dark brown rice syrup made by Mitoku. Other brands (often lighter in color) sometimes prevent the filling from setting firmly.

Cranapple-Currant Tart

This pie looks especially pretty when presented in a 10-inch tart tin with a removable base, but you can prepare it in a standard 9-inch pie plate just as well.

Oven: 15 to 20 minutes at 375°, plus 8 minutes stovetop

1 unbaked 9-inch pie crust (Oatmeal, page 369, or Nut Pie Pastry, page 367, work well)
1½ cups apple juice
1 cup finely diced apples, cored, peeled if desired
½ cup dried currants
3 tablespoons agar flakes
¼ teaspoon sea salt
1 cup cranberries, sorted through and rinsed
1 tablespoon arrowroot or kuzu
¼ cup cool apple juice or water

1. Set pie weights or beans into the pie crust and bake on the center rack of a 375° oven until lightly browned and crispy, about 15 to 20 minutes. Set on a rack to cool.

2. In a saucepan, bring the apple juice, apples, currants, agar flakes, and salt to the boil. Simmer, stirring occasionally, until the agar is completely dissolved, about 5 minutes.

3. Add the cranberries and cook until the cranberries and apples are tender but not mushy, about 2 to 3 minutes more.

4. In a small bowl, stir the arrowroot into the apple juice until it is completely dissolved. Stir it into the fruit mixture and simmer, stirring gently, until the mixture thickens slightly, about 5 to 10 seconds.

5. Transfer the filling to the prebaked pie shell. Let the pie cool to room temperature and set, about 2 hours (or place in the refrigerator for quick setting for about 1 hour).

6. For optimum taste, bring to room temperature before serving.

Mince Pie with
Twisted Lattice Pastry

Serves 6 to 8

A charming and very old-fashioned American pie, ideal for fall and winter holiday feasts.

Oven: 25 minutes at 400° plus about 20 minutes stovetop

Dough for 1 Whole Wheat Pie Pastry crust (page 368)
1 cup apple juice
1 tablespoon dark miso (optional, but creates a rich and complex taste)
1½ pounds unpeeled apples, cored and diced (about 4 cups)
½ cup raisins
½ cup dried currants
¼ cup orange juice
2 tablespoons lemon juice
1 tablespoon finely minced or grated orange peel (colored part only, organic if possible)
1 teaspoon finely minced or grated lemon peel (colored part only, organic if possible)
1 tablespoon apple cider vinegar
½ teaspoon ground cinnamon
¼ teaspoon each ground cloves, allspice, and ginger
2 tablespoons arrowroot or kuzu
¼ cup cool water

FOR THE GLAZE
1 tablespoon brown rice or maple syrup
1 tablespoon apple juice

1. Pinch off ⅓ of the pastry for the lattice top, and refrigerate in a covered container. Roll out the bottom pastry between sheets of waxed paper, taking care to peel off waxed paper and turning pastry over between rolls to prevent sticking.

2. Set the pastry into the pie plate, crimp the edges, and prick the bottom in a few places with a fork. Bake in a 400° oven for 10 minutes. Set on a rack to cool.

3. To prepare the filling, heat the apple juice Add the miso (if using), mashing it against the side of the pot to dissolve. Add the apples, raisins, currants, orange juice, lemon juice, orange and lemon peel, vinegar, and spices. Simmer covered until the apples are soft, but not mushy, and the raisins and currants are plump, stirring occasionally, about 10 to 20 minutes.

4. Dissolve the arrowroot in the water and stir it into the mixture until mixture thickens, about 2 minutes. Allow the filling to cool slightly as you roll out the remaining dough for the lattice crust.

5. Cut the rolled dough into six to eight ½-inch strips.

6. Pour the filling into the crust. Twist each strip just before you lay it down on top of the filling. Place 3 or 4 twisted dough strips about an inch apart and parallel to each other in one direction, and then place 3 or 4 strips across the first strips, in the opposite direction. (There is no need to interlace the strips.)

7. Bake the pie at 400° for 10 minutes. Mix the glaze ingredients and brush the pastry strips and edges and return to the oven for 5 minutes more. Allow to cool for about an hour before serving.

There is one elementary truth the ignorance of which kills countless ideas and splendid plans: that the moment one definitely commits oneself, then Providence moves too. All sorts of things occur to help one that would never otherwise have occurred. . . . Whatever you can do or dream you can, begin it. Boldness has genius, power and magic in it.

—Johann Wolfgang von Goethe

Pumpkin Pie

Serves 6 to 8

I love pumpkin pie and have done a fair amount of comparative tasting over the years. This filling is by far my favorite. It's light and rich tasting, with a pleasant texture and a robust squash taste, and just sweet enough.

The pie is best when it is baked in a nut crust. Since the pie needs time to cool and gel, plan on preparing it a half day in advance.

Oven: 30 minutes at 375°

1½ cups mashed baked winter squash or pumpkin (see Cook's Notes)
¾ pound (1½ cups mashed) firm tofu
½ cup maple syrup
1 teaspoon ground cinnamon
¼ teaspoon each ground nutmeg and ginger
⅛ teaspoon each ground allspice and cloves
½ teaspoon sea salt
2 tablespoons water (optional)
1 unbaked 9-inch pie crust, preferably Nut Pie Pastry (page 367)

GARNISHES
Tofu Whip (page 398) or Cashew Cream (page 398)
Freshly grated nutmeg

1. To prepare the filling, combine the squash, tofu, maple syrup, spices, and salt in a processor or blender, adding water only if the mixture seems very thick.

2. Pour the filling into the prepared pie crust and smooth it out with a spatula. Bake on the middle shelf of a preheated 375° oven for 30 minutes. Set on a rack to cool and firm up for at least 2 hours before serving. (If you are in a hurry, set the cooled pie into the freezer for 30 to 45 minutes.)

3. Cut the pie into 6 to 8 serving pieces and garnish with a dollop of Tofu Whip or Cashew Cream and nutmeg.

Cook's Notes: If you use pumpkin, make sure it is a pie pumpkin and not a huge jack-o'-lantern (the Halloween type), which is quite watery. If using squash, choose a sweet, flavorful variety such as butternut or kabocha. Discard the seeds or reserve them for roasting. Scoop out the cooked flesh and puree it. Don't use pressure-cooked or boiled squash for the pie filling, since it's likely to be too watery. For details on baking squash and pumpkin, see Ingredients A to Z.

Nut Pie Pastry

I recommend this crust for most of the pie recipes in this chapter. Thanks to Lissa De Angelis, associate director of the Natural Gourmet Institute for Food and Health in Manhattan, for sharing it. It's a foolproof recipe that's easy to handle and full of good flavor. The nuts give it a special something—use any kind you like.

If you have an extra pie plate, you might double the recipe and freeze one (either raw or baked) for future use.

¾ cup whole wheat pastry flour
¾ cup old-fashioned oatmeal (rolled oats)
½ cup finely chopped toasted almonds (blanching optional), walnuts,
  pecans, or sunflower seeds
¼ to ½ teaspoon ground cinnamon or ¼ teaspoon ground cardamom
Pinch sea salt
¼ cup canola oil
3 to 4 tablespoons maple syrup (depending on desired sweetness)
1 to 2 tablespoons water (optional)
Oil for preparing pie plate or tart tin

1. In a bowl, blend the flour, oatmeal, nuts, cinnamon, and salt.

2. In a liquid measuring cup, thoroughly whisk together the oil and syrup. (This can also be done in a blender.)

3. Make a well in the center of the dry ingredients and pour in the liquid. Stir with a fork to form a coarse dough, adding water if mixture seems dry. Do not overmix.

4. Flour your hands and press the dough thinly into the bottom and sides of an oiled 9-inch pie plate or 10-inch tart tin. You will have to press quite firmly to make the dough spread to cover all surfaces. Patch any torn or thin spots with dough pinched from the edges and reflour your hands as necessary.

5. Proceed as directed in individual recipes.

Whole Wheat Pie Pastry

Makes crust for one 9-inch pie or 10-inch tart

It's nearly impossible to create a truly light, flaky pastry crust using whole grain flour and oil rather than butter. For this reason, I usually prefer the preceding recipe for a crunchy nut crust that's pressed into the pie plate rather than rolled out. But there are times when a plain, basic crust is more appropriate to the filling. I found that once I was willing to drop any traditional pie crust expectations, I began to enjoy the less delicate but more wholesome taste and texture that this recipe produces.

This dough can be refrigerated for up to 3 days and frozen for up to 4 months.

*2 cups whole wheat pastry flour, or 1 cup whole wheat pastry flour and 1
    cup unbleached white flour (see Cook's Notes)*
¼ to ½ teaspoon sea salt

OPTIONAL FLAVORINGS
*½ teaspoon ground cinnamon, or ¼ teaspoon ground nutmeg, cloves,
    allspice, or cardamom*
*1 tablespoon finely minced or grated orange or lemon peel (colored part
    only, organic if possible)*

¼ cup canola oil
*3 to 5 tablespoons water or apple or other fruit juice (for a slightly
    sweet crust)*

1. In a bowl, combine the flour, salt, and flavorings (if using).

2. Drizzle in the oil and with your fingertips rub it gently into the flour mixture to create small pebble-sized pieces of dough.

3. Drizzle on 3 tablespoons of water while stirring. Gently press dough together to form a ball, drizzling on more water, if needed, until dough holds together. Press into a flattened disk.

4. If time permits, cover the dough with a damp cloth or place it in an airtight container and chill for about 45 minutes.

5. Just before needed, roll the dough out on a lightly floured board, rolling from the center toward the edge, and turning the pastry after every few rolls to prevent sticking. (You can also roll the dough between two pieces of waxed paper.)

6. Set the dough into a 9-inch pie plate or 10-inch tart tin, crimp the edges, and trim. Proceed as directed in individual recipe.

Cook's Notes: To lighten the crust, use half unbleached white flour, or sift the flours after measuring to aerate them. Another alternative is to make sure all of the ingredients are very cold and to handle the dough as little as possible.

Oatmeal Pie Pastry

This recipe produces a very satisfying, somewhat coarser, and sweeter crust than the whole wheat pie pastry recipe.

> 1 cup old-fashioned oatmeal (rolled oats)
> 1 cup whole wheat pastry flour or ½ cup whole wheat pastry and ½ cup
>   oat or barley flour
> ¼ teaspoon ground cinnamon or allspice
> ¼ teaspoon sea salt
> ¼ cup canola oil
> 2 tablespoons maple syrup
> 2 to 3 tablespoons apple juice or water

1. In a bowl, combine the oatmeal, flour(s), cinnamon, and salt.

2. In a measuring cup, whisk together the oil, maple syrup, and 2 tablespoons apple juice.

3. Pour the liquid into the dry ingredients and stir, then gently press to form a soft dough, adding extra liquid as needed to bind.

4. With moistened hands, press the dough into an oiled 9-inch pie plate or 10-inch tart tin and proceed as directed in individual recipes.

Triple Grain Granola

The advantage of making your own granola is that you can control the amount of oil and sweetness and, ideally, use all organic ingredients. (Although touted as healthful foods, many commercial granola mixes are loaded with sugar and fat.) Of course, it's much cheaper to make granola yourself—and very simple.

The possibilities are endless, but here's one to begin with. Unless you are heating up the oven for another purpose, the most fuel-efficient way to prepare granola is to pan-toast it. Make up a big batch and refrigerate it for up to 1 month or store it in the freezer for up to 8 weeks.

Skillet: 5 to 7 minutes
Oven: 20 to 30 minutes at 375°

1 cup each old-fashioned oatmeal (rolled oats), wheat flakes, and rye
*   flakes, or 3 cups oatmeal*
½ cup walnuts or almonds, coarsely chopped if desired
¼ cup unhulled sesame seeds
½ teaspoon ground cinnamon
¼ cup safflower or light sesame oil
⅓ to ½ cup (depending upon desired sweetness) maple syrup
2 teaspoons vanilla
½ cup raisins or currants (optional)

1. In a 10-inch (or larger) cast-iron skillet, combine the grains, nuts, sesame seeds, and cinnamon.

2. In a measuring cup, combine the oil, maple syrup, and vanilla, and pour over the dry ingredients while stirring. Mix well to blend.

3. To pan-toast: Toast over medium-high heat, stirring frequently, until the oats and nuts become crispy and brown, the sesame seeds begin to pop, and the maple syrup emits a burned-sugar aroma, about 5 to 7 minutes.

4. Stir in the raisins (if using). Cool to room temperature, stirring occasionally.

5. Transfer to a tightly sealed storage container.

Cook's Notes: If your skillet is smaller than 10 inches, pan-toast the granola in two batches.

To oven roast: Combine the oat-nut mixture and the rest of the ingredients (except for the dried fruit) in 1 large or 2 small cast-iron skillets or spread on 1 large jelly-roll pan. (Cookie sheets can also be used, but be careful to avoid spills when stirring.) Bake at 375° (the oven doesn't have to be preheated), stirring every 5 to 7 minutes, until grains are dry and crisp, about 20 to 30 minutes. Follows steps 4 and 5.

Variations

- Before toasting, add ⅓ cup sunflower seeds, ½ cup dried coconut, and/or ⅓ cup oat or wheat bran.
- After toasting is completed, add a variety of dried chopped fruits, such as apricots, pears, dates, or apple rings.

One-Minute Granola Pie Crust

Makes one 9-inch crust

This quick-and-simple crust can be made with either packaged or homemade granola. Unlike a flaky pie crust, this one requires no baking. It becomes moist and puddinglike while absorbing liquid from the filling. The crust also contributes a pleasing flavor and texture—especially if you use a high-quality granola.

This recipe works best with granola that doesn't contain pieces of dried fruit. I especially like to make it with Triple Grain Granola (page 370).

¼ *teaspoon oil*
¾ *cup granola, preferably without dried fruit*

1. Brush a 9-inch pie plate lightly with oil.

2. Using on-off pulses, buzz the granola in a food processor to break up any large lumps and create a fairly coarse meal. Spread the granola evenly on the bottom of the pie plate.

3. Use as a ready-to-go pie crust and ignore any instructions for prebaking in individual recipes.

Cookies

As far as I'm concerned, I can never have enough good cookie recipes in my file, or enough cookies in my cookie jar. What follows are my favorites, many of them with interesting variations. I hope they find their way into your cookie jar, but in all honesty I don't expect them to stay there very long.

Oatmeal Raisin Cookies

Makes about 2 dozen cookies

A moist and chewy cookie, full of good flavor—and a snap to prepare.

Oven: 17 to 20 minutes at 375°

2 cups old-fashioned oatmeal (rolled oats)
1½ cups whole wheat pastry flour
2 teaspoons double-acting, nonaluminum baking powder, such as Rumford
¾ teaspoon ground cinnamon
½ teaspoon freshly grated nutmeg
Generous pinch sea salt
¾ cup raisins
½ cup coarsely chopped walnuts
½ cup safflower or canola oil
½ cup apple juice
⅓ cup maple syrup
1 teaspoon vanilla

1. In a large bowl, combine the oatmeal, flour, baking powder, cinnamon, nutmeg, salt, raisins, and walnuts.

2. In a large measuring cup, combine the oil, apple juice, maple syrup, and vanilla. Pour the liquid into the dry ingredients and stir until all of the flour is absorbed.

3. Drop the batter by heaping tablespoons about 2 inches apart onto 2 oiled cookie sheets. Flatten each mound with the back of a spoon and with your fingers shape rough circles with a 2-inch diameter.

4. Bake on the center rack of an oven preheated to 375° until golden on the bottom and around the edges, about 17 to 20 minutes. (*Please note*: If you are baking both trays of cookies on different shelves at the same time, reverse the top and bottom trays after 9 minutes for more even browning.)

5. When the cookies are done, carefully lift them with a spatula and transfer to a rack to cool.

Variations

- Reduce the raisins to ½ cup and add ½ cup carob chips.
- Use chopped, pitted dates instead of raisins.
- Reduce the maple syrup to ¼ cup and add 2 tablespoons barley malt syrup for a slightly less sweet and more chewy cookie with a hint of molasses.

Peanut Butter–
Granola Cookies
Makes about 3½ dozen cookies

A wonderful recipe adapted from *The Natural Foods Cookbook* by talented whole foods chef Mary Estella. It tastes especially wholesome when prepared with Triple Grain Granola (page 370), but peanut butter fans will come back for seconds (and thirds) no matter what granola you use.

Kids will find these cookies are great to make, since they're shaped by hand and aren't offended if handled too much. A dollop of raspberry jam in the middle of each cookie is a tasty and very pretty touch.

Oven: 14 to 16 minutes at 350°

1 cup unsalted peanut butter at room temperature .
½ cup maple syrup
½ cup canola or safflower oil
¼ cup water
1 teaspoon vanilla
1½ cups Triple Grain Granola (page 370) or store-bought granola
    (coarsely chop any whole nuts)
2½ cups whole wheat pastry flour
¼ cup toasted sesame seeds (optional; see Cook's Notes)
1 teaspoon ground cinnamon
Pinch sea salt
¼ cup fruit-sweetened raspberry jam, approximately

1. In a processor or blender, blend the peanut butter, syrup, oil, water, and vanilla until fairly smooth. The blending can be done by hand but will take considerable effort.

continued

2. In a separate bowl, combine the granola with the flour, sesame seeds (if using), cinnamon, and salt. Stir the liquid ingredients into the dry mixture to create a soft, slightly dry dough. (Knead gently with your hands, if necessary, to incorporate all of the flour.)

3. Shape the dough into approximately walnut-sized balls. If the dough isn't holding together nicely, sprinkle on and knead in some more water.

4. Place the dough balls on 2 oiled cookie sheets about 2 inches apart, and press each one down with a fork (dip fork in cold water first) to create rounds about 2 inches in diameter and a scant ½-inch thick.

5. To make jam centers, press your thumb into the center of each cookie and fill the hollow with about ¼ teaspoon of jam.

6. Gently even out any jagged cookie edges with your fingers if desired.

7. Bake the cookies in the center of an oven preheated to 350° until light golden on the bottom, about 14 to 15 minutes for soft cookies and 15 to 16 minutes for crisper cookies. (*Please note*: If you are baking both trays of cookies on different shelves at the same time, reverse the top and bottom trays after 9 minutes for more even browning.) Cool for a few minutes on the cookie sheets and then transfer to a rack. (If the cookies crumble easily when moved, allow them to cool completely on the cookie sheets.)

Cook's Notes: Triple Grain Granola (page 370) contains sesame seeds, so it's not necessary to add more. But do add them to the cookie dough if you're using store-bought granola.

When I was four years old, my mother used to bring me a cookie every time she came home from the market. I always went to the front yard and took my time eating it, sometimes half an hour or forty-five minutes for one cookie. I would take a small bite and look up at the sky. Then I would touch the dog with my feet and take another small bit. I just enjoyed being there, with the sky, the earth, the bamboo thickets, the cat, the dog, the flowers. . . . I was entirely in the present moment with my cookie. . . .

It is possible to eat our meals as slowly and joyfully as I ate the cookie of my childhood. Maybe you have the impression that you have lost the cookie of your childhood, but I am sure it is still there, somewhere in your heart. Everything is still there, and if you really want it, you can find it.

—Thich Nhat Hanh, "Cookies of Childhood," *Peace Is Every Step*
(New York: Bantam, 1991).

Chocolate Chip Cookies

Developed by Peter Bergley—who has a great talent for making whole foods taste first rate—this is one delicious cookie that's very quick to prepare.

Oven: 12 to 15 minutes at 375°

2 cups whole wheat pastry flour
½ cup old-fashioned oatmeal (rolled oats)
½ teaspoon sea salt
¼ teaspoon baking soda
1 cup coarsely chopped walnuts
1 cup natural malt-sweetened chocolate chips or carob chips
½ cup maple syrup
½ cup canola oil
1 teaspoon vanilla
1 tablespoon water

1. In a large bowl, combine the flour, oatmeal, salt, and baking soda. Stir in the walnuts and chocolate chips.

2. In another bowl, mix the syrup, oil, vanilla, and water.

3. Stir the wet mixture into the dry ingredients just until the flour is absorbed. The batter will be fairly thick.

4. Drop by heaping teaspoons onto 2 oiled cookie sheets about 1 inch apart. Flatten with your fingers to a thickness of about ¼ inch.

5. Bake on the center shelf of an oven preheated to 375° until lightly browned on the bottom, about 12 to 15 minutes. (*Please note*: If you are baking both trays of cookies on different shelves at the same time, reverse the top and bottom trays after 9 minutes for more even browning.)

6. Transfer to a rack to cool.

Thumbprint Cookies

Makes about
1½ dozen cookies

Not only do these terrific cookies have great taste and texture, but the recipe invites endless delicious variations. Many thanks to author Mary Estella for sharing this recipe. Enjoy!

Oven: 18 to 20 minutes at 375°

1 cup old-fashioned oatmeal (rolled oats)
1 cup walnuts
1½ cups whole wheat pastry flour
½ teaspoon each ground cinnamon and allspice
¼ teaspoon ground cardamom
1 teaspoon baking soda
Pinch sea salt
½ cup canola or safflower oil
½ cup maple syrup
2 tablespoons freshly squeezed lemon juice
¼ cup fruit-sweetened raspberry (or other fruit) preserves

1. Combine the oatmeal and nuts in a food processor and process until the mixture resembles a coarse meal. Add the flour, spices, baking soda, and salt, and pulse a few times to mix well.

2. Add the oil, maple syrup, and lemon juice, and pulse a few times to create a soft dough.

3. Using your hands, roll dough into smooth balls about the size of a small walnut. Place about 2 inches apart on 2 lightly oiled cookie sheets. Gently press the balls to flatten them slightly.

4. With your thumb or index finger, make a "thumbprint" in the center of each cookie. Fill each hollow with ½ to 1 teaspoon of preserves. Wipe off any preserves that smear on the dough or cookie sheet.

5. Bake cookies in an oven preheated to 375° until lightly browned on the bottom and fragrant, about 18 to 20 minutes. (*Please note*: If you are baking both trays of cookies on different shelves at the same time, reverse the top and bottom trays after 9 minutes for more even browning.)

6. Carefully lift the cookies with a spatula and transfer to a rack to cool. When thoroughly cooled, refrigerate in an airtight container until needed.

Variations
- Use different kinds of preserves, even within one batch of cookies.
- Substitute toasted pecans or almonds for the walnuts.
- For a crunchier cookie, finely chop the nuts by hand.

376   **Recipes from an Ecological Kitchen**

- For LEMON-SESAME CRUNCH cookies, substitute ¾ cup toasted sesame seeds for the walnuts, eliminate the spices, and add 2 to 3 tablespoons finely minced or grated lemon rind.
- Instead of preserves, set a whole nut into the center of the cookie.

Anise Cookies with Pignoli

Makes about 2 dozen cookies

These pale and elegant cookies also come to you compliments of whole foods caterer and baker Peter Bergley. This is the recipe I turn to when preparing a sophisticated dinner and want to show everyone just how good whole grain, dairy-free treats can taste.

Oven: 12 to 15 minutes at 375°

1½ cups unbleached white flour
1½ cups brown rice flour
1 teaspoon aniseed, gently crushed in a mortar and pestle or coarsely
    ground in a spice grinder
Scant ½ teaspoon sea salt
½ teaspoon baking soda
½ cup toasted pignoli (pine nuts)
½ cup plus 2 tablespoons maple syrup
½ cup plus 2 tablespoons canola oil
1 teaspoon vanilla

1. In a bowl, combine the flours, aniseed, salt, baking soda, and pignoli.
2. In another bowl, thoroughly whisk together the maple syrup, oil, and vanilla.
3. Stir the wet ingredients into the dry mixture to form a soft dough.
4. Form the dough into balls about 1 inch in diameter and then press each ball into a round cookie about ¼-inch thick. Set cookies on oiled cookie sheets about 1 inch apart. (If some dry bits of dough remain in the bowl, drizzle on a tiny bit of water and gather scraps together to form a cookie.)
5. Bake on the center rack of an oven preheated to 375° until lightly browned on the bottom, about 12 to 15 minutes.
6. Transfer cookies to a rack to cool.
7. Refrigerate in a tightly sealed container until needed, up to 2 weeks, or freeze up to 3 months.

Steamed Puddings

Some of the most fun (and best eating) I've had while writing this book has been inventing recipes for puddings. The old-fashioned steamed pudding will make a comeback if I have anything to say about it. I'm not talking about the lard-infused cannonballs of Dickensian England. On the contrary, these puddings are quickly prepared and contain not a drop of added oil (except, of course, what's in the nuts). Eat them warm, or age them for 3 to 4 days in the refrigerator, bring them to room temperature, and enjoy their more mellow flavor. The texture varies from cakelike to quite moist, depending upon the unpredictable amount of liquid given off by the fruit and on the type of flour you use. Most recipes call for a combination of whole wheat pastry and unbleached white flours (which yields a light texture), but I have tried a few of the puddings using barley and spelt flours instead of white flour.

I have chef Alan Harding of Manhattan's Nosmo King to thank for reminding me how wonderful steamed puddings can be.

Before You Begin

Puddings are made by steaming batter in a tightly covered heatproof dish that sits on a rack over boiling water.

I use a 1-quart bundt pan and then unmold it for a very attractive presentation. You can also use a 5-cup soufflé dish or a 1- to 1½-quart heatproof casserole that will fit into the cooker.

The pan or dish should be securely covered by crisscrossing two long sheets of aluminum foil over the top. Tuck the foil under the bottom of the pan so that no moisture will enter the pudding. Lower the pan onto the rack in the cooker with the aid of a foil strip (page 10).

These puddings are delicious both warm and at room temperature—and some of my friends eat them straight out of the refrigerator for breakfast! To reheat, simply steam the pudding in the uncovered pan on a rack over boiling water until heated through, about 5 to 10 minutes. This technique is also great if the pudding dries out during cooking or storage.

The puddings don't unmold easily once they've cooled in the pan. Simply serve by scoopfuls directly from the pan. Believe me, no one will complain!

ECO-TIP: Save the aluminum foil strip to use again.

Steamed Cranberry Pudding

Serves 4 to 6

Here's chef Alan Harding's pudding recipe that started it all.

Serve warm or at room temperature with a dollop of Tofu Whip (page 398) or Cashew Cream (page 398) on top.

For additional instructions on making puddings, see page 378.

Pressure cooker: 25 minutes high pressure, 15-minute natural pressure release
Standard stovetop: 75 to 90 minutes

½ teaspoon canola oil and 2 teaspoons flour for preparing a 1-quart bundt pan or heatproof casserole
¾ cup whole wheat pastry flour
½ cup unbleached white flour
1 teaspoon baking soda
2 teaspoons finely minced or grated orange peel (colored part only, organic if possible)
¾ teaspoon ground cinnamon
¼ teaspoon ground cloves
⅛ teaspoon sea salt
2 cups coarsely chopped fresh or frozen (defrosted) cranberries
½ cup coarsely chopped walnuts
½ cup orange juice
½ cup maple syrup
Boiling water

1. Brush the oil on the bottom and sides of the pan or casserole and dust lightly with flour. Tip out any extra flour and set aside.

2. In a bowl, combine the flours, baking soda, orange peel, cinnamon, cloves, salt, cranberries, and walnuts. In a measuring cup, combine the orange juice and maple syrup. Stir the liquid into the dry ingredients just until all of the flour is absorbed.

3. Transfer the mixture into the prepared bundt pan or casserole. Wrap tightly with 2 sheets of aluminum foil crisscrossed on the top, ends long enough to tuck under the bottom of the pan.

4. Place a rack or trivet in the bottom of the cooker. Lower the pudding into the cooker with the aid of a foil strip (page 10) and set it on the rack. Add enough boiling water to reach halfway up the sides of the pan.

5. Lock the lid in place and over high heat bring to high pressure. Lower the heat just enough to maintain high pressure and cook for 25 minutes. Turn off the heat and allow the pressure to come down naturally for 15 minutes. Remove the lid, tilting it away from you to allow any excess steam to escape.

6. Remove the pan from the cooker by lifting it up with the aid of the foil strip and set it on a rack to cool slightly. Remove the top foil and, after all of the steam has escaped, run a knife around the edges. Turn pan over onto a platter and unmold. (Do not attempt to unmold while steam is still escaping, as the pudding might crack.)

7. Slice with a serrated knife and serve warm.

Standard Stovetop: Follow steps 1 to 3. Using a large pot with a tight-fitting lid, follow steps 4 and 5, replenishing water as needed. Steam until the pudding is set, about 75 to 90 minutes. Follow steps 6 and 7.

Apple Pudding

Serves 4 to 6

I love to make this pudding in the fall when apples are abundant and at their peak of flavor. For variety I sometimes use one tart apple and one sweet one.

Serve warm or at room temperature with a dollop of Tofu Whip (page 398) or Cashew Cream (page 398) on top.

For additional information on steamed puddings, see page 378.

Pressure cooker: 25 minutes high pressure, 15-minute natural pressure release
Standard stovetop: 75 to 90 minutes

*½ teaspoon oil and 2 teaspoons flour for preparing a 1-quart bundt pan or
    heatproof casserole*
¾ cup whole wheat pastry flour
¾ cup yellow cornmeal
1 teaspoon baking soda
*1 tablespoon finely minced or grated lemon peel (colored part only,
    preferably organic)*
½ teaspoon each ground cinnamon, ginger, and allspice
⅛ teaspoon sea salt
2 cups coarsely chopped, peeled, and cored apples
½ cup raisins
½ cup coarsely chopped walnuts or pecans
¾ cup apple juice
½ cup maple syrup
Boiling water

1. Brush the oil on the bottom and sides of the pan and dust liberally with flour. Tip out any extra flour. Set aside.

2. In a bowl, combine the flour, cornmeal, baking soda, lemon peel, spices, and salt. Stir to blend. Add the apples, raisins, and nuts, and toss until they are evenly distributed and coated with the flour.

3. In a measuring cup, combine the juice and maple syrup. Stir the liquid into the dry ingredients just until all of the flour is absorbed.

4. Transfer the mixture to the prepared bundt pan or casserole. Wrap tightly with 2 sheets of aluminum foil crisscrossed on the top, with ends long enough to tuck under the bottom of the pan.

5. Place a rack or trivet in the bottom of the cooker. Lower the pudding into the cooker with the aid of a foil strip (page 10) and set it on the rack. Add enough boiling water to reach halfway up the sides of the pan.

6. Lock the lid in place and over high heat bring to high pressure. Lower the heat just enough to maintain high pressure and cook for 25 minutes. Turn off the heat and allow the pressure to come down naturally for 15 minutes. Remove the lid, tilting it away from you to allow any excess steam to escape.

7. Remove the pan from the cooker by lifting it up with the aid of the foil strip and set it on a rack to cool slightly. Remove the top foil and, after all of the steam has escaped, run a knife around the edges. Turn pan over onto a platter and unmold. (Do not attempt to unmold while steam is still escaping, as the pudding might crack.)

8. Slice with a serrated knife and serve warm.

Standard Stovetop: Follow steps 1 to 4. Using a large pot with a tight-fitting lid, follow step 5. Bring to the boil, reduce the heat to medium, cover, and steam until the pudding is set, about 75 to 90 minutes, replenishing water as needed. Follow steps 7 to 8.

Celebrate Summer Fruit Pudding   Serves 4 to 6

This recipe is excellent to use with any soft seasonal fruit, such as plums, peaches, and nectarines. I've even had fantastic results with early spring rhubarb, cut into ¼-inch slices. It's not necessary to peel the fruit unless the skin is tough or unpleasantly thick.

Serve warm or at room temperature with a dollop of Tofu Whip (page 398) or Cashew Cream (page 398) on top.

For basic information on steamed puddings, see page 378.

Pressure cooker: 25 minutes high pressure, 15-minute natural pressure release
Standard stovetop: 75 to 90 minutes

½ teaspoon oil and 2 teaspoons whole wheat pastry flour for preparing a 1-
    quart bundt pan or heatproof casserole
1 to 1¼ cups whole wheat pastry or barley flour, divided
¾ cup granola, store-bought or Triple Grain (page 370)
1 teaspoon baking soda
⅓ cup raisins
½ cup walnuts
1 tablespoon finely minced or grated orange peel (colored part only,
    preferably organic)
½ teaspoon ground cinnamon
¼ teaspoon freshly grated nutmeg
⅛ teaspoon sea salt
2½ cups sliced or diced fresh soft fruit, peeled if desired
¾ cup orange juice
⅓ to ½ cup maple syrup (amount depends upon the sweetness of the
    granola and of the fruit; start with ⅓ cup and add more if needed)
Boiling water

1. Brush the oil on the bottom and sides of the pan and liberally dust with flour. Tip out any extra flour. Set aside.

2. In a bowl, combine 1 cup of the flour, granola, baking soda, raisins, walnuts, orange peel, cinnamon, nutmeg, and salt. Stir in the fruit.

3. In a liquid measuring cup, combine the orange juice and maple syrup. Stir the liquid into the dry ingredients just until all of the flour is absorbed. If the batter is very thin, stir in the additional ¼ cup flour.

4. Transfer the mixture into the prepared pan. Wrap tightly with 2 sheets of aluminum foil crisscrossed on the top, with ends long enough to tuck under the bottom of the pan.

5. Place a rack or trivet in the bottom of the cooker. Lower the pudding into the cooker with the aid of a foil strip (page 10) and set it on the rack. Add enough boiling water to reach halfway up the sides of the pan.

6. Lock the lid in place and over high heat bring to high pressure. Lower the heat just enough to maintain high pressure and cook for 25 minutes. Turn off the heat and allow the pressure to come down naturally for 15 minutes. Remove the lid, tilting it away from you to allow any excess steam to escape.

7. Remove the pan from the cooker by lifting it up with the aid of the foil strip and set it on a rack to cool slightly. Remove the top foil and, after all of the steam has escaped, run a knife around the edges. Turn over onto a platter and unmold. (Do not attempt to unmold while steam is still escaping, as the pudding might crack.)

8. Slice with a serrated knife and serve warm.

Standard Stovetop: Follow steps 1 to 4. Using a large pot with a tight-fitting lid, follow step 5. Bring to the boil, reduce the heat to medium, cover, and steam until the pudding is set, about 75 to 90 minutes, replenishing water as needed. Follow steps 7 to 8.

The biodynamic/French intensive method of horticulture is a quiet, vitally alive art of organic gardening which relinks people with the whole universe—a universe in which each of us is an interwoven part of the whole. People find their place by relating and cooperating in harmony with the sun, air, rain, soil, moon, insects, plants and animals rather than by attempting to dominate them. All these elements will teach us their lessons and do the gardening for us if we will only watch and listen. We each become gentle shepherds providing the conditions for plants' growth.

—John Jeavons, *How to Grow More Vegetables*
(Berkeley: Ten Speed Press, 1982).

Date-Nut Pudding

This and the following two recipes offer versions of steamed puddings using dried fruit rather than fresh. It's easy to keep the ingredients on hand to make these quick and elegant last-minute desserts. Top them with some Tofu Whip (page 398) or Cashew Cream (page 398).

For additional information on steamed puddings, see page 378.

Pressure cooker: 25 minutes high pressure, 15-minute natural pressure release
Standard stovetop: 75 to 90 minutes

½ teaspoon oil and about 2 teaspoons flour for preparing a 1-quart bundt
   pan or heatproof casserole
1 cup whole wheat pastry or barley flour
½ cup unbleached white flour
1 teaspoon baking soda
¼ teaspoon ground cloves
¼ teaspoon ground nutmeg
¼ teaspoon ground allspice
⅛ teaspoon sea salt
1 cup tightly packed chopped, pitted dates (see Cook's Notes)
½ cup toasted walnuts or pecans, coarsely chopped
1¼ to 1½ cups apple or pear juice (see Cook's Notes)
2 to 4 tablespoons maple syrup (optional)
Boiling water

1. Brush oil on the bottom and sides of the pan or casserole and dust liberally with flour. Tip out any extra flour and set aside.

2. In a bowl, combine the flours, baking soda, cloves, nutmeg, allspice, and salt. Stir in the dates, taking care to coat the pieces with flour. Add the nuts and juice, stirring just until all of the flour is moistened. Taste and add maple syrup if extra sweetness is desired.

3. Transfer the mixture into the prepared bundt pan or casserole. Wrap tightly with 2 sheets of aluminum foil crisscrossed on the top, and with ends long enough to tuck under the bottom of the pan.

4. Place a rack or trivet in the bottom of the cooker. Lower the pudding into the cooker with the aid of a foil strip (page 10) and set it on the rack. Pour in enough boiling water to reach halfway up the sides of the pan.

5. Lock the lid in place and over high heat bring to high pressure. Lower the heat just enough to maintain high pressure and cook for 25 minutes. Turn off the heat and allow the pressure to come down naturally for 15 minutes. Remove the lid, tilting it away from you to allow any excess steam to escape.

6. Remove the pan from the cooker by lifting it up with the aid of the foil strip and set it on a rack to cool slightly. Remove the top foil and, after all of the steam has escaped, run a knife around the edges. Turn over onto a platter and unmold. (Do not attempt to unmold while steam is still escaping, as the pudding might crack.)

7. Slice with a serrated knife and serve warm.

Standard Stovetop: Follow steps 1 to 3. Using a large pot with a tight-fitting lid, follow step 4. Bring to the boil, reduce the heat to medium, cover, and steam until the pudding is set, about 75 to 90 minutes, replenishing water as needed. Follow steps 6 to 7.

Cook's Notes: Plump, medjool dates are the king of dates as far as I'm concerned, richer and creamier than the more common deglet noors.

Store dates in the freezer to keep them fresh. Chop them when they're partially frozen, or roll them in a bit of flour first, then snip them with kitchen shears.

Use the maximum amount of liquid for a moister texture or if the dates are very dried out.

Variation: TUTTI-FRUTTI PUDDING: Instead of dates, try ½ cup *each* of chopped dried apricots, prunes, and apples.

> The responsible consumer must also be in some way a producer. Out of his own resources and skills, he must be equal to some of his own needs. The household that prepares its own meals in its own kitchen with some intelligent regard for nutritional value, and thus depends on the grocer only for selected raw materials, exercises an influence on the food industry that reaches from the store all the way back to the seedsman. The household that produces some or all of its own food will have a proportionately greater influence.
>
> —Wendell Berry, *The Unsettling of America*
> (San Francisco: Sierra Books, 1986).

Down-Home Bread Pudding

Serves 6 to 8

This lovable dessert is comfort food at its best, and the most delicious way I know to transform stale bread.

This pudding is especially tasty with whole wheat sourdough or raisin bread, but can be made with any kind of leftover bread, including rye.

Prepare this pudding in a 2-quart heatproof casserole that fits into the cooker with at least ½ inch to spare around the perimeter.

Pressure cooker: 20 minutes high pressure, 10-minute natural pressure release
Standard stovetop: 75 to 90 minutes

6 to 8 thin slices of a large, round country loaf or 14 to 16 slices of an Italian or French loaf, stale or air-dried for 12 to 14 hours
3 cups apple or pear juice (see Cook's Notes)
1 cup (4 ounces) raw, unsalted cashews
Grated or finely minced peel (colored part only) of 1 orange, preferably organic
½ teaspoon ground nutmeg
¼ to ½ teaspoon ground cardamom
Pinch sea salt
½ cup coarsely chopped hazelnuts (toasted are especially nice) or walnuts (optional)
2 cups chopped mixed dried fruit (see Cook's Notes)
2 tablespoons fruit-sweetened strawberry or raspberry preserves

1. Break each bread slice into 2 to 3 pieces. Set aside.

2. In a blender or food processor, combine the juice, cashews, orange peel, nutmeg, cardamom, and salt, and blend until smooth.

3. Place a layer of bread on the bottom of the casserole. Douse liberally with the juice mixture. Distribute some nuts (if using) and dried fruit on top. Continue layering bread, juice, nuts, and fruit, taking care to end with a bread layer. Gently press the ingredients down into the liquid so that all of the bread is submerged.

4. Cover with a sheet of aluminum foil large enough that the ends can be tucked under the bottom of the casserole. (At this point, you can set the uncooked pudding aside for up to 2 hours before cooking.)

5. When ready to cook the pudding, place the rack and 2 cups of water in the cooker. Lower the casserole into the cooker with the aid of a foil strip (page 10). Lock the lid in place and over high heat bring to high pressure. Lower the heat just enough to maintain high pressure and cook for 20 minutes. Turn off the heat and allow the pressure to come down naturally for 10 minutes. Remove the lid, tilting it away from you to allow any excess steam to escape.

6. If not serving immediately, let the pudding sit in the cooker with the lid ajar to stay warm. When ready to serve, lift the casserole from the cooker with the aid of the foil strip. Remove the aluminum foil from the casserole and brush the top with the preserves. Serve warm in hearty scoopfuls. (After the pudding sits for a while, it usually firms up enough to be sliced.)

Standard Stovetop: Follow steps 1 to 4. Using a large pot with a tight-fitting lid, follow the first two instructions in step 5. Bring to the boil, then cover and reduce heat to medium. Steam until the pudding is set, about 75 to 90 minutes, replenishing water as needed. Follow step 6.

Cook's Notes: If the fruit is very dried out, add an extra ⅓ cup of juice.

Variation: PEACH BREAD PUDDING: Use 2 cups of dried peaches instead of the mixed dried fruit, and 3 cups of peach juice instead of apple juice. Peach preserves or a complementary topping also work well. This approach allows you to make a wide variety of single-fruit bread puddings, such as apple, pear, or apricot.

Raisin-Rice Custard Pudding **Serves 6**

This is a wonderfully rich and moist (but not too liquid) rice pudding. If you like to gild the lily, top it with a dollop of Tofu Whip (page 398). Serve the pudding warm, right from the casserole.

Leftovers, by the way, are great for breakfast. Reheat the pudding in a small dish set on a rack over boiling water. Steam until heated throughout, about 4 to 5 minutes.

> **Pressure cooker:** 25 minutes high pressure, 10-minute natural pressure release
> **Standard stovetop:** 75 to 90 minutes

1 cup (4 ounces) raw, unsalted cashews
3 cups water
3 tablespoons maple syrup, approximately
1 teaspoon ground cinnamon
¾ teaspoon ground ginger
¼ to ½ teaspoon ground cardamom
Pinch sea salt
1 cup brown basmati or long-grain brown rice
½ cup raisins or dried currants (slightly less sweet)
Additional maple syrup to taste

continued

1. In a blender (preferably) or food processor, combine the cashews, water, maple syrup, spices, and salt, and process to create a smooth, milky texture. (A processor will not make a very smooth mixture; this is not important.) Place the rice and raisins in a 1½- to 2-quart casserole that fits into the cooker, with at least ½ inch to spare around the perimeter. Add the liquid and stir.

2. Set the rack and 2 cups of water into the cooker. Transfer the covered casserole to the cooker with the aid of a reusable foil strip (page 10).

3. Lock the lid in place and over high heat bring to high pressure. Lower the heat just enough to maintain high pressure and cook for 25 minutes. Turn off the heat and allow the pressure to come down naturally for 10 minutes. Remove the lid, tilting it away from you to allow any excess steam to escape.

4. Stir well to distribute any nut bits that have floated to the top. If the rice is not quite tender, replace the lid and continue to steam in the residual heat until done. If the rice isn't sweet enough, stir in more maple syrup to taste, or pour some syrup on top of each serving. Serve warm.

Standard Stovetop: Using a heatproof casserole that will fit into a large pot, follow steps 1 and 2. Cover the pot and bring the water to the boil. Reduce the heat to medium and steam until the rice is tender and the liquid has become puffy and custardlike, about 75 to 90 minutes. Replenish the water in the bottom of the pot as needed. Follow step 4.

He will never go to heaven who is content to go alone.

—Boethius, A.D. 450

Winter Dried and Fresh Fruit Compote

Serves 4 to 6

This dish stands on its own as an elegant dessert or as a superb topping for waffles, pancakes, or whole grain cereals. It's not a fussy recipe, so use up whatever dried fruits you have on hand. If they're bone-dry, simmer them in the water while you're preparing the fresh fruits. Otherwise, cook all of the ingredients together.

Pressure cooker: 3 minutes high pressure
Standard stovetop: 15 to 20 minutes

1 cup water
4 thin slices lemon, preferably organic
1 tablespoon plus 1 teaspoon freshly grated ginger
1 cinnamon stick, cut in two
6 dried figs, trimmed and quartered
12 dried peach or apricot halves
10 pitted prunes, halved
⅓ cup raisins
5 medium apples, peeled, cored, and quartered
5 plums, pitted and halved, or 4 pears, peeled, cored, and quartered

1. Place all of the ingredients in the cooker.

2. Lock the lid into place. Over high heat bring to high pressure. Lower the heat just enough to maintain high pressure and cook for 3 minutes. Reduce the pressure with a quick-release method. Remove the lid, tilting it away from you to allow any excess steam to escape.

3. Remove the cinnamon stick and serve warm.

Standard Stovetop: In a saucepan, follow step 1. Bring to the boil, cover, and reduce heat. Simmer until the dried fruits are very soft and the fresh fruits are tender, about 15 to 20 minutes. Follow step 3.

Summer Fruit Compote

Here's a quick and refreshing way to use any plums, peaches, apricots, or other summer fruit that have become bruised or overripe.

Serve the compote chilled on its own or at room temperature as a topping for Lemon Poppy Seed Cake (page 352).

Pressure cooker: up to high pressure, 10-minute natural pressure release
Standard stovetop: 20 to 25 minutes

2 to 2½ pounds mixed soft fruit, such as peaches, nectarines, and plums, pitted and quartered (remove any bruised spots)
1 cup fruit juice (white grape is nice) or water
4 thin slices of lemon, preferably organic
Maple syrup to taste (optional)

1. Place the fruit, juice, and lemon slices in the cooker.

2. Lock the lid into place. Over high heat, bring up to high pressure. As soon as high pressure is reached, shut off the heat and allow the pressure to come down naturally for 10 minutes. Quick-release any remaining pressure. Remove the lid, tilting it away from you to allow any excess steam to escape.

3. Stir in maple syrup to taste, if added sweetness is desired.

Standard Stovetop: In a 3-quart saucepan, follow step 1. Bring to the boil, then cover and reduce heat. Cook gently until the fruits are soft and puffy, about 20 to 25 minutes. Follow step 3.

Variations

- For a sweeter compote, add ¼ cup raisins or dried currants.
- Add 3 to 4 thin slices of fresh ginger.
- Add ¼ teaspoon ground cardamom.

Applesauce

I like straightforward applesauce recipes because they allow the taste of the fruit to emerge in full splendor.

Peel and core the apples before cooking if you want the dish to remain chunky. For a smooth applesauce, just quarter the apples and press them through a sieve or food mill after cooking.

For a truly memorable result, use a variety of apples so that the flavor is complex but quintessentially apple. If necessary, squirt on some fresh lemon juice and add lemon peel to perk up lazy flavors.

Pressure cooker: up to high pressure, 10-minute natural pressure release
Standard stovetop: 25 to 30 minutes

2½ to 3 pounds apples, quartered (peeled and cored, if desired)
½ cup apple juice or water (see Cook's Notes)
3 to 4 thin slices of lemon
Maple syrup, lemon juice, and lemon peel to taste (optional)

1. Place the apples, juice, and lemon slices in the cooker.

2. Lock the lid into place. Over high heat bring to high pressure. Turn off the heat and allow the pressure to drop naturally. (Do not use a quick-release method, which is likely to cause spouting at the vent.) Remove the lid, tilting it away from you to allow any excess steam to escape.

3. Remove the lemon slices, and pass the apples through a food mill or sieve, if desired.

4. Add maple syrup, lemon juice, and lemon peel to taste, if desired.

Standard Stovetop: In a large saucepan, proceed with step 1. Bring to the boil, cover, and lower the heat. Simmer until the apples are puffy and very tender, about 25 to 30 minutes. If the mixture seems quite dry, add a bit more juice or water. Follow steps 3 and 4.

Cook's Notes: Even if your cooker requires 1 cup of liquid to come up to pressure, it will probably work well with only ½ cup, since the apples release so much moisture.

Variations

- PEAR SAUCE: Substitute an equivalent amount of pears for the apples. Add 2 to 3 teaspoons freshly grated ginger, if desired.
- RHUBARB APPLESAUCE: Add 1 pound of rhubarb cut into ½-inch slices, or substitute 1 pound of rhubarb for an equal weight of apples. Since rhubarb is tart, you may want to add a sweetener after cooking.

Rhubarb Raisin Crumble

One day I had a lot of rhubarb on hand and not a lot of time. This simple dessert was the result. It is great served right out of the oven and makes a magnificent leftover: Overnight refrigeration gives it a puddinglike texture.

This recipe makes a big batch, but cut it in half if you're not planning to feed an army.

Delicious served warm with a dollop of Tofu Whip (page 398) on top.

Oven: 25 to 30 minutes at 375°

3 pounds rhubarb, trimmed and cut into 1-inch slices (discard any leaves, which are poisonous)
½ cup fruit-sweetened strawberry preserves
½ cup raisins
1 tablespoon finely minced or grated orange peel (colored part only, organic if possible)
1 teaspoon ground cinnamon
2 cups Triple Grain (page 370) or store-bought granola, preferably maple walnut
Maple syrup to taste

1. Combine the ingredients in a heatproof pan measuring 13 × 8 × 2 inches. (The mixture will seem very dry; don't be concerned; the rhubarb will give up considerable liquid as it cooks.)

2. Place the pan in a cold oven, set the temperature to 375°, and bake uncovered for 15 minutes. Stir and continue baking until rhubarb is tender but still firm, about 10 to 15 minutes more.

3. Add maple syrup to taste if more sweetness is desired.

Peaches with Fresh Raspberry Sauce Serves 4

Sometimes I'm so busy cooking that I forget how refreshing and elegant a plate of beautifully arranged peach slices with fresh raspberry sauce can be. This is particularly true on summer days when even lifting a fork feels like an effort. Serve the sauce within a half day of preparing it.

1 pint raspberries
1 to 2 teaspoons finely minced lemon peel (colored part only, organic if
*   possible; optional)*
1 to 2 tablespoons lemon juice
Maple syrup to taste (optional)
4 large, ripe peaches, sliced

1. In a blender or processor, puree the berries.

2. Pass the puree through a fine sieve to remove the seeds.

3. Blend in lemon peel (if using), lemon juice, and maple syrup to taste, if desired. Make a puddle of sauce on pretty dessert plates and arrange the peach slices on top.

Variations

- Substitute kiwis, strawberries, or blueberries for the raspberries.
- Use the sauce over Lemon Poppy Seed Cake (page 352) rather than with fresh fruit.

Pineapple Granita

A couldn't-be-easier summer dessert that will cool down the cook and guests alike. The secret to success is a sweet, perfectly ripe pineapple.

1 large, ripe pineapple
Maple syrup to taste
Strawberry slices or mint leaves

1. Cut off the top and slice the pineapple into quarters. Slice off the sliver of hard core on the top of each quarter.

2. With a serrated knife, using a sawing motion, slice the flesh from the skin. Cut each boat-shaped quarter into thin slices.

3. Set the slices into a well-sealed container and freeze overnight. (The pineapple can be stored in the freezer for up to 3 weeks.)

4. Remove from the freezer about 10 minutes before serving.

5. Just before serving, put the pineapple into a blender or food processor and process to a coarse puree. Add maple syrup if extra sweetness is desired.

6. Serve immediately, garnished with strawberry slices or mint leaves.

Variations

- For a BANANA SORBET, peel and slice very ripe bananas (they should have lots of brown spots on them). Freeze bananas overnight and puree as directed above. A dash of vanilla or a light dusting of nutmeg is nice. Sweeten with maple syrup, if desired.
- For a creamy PINEAPPLE BANANA SORBET, freeze a very ripe, sliced banana with the pineapple and puree both fruits together.
- Experiment with using frozen fresh strawberries, raspberries, and blueberries.

Ginger-Poached Rhubarb

Rhubarb always signals spring to me. I love its tart taste and complex texture—silken and fibrous at the same time.

Since rhubarb releases considerable liquid as it cooks, I prefer not to cook it in a pressure cooker, which would require adding a cup or so of liquid.

Standard stovetop: 15 minutes

2 pounds rhubarb (7 large stalks)
⅓ cup apple juice, approximately
½ cup raisins
2 tablespoons freshly grated ginger
½ teaspoon ground cinnamon
2 to 4 tablespoons maple syrup

1. Trim rhubarb stalks, top and bottom. (Discard any leaves, which are very poisonous.) Cut the rhubarb into 1-inch slices.

2. In a saucepan, combine the rhubarb with the remaining ingredients except the maple syrup. Bring to boil, then simmer, covered, until the rhubarb is tender, about 15 minutes. If the mixture becomes dry, add a bit more apple juice.

3. When the rhubarb is tender, stir in maple syrup to taste.

Cook's Notes: Some people prefer their rhubarb cooked to a thick, soupy consistency. I like mine tender but still holding its shape. When you can easily pierce them with a fork, taste the stalks at various stages to determine what consistency you prefer.

Carob Frosting

**Makes about 2 cups,
enough to frost and fill a 2-layer cake**

Here is a creamy, rich frosting with a deep chocolate color. It spreads like a dream when at room temperature, and may be stored in the refrigerator for up to 1 week. You can halve this recipe to frost 2 dozen cupcakes or a single layer cake.

Thanks to Laura Litterello, of the Natural Gourmet Institute for Food and Health in New York City, for this sumptuous frosting recipe.

1 cup cashew or almond butter at room temperature
6 tablespoons maple syrup
2 teaspoons vanilla
6 tablespoons roasted carob powder, sifted
3 to 6 tablespoons soy milk

1. In a food processor (preferably) or blender, mix the nut butter with the maple syrup and vanilla. Process until smooth.

2. Add the carob powder and pulse on and off until the ingredients are thoroughly combined.

3. Blend in just enough soy milk to achieve a spreading consistency.

Coconut Icing

Makes about ¾ cup, enough to frost the top of a 9-inch cake

A luxurious alternative, especially delicious on Carrot Cake (page 354).

Stovetop: 15 minutes

¾ cup plus 2 tablespoons apple juice, divided
½ cup dried (unsweetened), shredded coconut
2½ teaspoons arrowroot
Pinch sea salt
Maple syrup to taste (optional)

1. In a 2-quart saucepan, simmer the ¾ cup of apple juice and coconut, covered, until the coconut softens slightly, about 10 minutes. (Alternatively, soak the coconut in the apple juice overnight and simmer for about 2 minutes.)

2. Dissolve the arrowroot in the 2 tablespoons of apple juice. Stir this mixture and the salt into the coconut, and simmer uncovered until thickened, about 5 minutes.

3. Add maple syrup, if desired.

4. Cool slightly, then pulse in a food processor to create a coarse paste. Set aside to cool completely before frosting the cake.

Date Glaze

Makes 1¼ cups, enough to glaze the top and sides of a 9-inch cake

Try this distinctive topping on Carrot Cake (page 354).

Stovetop: about 15 minutes

1 cup loosely packed, pitted dates (preferably medjools)
1 cup plus 2 tablespoons water, divided
3 tablespoons sesame tahini
2 teaspoons arrowroot

1. Combine the dates and 1 cup of water in a 2-quart saucepan and bring to the boil. Reduce the heat, cover, and simmer until the dates are very soft, about 10 minutes.

2. Transfer the mixture plus the tahini to a food processor and puree until smooth. Return to the pot and bring to the boil.

3. Dissolve the arrowroot in the remaining 2 tablespoons of water.

4. Reduce the heat under the date puree, stir in the arrowroot, and continue to simmer until the mixture thickens to a porridgelike consistency, stirring frequently, about 3 to 5 minutes.

5. Set aside to cool before frosting the cake.

Cashew Cream

Makes about ¾ cup

This recipe comes to us courtesy of the Natural Gourmet Institute for Food and Health in New York City. It makes an irresistibly rich topping for pies and tarts. The mixture comes out slightly smoother when made in a blender, but the food processor also does a creditable job.

1 cup raw, unsalted cashews
¼ cup water, approximately
2 to 3 tablespoons maple syrup
1 teaspoon vanilla

1. Coarsely chop the nuts in a blender or food processor. With the motor running, gradually add the water, 2 tablespoons maple syrup, and vanilla.

2. Taste and add additional maple syrup, if desired. Continue processing until the mixture achieves a consistency similar to whipped cream. Add a bit more water if needed.

Tofu Whip

Makes about 2 cups

It's light, fast, and a perfect complement to pies, puddings, and fruit compotes. Tofu Whip can be stored in the refrigerator for up to 1 week; if the mixture separates, blend it thoroughly before using. The recipe may be cut in half.

1 pound firm or extra-firm tofu, drained and cut into chunks
¼ cup maple syrup
1 tablespoon vanilla
1 to 2 tablespoons water (optional)

1. In a food processor or blender, blend all of the ingredients until very creamy, adding water if needed to achieve a whipped cream consistency. Refrigerate until needed.

Variation: Instead of maple syrup, try 3 to 4 tablespoons of fruit-sweetened preserves and some finely minced citrus peel. Choose the fruit and citrus flavors to complement the dessert.

Ingredients A to Z

In this alphabetical listing, I have provided some personal observations on the ingredients used in this book, plus my recommendations for selection, storage, and cooking times.

Please keep the following points in mind when using this glossary:

1. The use of small capital letters within an entry indicates that the ingredient has an entry of its own.
2. Vegetable cooking times for both pressure cooking and steaming are calculated from the moment that the vegetables are placed on a rack over *already boiling* water and the cover set in place.
3. For basic instructions on wok cooking, turn to pages 10–12, for pressure cooking, pages 8–10, and for steaming, page 12.
4. When preparing fruits or vegetables for cooking, see "To Peel or Not to Peel," page 6.

5. Plastic bags are frequently suggested as a convenient way to store fruits and vegetables. Try to rinse out and recycle them whenever possible; however, discard any plastic bags that have been used for storing meat as they may contain bacteria.
6. If you cannot locate an ingredient locally, check Mail-Order Sources, page 475.

Acorn Squash (Table Queen): A roundish, ribbed WINTER SQUASH that has a deep green or orange skin and pale yellow-orange flesh. It is rarely as flavorful, sweet, or creamy as many other winter squashes, but it has the ideal shape to stuff and bake—perhaps its best use. *Se-*

lect firm squash, heavy for its size, with stem intact and dull skin. (Shiny skin usually indicates that it's been waxed.) *Allow* 6 to 8 ounces per person. *Store* in a cool, dry spot or refrigerate for up to 3 months. *Prepare for cooking* by lightly scrubbing (if pressure cooking) or peeling (if using other cooking techniques or if not organic). To peel, cut into crescents, remove seeds, and cut away peel with a sharp paring knife.

Pressure cooking:
Unpeeled, halved, and seeded: 6 to 7 minutes high pressure

Unpeeled, halved, seeded, and cut into ½-inch crescent-shaped slices: 3 to 4 minutes high pressure

Peeled (if desired), seeded, and cut into 1½-inch chunks: 3 to 4 minutes high pressure

With small acorn squash (under 1½ pounds), the skins become tender enough to eat after 3 minutes under high pressure.

Steaming:
Peeled, seeded, and cut into ½-inch crescent-shaped slices: 9 to 12 minutes

Baking:
Halved, seeded, and set, cut side down, on a lightly oiled shallow baking pan: 30 to 45 minutes at 400°. Drizzle with maple syrup and sprinkle with ground cinnamon or nutmeg before serving, if desired.

Aduki (Adzuki, Azuki) Beans: Long esteemed as a healing food in Japan, these small brownish-red beans with elegant slender white stripes are now cultivated in America; organically grown beans are available. The little polished adukis imported from Japan are sold in well-stocked health food stores for about triple the price of the American beans. They are thought to be more nutritious, but I've found no dramatic difference in taste and don't consider them worth the price.

Adukis are considered to be more digestible than most other beans; they are also a good source of B vitamins, potassium, iron, and calcium.

Adukis turn from firm to mushy in a flash in the pressure cooker, so it's best to cook them under pressure for the minimum recommended time and then finish them off by simmering. Reserve the nutritious cooking liquid and drink it as a broth or use it as part of the stock for soup. See BEANS and the bean cooking chart, page 175.

Agar (Agar-Agar, Kanten) and Irish Moss (Carrageen): Both of these SEA VEGETABLES are valued as gelling agents. Agar creates a firmer gel, is more readily available than Irish moss, and is the only one used in the recipes in this book. It is most commonly sold in the form of flakes or in bars, and it is taste-free. Agar is a fine source of iodine, calcium, iron, phosphorus, and vitamins.

Add 2 tablespoons of agar flakes per cup of *simmering* liquid to be gelled (if the liquid is citrus, use 3 tablespoons). Continue simmering, stirring occasionally, until the agar has dissolved. Allow about 1 hour gelling time at room temperature or 35 minutes in the refrigerator.

Many cooks prefer the long, rectangular agar bars, but I find the flakes more convenient to use. The bars are first rinsed and shredded into bits before they are dissolved in a hot liquid.

Alaria: A sea vegetable harvested off the coast of Maine, it is similar to WAKAME, although often considerably tougher, especially its fibrous central rib, which should be removed after soaking the alaria in boiling water for 15 minutes. Alaria requires cooking, while most wakame can be eaten after it is softened in water. See SEA VEGETABLES for general storing and cooking instructions.

Alfalfa Sprouts: See SPROUTS.

Allspice: A tiny dark brown berry native to the West Indies whose name derives from its flavor, which suggests a combination of CINNAMON, NUTMEG, and CLOVES. Try it in baked goods and desserts; allspice marries especially well with fruit. Also tasty with pureed SWEET POTATOES and SQUASH. Purchase whole berries and grind as needed for the most vibrant taste; see SPICES and Flavorprints, page 4.

Almond Butter: My all-time favorite nut butter, this spreadable paste made of ground ALMONDS is at its most flavorful when prepared from toasted almonds. (Don't confuse almond butter with almond paste, which is sweetened and resembles marzipan.)

Almond butter makes a great spread on bread or rice crackers, and it is a nice thickener and flavoring agent in cake icings. Refrigerate once opened; store up to 4 months. Optimum choice: unsalted, toasted, crunchy-style, and ground from organic nuts. See NUT BUTTERS.

Almonds: Kernels of the fruit of the almond tree, almonds stay freshest when purchased in the shell. If shelling them involves too much work, buy them unblanched (with their thin brown skins intact, protecting freshness and flavor), preferably from a refrigerated case. To blanch almonds, drop them in boiling water for 10 to 20 seconds and then "shock" them in cold water to loosen and slip off the brown skins. See NUTS AND SEEDS.

Amaranth: A tiny seed—usually yellow-brown—that is high in protein and two essential amino acids, lysine and methionine. Because the seeds are so small, the best way to rinse them is by swooshing in cold water and then pouring the mixture through a strainer lined with cheesecloth—a messy task. I purchase packaged organic amaranth, which seems quite clean, so I rarely rinse it.

Cooked amaranth has the crunch and appearance of caviar. As a breakfast cereal or a gritslike side dish (page 70), amaranth has the irresistible aroma of fresh CORN. Eaten alone, however, it tastes a bit grassy and benefits by being cooked with GARLIC or fresh GINGER (for a savory dish), or MAPLE SYRUP and CINNAMON (for a sweet dish). When a tablespoon of amaranth is cooked with a cupful of RICE, it adds a welcome crunch but also a noticeable stickiness.

Because it releases a starchy substance during cooking, a small amount of amaranth added at the beginning does a nice job of thickening soups and stews. However, this starchy substance makes it virtually impossible to toss amaranth in a grain salad or prepare it pilaf fashion. You can make miniature popcorn by popping amaranth in an ungreased, heavy skillet, but I don't find it worth the trouble.

I have seen gorgeous fresh red amaranth leaves growing in organic gardens, but haven't yet had the opportunity to try them. I'm told that another variety with green leaves and deep pink around the central rib is sometimes sold in Oriental markets in the U.S. In Asia amaranth leaves are highly regarded and steamed or stir-fried like SPINACH. See AMARANTH FLOUR and GRAINS.

Amaranth Flour: Because of its impressive protein profile, amaranth flour is added to many crackers and cookies and some PASTAS sold in health food stores. Make amaranth flour at home by grinding small amounts as needed in a spice grinder. You can safely substitute ¼ cup of amaranth flour for WHOLE WHEAT PASTRY FLOUR in any savory baked goods. Because it has a slightly grassy taste, I don't recommend using it in cakes or desserts. See FLOUR.

Amasake: A naturally sweet fermented beverage made by introducing a rice-based culture called *koji* into cooked sweet glutinous rice. This refreshing drink is in the refrigerated section of health food stores and can be substituted for fruit juice in baked goods. In summer blend amasake with fresh fruit for a smoothie. In winter prepare a comforting cocoalike drink by heating 1 cupful of amasake with 1 heaping teaspoon of Cafix and roasted CAROB powder to taste.

Anasazi Beans: A native American maroon-and-white speckled bean about the size of a pinto, which can be used as a substitute. Readily available in health food stores, anasazis have a slightly sweet flavor and work well in Southwestern and Mexican-style bean dishes. You can substitute PINTOS in any recipe calling for anasazis. See BEANS and the bean cooking chart, page 175.

Ancho Chilies: These earthy-red chilies are actually poblano chilies in dried form. They are a principal ingredient in most authentic CHILI POWDER. Once you have tasted your own blend of high-quality roasted CHILI PEPPERS and HERBS, you will probably never again purchase a commercial chili powder. A great mail-order source is Los Chileros de Nuevo Mexico. See CHILI PEPPERS and CHIPOTLES.

Anise, Star: See STAR ANISE.

Aniseed: A small greenish-brown seed with a slender tail and a slightly sweet licorice flavor. It's great in cookies and pairs remarkably well with CELERY, CHESTNUTS, and RICE. See SPICES and Flavorprints, page 4.

Appaloosa Beans: Small brown-and-white speckled beans grown in the American Northwest, with a mild flavor that makes them a pleasing (and pretty) alternative to WHITE BEANS in sauces and salads.

Apple Butter: A delicious nondairy spread made by cooking down APPLES, SPICES, and a SWEETENER until thick. Purchase organic brands.

Apple Cider/Juice: When it's in season, opt for freshly made cider, which is sweeter and more full of vibrant flavor than any purchased apple juice. If you own a juicer, you can extract the juice when needed. Next best, choose store-bought juice that is labeled 100 percent pure organic, expressed from whole fruit (not concentrate) and has no sugar added. If you use juice only for occasional baking, freeze extra in 1- or ½-cup portions.

Apples: Available year round, this all-American fruit (apples were actually brought here by colonists from England) is at its crispy-crunchy best in the fall. Apples are a good source of vitamin A. My current favorite apples include crisp-tart Macouns, Winesaps, Granny Smiths, and Jonathans. For baking, I like Cortlands, Northern Spies, Golden Delicious, and Rome Beauties. Ask your local growers what varieties are best for what purposes and request information on which, if any, pesticides were used in their cultivation. (Many growers tell you that it's impossible to grow apples without spraying them, but this is untrue.) Depending upon the answer, determine whether to peel the fruit before eating it.

Select firm apples free of bruises. *Store* apples in a plastic bag in the refrigerator for up to 10 days. If left for more than a day or two at room temperature, apples continue to ripen and become soft. Overripe or bruised fruit can be made into homemade Applesauce (page 391).

Apples, Dried: At their best, dried apples are delicious and intensely flavored; purchase organic apples packaged without preservatives (such as sulfur dioxide) and sold from a refrigerated case; dried apples have a high fiber content and are great for snacks. See DRIED FRUIT.

Apricots: Grab those fresh apricots during the midsummer months when they're available: If you can find tree-ripened specimens, they're truly nectar for the gods. Since more than 90 percent of apricots in the United States are grown in California and ripe apricots don't travel well, you're better off with the dried version (see below). Apricots are a superb source of vitamin A.

Select plump, aromatic fruit with a rich golden-orange hue and a smooth, unbroken skin. Once completely ripe, *store* apricots up to 2 days in a plastic bag in the refrigerator.

Apricots, Dried: Dried apricots are a superior source of vitamin A and make a good snack unless you are sensitive to their concentrated sweetness. Avoid buying most imported apricots (many come from Turkey) because they have been treated with sulfur dioxide, which turns them bright orange. Opt for organic fruit, free of preservatives, and sold from a refrigerated case; they are brownish in color. See DRIED FRUIT.

Arame: A sea vegetable with large leaves, arame is thinly sliced and sold in a dried form that suggests charcoal-black angel-hair PASTA. Since it is precooked before it is dehydrated, arame requires very little actual cooking time and is one of the mildest-tasting sea vegetables. It is a fine source of protein and minerals, especially calcium and potassium. See SEA VEGETABLES.

Arrowroot: A powdery thickening agent derived from a tropical starchy tuber of the same name. Arrowroot has no taste and becomes clear when cooked, making it an ideal thickener for sauces. It can be used in equal amounts as a substitute for KUZU. To prevent clumping, dissolve arrowroot in a small quantity of cold water before adding it to a hot liquid. Arrowroot is sometimes used as a binder in egg-free

baking. *Store* well sealed in a cool, dry place.

Artichokes (Globe Artichokes): Artichokes are at their best in the spring. *Select* dense specimens with tightly layered leaves and a fresh green hue. If their leaves are shriveled or olive-colored, pass them by. For best results, use medium artichokes; the outer leaves of large ones can become overcooked by the time the heart is tender. *Allow* 1 medium or large artichoke per person. *Store* in a plastic bag in the refrigerator for 2 to 3 days. *Prepare for cooking* by pulling off tough outer leaves and trimming the bottoms so the artichokes will sit flat on the steaming rack. To *serve*: Eat the artichoke leaf by leaf, scraping off the soft flesh between your teeth. Dip leaves into garlic-scented OLIVE OIL or a vinaigrette, if desired.

Once you have stripped off all the leaves, scrape away the inedible furry choke and quarter or slice the heart. Eat plain or dip into a vinaigrette dressing. Very yummy, low in calories, and high in potassium and vitamins A and C.

Artichokes are properly cooked when an inner leaf pulls off with a gentle tug, and you can strip off the flesh easily.

Pressure cooking:
Large (9 to 10 ounces): 9 to 11 minutes high pressure
Medium (6 to 8 ounces): 6 to 8 minutes high pressure
Baby (1 ounce each): 3 to 4 minutes high pressure

Fit 3 to 4 artichokes side by side on a rack or stack them pyramid fashion.

Steaming:
Large: 35 to 40 minutes
Medium: 25 minutes
Small: 15 minutes

Arugula (Rocket, Rugula): An elongated green leaf with a flavor that ranges from mildly biting to sharp and mustardy. *Se-*

lect young and tender bunches with bright green, perky leaves. *Store* up to 2 days in a glass or small pitcher with the roots submerged in water and a plastic bag over the leaves. *Prepare for eating* by cutting off the roots and lower stems and swooshing arugula vigorously in two or three changes of water to remove the sand. Spin dry.

Use arugula in a mixed green salad or in equal parts with RADICCHIO and BELGIAN ENDIVE. Like BEET GREENS or WATERCRESS, it makes a colorful and tasty addition to soups and vegetable stews when stirred in just before serving.

Asparagus: Asparagus—nature's proud trumpeters of spring's arrival—cook (and overcook!) so quickly that it is best to steam or stir-fry them: Pressure-cooking is too risky. *Select* asparagus with tightly closed tips and bright green stalks. *Allow* 4 to 6 ounces per person. Cook them as soon after purchase as possible. If you need to *store* them for more than a day, take Marian Morash's advice in *The Victory Garden Cookbook*: Slice ¼ inch off the bottoms and stand upright in water so they can drink it up like cut flowers. Cover the tops with a plastic bag. *Prepare for cooking:* Snap off the toughest part of the bottoms and peel nubby parts from the stalks. Instead of discarding the tough bottoms, consider making Spring Asparagus-Celery Stock (page 28).

Steaming:
Thick stalks: 3 to 6 minutes
Slender stalks: 1 to 2 minutes

If serving asparagus cold, immediately refresh stalks under cold water.

Stir-frying:
Thick stalks, cut into ½-inch slices on the diagonal: 1 to 2 minutes, plus 1 to 2 minutes wok steaming
Slender stalks, cut into ½-inch slices on the diagonal: 1 to 2 minutes

Avocados (Alligator Pears): The only avocado worth eating is the small, black, bumpy-skinned variety called Haas. The larger Fuerte avocado has a bright green, smooth skin and flesh that is quite watery, a far cry from the dense a d creamy texture that makes avocados such a treat. Mashed avocado makes a superb sandwich spread; it also adds an appealing creaminess to salad dressing (page 297).

For eating on their own or cut up for salads, *select* firm avocados with no mushy areas. When ripe, they feel pliant to a gentle touch. To ripen at home, place the avocados in a paper bag and store them at room temperature. (Soft, over-ripe avocados are often reduced in price and are great for making a vinaigrette or guacamole). Once they are ripe, *store* in the refrigerator until shortly before needed. *Serve* at room temperature for optimum flavor. Cut them open just before serving or sprinkle generously with lemon juice to avoid discoloration upon contact with the air.

Azukis: See ADUKI BEANS.

Baking Powder: A leavening agent composed of baking soda, an acid (calcium acid phosphate or cream of tartar), and cornstarch or ARROWROOT to absorb moisture. Double-acting baking powder releases carbon-dioxide gas bubbles immediately upon contact with liquid and again when heated. These bubbles create air pockets, which helps achieve a light and crumbly texture in baked goods.

Whenever a recipe in this book calls for baking powder, a double-acting and nonaluminum brand is specified. Recommended are Rumford and Featherlight, now widely available in health food stores. If using another brand, check the label to make sure it doesn't contain sodium aluminum sulfate, which may be harmful to health.

Baking powder is more perishable than one might believe. Check the expiration date on the bottom of the can before purchasing. Store in an airtight container in a cool, dry place for 4 to 6 months. If in doubt about its potency, mix 1 teaspoon powder with ⅓ cup hot water. Vigorous bubbling indicates that it's okay.

Baking Soda (Bicarbonate of Soda): When baking soda comes in contact with an acid (such as apple or lemon juice) and a liquid, it produces carbon-dioxide gas bubbles, causing dough to rise. Once this chemical reaction takes place, the batter should be set in the oven as soon as possible. Baking soda can work alone (as long as an acid is present) or in conjunction with baking powder to produce a light-textured product, but use it sparingly to avoid an unpleasant aftertaste.

Don't be tempted to add a pinch of baking soda to vegetables to keep them a bright green, as suggested by many old cookbooks. Recent tests have shown that this practice destroys vitamin C.

Check the expiration date before purchasing (baking soda does not last indefinitely), and *store* in a well-sealed container in a dry place.

Balsamic Vinegar: See VINEGAR.

Banana Chips/Dried Bananas: These seemingly healthful snacks are often available in health food stores, but beware—they are usually cooked in coconut oil (a saturated fat) and sweetened with sugar or honey. Ask your health food store to locate Plantation brand dried unsweetened organic bananas, which are delicious in morning cereal and muffins.

Bananas: Most bananas are picked green and then sprayed with ethylene gas to speed ripening. This seems unnecessary, since bananas ripen perfectly well when left at room temperature for a few days. Stores specializing in organic produce often sell ungassed bananas, but they may not be worth the added price, since the process of gassing is not likely to be harmful: It simulates the ethylene that bananas produce naturally as they ripen on the tree. *Select* unblemished bananas still attached to the stem; those that have broken off may not ripen properly. Ripen and *store* at room temperature. After peeling bananas, sprinkle with lemon juice to prevent browning.

My favorite way to eat bananas is to let them get very ripe (full of brown spots), peel and freeze them in chunks, then blend them with some AMASAKE or fruit juice to make a thick summertime drink.

Banana Squash: A very large winter squash with a golden, gray, or green skin, orange or tan flesh, and an elongated bananalike shape. It can be prepared and cooked like any other winter squash and is nice for pumpkin pies. See WINTER SQUASH.

Barley: An ancient grain that is one of the most appealing and digestible. Barley is mild and delightfully chewy; it deserves more attention in the whole foods kitchen!

Before being processed, this short, plump grain has two inedible hulls and a bran layer (the aleurone) covering its central white "pearl." The bran layer is rich in protein, fiber, and B vitamins.

UNHULLED BARLEY is the best to use for sprouting and is available by mail order. Nowadays, well-stocked health food stores carry either HULLED or "WHOLE" barley (only the inedible hulls are removed) and PEARL BARLEY (the hulls and most of the bran are removed). HULLED BARLEY (also known as SCOTCH or POT BARLEY) is nutritionally superior to pearl barley, but is chewier and requires longer cooking.

If you are a newcomer to whole grains, start with the pearl barley sold in health food stores, which is noticeably darker and less processed (that is, some of the bran is left intact) than the supermarket variety. See GRAINS and the grain cooking chart (page 67) for cooking instructions and timing. For HATO MUGI BARLEY, see JOB'S TEARS.

Barley Flakes: An alternative to rolled oats, these flakes are made of pearl barley, lightly toasted, and then flattened between rollers. Since they are precooked, barley flakes make a fast and tasty breakfast cereal. They have a delicate taste and none of the stickiness of OATMEAL. I love them! Try barley flakes instead of pearl barley in quick soups and stews, and instead of rolled oats in savory pie crusts.

Barley Flour: I enjoy the sweet taste and relative lightness of barley flour, and find it a welcome addition to whole grain muffins. A simple way to make fresh barley flour is to spin BARLEY FLAKES in a food processor; see FLOUR.

Barley Malt Syrup: Extracted from sprouted, roasted BARLEY, this thick, amber-colored sweetener tastes like a cross between MOLASSES and honey. It adds a nice flavor dimension to baked beans, squash pies, and savory baked goods. Barley malt is about 50 percent as sweet as sugar, and because its sugars are complex, it enters the bloodstream gradually, thus allaying sugar rushes. Select organic pure barley malt (read the label to be sure that corn syrup is not included). Measure from an oiled spoon or cup to avoid waste and a messy cleanup.

Do not confuse barley malt syrup with barley malt powder, a much more concentrated sweetener. See SWEETENERS.

Basil: When basil is in season, I buy large bunches and set the sandy roots into a large vase of water. Basil perfumes my kitchen and numerous summer salad recipes. To *store* fresh basil longer than a day or two, place the root ends into a pitcher of water and cover the leaves with a plastic bag; it will last in the refrigerator for up to a week, although the flavor will diminish daily. Most basil has green leaves, but occasionally a purple-leafed variety known as opal basil can be found.

When fresh basil is not available for salads, I suggest substituting an equal quantity of another fresh herb rather than using dried basil. If you have extra basil leaves that are about to dry out, chop them finely and make an herb vinaigrette—a tasty way to preserve their aromatic flavor for a week or so.

Basmati Rice: See RICE, BASMATI.

Bay Leaves: Highly aromatic, herbaceous leaves of the bay laurel tree. One is usually enough to add good flavor to soups, stews, and GRAINS. Take care to remove bay leaves before serving as they are not meant to be eaten. See HERBS and Flavorprints, page 4.

Bean Curd: See TOFU.

Beans: There are three main types of beans:

1. Fresh beans eaten with edible pods intact, such as green beans (also known as string beans). See GREEN BEANS for further information.
2. Fresh beans with inedible pods, such as green peas, fava beans, and cranberry beans. See BEANS, FRESH SHELLED for additional information.

3. Beans that have been dried, such as pinto and chick-peas. The following information relates to this third type.

Unless a reliable organic packaged brand is available, shopping for beans requires as much attention as selecting fresh fruit. *Select* beans that are brightly colored and whole; faded color indicates the beans are old, broken beans suggest rough handling. Once a bean's skin is broken, taste and the quality of its nutrients diminishes.

It is usually less expensive to purchase beans in bulk, although for certified organic beans you may have to choose 1-pound packages (Shiloh Farms is a personal favorite). If your local health food store does not carry bulk beans that meet the criteria listed above, you are better off buying them in 1-pound packages or ordering them by mail from one of the sources listed on page 475.

Store beans in bottles or tightly closed plastic bags in a cool place, and they will be fine for a year or so. Keep in mind, though, that the older the bean, the drier and harder it becomes. "Aged" beans will absorb more water and take longer to cook. Their flavor may not be as vibrant but their nutritional value will remain intact. Once cooked, beans last well for 3 to 4 days under refrigeration, and they freeze beautifully.

For more information and cooking instructions, see pages 172–178. See also the bean cooking chart (page 175) and individual listings under ADUKI BEANS, ANASAZI BEANS, BLACK-EYED PEAS, BLACK BEANS, CANNELLINI BEANS, CHICK-PEAS, FAVA BEANS, FLAGEOLETS, GREAT NORTHERN BEANS, KIDNEY BEANS, LENTILS, LIMA BEANS, MUNG BEANS, PEAS, DRIED, PINTO BEANS, SOYBEANS.

Beans, Fresh Shelled: This category includes CRANBERRY BEANS, FAVAS, LIMAS, and various other fresh beans sold in their pods. When you spot them in the market, buy them for a real treat. *Select* fresh-looking pods that are bulging with beans yet are tightly shut. *Allow* ½ to ¾ pound unshelled beans per person. (One pound of unshelled beans yields ¾ to 1 cup of shelled beans.) *Store* no more than a day or two in a tightly sealed container in the refrigerator. *Prepare for cooking* by shelling and rinsing beans.

Boiling:
Boil, lid on, in water to half cover until tender, about 10 to 12 minutes for lima beans and slightly longer for cranberry and fava beans. (*Note:* Fava beans, except for the youngest, must be peeled after they are cooked as the skins are very tough.)

Bean Sprouts: This term usually refers to mung bean sprouts, commonly used in Chinese cooking; it is also a generic term for any sprouted beans. See SPROUTS.

Beet Greens: These greens are very perishable and must be used within a day or two. They last slightly longer when left attached to the BEETS. Beet greens taste a lot like spinach and can be selected and cooked in the same way (see SPINACH). However, because a bunch of beets yields only ½ to 1 ounce of greens, I generally use them as a garnish or add them at the last minute to soup. (Ask your greengrocer to save discarded beet greens and you'll come home with enough to serve an army!) *Prepare for cooking* by trimming off the fibrous red stems and coarsely chopping any large leaves. For cooking instructions, see Basic Sautéed Greens, page 254.

Beets: I find beets delicious and so gorgeous to behold. I love stirring small quantities of raw grated beets into GRAINS to turn them a magnificent scarlet (see Scarlet Quinoa, page 97). *Select* firm beets without bruises or dents; perky beet greens offer the best indication of freshness. If cooking the beets whole, use those of approximately equal size. *Allow* 6 to 8 ounces per person. If the greens are available and in good condition, see BEET GREENS. Cut off all but 1 inch of the stem, and *store* the beets in a tightly sealed container for up to 2 weeks. *Prepare for cooking* by scrubbing gently but thoroughly. Slip off skins after cooking, if desired. *Serve* cooked beets sliced and tossed with a vinaigrette dressing.

Pressure cooking:
Medium-large whole beets (5 to 6 ounces each): 20 to 22 minutes high pressure
Small whole beets (3 to 4 ounces each): 11 to 13 minutes high pressure
¼-inch slices: 3 to 5 minutes high pressure

When preparing whole beets, use a minimum of 2 cups of water in the bottom of the cooker, since the cooking time is fairly long. Except for aesthetic reasons, you don't have to peel the cooked beets, since the pressure cooker tenderizes the skins.

Boiling:
Boil, lid on, in water to cover until tender when pierced with the tip of a knife, about 20 to 40 minutes, depending upon the size.

Baking:
A delicious way to prepare beets with intense flavor, but impractical unless the oven is being used for another purpose (such as baking a cake). Place unpeeled beets (small or medium ones are best; the large ones take too long to cook) in a heavy, covered ovenproof casserole with 1½ inches of water on the bottom, and bake until tender, about 1 hour. Water may need replenishing about halfway through cooking. Peel before serving, if desired.

Belgian Endive: See ENDIVE.

Bell Peppers (Sweet Peppers): Sweet bell peppers come in a variety of colors, green, yellow, red, and orange being the most common. They are a fine source of vitamin C. Red peppers, my personal favorite, are green peppers that have been left on the vine to ripen and sweeten further. Chopped, raw peppers add specks of lively color to bean and grain dishes, and they are especially tasty when roasted (see ROASTED PEPPERS). *Select* firm peppers without blemishes or soft spots. Peppers should be naturally glossy, not waxed. *Store* in a plastic bag in the refrigerator for up to 4 days. *Prepare for cooking* by halving from bottom to stem and plucking out stem, seeds, and large white membranes.

Stir-frying:
Cut into ½-inch dice: 3 to 4 minutes

Berries: Raspberries, blueberries, blackberries, and strawberries are among the greatest delights of summer, and anyone who has been fortunate enough to eat them right from the bush knows that they are best when just picked and slightly warmed by the sun. Berries are among the most delicate of fruits. When purchasing them, it's often a toss-up between buying those that are slightly crushed and those that are hard and lacking in flavor (because they have not been left to ripen on the bush). Your best bet is to *select* pints of berries in which the majority are holding their shape and have vivid color—good indicators of ripeness and intense flavor. Ideally, they should be kept at room temperature and eaten within 6 hours. Otherwise *store* them in the refrigerator, loosely covered with a kitchen towel, for up to 2 days. You can also freeze blueberries and strawberries in a single layer and then transfer them for longer freezer storage to a well-sealed container; store for up to 4 months.

Bifun: Clear Chinese-style rice noodles made from rice flour and potato starch; also known as rice vermicelli. Boil bifun for 3 to 5 minutes or steep in boiling-hot water for 10 to 20 minutes. (Check package instructions.) A delicious addition to soups and stir-fried dishes, and great for camping trips too!

Black Beans (Black Turtle Beans): These sturdy beans are among the most soul-satisfying of the common beans. Their earthy, mildly sweet taste and dense texture hold up beautifully against the assertive hot seasonings of Brazilian, Caribbean, and Mexican kitchens. They make a superb soup (page 55). The black skins turn to maroon or reddish brown when cooked, contrasting dramatically with fresh CORN or GREEN OLIVES in a bean salad.

Black Beans, Fermented (Salty Black Beans): A little of this Chinese specialty—small black SOYBEANS preserved in SALT—goes a long way. About 1 tablespoon adds a deliciously complex flavor to stir-fries. Chop the beans finely to disperse their flavor.

If you like the taste but want to reduce the salt, soak the beans briefly in water before using. Fermented black beans last for about a year in a well-sealed jar under refrigeration. They are readily available in Oriental groceries or through mail order (page 475).

Black-eyed Peas (Black-eyed Beans): These much underestimated beans are among my all-time favorites for their full flavor and down-to-earth taste. Probably introduced to the United States by slaves from Africa, this small, beige bean with its characteristic black eye is relatively quick-cooking and requires no presoaking. A must for the traditional Hoppin' John Salad (page 216) and great spiced with jalapeño peppers (page 178). Try it in a soup with collards (page 41).

Black Sesame Seeds: See SESAME SEEDS.

Black Soybeans: See SOYBEANS, BLACK.

Blue Corn, Blue Cornmeal: See CORN, BLUE.

Bok Choy (Chinese White Cabbage): A handsome, quick-cooking vegetable with long, billowing green leaves and slender ivory-white or green stalks, bok choy makes a welcome addition to stir-fry dishes. It is an impressive source of calcium. *Select* heads with unblemished stalks and sprightly leaves. *Allow* at least 6 ounces per person, since the volume shrinks more than 50 percent when cooked. *Store* in the refrigerator in a tightly sealed plastic bag for no longer than 2 days. For preparation and stir-frying, see Basic Sautéed Greens, page 254.

Bragg Liquid Aminos: This is a *very tasty* soy-sauce–like condiment made by extracting amino acids from organic SOYBEANS. Its flavor is more winelike and complex than most soy sauces. It is salty, so sprinkle sparingly. (There is no added salt, but 125 milligrams of sodium per ½ teaspoon comes from the natural sodium in the soybeans.)

Unlike SOY SAUCE, Bragg Liquid Aminos is not fermented, making it an ideal seasoning for those who suffer from yeast sensitivities. Delicious added to stir-fries or plain-cooked GRAINS. It is readily available in health food stores.

Bran: The fiber-rich layer just below the hull of a grain that protects the nutrient-rich endosperm. Bran is a fine source of carbohydrates, calcium, and phosphorus, and is one of the many good reasons to eat whole grains.

Broccoli: I treat broccoli florets and stalks as two separate vegetables. Since the stalks take longer to cook than the florets, they must be tossed into the pan a few minutes beforehand. Alternatively, slice the stalks very thinly and leave the florets large. *Select* broccoli with tight, dark florets that have no yellow or brown spots; avoid those with thick, woody stalks. *Allow* 4 to 6 ounces per person. *Store* in a plastic bag in the refrigerator for up to 3 days. *Prepare for cooking* by cutting the florets and about 2 inches of the stalk from the remainder of the stalk. Peel any older, thick stalks to expose the lighter green, tender flesh underneath.

Boiling is a surprisingly effective way to cook broccoli and my preferred method.

Pressure cooking:
Large florets (3½ inches across the top): 2 to 3 minutes total cooking time
Stalks, peeled, cut into ⅛-inch slices: 2 to 3 minutes total cooking time

Boiling:
Stalks, peeled, cut into ½-inch slices: 4 to 5 minutes*
Medium florets (2 inches across the top): 3 to 4 minutes

Stir-frying:
Stalks, peeled, cut into ¼-inch slices: 2 to 3 minutes
Small florets (1 inch across the top): 1 minute, then 2 to 3 minutes wok steaming

Broccoli Rabe (Rapini): An assertive green with a slightly bitter edge and small buds that resemble broccoli florets. *Select* only bunches with sprightly green leaves and use as quickly as possible. *Store* up to 3 days in a plastic bag in the refrigerator. *Prepare for cooking* by trimming and coarsely chopping stems and leaves. For cooking instructions, see Basic Sautéed Greens, page 254.

Brown Basmati Rice: See RICE, BASMATI.

Brown Beans (Swedish Beans): Scandinavian immigrants brought their beloved small brown beans with them when they settled in the Midwest. These beans can be pureed with a bit of MAPLE SYRUP and served as an interesting alternative to mashed SWEET POTATOES. They also work nicely as a stand-in for NAVY BEANS in Chili "Barbecued" Beans (page 200).

Brown Rice: See RICE, BROWN.

Brown Rice Cream: A coarsely cracked brown rice that cooks up quickly into a cereal and makes an excellent thickener for soups and stews. Although available in packaged form, it's simple to make at home: first toast the brown rice at 350° until it darkens and becomes aromatic, about 12 to 15 minutes. Then crack it into tiny pieces in a blender or spice grinder.

Brown Rice Flour: A finely milled flour made of brown rice; the hull and some of the BRAN have been removed. Brown rice flour adds a subtle nutty quality to baked goods and is especially delicious in cookies and pancakes. See FLOUR.

Brown Rice Vinegar: Buy a fine-quality, organic, unrefined brown rice vinegar, and you'll be amazed by its subtle complexity of flavor. See VINEGAR for a detailed description.

Brussels Sprouts: Brussels sprouts are among those vegetables that people love to hate, so it's special fun to change minds by selecting and cooking these little cabbages with care. Old or overcooked Brussels sprouts do merit strong aversion. *Select* firm, bright green, very small sprouts. For a surprising taste treat try very fresh, baby sprouts raw! *Allow* ¼ pound per person. *Store* in the refrigerator in a perforated plastic bag for up to 2 days. *Prepare for cooking* by trimming the stem ends and removing any yellow, torn, or brown-edged outside leaves. With the tip of a paring knife, cut a shallow X into each stem end. Uniform size ensures even cooking, but if the size varies considerably, cut the larger ones in half. Rinse thoroughly.

Pressure cooking:
Large (about 2 inches long): 4 to 5 minutes total cooking time

---

*If cooking stalks and florets together, boil stalks for 1 minute before adding florets.

Small (about 1½ inches long): 3 to 4 minutes total cooking time

Steaming:
Large: 10 to 12 minutes
Small: 6 to 8 minutes

Stir-frying:
See Vinaigrette-Wokked Brussels Sprouts (page 245).

Buckwheat (Kasha): The most commonly available form of buckwheat, KA-SHA is hulled and toasted. It has a deep amber color and an assertive, complex flavor and aroma that people either love or hate. Hulled groats have a distinctive heart shape, unlike any grain you've ever seen. Kasha comes in various grades from coarse to fine; since it cooks so quickly, there seems no advantage to selecting anything but whole groats (or the coarse grind as a second-best choice), unless you want a porridgy breakfast cereal.

Less commonly available are RAW BUCKWHEAT GROATS, creamy-colored hulled buckwheat that is untoasted and whose flavor is considerably milder than kasha. Cook them plain or dry-toast them in a skillet to bring up the flavor. WHOLE BUCKWHEAT SEED (with the hull intact) is best for sprouting and is available from mail-order sources. Buckwheat is high in protein, with significant amounts of iron, B vitamins, and calcium. See Basic Buckwheat, page 76, and GRAINS.

Buckwheat Flour: When made from toasted BUCKWHEAT, this flour is a dark tan and has a strong taste. It is traditionally used for making Japanese SOBA noodles and the Russian crepes called *blini*. If made from untoasted buckwheat, the flour is lighter and has a milder taste. Either type adds a hearty heaviness and distinctive flavor to pancakes and baked goods. Use with discretion. See FLOUR.

Bulgur (Bulgar, Bulghur) Wheat: After the WHEAT BERRIES' hulls and BRAN are removed, the berries are steamed, dried, and then crushed to create light brown gritlike pieces of uneven size and shape. Although it has undergone a fair amount of processing, bulgur has good texture and wholesome flavor and is ideal for newcomers to natural foods. Also, the popularity of tabbouleh has made it somewhat familiar.

Bulgur comes in various grinds, the two most common being medium and fine. Unfortunately, the grind of bulk bulgur is often not indicated. Compare it with the medium-ground bulgur packaged by Arrowhead Mills to distinguish. Medium and coarse bulgur have a chewy texture and are my personal favorites for making tabbouleh. Fine bulgur has a light fluffiness resembling COUSOUS. To my mind, it is overly processed and lacks character, but most packaged mixes for tabbouleh contain it.

Despite what many cookbooks tell you, steeping medium-ground bulgur for an hour or so in boiling water is not a consistently reliable way to "cook" it thoroughly. It must actually be cooked over heat (page 104). Steeping does work effectively for finely ground bulgur.

It is easy to confuse bulgur with cracked wheat because the two can look almost exactly alike, depending upon how they are processed. See CRACKED WHEAT and GRAINS.

Burdock: Much favored by the Japanese, this long, thin, brown-skinned root grows wild throughout much of the United States. *Select* slender roots that are heavy for their size; they are the sweetest and least fibrous. Fresh burdock is more pliant than other root vegetables; avoid any that look shriveled or moldy.

In *Uncommon Fruits and Vegetables*, Elizabeth Schneider advises that burdock can be *stored* up to 3 days, wrapped in a dampened cloth, and then covered tightly with plastic. *Prepare for cooking* by scrubbing the root to remove any dirt; trim off any dried-out tops and bottoms. Whittle burdock into longish chips with a sharp paring knife as if sharpening a pencil. *To cook*, sauté a large chopped ONION in a little oil and braise the burdock with an approximately equivalent amount of CARROTS cut the same way as the burdock (but slightly thicker) in a cup of vegetable stock for 4 minutes under high pressure. Toss in 1 teaspoon of TOASTED SESAME OIL and add TAMARI SOY SAUCE to taste. An unusually tasty dish.

Buttercup Squash: A variety of roundish winter squash with a dark green skin and a slightly sunken pale grayish "lid." Its orange flesh is tasty and very sweet. For cooking instructions, see WINTER SQUASH.

Butternut Squash: A thick-necked, camel-colored squash with a bulbous bottom, butternut squash is readily available and a personal favorite. Its bright orange flesh adds a cheerful burst of color to any dish, and it is sweet and creamy. See WINTER SQUASH.

Cabbage: Cabbage is a victim of bad public relations because it usually is overcooked, which results in pungent odors and an unpleasant taste. Treated with care, however, cabbage is a delight, both raw and cooked.

For coleslaw or to steam in wedges, *select* tight, round heads of green or red cabbage that feel heavy for their size. *Allow* ¼ pound per person. A 1½-pound cabbage yields approximately 6 to 7 cups of shredded cabbage. *Store* cabbage in a plastic bag for up to 10 days in the refrigerator. *Prepare for cooking* by pulling off wilted or blemished outside leaves. Rinse, cut into quarters, and slice off core. If desired, shred the cabbage by slicing very thinly along the length.

Red cabbage is tougher than green cabbage and requires slightly longer cooking and marination times (for example, when making slaw). Slice red cabbage with a stainless-steel knife to avoid discoloration. To retain its color, red cabbage must be cooked with an acid, such as VINEGAR or APPLE JUICE.

Pressure cooking:
1 large cabbage (about 3 pounds), quartered: 3 to 4 minutes total cooking time

Steaming:
Wedges, set on a rack over boiling water: 6 to 8 minutes

Stir-frying:
Shredded: 1 minute, then 3 minutes wok steaming.
See also BOK CHOY (CHINESE CABBAGE), BRUSSELS SPROUTS, and NAPA (CHINESE) CABBAGE.

Cannellini Beans: White oval-shaped beans prized in Italy, cannellini are the beans of choice for the dish called *pasta e fagioli*. Their creamy texture makes them a good candidate for spreads and purees, and they are delicious marinated whole in OLIVE OIL, BALSAMIC VINEGAR, and minced fresh BASIL or ROSEMARY. For a beautiful summer salad, toss in a few chopped TOMATOES or OLIVES. If cannellini are unavailable, NAVY BEANS are a good substitute. See BEANS and bean cooking charts, pages 175 and 177.

Canola Oil: Expressed from rapeseed, canola oil is lower in saturated fat than any other oil and contains cholesterol-lowering Omega-3 fatty acids. It is tasteless, which makes it a good choice for baking and some salad dressings. See OILS.

Capers: These little pickled flower buds add a salty punch to bean and grain salads—much the way chopped OLIVES do. You are more likely to find them in a gourmet shop than in a health food store.

Taste them first, and if they are too "pickley," give them a quick rinse.

Caraway Seeds: Aside from their traditional use in rye bread, caraway seeds are delicious with CABBAGE or sauerkraut and give a hearty, Eastern European stamp to soups and stews. Use these pungent little seeds with discretion— about ½ teaspoon flavors a dish to serve 6. It's easy to mistake them for the slightly lighter and longer CUMIN SEEDS; unless your jars are labeled, be sure to sniff them first before using! See SPICES and Flavorprints, page 4.

Cardamom: I have to admit that cardamom is one of my all-time favorite spices. Used with discretion, it adds a complex sweet-spiciness to baked goods and cuts through the flavor and texture of oil with sharp, palate-cleansing zeal. However, if you use too much of it, the camphorlike undertone of cardamom overpowers a dish and is reminiscent of cough syrup.

If you love cardamom as much as I do, you'll want to buy it whole—an ounce at a time for maximum freshness. Opt for green pods (the white ones are bleached for aesthetic reasons only) and open each with your fingernail to reveal the tiny black seeds. Grind the seeds as needed for baked goods. For soups or stews, the whole pod can be gently crushed and added. Cardamom is a common ingredient in CURRY POWDER. See SPICES and Flavorprints, page 4.

Carob (St. John's Bread): Although touted as a chocolate substitute, carob tastes as much like chocolate as yogurt tastes like sour cream. However, you might enjoy the natural sweetness of carob in its own right.

Carob powder is made by grinding and roasting the pods of a tropical tree. The powder forms lumps, so it's necessary to sift it before using. Carob is also available in chips. Carob is a fine source of calcium, magnesium, iron, and vitamins A and B. It has only 4 percent fat and contains none of the caffeinelike stimulant present in cocoa powder. *Store* carob in a well-sealed container in a cool, dry place.

Carrageen: See AGAR.

Carrots: Carrots are a most versatile vegetable, and my vegetable bin almost always contains them. Inexpensive, pretty, and easy to store, carrots add delightful flavor and color to a wide range of dishes. *Select* firm carrots without any black or softened areas and with no cracks or hairy roots. Carrots with green tops still attached are probably the freshest, but remove the tops for storage as they continue to draw moisture and wilt the carrots within a day or two. Except perhaps for home juice-making, avoid huge carrots, which have hard central cores and can be quite bitter. *Allow* ¼ pound per person. *Store* in a plastic bag in the refrigerator for 2 to 3 weeks. (Limp carrots can be used in stock and soups.) *Prepare for cooking* by scrubbing well and trimming off top and root end. Peel, if desired (see page 6). Carrot tops, if impeccably fresh, may be chopped very fine, quickly sautéed, and sprinkled with TOASTED SESAME OIL and TAMARI SOY SAUCE.

Pressure cooking:
Large carrots, cut into 2-inch chunks: 4 to 5 minutes high pressure
¼-inch slices: 1 minute high pressure
Carrots hold their shape nicely when pressure-cooked for longer periods of time in soups and stews.

Steaming:
¼-inch slices: 5 to 8 minutes

Stir-frying:
¼-inch slices, on the diagonal: 4 to 6 minutes, then wok-steamed 3 to 4 additional minutes

Cashews: Cashews' high fat content gives them a luscious richness suitable for making Cashew Cream (page 398) and nut milks such as the one used in Raisin-Rice Custard Pudding (page 387). Although they are more expensive, for optimum freshness *select* whole raw nuts rather than pieces; they should be crisp. Roast them as needed. See NUTS AND SEEDS.

Cauliflower: Cauliflower is a mild-tasting vegetable that must be eaten very fresh or it has an off-taste. *Select* creamy-white tight heads that are blemish-free and have bright green outer leaves. *Allow* 1 large head for 4 to 6 people. *Store* no more than a day or two in the refrigerator in a perforated plastic bag. Since cauliflower needs to breathe, remove any tightly sealed wrap as soon as you purchase it. *Prepare for cooking* by cutting away the outer leaves. Turn cauliflower upside down and cut large clusters of florets from the central stalk. Break or cut florets into approximately equal size for even cooking. Cut away any brown spots.

Pressure cooking:
Large florets (about 2½ inches across the top): 2 to 3 minute total cooking time
Small florets: not advised due to risk of overcooking

Steaming:
Large florets: 6 to 10 minutes

Stir-frying:
Small florets: 1 minute plus 4 to 5 minutes wok steaming. (For quicker stir-frying, cut the florets into ½-inch slices.)

Cayenne: Ground red chili pepper. See CHILI PEPPERS.

Celeriac (Celery Root, Knob Celery): Celeriac is a brown-skinned, knobby, baseball-sized vegetable with hairy roots. When eaten raw, it has a sweetness and delightful crunch reminiscent of CELERY heart. When cooked, its texture and taste are more like POTATO. Celeriac deserves more recognition for both its good taste and the fact that it is a richer source of fiber, iron, and B vitamins than celery. *Select* the smallest specimens you can find, since large celeriac is often spongy in the center. *Prepare for cooking* by cutting off the two ends, then use a sharp vegetable peeler or paring knife to remove the skin. If not cooking celeriac immediately, set in cold water along with 3 to 4 tablespoons of freshly squeezed lemon juice to prevent browning. Many people prefer celeriac raw to cooked: For an elegant and unusual salad, cut it into matchsticks and marinate (to tenderize it) for a few hours in Maple-Mustard Dressing (page 293).

Pressure cooking:
½-inch dice: 3 to 4 minutes total cooking time

Steaming:
Peeled, cut into ½-inch dice: 4 to 6 minutes

Celery: Like CARROTS, celery is a staple in my vegetable bin. It lends an herbaceous undertone to soups and stews, and I love the crunch it gives to salads and Celery Slaw (page 286). *Select* crisp, firm stalks that are unblemished and free of cracks; any leaves should be perky and bright green. *Store* in a perforated plastic bag in the refrigerator for up to 1 week. Slightly limp celery can be crisped by placing it in ice water for a few hours. *Prepare for cooking* by trimming the top and bottom and stripping off tough strings from outer ribs. Discarding the leaves is optional; they are flavorful but can be slightly bitter so taste before tossing in the pot.

Pressure-cooking time is offered if you want to include celery in a briefly cooked recipe, but pressure-cooking or steaming celery on its own is not recommended as it robs the celery of its distinctive flavor.

Pressure cooking:

1-inch slices: 3 to 4 minutes total cooking time

Celery holds its shape nicely when pressure-cooked for longer periods of time in soups and stews.

Stir-frying:

Cut into ⅛-inch slices on the diagonal: 2 to 3 minutes

Celery Seeds: Small green-brown seeds that are actually the fruit of wild celery. The flavor is reminiscent of celery leaves. These seeds are slightly bitter when fresh and *very bitter* when stale, so always taste them before using and add them with discretion. A pinch can impart an impish burst of flavor to a dip, soup, or vegetable stew.

Chard: See SWISS CHARD.

Chervil: An aromatic herb with a flavor reminiscent of TARRAGON. The lacy, fern-like leaves are especially lovely when fresh.

Chestnuts: I love chestnuts and was delighted to discover that for all of their rich taste and texture they are remarkably low in fat. After years of enjoying them freshly roasted in the fall, I discovered dried chestnuts, which are now nationally distributed in health food stores and are available year round. (They can also be found in some gourmet shops, but do not confuse dried chestnuts with the canned or bottled peeled chestnuts; the latter are much more expensive.)

Dried chestnuts make a superb smoky-sweet addition to beans and grains (pages 204 and 129). They are sold already peeled and last for a year or two when stored in the refrigerator or freezer. I cook them with other ingredients (as in Wild Rice with Chestnuts, page 140) so that their delicious flavor infuses the entire dish. Presoak the chestnuts if you wish to cut the cooking time by two thirds. A properly cooked

chestnut is soft and slightly mealy, with little to no crunch.

Select fresh chestnuts that look plump, feel firm and heavy, and have a nice sheen. *Store* them for 3 to 4 days in a cool place in a brown paper bag. (Do not refrigerate; this makes them difficult to peel.) *Prepare fresh chestnuts for cooking* by making a slit with the tip of a paring knife on the flat side of each shell.

Pressure cooking:

Fresh, with shell intact: Bring 2 to 3 quarts of water to boil in the cooker, then add the chestnuts. Cook 6 minutes under high pressure. Use a quick-release method. Drain chestnuts, When cool enough to handle, peel off the shells and brown papery inner skins.

Peeled, dried: 20 to 22 minutes high pressure

Peeled, dried, soaked overnight: Discard any brown skins that float to the top; cook 7 to 10 minutes under high pressure.

For each cup of dried chestnuts, use 3 cups of water.

Roasting:

Put slit side up in a shallow pan and bake at 375° until the slit opens slightly and the flesh is soft, about 20 minutes. Cool slightly. Peel by pressing the ends of each chestnut between your thumb and second finger until it bursts open.

Chick-peas (Garbanzos): Chick-peas have a round mini-walnut shape, beaklike tip, and creamy-beige color. At their best, chick-peas have a characteristic nutty flavor, firm yet creamy texture, and subtly sweet taste. The perfectly cooked chick-pea offers just a slight resistance to the tooth at first bite (accentuating the nutty flavor), then melts into a dense, creamy texture.

Chick-peas are used to make the Middle Eastern spread Hummus (page 312), and can be added to soups, and Indian curries. See BEANS and the bean cooking charts, page 175 and 177.

Chili Peppers: Chili peppers are available both fresh and dried. They range in taste from mild to scorchingly hot, and there is considerable variation of "heat" within any given chili type.

The real heat resides in the seeds and surrounding membranes; removing them tones down the potency. You *must* wear rubber gloves when working with chili peppers; if you forget to do this and rub your eyes, you will never forget again! *Select* firm, plump, unblemished chili peppers. *Store* them in the refrigerator for up to 5 days.

An excellent mail-order source of high-quality dried chilies is Los Chileros de Nuevo Mexico (page 476). See ANCHO CHILIES, CHIPOTLES, and JALAPEÑOS for descriptions of a few of my favorites.

Chili Powder: A blend of ground chilies (from mild to hot), OREGANO, CUMIN SEEDS, GARLIC, and SALT. Taste before using and make sure powder isn't stale or bitter. If your chili powder is old and the flavor has faded, you may need to add more than is called for in the recipe— or better yet, treat yourself to a fresh batch.

Chipotles: Dried and smoked JALAPEÑOS, chipotles add mild to intense heat (as chance would have it) and delightful smokiness to chili.

Chives: This hollow-stemmed, slender green member of the onion family makes a delicate addition to bean and grain salads and a lovely garnish. Always use fresh chives raw, for their flavor is mild and gets lost in cooking. *Select* vibrant green, perky chives that show no signs of browning. *Store* them in a plastic bag in the refrigerator for up to 5 days and snip as needed. *Select* freeze-dried chives that are a lively green and *store* them in a tightly sealed glass bottle in a dark place.

Cilantro (Chinese Parsley): See CORIANDER LEAF.

Cinnamon: The dried bark of a tree in the evergreen family, cinnamon is one of the few spices whose flavor holds up reasonably well when ground. You can, however, keep the "sticks" on hand and grind small pieces as needed. Extremely versatile cinnamon marries successfully with RICE, BEANS, CHILI PEPPERS, fruits, and sweet baked goods. See SPICES and Flavorprints, page 4.

Cloves: These dried, unopened buds of an evergreen tree are brownish-red and nail-shaped. A few go a long way toward imparting a sharp, aromatic taste. Cloves are most often used in desserts, but they also work well with sweet vegetables, such as BEETS, SWEET POTATOES, and SQUASH. A traditional way to flavor beans is to cook them with a clove-studded ONION. Or stud an orange with cloves for Nosmo King's Moroccan Chili (page 188). In each case, about 6 to 8 cloves will be sufficient. See SPICES.

Coconut: I like to keep desiccated (dried), shredded coconut on hand to add an exotic touch to RICE or vegetables. *Select* unsweetened coconut, ideally from a shop that stores it under refrigeration. *Store* shredded coconut in the freezer, since its high concentration of saturated fat makes it go rancid quickly. If only flaked coconut is available, grind it finer in a blender, if desired.

Collards (Collard Greens): This soul-food ingredient deserves to be better known in kitchens beyond Dixie; it has a flavor similar to KALE (although more assertive), and is an excellent source of calcium, iron, and vitamins A and C. *Select* the smallest leaves available, since they are the most tender and mildest tasting. (Large, more mature greens require a longer cooking time and sometimes have a slight bitter edge.) Avoid collards with yellowed edges or brown spots. *Store* in a plastic bag in the refrigerator for up to 4 days. *To prepare for cooking*, discard the stems. Wash the leaves thoroughly and chop them coarsely. Boiling is the most effective method for tenderizing collards; blanch them first if you intend to use them in a sauté or stir-fry. For further information on cooking greens, see pages 252–253.

Coriander Leaf (Cilantro, Chinese Parsley): This fresh green herb looks somewhat like flat-leafed Italian PARSLEY, but its leaves are broader and not as long. Once you sample a leaf, however, you cannot mistake it for parsley as its potent aromatic taste is unique—adored by many, detested by others. I like it, and find that almost any savory dish can be turned from dull to delicious with a generous amount of fresh coriander. (If you do not care for it, you can substitute fresh parsley for coriander called for in the recipes.) *Store* fresh coriander in the refrigerator, stems down, in a glass of water; cover the leaves with a plastic bag. It will last up to a week this way, although its flavor will diminish daily. I have tried dried coriander and find it so lacking in flavor as to be useless.

Coriander Seeds: Taste nothing like the leaf, although they come from the same plant. These small, round, tan, ribbed seeds are an important ingredient in CURRY POWDER and add a slightly sweet, fragrant quality to GRAINS and baked goods. For optimum taste, purchase whole seeds and grind as needed, but do grind thoroughly as bits of hull that end up in a dish can be unpleasantly woody. See SPICES and Flavorprints, page 4.

Corn, Blue: Recognized by its striking purple-blue or grayish kernels, blue corn is sacred to the Hopis, who use it to make their paper-thin piki bread. Blue cornmeal is grayish blue (it imparts this characteristic color to baked goods) and is more delicate in flavor and finer in texture than yellow CORNMEAL. It is readily available in health food stores. See FLOUR.

Corn, Fresh Sweet: When summer rolls around, look for the freshest, most local corn you can find. *Select* ears with husks intact to preserve freshness; the husks should be moist and pliant, not brittle and shriveled. *Allow* 1 to 2 ears per person. *Store* in perforated plastic bags in the refrigerator for up to 2 days. *Prepare for cooking* by removing the husks and silks.

As corn ages, its sugars turn to starch and it becomes less appealing to eat off the cob. I prefer to strip off the cooked kernels to use in bean or pasta salads.

To cut the kernels from cooked corn, stand one end of the ear in a shallow bowl and, with a horizontal zigzag motion, use a serrated knife to strip the kernels from top to bottom. Repeat until the entire ear is stripped bare. One large ear of corn yields approximately 1 cup of kernels.

Pressure cooking:
Set a few husks on the steaming rack. Break the cobs in half, if necessary, to fit into the cooker. Layer in pyramid fashion on the rack.
Corn on the cob (old, large): 3 to 4 minutes total cooking time
Corn on the cob (young, fresh): 2 to 3 minutes total cooking time

Steaming:
Prepare as for pressure cooking.
Corn on the cob (old, large): 7 to 10 minutes
Corn on the cob (young, fresh): 4 to 5 minutes

Roasting:
This method of cooking corn is surprisingly delicious. Strip off the husks but leave them attached at the bottom. Re-

move the cornsilk and put the husks back into place. Soak the ears in water for 5 to 10 minutes. Bake on the rack of a preheated 375° oven until tender, about 15 to 20 minutes. Set a cookie sheet under the rack to catch any drippings.

Corn Grits: broken-up pieces of dried corn. The recipes in this book have been tested with coarse *yellow* corn grits, such as those nationally distributed by Neshaminy Valley. The grits distributed Arrowhead Mills are slightly finer and produce a creamier POLENTA. *Store* in the refrigerator or freezer. See Basic Polenta (page 78).

Cornmeal: Dried field (dent) corn ground into a coarse flour and used for corn bread or traditional POLENTA (cornmeal porridge). In baking, use no more than half cornmeal for the total amount of flour as it produces a crumbly product. Like any whole grain flour, cornmeal becomes rancid quickly and should be stored in the freezer; use within 3 months. (If it's been stored longer than that and it tastes bitter, throw it out!) Avoid DEGERMINATED CORN FLOUR, which has been robbed of its germ in order to give it an extended shelf life. Instead, consider HIGH-LYSINE CORNMEAL, a relatively new hybrid that improves corn's amino acid balance, making it a more complete protein. It also doesn't get rancid as quickly as other varieties of cornmeal.

Corn Oil: A golden, buttery-colored oil extracted from the germ of corn kernels. It has a faint corn taste. Because all but the most highly refined corn oils are too heavy for baking and not ideal for frying, I don't use it. See OILS.

Couscous: Traditional couscous, a staple of North Africa, is made of durum (hard) WHEAT stripped of its BRAN and germ. The exposed endosperm is then made into a paste that is steamed and dried in the form of granules. Many health food stores now carry a whole wheat couscous distributed by Neshaminy Valley. This product is brown rather than cream-colored because it is made from the whole grain. The recipes in this book call for "old-fashioned" whole wheat couscous, not the quick-cooking kind.

Cow Peas: See BLACK-EYED PEAS.

Cracked Wheat: Made from whole WHEAT BERRIES cracked into pieces ranging from coarse to fine. Cracked wheat cooks much faster than whole wheat berries and makes a quick breakfast cereal. Unlike BULGUR, coarsely cracked wheat is not precooked and can *never* be "cooked" effectively by steeping it.

For optimum freshness and nutritional value, if possible crack the whole wheat berries yourself in a grain mill, coffee grinder, or heavy-duty blender just before cooking. Sift out any fine flour and simmer the cracked wheat (you can toast it first), covered tightly, in 2 parts boiling water to 1 part wheat until the wheat is tender and liquid is absorbed, about 20 minutes.

Because it is more readily available, I have used only Arrowhead Mills bulgur wheat to test the recipes in this book. See BULGUR.

Cranberries: Since cranberries freeze so well, I try to keep a supply of them for at least 4 months after Thanksgiving, since they can be tricky to find after November. There's no need to defrost them before adding them to a batter, and they add beautiful color and a refreshing tartness to cakes, puddings, and relishes. Fresh cranberries are notably high in vitamin C. *Select* cranberries that are firm enough to bounce; discard any soft, shriveled, or discolored berries. Fruit-sweetened dried cranberries are sometimes available in health food stores and can be substituted for RAISINS in baked goods.

Cranberry Beans: Occasionally available fresh, cranberry beans are most often sold dried. They are distinguished by the pinkish-red blotches on their beige skins. These very pretty beans unfortunately lose most of their bright color in cooking. See BEANS, FRESH SHELLED, for cooking instructions, and the bean cooking charts (pages 175 and 177) for dried beans.

Croutons: Making croutons is a great way to recycle leftover or stale bread. Croutons add delicious crunch to soups and salads. Since they defrost very quickly, you can store them in the freezer (for up to 3 months) to use when needed.

**Whole Grain
Herb-Garlic Croutons:**

Makes 2 cups

¼ cup olive oil
½ teaspoon dried leaf oregano
½ teaspoon finely chopped garlic
⅛ teaspoon sea salt
8 slices (about ½-inch thick) whole wheat Italian bread

In a small bowl, combine the oil, oregano, garlic, and salt. Brush a thin layer of this mixture onto both sides of the bread. Cut the slices (stack them up and do a few at a time) into ½-inch cubes. Toast in a pie plate in the oven or on the tray of a toaster oven set to 375° until crispy, stirring once or twice, about 2 to 5 minutes, depending upon the age of the bread.

ECO-TIP: Bake these croutons in the oven while baking other things; otherwise use the toaster oven.

Cucumbers: Since it's almost impossible to find unwaxed large cucumbers, I opt for the small, light green pickling cucumbers called Kirbies. They are sweeter and denser, and are never waxed. Since their skins are delicate, I generally don't peel them. *Select* firm cucumbers that show no signs of shriveling. *Store* in a perforated bag in the refrigerator for up to 4 days. *Prepare for eating* large cucumbers by peeling off waxed skins. Before slicing them, cut them in half lengthwise and remove the seeds. If cucumbers are bitter, sprinkle with SALT and allow to sit for 15 to 30 minutes to release liquid. Squeeze lightly in a clean kitchen towel before serving. For an unusual recipe featuring cucumbers, see Marinated Cucumber-Dill and Wakame Salad, page 278.

Cumin Seeds (Comino): This tiny brown seed looks a bit like CARAWAY except that it lacks the curve. A predominant spice in CHILI POWDER, curries, and Middle Eastern and Mexican food, cumin is shown to best advantage when the seeds are used whole or ground into powder as needed. See SPICES and Flavorprints, page 4.

Currants, Dried (Zante Currants): Made by drying Zante grapes, currants are smaller and less sweet than RAISINS. This makes them a nice alternative in grain and vegetable dishes as well as baked goods. Organic currants are available. An equal amount of raisins can be substituted in recipes calling for currants. See DRIED FRUIT.

Curry Powder: A blend of spices that varies in taste and "heat" from producer to producer. Most curry powders include CUMIN, CORIANDER and MUSTARD SEEDS, FENUGREEK, red chilies, BLACK PEPPERCORNS, and TURMERIC. I prefer to use a mild curry powder and add some CAYENNE or crushed red pepper to taste. Be sure to taste your curry powder before using it; any bitterness indicates that it's time to throw it out.

Daikon: Long prized in Japan, this white carrot-shaped radish has in recent years become more available in the United States. Raw daikon is said to aid in the digestion of oils. I prefer to eat it raw to enjoy to the fullest its radishlike bite. Just before serving, scrub daikon gently and then grate it. Toss it into a salad or serve it by itself in mounds, lightly sprinkled with UMEBOSHI VINEGAR, lemon juice, or SOY SAUCE. Alternatively, slice the daikon into ½-inch rounds to use as a "cracker" base for an interesting spread (see pages 309–316). Daikon cubes cook quickly and lose their bite: Add them to a stir-fry for the last 1 to 2 minutes of cooking. Large and slightly tougher than KALE, fresh DAIKON GREENS can be steamed in the water clinging to their leaves and eaten plain or sautéed in garlicky OLIVE OIL. They can also be substituted for kale or COLLARDS in soups, but are quite perishable, so use them within a day or two. *Store* them in a tightly sealed plastic bag in the refrigerator. Daikon seeds can be sprouted to add zest to salads.

Dried Daikon, thinly shredded, is available packaged in many health food stores. Because it is sun-dried, the flavor is sweeter and more intense than fresh daikon and works nicely in root-vegetable stews. Or soak dried daikon in boiling water until soft (about ½ hour), chop, and add to salads. Be sure to store an opened package in a tightly sealed container.

Daikon Pickles, available in vacuum-sealed packages, are large pieces of daikon pickled in SALT and rice bran according to an ancient Japanese technique. Slice off about 1½ inches, rinse lightly, then slice into long, thin strips. Although rather salty, they are a rich source of B vitamins and considered an aid to digestion when eaten after a meal.

Sushi Daikon, sold in many health food stores, is pickled in SOY SAUCE and very thinly sliced; scatter the thin slivers at random in brown-rice sushi rolls for crunch and wake-up flavor.

Dates: Until I made a chance stop in the desert town of Indio, California, the only dates I'd ever tasted were the dried, chewy deglet noors sold in supermarkets. Was I in for a delightful surprise after tasting luscious, plump, and moist medjools and silken honeyed barhis. Although medjools are often available in the refrigerator section of natural food stores and gourmet shops, barhis and other less common varieties are quite perishable and usually have to be mail-ordered (see page 476) just after the September harvest. These special dates are best appreciated when eaten out of hand, and two or three make a dessert by themselves. Barhis are too creamy to use in baked goods, but I often use chopped medjools instead of deglet noors in Date-Nut Pudding (page 384). *Store* fresh dates in the freezer and dried dates in the refrigerator for up to 6 months.

Delicata Squash: This is a cheerful-looking cucumber-shaped squash with bright yellow skin and green or deep orange stripes. Its pale orange flesh is sweet, creamy, and dense. Next to KABOCHA, delicata is my favorite squash. See WINTER SQUASH.

Dill: A lacy-leafed herb that is delicious in salads and soups. Eat it uncooked or add it at the end of cooking, since its flavor is quickly diminished by heat. *Select* sprigs that show no signs of limpness or brown edges. *Store* in the refrigerator, roots submerged in a glass of water, leaves covered with a plastic bag, for up to 5 days. (The flavor will lessen daily.)

Dried Dillweed is one of the few forms of dried herbs I find to be a viable alternative to the fresh herb. See HERBS, DRIED.

Dried Currants: See CURRANTS, DRIED.

Dried Fruit: Drying fresh fruit (that is, extracting most of the moisture) is a terrific way to preserve it for a long time— if the preserving is done naturally. Unfortunately, much of the dried fruit available has been treated with sulfur dioxide (which retains moisture and bright color) and packaged with an additional preservative. Sulfur dioxide can cause severe allergic reactions and other nasty physical side effects. If fruits are not organically grown and are preserved by these common techniques, they just end up being a concentrated source of chemicals.

It seems worth the extra money to purchase organically grown fruit that has been dried by a natural process (either by the sun or in a low-heat dehydrator) and untreated with chemicals or preservatives of any kind. If you have a solar box cooker or a dehydrator, you can dry your own fruit. Such fruits will look darker and be drier (and therefore chewier) than you are perhaps accustomed to—but the bonus is that they are more intensely flavored.

Although organic dried fruits are more expensive, they are quite a bargain when you realize that it takes 9 pounds of APPLES to make 1 pound of dried apple rings.

Try, whenever possible, to buy domestically grown dried fruit, because imported varieties must be fumigated before entering our borders. Since dried fruits are so sweet and flavorful, it's gilding the lily to buy them dipped in a sweetener—as is often the case with dried fruits sold in bulk in health food stores. (If in doubt, inquire.)

Although dried fruits can be well sealed and stored in a cool spot for a couple of months, they keep better and last up to 6 months in the refrigerator, wrapped in a plastic bag, which is then set into a tightly sealed container.

If the fruit becomes very dry, you can add it to a liquid dish like a soup or stew. If you wish to add dried fruit to a grain recipe, where the amount of liquid is carefully calculated, pour boiling water over the dried fruit first and let it steep, covered, until plump. Dried-out fruits are a perfect excuse to make a compote (page 389). See APRICOTS, CURRANTS, DATES, PRUNES, and RAISINS.

Dried Mushrooms: See MUSHROOMS.

Dulse: Second to NORI, dulse is probably the SEA VEGETABLE that has the most immediate appeal to North American palates. Dried dulse is a deep red color and is sold in the form of wrinkled leaves. It has a rich taste and a salty zest. Unlike most sea vegetables, dulse needs no cooking. I usually give dulse a quick rinse to remove any dust and excess salt, but some folks I know snack on it straight from the package (quite salty!). Add a few snipped leaves to soups and stews just before serving. Maine Coast Sea Vegetables has recently begun producing hickory-smoked dulse. A few shredded leaves stirred into cooked bean soups add an intriguing smoky flavor. For other suggestions, see page 263.

Eggplant: Eggplant comes in a variety of sizes, colors, and forms, the most common being pear-shaped and purple-skinned. *Select* shiny, blemish-free eggplant that feels heavy for its size and bounces back when gently pressed. Avoid very large eggplants, which tend to have many seeds and spongy flesh. *Store* in the vegetable bin of the refrigerator for 1 to 2 days at most. Because eggplant soaks up oil like a sponge, I prefer to bake or steam it and serve it as a puree. It is delicious with a bit of OLIVE

OIL, lemon juice, GARLIC, SALT, and pepper, or in Babaghanoush (page 317). One and a half pounds of eggplant yield approximately 2 cups of cooked, pureed flesh.

Prepare for cooking by peeling, unless the eggplant is to be baked. To avoid excess moisture in a mixed vegetable dish containing eggplant, sprinkle the cubed vegetable with salt and allow it to drain for about 30 minutes. Press out excess moisture in a clean kitchen towel.

Pressure cooking:
Peeled and cut into 1½-inch chunks: 2 to 3 minutes total cooking time
Peel the eggplant as the skin doesn't soften sufficiently during the brief cooking time.

Steaming:
Peeled and cut into 1½-inch chunks: 5 to 7 minutes

Baking:
1 medium (1½ pounds) whole eggplant, skin pricked and put in a baking dish: 30 to 40 minutes at 425°

Broiling:
First bake as directed above. Then place the whole eggplant under the broiler and rotate until it is charred all around. Slip off the skin before pureeing.

Endive (Belgian Endive): Grown in the absence of light, endive comes in tight miniature bunches of pale white leaves, each trimmed with a delicate tinge of yellow. The leaves are very slightly bitter and are a highly esteemed addition to salads. The whole leaves also make elegant barquettes when stuffed with bean purees. *Select* firm, crisp heads with no brown edges. *Store* in a plastic bag in the refrigerator for up to 4 days.

Escarole: This popular Italian vegetable looks something like a relaxed head of LETTUCE, its broad, wavy green leaves hanging loosely from the central core. The leaves are slightly bitter and deli-cious in a sauté (see Basic Sautéed Greens, page 254) and in soup (page 46). For selection, storage, and cooking of greens, see pages 252–254.

Fava Beans: Fava beans are most readily available dried, although fresh favas in long, fat green pods make a brief appearance in Italian and specialty markets during the spring. Dried favas are oversized and chunky beans with rust-brown skins and a narrow black stripe at one end. Favas' deep, rich, earthy flavor is slightly suggestive of split peas, and they have a soul-satisfying, potatolike texture. No wonder they have been a staple of the Middle East and Mediterranean countries for millennia.

Favas have never been as popular in the United States, probably because their tough, leathery skins must be removed prior to eating (unless making a puree). But they do look beautiful on a plate, so I sometimes serve them by themselves as an appetizer and invite friends to peel and eat as they go. You are more likely to find favas in a Middle Eastern grocery than in a health food store; they can also be mail-ordered. See FUL MEDAMES and the bean cooking charts, pages 175 and 177. For fresh favas, see BEANS, FRESH SHELLED.

Fennel: This bulbous, celery-colored vegetable with its long, light green stalks and feathery fronds deserves to be better known. I love the crunch and delicate sweet licorice taste of fresh fennel, thinly sliced and eaten plain or perhaps drizzled with a little OLIVE OIL as a side salad. The stalks are often too fibrous to eat raw, but can be cooked in soup or stocks. If quite fresh, the fronds can be chopped and used as garnish. *Select* small to medium-sized fennel that is firm and free of brown spots, preferably with stalks still attached. Cut the stalks from the bulb and *store* them separately in plastic bags in the refrigerator for up to 4 days (the stalks are more perishable than the bulbs). *Prepare for eating* by trimming the base of the bulb. Remove any blemished outer layers. To eat raw as finger food or a side salad, cut into thin slices across the width (remove the core as you go). When adding to a tossed salad, quarter and slice fennel along the length of each quarter to create small strips.

Although many people enjoy braised fennel, I have always been disappointed at the dramatic loss of taste when fennel is cooked. If you wish to try cooked fennel, check CELERY for approximate cooking times.

Fennel Seeds: Long, brownish-green ridged seeds with an anise flavor. Opt for whole seeds and grind as needed. See SPICES and Flavorprints, page 4.

Fenugreek: Yellowish-brown pebble-shaped seeds distinguished by a slit running down the center. Fenugreek is slightly bitter, with a taste reminiscent of CELERY. It is a common ingredient in CURRY POWDER and other Indian preparations. For optimum taste, dry-toast before grinding. See SPICES and Flavorprints, page 4.

Fermented Black Beans: See BLACK BEANS, FERMENTED.

Fiddlehead Ferns: These green "snails" of the vegetable kingdom are in season for only a few short weeks in the spring (the precise time varies regionally). They have a delightful appearance and crunch, and taste like a cross between ARTICHOKES and ASPARAGUS. *Select* sprightly green, firm, tightly closed specimens. *Store* in a plastic bag in the refrigerator for a maximum of 2 days. *Prepare for cooking* by swooshing vigorously in water

so that the papery brown casing comes loose, then slice off all but about ¼ inch of the tail.

Cook and *serve* fiddleheads simply: Immerse them in boiling water for 2 to 4 minutes until tender-crisp (the water will turn brownish), drain, and eat plain or tossed in a little OLIVE OIL or a simple vinaigrette dressing. Or try them instead of asparagus in Risotto (page 152).

Figs: Fresh figs are exquisitely delicious but very perishable, so eat them within a day or two of purchase. Two of the numerous types available are yellowish green-skinned calimyrna and deep purple black mission. *Select* plump, soft fruit, free of bruises, and heavy for their size. *Store* fresh figs wrapped in a kitchen towel for up to 2 days in the refrigerator. For selection and storage of dried figs, see DRIED FRUIT.

Filberts: See HAZELNUTS.

Five-Spice Powder: A Chinese spice blend, usually composed of CINNAMON, CLOVES, FENNEL SEEDS, SZECHUAN PEPPERCORNS, and STAR ANISE, and available in Oriental groceries. It adds a distinctively exotic accent to stir-fries. Experiment with making your own blend, using proportions of your choice. Use with discretion as these spices are potent.

Flageolets: Slender, pale green or mustard-yellow (less common) beans with a subtle taste. Flageolets are highly esteemed in France, but it's difficult to find them fresh in this country, and dried flageolets command a steeper price than the average legume. *Cook* dried flageolets as you would any bean (see pages 173–178 and the bean cooking chart, page 175). *Serve* them warm or at room temperature with just a drizzle of light OLIVE OIL and a bit of SALT.

Flax Seeds: A food that *The Wall Street Journal* predicted "may emerge as the next exotic 'health' food to reach the tables in U.S. homes" (1/14/91). Flax seeds are richer than soybeans in Omega-3 fatty acids and are an excellent source of vitamin E. They have a sweet, nutty flavor and make a good binder in eggless baked goods (pages 333–347 and 352–354). Because of their high oil content, flax seeds are prone to rancidity; *store* them whole in the freezer for up to 3 months and grind as needed. They have a laxative effect, so eat flax seeds in moderation.

Flour: Flour is the ground meal of GRAINS. Once the oil-rich germ of each grain is exposed through milling, whole grain flours begin to oxidize and lose nutrients. *Select* flours made from organically grown grains that have been stone-ground (the preferred milling process because it avoids the extremes of heat that destroy nutrients). If possible, purchase flours from shops that store them under refrigeration or have a rapid turnover. *Store* flours in a tightly sealed container in the freezer (preferred) or refrigerator for up to 4 months (mark the date of purchase on the package). After that time, taste flours before using and discard if they have developed any bitterness. For optimum freshness, grind your own flour as needed. Use a blender to grind small whole grains, such as AMARANTH, MILLET, QUINOA, and TEFF, or flakes such as BARLEY, OATS, and RYE. To *enhance flavor*, toast flour lightly in a cast-iron skillet, stirring constantly, over medium-high heat just until it emits a toasted aroma. Immediately transfer it to a bowl. Toasted flours are likely to absorb slightly more liquid than the recipes call for. For a brief description of individual flours, see page 322.

Fresh Shelled Beans: See BEANS, FRESH SHELLED.

Fruit, Dried: See DRIED FRUIT.

Fu: An ancient meat substitute developed by Buddhist vegetarian monks, fu are small dried cakes of WHEAT GLUTEN. (Broadly speaking, fu could be defined as dried SEITAN.) *Store* in a cool, dry place until infinity. *Prepare for cooking* by reconstituting fu in water, then squeezing out excess liquid. Simmer with soups and stews for an extra zap of protein, a nice bit of chewiness, and a subtle sweet taste.

Ful Medames: Resembling miniature FAVAS, these small brown flavor-packed beans are a staple of Egyptian cooking. They have given their name to a delicious parsley-flecked stew (page 193) that is eaten all times of the day or night in the land of the Pharaohs. Like favas, ful medames have tough skins that a pressure cooker can just barely tenderize. Their rich flavor more than compensates for their tough exteriors, but if you prefer, you can substitute BLACK-EYED PEAS for ful medames in recipes. Alternatively, you can peel the cooked beans if time and temperament permit.

Garlic: I can't imagine cooking without garlic, so I was pleased to learn from *The New York Times* (9/4/90) that "preliminary studies suggest that garlic may offer a wide range of health benefits." When I discovered ROASTED GARLIC (see below), I found the mellow alternative to raw garlic that I'd been looking for. *Select* plump, firm, tightly packed heads (also called bulbs) of garlic. *Store* them, uncovered, in the vegetable bin or butter keeper of the refrigerator for up to 2 months, breaking off individual cloves as needed. (Garlic is too old and bitter to use when the cloves have shriveled and produced little green sprouts.) *Prepare for cooking* by peeling each clove. When cooked whole, garlic cloves have a much more subtle flavor than when they are chopped. Since fresh garlic is so readily available, avoid garlic powder and other dried garlic products. I find them unsatisfactory substitutes for the real thing.

Garlic, Roasted: Roasted garlic is a snap to prepare and adds a mellow and complex flavor to uncooked dressings and sauces. Once prepared, it can be refrigerated, unpeeled, in a well-sealed container for up to 2 weeks.

Roasted garlic makes a great snack spread on whole grain bread or crackers. For a do-it-yourself hors d'oeuvre, simply set out the warm roasted head and invite guests to help themselves to a clove or two. With a little gentle pressure, the garlic puree is easily squeezed out of each clove.

If you discover that you love roasted garlic, why not prepare a few heads at a time. Then you'll always have some on hand for preparing salad dressing or stirring into soup at the last minute.

1 large, firm head of garlic
1 teaspoon olive oil

Peel off as much papery skin as will come off easily while still keeping the head intact. Brush the garlic liberally with olive oil. Place it in a small, shallow baking dish in the toaster oven and roast at 375° until the outside is lightly browned and the innermost cloves are soft, about 20 minutes. Refrigerate in a sealed container for up to 2 weeks.

Ginger, Dried: The ginger used for baked goods and curries is ground from dried ginger root. Its potent flavor has a longer shelf life than most ground spices. However, because the taste and intensity differ from FRESH GINGER, it cannot be substituted for the latter. In all recipes that call for ground ginger the ingredient should be ground *dried* ginger; recipes calling for freshly grated ginger intend that *fresh* ginger be used.

Ginger, Fresh: Second only to GARLIC, fresh ginger plays a dominant role in my cooking, and I am almost never without a piece of this light brown knobby root. *Select* a plump piece of ginger with smooth skin (I usually break off and purchase a "finger" of the size I need). The freshly broken end should release a fresh and pungent fragrance and feel moist to the touch. Select young ginger (which has thin skin); older ginger tends to be quite fibrous. *Store* ginger, uncovered, in the vegetable bin or butter keeper of the refrigerator for 2 to 3 weeks. Should a section get moldy, simply cut it away. If fresh ginger is not always available, buy a large piece whenever you can and follow Barbara Tropp's advice, offered in *The Modern Art of Chinese Cooking*:

"Refrigerate the ginger in a small brown paper bag sealed tightly in plastic. Replace the paper bag each time it gets moist, and the ginger will last for months. Another effective technique of long-term storage is to submerge the peeled knob of ginger in dry sherry." Slice off pieces as needed. *To prepare for cooking*, rinse off just the section you'll be using, and rub one end of the whole piece against a fine grater until the desired amount is achieved. Unless the skin is shriveled, it's not necessary to peel ginger.

When little bits of grated ginger might detract from the texture of a dish, adding fresh ginger juice at the end of cooking is the answer. *To make ginger juice*, grate fresh ginger very finely and squeeze it tightly in your hand directly into the dish you are making. About 2 tablespoons of grated ginger produce ¼ teaspoon of ginger juice (the flavor is quite intense).

Unfortunately, there is no good substitute for fresh ginger. DRIED GINGER has quite a different flavor.

Gluten: Gluten is a protein found in WHEAT and, to a considerably lesser extent, in OATS, RYE, TRITICALE, and BARLEY. When kneaded in bread dough, gluten becomes as elastic as a rubber band and captures gas bubbles released by the yeast. These pockets of gas cause the bread to rise. A less common use of gluten is in the preparation of the "wheat meat" known as SEITAN.

In recent years, some people have discovered that they are allergic to gluten and have shifted their diets to gluten-free grains, including MILLET, RICE, AMARANTH, and QUNIOA.

Gomasio: See SESAME SEASONING SALT.

Grains: These edible seeds are typically members of the grass family. They are high in protein, minerals, and fiber, and relatively low in fat. As complex carbohydrates, grains are filling and enter the bloodstream slowly, providing sustained energy. For complete information on selection, storage, and cooking of grains, see pages 63–65. See also BARLEY, BUCKWHEAT, CORN, JOB'S TEARS, KAMUT, MILLET, OATS, QUINOA, RICE, RYE BERRIES, SORGHUM, SPELT, TEFF, TRITICALE, WHEAT, and WILD RICE.

Great Northern Beans: These large WHITE BEANS are harvested in the Midwest. They hold their shape nicely in cooking and have a mild flavor. Use them in assertively flavored dishes, such as Chili "Barbecued" Beans (page 200). See BEANS and the bean cooking charts, pages 175 and 177.

Green Beans (Snap Beans): Tender fresh green beans are so sweet they can be eaten raw out of hand. After being stored for a few days, they benefit from a quick steaming. *Select* bright green beans that break in two with a snapping sound and are free of blemishes. The slimmer the better. *Allow* ¼ pound per person. *Store* in a tightly sealed container or plastic bag in the refrigerator for up to 3 days. *Prepare for cooking* by snapping or slicing off the ends and cutting into 2 to 3 pieces, if you wish.

Pressure cooking:
Young, tender beans, whole: 2 to 3 minutes total cooking time
Old, tough beans, whole: 1 to 3 minutes high pressure

Steaming:
Young, tender beans, whole: 6 to 8 minutes
Old, tough beans, whole: 10 to 12 minutes

Stir-frying:
Cut into ¾-inch pieces: 1 minute stir-fried, then 3 to 5 minutes wok-steamed

Green Onions: See SCALLIONS.

Green Peas: See PEAS, GREEN.

Greens: The edible leaves of a number of plants, greens are low in calories and an excellent source of fiber, vitamins, and minerals. (Kale and collards are particularly fine sources of calcium, beta carotene, and vitamin A.) Greens vary from small to large and tender to tough, depending upon age and variety. For selection, storage, and cooking of greens, see pages 252–254; for descriptions, see individual listings under BEET GREENS, BROCCOLI RABE, COLLARDS, ESCAROLE, KALE, MUSTARD GREENS, and SPINACH.

Grits: See SOY GRITS and CORN GRITS.

Groats: Whole grains whose inedible outer hulls have been removed. For example, OAT GROATS are hulled oats.

Harusame (Saifun, Bean-Thread Noodles, Cellophane Noodles): Clear noodles made of the flour of finely ground

MUNG BEANS. They have a slippery texture and are usually added at the last minute to soups; however, they also provide an intriguing alternative to regular PASTA in pasta salads and are good in stir-fries. To "cook" harusame, steep noodles for 5 to 8 minutes in a pot of just-boiled water; if not sufficiently tender, simmer for a few minutes. Shock the noodles in cold water as soon as they are tender but still somewhat chewy. Drain thoroughly and coat with sauce or a bit of oil immediately to prevent sticking. Saifun are sold in 2- to 3-ounce packages; because the noodles expand considerably after steeping, you can figure on about 1½ ounces per person. Store at room temperature, well sealed, for up to a year.

Hato Mugi Barley: See JOB'S TEARS.

Hazelnuts (Filberts): A delicious nut shaped like a large chick-pea. Hazelnuts have a slightly bitter brown skin, which should be removed before eating. Toast the nuts at 350° for 5 to 6 minutes and remove the skins by rubbing the nuts in a kitchen towel. See NUTS AND SEEDS.

Herbs: The leaves and stems of plants used in cooking to add their characteristic flavor. Use FRESH HERBS whenever possible—consider growing your own—as they have the power to turn an ordinary dish into a star. Use 3 to 5 times more fresh herbs than dried (except for tarragon, which is often stronger when fresh). For optimum flavor, add all or at least half of the chopped herbs at the end of cooking, tasting as you go. The best way to *store* fresh herbs is to snip the bottom of the stems and set them (unwashed) in a jar of water. Cover herbs with a plastic bag, tucking the ends of the bag under the jar, and store in the refrigerator. They will last 5 to 7 days, but begin to lose flavor after the third day (use more, as required). *To prepare for cooking or eating*, rinse herbs thoroughly by swooshing them in water. Spin in a salad spinner or pat dry in a kitchen towel before chopping.

DRIED HERBS have a more concentrated flavor than fresh herbs, and are best used when cooked or marinated. They do not work as well when added to dishes just before serving. To maximize their potency, before adding the herbs, rub them between your fingers to release the essential oils.

If possible, buy dried herbs in small quantities (about ½ to 1 ounce), since their vibrant taste lasts only a few months. The recipes in this book call for the crushed leaves of dried herbs rather than ground herbs, which lose flavor more rapidly. To find out if your dried herbs are sufficiently fresh, rub them between your palms. They should emit a distinctive aroma. If they do not, dump every last leaf. *Store* herbs in tightly sealed glass bottles (preferably dark glass) in a cool place away from the light.

Choose herbs that are domestically grown, preferably organic, since imported herbs are generally fumigated (by law) with ethylene oxide before they enter the United States. Avoid buying dried herbs that have been irradiated; most sold in health food stores have not been, but check the label or, if buying them loose, ask the manager. The range in quality and taste of dried herbs is quite remarkable, and it's well worth seeking out the best. For two excellent mail-order sources, see page 476. See BASIL, BAY LEAVES, CHERVIL, CHIVES, CORIANDER, DILL, FENNEL SEEDS, LEMONGRASS, MARJORAM, MINT, OREGANO, PARSLEY, ROSEMARY, SAGE, SUMMER SAVORY, TARRAGON, THYME, and WINTER SAVORY.

Hijicki (Hizicki): Hijicki is the most elegant of SEA VEGETABLES. In its dry form, the gossamer black filaments are even thinner than angel hair PASTA. When rehydrated, hijicki quadruples in size and resembles long strands of thick black spaghetti. Soak hijicki for 10 to 15 minutes, then drain and rinse before cooking to diminish its pronounced briny taste. Toss small amounts of cooked, chopped hijicki with GRAINS or BEANS, or serve it in small portions on its own, sprinkled with TOASTED SESAME OIL, a few toasted SESAME SEEDS, and BRAGG LIQUID AMINOS or TAMARI SOY SAUCE. Hijicki is an excellent source of calcium, and like many sea vegetables is high in iron and protein. For additional information and recipe, see pages 263 and 264.

Hokkaido Pumpkin: See KABOCHA SQUASH.

Horseradish: A gnarled beige-brown root renowned for its sharp bite, this sinus-clearing member of the mustard family perks up any dull dish. Stir a bit of horseradish—freshly grated or prepared—into a bean puree (page 311), POTATOES, grain salads, or dressings, and your dishes will have flavor and great pizzazz. The mustard oil that gives horseradish its heat dissipates quickly, so for the most vibrant taste, grate the horseradish as needed. As soon as a bottle of prepared horseradish is opened, its potency diminishes rapidly; just add as much as you need to achieve the desired balance of taste.

Fresh horseradish is easiest to find in the spring just before the Jewish holiday of Passover, during which it plays a traditional role on the Seder plate. *Select* a firm root without soft spots or sprouts. *Store* in a plastic bag in the refrigerator for up to 2 weeks; wrap tightly in plastic and freeze for up to 4 months (freezing causes some loss of pungency). *To prepare for use*, peel and grate, preferably in a food processor. Avoid breathing in the volatile oils while grating as they are very

pungent and can actually burn sensitive tissue.

Occasionally you will find prepared organic horseradish for sale in the refrigerated section of a health food store, but it's easy to make your own: Peel off the skin and the green layer underneath. Grate horseradish in a processor (to prevent copious tears) or by hand. Stir in a few tablespoons of white wine or APPLE CIDER VINEGAR and add a pinch of SALT. For red horseradish, stir in a small, raw, finely grated beet. Refrigerate in a tightly sealed bottle for up to 3 weeks.

Hubbard Squash: A large, longish, irregularly shaped winter squash with a gray-green bumpy skin and orange flesh. Not a squash I go out of my way for, but pleasant enough for purees. See WINTER SQUASH.

Jalapeños: Small, plump green chili peppers, broad at the stem and narrow at the bottom. The seeds and veins contain most of the heat, and some or all can easily be removed, if desired. Jalapeños range from quite mild to fairly hot, and it's a gamble what you'll end up with. *Select* firm, unwrinkled, unblemished peppers. *Store* in a plastic bag in the refrigerator for up to 5 days. Always wear rubber gloves when handling jalapeños. See CHILI PEPPERS.

Jerusalem Artichokes (Sun Chokes): A brown-skinned, iron-rich tuber that looks like FRESH GINGER. Jerusalem artichokes, sliced and eaten raw in a salad or quickly stir-fried with other vegetables, have the delightful crunch of water chestnuts. Their nutty sweetness becomes apparent when they are baked. Be forewarned, however, that they can cause extreme flatulence in some people; eat only small amounts until you determine how your body reacts to them.

Select tubers that are firm to the touch. *Allow* 4 to 6 ounces per person if serving as a vegetable. *Store* in a perforated plastic bag in the refrigerator for up to 10 days. *Prepare for cooking* by scrubbing well; it is not necessary to peel them.

Pressure cooking and steaming are not recommended as Jerusalem artichokes turn quickly to mush.

Baking:
Medium-sized chokes, lightly brushed with olive oil: 20 to 25 minutes at 400°

Job's Tears (Hato Mugi Barley): This Oriental grain resembles pearl barley but is larger and has a distinctive light brown indentation running down the center. Job's Tears have a delightful chewiness and are higher in protein than brown rice. They are also a good source of iron and calcium. I like to add them in small quantities to soups and stews; they are especially delicious with SPLIT PEAS. Avoid buying Job's Tears in Oriental markets as they are often of inferior quality. Unfortunately, this grain is not always available in health food stores because of the difficulty in locating a high-quality product. They are sometimes available by mail order from Gold Mine. For information on selection, storage, and preparation for cooking, see page 82.

Juniper Berries: An intriguing spice that is too little known in the American kitchen. These black berries are slightly larger than PEPPERCORNS and have smoother skins. Their unique flavor is bittersweet (like gin, for which they are the main flavoring) with a suggestion of resin. Used with discretion, they add an unforgettable taste to dishes such as Red Cabbage Slaw (page 284). Try a Greek approach: braise POTATOES with lots of GARLIC and a smattering of crushed juniper berries.

Kabocha Squash (Hokkaido Pumpkin): My all-time favorite squash! Although not as readily available as other varieties of winter squash, kabocha is well worth looking for. Almost a dead ringer for BUTTERCUP SQUASH, kabocha is round and dark green with occasional orange splotches or light green stripes running down the sides; it lacks the small indented lid characteristic of buttercup. Kabocha's orange flesh is sweet and starchy, making it a full-flavored vegetable to serve on its own. Pressure cooking and steaming do a nice job of tenderizing the tough skin, so it's not necessary to peel it. Do scrub it well, however, as kabocha sometimes has hard brown spots that do not soften in cooking. For selection, storage, and cooking instructions, see WINTER SQUASH.

Kale: It's a rare week that I don't eat kale, since it is a very satisfying green and one of the most readily available. Kale is a fine source of calcium, beta carotene, vitamin A, and iron, and is particularly delicious when picked after the first frost, when its flavor becomes sweeter and more mellow. *Select* perky leaves that show no signs of drooping or turning yellow. *Store* in a plastic bag in the refrigerator for up to 4 days. *Cook* thick stems, cut into ¼-inch slices, a minute or two longer than the chopped leaves. For further information on cooking greens, see pages 252–254.

Kamut: An even more ancient grain than WHEAT, plump golden kamut is making a comeback in modern diets because of its impressive nutritional profile, delicious taste, and texture. Grains of kamut are almost three times the size of whole WHEAT BERRIES, and ounce for ounce they are higher in protein and minerals, most notably magnesium and zinc. Kamut has a buttery taste and a pleasing chewiness. Some people who are allergic to wheat find kamut is easier to digest. Kamut flakes cook up like OATMEAL, and kamut flour yields a whole grain PASTA with a superior texture. For further information and cooking instructions, see page 87.

Kasha: See BUCKWHEAT.

Kelp: A large family of sea vegetables often sold in powdered form. Kelp makes a flavorful seasoning and provides a mineral-rich alternative to SALT. Kelp is notably high in calcium and iodine. Members of the kelp family include ARAME, KOMBU, PACIFIC COAST OCEAN RIBBONS, and WAKAME; see SEA VEGETABLES and individual listings.

Kidney Beans: Although kidney beans come in numerous colors and sizes, it's the handsome deep red variety that has become an all-American favorite. Full of good flavor, it's the lead player in New Orleans rice and beans and, of course, in Southwestern chili. Kidney beans hold their shape well, making them a good choice for vegetable stews and bean salads. See BEANS and the bean cooking charts, pages 175 and 177.

Knob Celery: See CELERIAC.

Kombu: A sea vegetable generally sold in wide, dark green dehydrated strips that expand considerably upon soaking or cooking. *Prepare for cooking* by rinsing quickly. Kombu contains glutamic acid, a natural flavor enhancer, so add a strip of it to soups and stews instead of salt. In addition, many believe that adding kombu to BEANS and GRAINS improves their digestibility and nutritional value. Like most sea vegetables, kombu is high in iodine and a fine source of minerals. See SEA VEGETABLES.

Kuzu (Kudzu): A root starch from a vine of the same name. Kuzu is sold in dainty packets containing small white chunks. It is an odorless thickener that can be substitute in equal amounts for arrowroot. For cooking instructions, see ARROWROOT.

Kuzu Kiri: Clear Japanese noodles traditionally made of the starchy root of the KUZU plant (believed to have considerable medicinal benefits). Presumably to avoid the prohibitive costs of processing kuzu, most kuzu kiri are made of potato starch instead. *To cook*, add noodles to a generous potful of boiling water, slowly stirring to prevent sticking. Simmer gently until tender (but still chewy), about 5 minutes. Drain and rinse immediately in cold water. Kuzu kiri are delicious in soups. For cold PASTA salads, toss them with a simple dressing of TAMARI SOY SAUCE and TOASTED SESAME OIL and top with finely chopped SCALLION greens. *Note*: If you don't plan to dress the noodles immediately, toss them in a bit of oil to avoid sticking.

Leeks: These members of the onion family are easy to cook and absolutely delicious. *Select* leeks with perky green tops and blemish-free white bottoms. For braising whole (rather than chopping), choose slender leeks, which are the most tender. *Store* in a plastic bag in the refrigerator for up to 10 days. *Allow* 2 to 3 slender leeks per person when serving whole.

I treat leeks as two vegetables: the white part, which can be braised on its own or chopped like onions and incorporated into stir-fries or other quick-cooking dishes; and the green part, which requires longer cooking to become tender and imparts a delicious flavor to stocks, soups, and stews. Leek greens can be cooked whole and removed before serving, or they can be chopped very finely and incorporated into the dish. *Prepare for cooking* by removing any tough or yellowed outer leaves. Cut off all but about 2 inches of the greens and make a slit about three quarters down the center of the white part in the direction of the root. Under cold running water, gently separate the layers to wash away the sand (leeks are usually quite sandy!). Trim off and discard the root end. Drain thoroughly, then slice or chop as directed in the recipe.

Pressure cooking:
Large, whole leeks (over 1½-inch diameter): 3 to 4 minutes total cooking time
Small, whole leeks (under 1¼-inch diameter): 2 to 3 minutes total cooking time

Steaming:
Small, whole: 5 to 6 minutes

Stir-frying:
Cut into ¼-inch slices: 2 to 3 minutes

Legumes: A large family of plants that includes BEANS, LENTILS, PEANUTS, and PEAS. Although there are considerable differences among them, they grow in a similar way: Each pod splits open when ripe and contains a single row of seeds. See individual listings.

Lemongrass: Lemongrass, which comes from Southeast Asia, contributes a fragrance and taste that suggest lemon PEEL. (A bit of freshly grated lemon peel makes a viable substitute.) Fresh lemongrass—much preferred to dried—is a long greenish stalk with a small bulb at the bottom. In this form, it is often available in Asian markets, and can be tightly wrapped and frozen quite effectively for up to 3 months. Do not be concerned if it turns pinkish.

Prepare for cooking by pulling off the tough outer layer. Thinly slice the bulb and fleshier part of the stalk and add to GRAINS, soups, and stews. Since lemongrass remains hard after cooking, remove any large pieces before serving. Better yet, before adding it to soups or stews, tie sliced lemongrass loosely in a small cheesecloth bundle or place it in a large stainless tea ball. Follow the same procedure with dry lemongrass, which is now available in most health food stores.

Lemon Peel: See PEEL.

Lemons: The juice of this bright yellow citrus fruit is a marvelous natural flavor enhancer and a vibrant, flavorful acid to use in salad dressings. *Select* thin-skinned lemons that are pliant to the touch and feel heavy for their size. *Store* in the vegetable bin of your refrigerator for up to 2 weeks.

Before extracting the juice, consider removing the PEEL and freezing it for future use. It is best to use only the peels of organically grown lemons. To extract the maximum amount of juice, before squeezing, roll the lemon firmly back and forth on the countertop. One large lemon yields 2 to 4 tablespoons of juice (depending upon type and time of year) and at least 1 tablespoon of finely grated lemon peel.

Lentils: A very ancient legume. There are dozens of varieties, all of which cook quickly without presoaking. Lentils are extremely high in protein.

The most common lentil is the BROWN LENTIL, which has a slightly peppery taste. GREEN LENTILS are about the same size but are olive green and somewhat milder in taste. For a real treat, try LENTILS LE PUYS, a diminutive French variety that has a slight sweetness and holds its shape beautifully. These are available in gourmet shops and by mail order.

RED (EGYPTIAN) LENTILS start out an appealing bright orange but, alas, turn brown after cooking under pressure. They are slightly smaller and rounder than brown lentils, and because they are hulled (stripped of their seed coats), cook more quickly and turn to mush the minute they are properly cooked. For this reason, they are best suited to soups or purees. Their flavor, which is slightly milder than brown lentils, suggests SPLIT PEAS. If your health food store does not carry red lentils, they are available in Middle Eastern groceries and by mail order.

Pink masoor dal and yellow toovar dal are two hulled varieties of lentil used in Indian cuisine and can be purchased in Indian groceries. Like red lentils, they cook more quickly than the brown or green lentils.

Lettuce: The generic term for certain types of salad greens. Here are the main varieties:

Butterhead: round, loosely formed heads with wavy leaves that have a buttery texture and a delicate taste. Bibb and Boston are typical examples.

Iceberg: tightly formed heads with crisp and crunchy leaves and a very mild taste

Loose-leaf: loosely formed, medium-long heads with ruffle-edged, tender leaves. Red-tip leaf lettuce looks particularly pretty in a salad.

Romaine (Cos): loosely formed heads with elongated leaves that have a very crisp texture

Select heads with perky leaves that are free of brown spots or withered edges. *Prepare for eating* by twisting out the core and separating the leaves. Dunk delicate lettuces in a large bowl of cold water. (I use the outside bowl of my salad spinner.) Swoosh firmer leaves vigorously. You may need to change the water a few times if lettuces are very sandy. Spin lettuce as dry as you can. Eat the same day, if possible. *Store,* loosely wrapped in a clean kitchen towel, in a plastic bag in the vegetable bin of the refrigerator for up to 3 days. Discard any brown or withered leaves before eating.

Lima Beans (Butter Beans): These popular white dried beans, with their delicate, sweet taste, are available in two distinct varieties: large and small. Large limas (Fordhooks) are a personal favorite for their starchy, creamy texture and impressive size. The trick to cooking the beans properly is first to soak, then cook them in salted water (a no-no for most other beans) in order to keep their delicate skins intact (see instructions on page 206). Once the lima skins loosen, the beans quickly turn to mush and are best used for purees or to thicken soups or stews. Fresh Forkhooks (large limas) can be shelled and boiled until tender (see BEANS, FRESH SHELLED).

Baby limas take about the same amount of time to cook, have more tenacious skins, and are very tasty: It just depends on whether your mood is Lilliputian or Gargantuan. See BEANS and the bean cooking charts, pages 175 and 177.

A wonderful variety of limas that has recently become more available is the Calico or Dixie Speckled Butter Bean, a medium-sized lima with bold blotches of deep red. Although the color fades somewhat during cooking, this tasty and pretty bean makes an enjoyable change from the norm.

Lupini Pasta: A high-fiber pasta based on the flour of the sweet lupin bean. It has a very faintly bitter taste (disguised by most sauces), but is high in protein and never sticks to itself, as do most other types of pasta. See LUPINS.

Lupins: The ancient lupin bean, enjoyed in Europe, is extremely bitter in its natural state and must be processed before eating to remove the offending alkaloid. However, over the last few decades, a sweet lupin has been developed in the United States that rivals the soybean in protein, but is more easily digested. Lupins are higher in calcium than SOYBEANS and provide a good source of iron, among other minerals. Sweet lupins, which have only the slightest hint of bitterness, are now available primarily in the form of LUPINI PASTA.

Mace: This spice is the webbed outer covering of the NUTMEG seed. It is similar in taste to nutmeg but somewhat more pungent. Mace is almost exclusively sold in ground form, although "blades" are sometimes available. Nice in spicy muffins, but use it with discretion. See SPICES.

Mansan Tamari: See TAMARI SOY SAUCE.

Maple Syrup: This delicious sweetener is traditionally made by boiling sugar maple sap until it becomes thick. (Nowadays a mechanical reverse-osmosis process is more often used.) It is very expensive because it takes an average of 35 gallons of sap to produce 1 gallon of syrup. Opt for organic, guaranteeing that parafomaldehyde pellets were not used by harvesters to increase the yield.

I see no reason to purchase the most costly Fancy or Grade AA syrup as it is very thin and has an extremely mild taste. I prefer the less expensive Grade A or Grade B Dark Amber syrup, for its deep color and luscious maple flavor. Avoid "maple-flavored" syrups, which are less expensive because they are a mixture of maple syrup and another sweetener, usually corn syrup. *Store* maple syrup in the refrigerator after the jug is opened. If the syrup comes in a tin, transfer it to a glass bottle for long-term storage.

Marjoram (Sweet Marjoram): A delightful herb, popular in Mediterranean cuisine, that is faintly reminiscent of OREGANO. Try it as a seasoning for GREEN BEANS or LIMAS. See HERBS.

Millet: Hulled millet is a versatile grain, which, when dry-cooked (page 89), makes a fluffy and whole-grain alternative to COUSCOUS. Moist-cooked, it's nice to use for stuffings or savory burgers (page 90).

If you've tasted this tiny yellow beadlike grain and put it on your "avoid" list, it was probably improperly cooked. Most recipes call for 3 to 4 cups of water per cup of millet: The result is a bland, stodgy porridge.

The trick to cooking millet is first to toast it until it's lightly browned and emits a toasty aroma. Use either a dry skillet or sauté the millet with a tablespoon of oil. Either procedure enhances the taste and helps keep the cooked grains separate—especially if oil is added.

Second, be stingy on the cooking water. For fluffy millet, use only 1¾ cups water per cup of dry millet and 2¼ cups for moist millet. For further details, see the recipe for Reliably Fluffy Millet, page 89.

Since millet is relatively bland, it takes well to a variety of seasonings. When serving it plain, cook it with vegetable stock instead of water. If the millet tastes bitter, it's a sure sign that the grain is rancid and should be thrown away. For selection, storage, and cooking tips, see pages 63–65.

Millet Flour: Made of ground whole MILLET, this flour is sold in health food stores. However, I advise grinding your own, as needed, in a spice grinder or coffee mill, since millet flour turns rancid and bitter more rapidly than most other flours. To add a complement of vitamins and minerals, use a small quantity of millet flour—about ¼ to ½ cup—to replace an equivalent amount of WHOLE WHEAT FLOUR in savory baked goods. (The texture of the final product will be slightly denser.)

Mint: Fresh mint adds an appealing vitality to grain salads, and dried mint is one of the few herbs that make an acceptable substitute for fresh herbs in uncooked dishes. Be sure, however, to use spearmint rather than peppermint, or you may end up with a dish that tastes like toothpaste! See HERBS.

Mirin (Rice Wine): A sweet, low-alcohol Japanese cooking wine made by fermenting sweet glutinous rice with water and a grain-based catalyst called *koji*. Mirin adds an interesting flavor dimension to sauces and to MANSAN TAMARI soy sauce. It also makes a nice, shiny glaze for pie crust. Although it is unlikely that you will find an inferior product in a health food store, read the label to make sure the mirin has not been artificially sweetened with corn syrup or sugar.

Miso: This salty fermented paste is a fine source of high-quality protein, and is prized in Japan for its ability to aid digestion. Connoisseurs speak of misos and their special properties the way oenophiles discuss the vintages of fine wines.

Miso is available in a mind-boggling array of colors and tastes. A good, basic, all-around miso is country or mellow barley miso. For the faint of heart, sweet chick-pea miso is a milder choice. (It is sometimes referred to as "light" or "blond" miso.) If available, *select* unpasteurized miso, which must be stored in the refrigerator. Its flavor and nutritional value are superior to pasteurized misos that are sold in vacuum packs.

Stirring in a tablespoon of miso at the end of cooking imparts an extraordinarily complex flavor to almost any dish. Just dissolve the miso in a small bit of liquid from the dish (or use water, if no liquid is available) and stir this mixture back in. Avoid boiling once the miso has been added to a dish, as intense heat destroys its healthful enzymes. Miso may be thought of as an alternative to plain sea SALT; depending on the type of miso, the salt content ranges from 6 to 12 percent.

If you enjoy the saltiness and winelike flavor of miso as much as I do, you may want to have a few different types on hand. It's fun to mix them together for an even more complex taste.

There are three main categories of miso:

1. *Sweet miso* is light and yellowish in color and only 6 percent salt.
2. *Mellow miso* is reddish brown and approximately 9 percent salt.
3. *Country miso* is dark brown and contains 12 percent salt.

Additional information on miso is found in the comprehensive *Book of Miso* by William Shurtleff and Akiko Aoyagi.

Mochi: Mochi is made from cooked sweet RICE that is pounded until it becomes quite sticky. Flat rectangles of prepared mochi can be found in the refrigerator or freezer section of most health food stores. Cut mochi into 1½-inch squares and slowly brown on each side in a preheated, covered, ungreased cast-iron skillet over low heat. The mochi will puff up and become brown and crunchy on the outside while remaining soft and chewy on the inside; it makes a filling snack, a nice substitute for bread, and an unusual dumpling for soup. There is a significant difference among brands, so shop around until you find your favorite.

Molasses: Molasses is a by-product of sugar cane manufacture. Although molasses contains valuable vitamins and minerals (notably iron and calcium), it is also likely to contain traces of the pesticides used in sugar cane production. In addition, there is evidence that the minerals are not readily assimilated by the body.

For these reasons and the fact that it plays havoc on my blood-sugar level, I don't use molasses. Although it is not as rich in flavor as molasses, BARLEY MALT SYRUP makes a more-than-satisfactory substitute.

Monukka Raisins: See RAISINS.

Mung Beans: These tiny pea-shaped khaki-green beans are most familiar in their sprouted form (see below), but they cook up quickly without presoaking and make pleasing soups and purees. Health food stores carry the organic whole beans, while in Indian markets, they can also be found split and hulled. Dried mung beans are ground into flour and made into clear noodles called HARUSAME.

Mung Bean Sprouts: A delightful addition to salads and Chinese stir-fries, mung bean sprouts are usually available fresh in Oriental groceries. But compared to home-grown sprouts (page 287) the store-bought kind will seem waterlogged. The nutritional profile of mung beans is transformed when they are sprouted: Their protein content drops dramatically but their vitamin content improves. The sprouts are highly perishable and should be eaten within a day or two of purchase or harvest. See SPROUTS.

Mushrooms: Because of their mild taste and limited storage potential, I use the common button mushrooms only on occasion, and favor dried mushrooms (see below) in most of my cooking. *Select* fresh mushrooms that are firm and unblemished, with caps that are closed around the stem. They should have little to no odor and the skin should not be slimy. *Store* them unwashed in the refrigerator in a paper bag, kitchen towel, or perforated plastic bag (to allow them to breathe) for up to 3 days. Mushrooms lose moisture when cooked and shrink considerably. *Allow* about ¼ pound per person when serving as a vegetable.

Stir-frying:
¼-inch slices: 3 to 4 minutes

Dried mushrooms are convenient to have on hand as they add a rich flavor to soups and stews and last indefinitely when stored in a well-sealed container in a cool, dry place. Many supermarkets carry dried wild mushrooms in ½-ounce containers and most health food stores sell dried SHIITAKE. The flavor and intensity of dried mushrooms vary dramatically. Reconstitute an unfamiliar variety in water and taste it before determining how much to use in cooking. Dried mushrooms tend to be sandy. If necessary, *prepare for cooking* by soaking in water until soft and swooshing around to release any clinging sand. Strain the tasty soaking liquid through cheesecloth (or pour it carefully so as to leave any sediment on the bottom of the bowl) and substitute it for part of the cooking liquid.

Mustard: Prepared mustard is made by blending dried mustard seed, VINEGAR, and spices. One of the highest-quality mustards is the French Dijon; it is a staple in my kitchen. Excellent Dijon-style mustards are now being produced in the United States. Most mustards are smooth pastes; I prefer country mustards, which are made from coarsely ground seeds and have a bit of crunch.

Stir in a teaspoon or two of a high-quality mustard at the end of cooking (long cooking or intense heat will dissipate its strength) to bring up flavor in even the blandest dish. I like to keep at least two or three kinds of mustard on hand, and sometimes add a bit of each. Explore the wide range of flavorful organic mustards now available.

Dry Mustard: Ground mustard seeds. The most commonly obtainable is Colman's, a traditional English mustard that is fairly hot. Use Colman's rather than Chinese dry mustard when preparing the recipes in this book.

Mustard Greens: These curly-edged leaves have a spicy bite that makes them a delicious addition to soups and stir-fries. Like all greens, they are a fine source of calcium; they also have noteworthy amounts of iron and vitamins A and C. Very young greens can be used raw in salads, but most require cooking to become tender. *Select* vibrant green leaves that show no signs of wilting or yellowing. Avoid bunches with thick stems, indicating age and toughness. *Store* unwashed in a tightly sealed plastic bag in the refrigerator for up to 2 days. For further information, see pages 252–254.

Napa (Chinese) Cabbage: One of the most readily available varieties of Chinese cabbage has fluffy, elongated leaves and a shape that vaguely resembles romaine lettuce. It cooks more quickly, is sweeter and milder than head cabbage, and makes a delicious addition to stir-fries. For information on selection and storage, see BOK CHOY. For cooking instructions, see Basic Sautéed Greens (page 254).

Natto: Its stringy texture, musty smell, and strong "cheesy" taste make this most unusual fermented soyfood definitely an acquired taste. The good news, however, is that natto is high in protein and a fine source of iron, calcium, and B vitamins. The Japanese mix it with a bit of MUSTARD or chopped SCALLION and use it as a condiment with RICE. You may find natto in the freezer section of your health food store, if at all. Thaw just before needed as it will continue to ripen and ferment after defrosting.

Navy Beans (Pea Beans): Technically, pea beans are smaller than navy beans, but the names are often used interchangeably. These creamy little egg-shaped beans are best for making quintessential baked beans. Although some cookbooks tell you that these beans require long, slow cooking, they do just fine in the pressure cooker. Because navy beans do not hold their shape reliably well after cooking, they are ideal for purees but not for bean salads. Although slightly larger, GREAT NORTHERN BEANS can be substituted (just increase cooking time as indicated in the bean cooking charts, pages 175 and 177). See BEANS.

Nigari: The traditional coagulating agent used in making tofu. Nigari is derived from seawater and is primarily composed of magnesium chloride and some trace minerals.

Noodles: See PASTA.

Nori (Sea Lettuce; Green Laver): The sea vegetable nori is usually sold in paper-thin, flat, dark greenish-brown sheets. It is a fine source of protein, vitamins, and minerals, especially calcium and iron. Nori has a mildly briny flavor and is ideal for wrapping sushi rolls, floating in soups and stews, or cutting into thin strips for garnishing green salads. Shredded nori also makes a nice addition to bean and grain salads and hot PASTA. You can use scissors to shred nori, but I find it easier to do it by hand: First, tear the nori into quarters. Place the quarters in a stack and continue tearing the stacks in half until you have tiny pieces. When adding shredded nori to a cooked dish, sprinkle it in while stirring to avoid clumps.

You can buy pretoasted nori (the words "sushi nori" on the package mean the nori has already been toasted), but it is usually more economical to toast it yourself. Just pass each sheet quickly over a gas flame or electrical element on your stove until the color turns from purple-black to greenish-brown. Roasting tenderizes nori and enhances its flavor, but is optional.

Some domestic nori is available in its more "wild" state: shriveled purple-green leaves that taste and smell as if they've just come out of the sea. In this form nori is less expensive and great for nibbling out of hand (it's quite chewy!) or roasting and crumbling to use as a condiment. Try sprinkling some roasted nori flakes on your next batch of popcorn. For a nori-flavored condiment, see Variation under SESAME SEASONING SALT.

Nut Butters: The thick pastes made by grinding nuts. The good news is that nut butters are fiber-rich and a concentrated source of protein; the bad news is that they are very high in fat. Toasted nut butters are the most intensely flavored, but heat causes some loss of nutrients. *Select* unsalted, organic nut butters, if possible.

As opposed to supermarket nut butters, which use hydrogenated oil as an emulsifier, natural nut butters need to be stirred to distribute the oil that rises to the top after bottling. You can also pour off the extra oil and use it in a salad dressing; this will result in a slightly drier nut butter. *Store* nut butters in the refrigerator to retard rancidity. A bitter taste or musty smell indicates that the nut butter is past its prime.

Delicious homemade nut butters can be made by grinding freshly roasted nuts in a blender. Health food stores now carry a range of delicious nut butters, including delicate hazelnut and rich cashew. See ALMOND BUTTER, PEANUT BUTTER, and SESAME BUTTER.

Nutmeg: The large, dried brownish seed of the fruit of the nutmeg tree. Grind fresh nutmeg as needed on a small grater to release its spicy-sweet aroma. Nutmeg adds a delightful burst of flavor to baked goods and is delicious lightly dusted on SPINACH and SWEET POTATOES. See SPICES and Flavorprints, page 4.

Nuts and Seeds: Nuts are a good source of protein, but their high oil content makes them very perishable. For maximum freshness purchase nuts in the shell and remove the nutmeats as needed. Next best, purchase shelled nuts from a shop that has a quick turnover and/or refrigerates them. Freeze nuts in tightly sealed containers and use within 4 months. *Select* nuts that have a crisp texture and are plump and of uniform color. See ALMONDS, CASHEWS, CHESTNUTS, PINE NUTS, PUMPKIN SEEDS, SEEDS, SESAME SEEDS, SUNFLOWER SEEDS, and WALNUTS.

Toasting Nuts and Seeds

Toasting nuts dramatically enhances their flavor and gives them even more crunch, but heat slightly diminishes their nutritive value and makes them prone to rancidity. For the latter reason, I toast nuts in small quantities as needed and use them in recipes where the added flavor will really count.

Nuts can be toasted by stirring them over medium-high heat in a heavy (ungreased) skillet. However, this is one of the instances when I find it more efficient and practical to use my toaster oven. Nuts can go from browned to burned in the blink of an eye, so I like having them at eye level and in constant view.

These timings are for nuts and

seeds taken directly from the freezer and spread out in one layer on the thin baking tray that comes with the toaster oven. Set the timer as soon as you pop the nuts into the toaster oven, set at 350°; no preheating is necessary. Stir once or twice during toasting to expose all sides. The nuts are toasted when they emit a toasted aroma and turn a shade darker or, in the case of seeds, begin to pop and crackle.

Cool and refrigerate or freeze until needed. If using a standard oven for toasting, plan ahead to do it when the oven must be used for some other purpose.

Consider these timings approximate; always pay close attention and keep your sniffer on the alert.

Nuts:
Blanched almonds: 6 to 7 minutes
Hazelnuts (filberts): 5 to 6 minutes
  After toasting, remove the brown papery skins by rubbing the nuts gently in a clean kitchen towel.
Pecans: 3 to 4 minutes
Pine nuts (pignoli): 4 to 5 minutes
Walnuts: 5 to 6 minutes

Seeds:
Pumpkin: 5 to 6 minutes
Sesame: 5 to 6 minutes
Sunflower: 5 to 6 minutes

Oat Bran: The bran layer of the oat groat, just under the hull. Like wheat bran, oat bran is high in soluble fiber and makes a nice alternative in baked goods. Studies indicate that oat bran can lower blood cholesterol, but you might keep in mind that OAT GROATS and STEEL-CUT OATS also contain BRAN—perhaps in more appropriate amounts for the body to absorb in one meal. *Store* oat bran in the refrigerator in a tightly sealed container.

Oat Flour: The flour you purchase has been made by grinding whole OAT GROATS. A quick and easy substitute when you need only a small amount is to grind OATMEAL at home in a food processor or blender. One and a quarter cups of oatmeal yield 1 cup of flour. Oat flour adds sweetness and a pleasant texture to baked goods when used in moderation. (Adding more than 20 percent oat flour will result in a heavy product.) A bonus is oats' natural antioxidant, which prolongs freshness in baked goods. *Store* in a tightly sealed container in the freezer for up to 4 months. See FLOUR.

Oat Groats (Whole Oats): The whole grain with only the two inedible outer hulls removed. This high-protein grain can be cooked whole or ground into flour. Whole oat groats are chewy even when tender, much akin to WHEAT BERRIES, but with a distinctively sweet oat flavor. To sidestep chewiness and shorten cooking time without loss of flavor, try STEEL-CUT OATS. *Store* oat groats in a tightly sealed container in the freezer for up to 6 months. See GRAINS.

Oatmeal (Rolled Oats): Sometimes called "old-fashioned oatmeal," oatmeal is prepared by steaming OAT GROATS and passing them between rollers to flatten them. Aside from making a delicious breakfast cereal, oatmeal can be used to thicken soups and sauces. The recipes in this book call for rolled oats, not the quick-cooking kind, which has undergone further processing. See GRAINS.

Ocean Ribbons: See PACIFIC COAST OCEAN RIBBONS.

Oils: Oils are extracted from nuts, grains, seeds, and—in the case of OLIVE OIL—from fruits. Although at best they are highly refined foods, you can exercise considerable choice in the method of extraction and degree of refinement when making a selection.

Most supermarket oils are a clear golden color and free of taste and aroma. This is because they have been through a multistep refining process that includes extraction through the use of a hexane solvent, degumming to separate out cloudy substances, bleaching to remove pigments, and deodorizing to dispel any aroma. Experts in natural foods express concern that the high heat involved in many of these steps destroys nutrients and essential fatty acids and, more important, demolishes the oil's antioxidants (naturally occurring chemicals that neutralize injurious molecules known as free radicals).

Health food stores and some supermarkets now carry a range of less refined oils. Some of these oils have been extracted mechanically in an expeller press, which bypasses the need for a hexane solvent. In addition, they have not been exposed to the degree of heat that might destroy essential fatty acids and some nutrients. The trade-off is that these oils are more prone to becoming rancid.

The labeling of oils causes much confusion, so I would like to focus on the oils I presently consider most healthful and practical for particular purposes. For sautéing and salad dressings when I want to add flavor, I prefer an aromatic, fruity virgin OLIVE OIL, either from California or Italy. Full flavor in olive oil is often revealed by a rich green or golden color. When I want to use a no-taste oil for the same purposes, I choose an unrefined, expeller-pressed CANOLA OIL or a high-oleic (high in monounsaturated fat) SAFFLOWER OIL. For stir-fries containing Oriental seasonings, either a fragrant PEANUT OIL or canola oil works best. For salad dressings that are enhanced by nuttiness, I like light SESAME OIL or TOASTED SESAME OIL (for a much stronger taste). On occasion, I will also use walnut or hazelnut oils imported from France. I buy expeller-expressed organic oils whenever possible.

With the exception of olive oil, these relatively unrefined oils *must be refrigerated before and after opening* because their chemical composition breaks down upon contact with air and light. Date the bottle when you buy it, and if you've stored the oil for more than 4 months, test it for rancidity before using it. A rancid oil tastes bitter and causes a burning sensation at the back of the throat. It also has an off, sometimes unpleasant odor.

You can write to Spectrum Naturals, a producer of high-quality oils, for a useful set of brochures on oils. Their address is 133 Copeland Street, Petaluma, CA 94952.

Okra: Okra is a vegetable that some people love to hate. I am convinced that those who dislike okra have never eaten it properly cooked. You can keep okra's gooeyness to a minimum by doing the following: *Select* only small (under 2 inches long), tender, bright green pods and plan to cook them whole. Eat okra as soon after purchase as possible; if necessary, *store* up to 2 days in a perforated plastic bag in the refrigerator. *Allow* ¼ pound per person. *Prepare for cooking* by trimming on the line where the stem meets the pod. When the cooking water boils, add a tablespoon of VINEGAR. (*Note*: Cook okra in a nonreactive pot, such as stainless steel, to prevent discoloration.) Okra is delicious, warm or at room temperature, when tossed in a vinaigrette dressing. It also marries beautifully with boiled RICE and a lacing of tomato or hot sauce.

Pressure cooking:
Whole small, tender pods: 2 to 3 minutes total cooking time

Steaming:
Whole small, tender pods: 12 to 16 minutes

Boiling:
Whole small, tender pods: 5 to 8 minutes

Olive Oil: Olive oil has great flavor and a high smoke point (which means that it doesn't burn easily). It is also one of the least processed oils. For these reasons I favor it almost exclusively for cooking and salad dressings. *Select* cold-pressed olive oil. In general, the lighter the color, the more delicate the flavor. I choose a fruity greenish oil that is full-flavored. Although olive oil is more shelf-stable than most, I prefer to keep it refrigerated. Since it congeals when cold, I keep about a cupful at room temperature in a small pitcher near the stove. See OILS.

Olives: I'm crazy about olives. They add an appealing salty punch to bean and grain salads and make attractive garnishes. If you haven't yet explored the world of olives, you're in for a treat. The varieties are endless. Among my favorites are intensely flavored oil-cured black olives, plump, purplish Greek Kalamatas, and good-quality green Spanish olives. If the olives you purchase are too bland, try marinating them overnight with OLIVE OIL and one or more of the following: a crushed clove or two of GARLIC, ½ teaspoon dried ROSEMARY or OREGANO leaves, and a generous pinch of crushed red pepper flakes.

Onions: Like GARLIC and CARROTS, onions are a staple in my kitchen. I love the sweet and complex flavor that they add to food. When I'm feeling lazy, I simply toss them into the pot with the other ingredients. When I want more intense flavor, I brown them in a bit of oil first.

Since onions can be a nuisance to peel, I usually opt for large yellow onions so that one is enough for any given dish. Large onions also tend to be sweeter than smaller ones. By my calculations, 1 large onion equals about 1½ cups coarsely chopped. When making a soup or stew, you don't have to be precise. Extra chopped onions can be frozen, al-

though there will be considerable loss of flavor.

Select firm onions that show no signs of sprouting. *Store* them up to 1 week at room temperature in the coolest, best-ventilated part of the kitchen. For longer storage, choose a colder spot (ideally about 50° Fahrenheit). If you need to refrigerate them, place the onions in a paper bag rather than a plastic one, preferably away from LETTUCE and other moist vegetables.

Small white onions and pearl onions are delightful to add to soups and stews or to cook on their own and toss in OLIVE OIL and FRESH HERBS.

Pressure cooking:
Medium small white, whole, peeled (2 ounces each): 4 to 5 minutes under high pressure
Small white (pearl), whole, peeled (¼ to ½ ounce each): 1 to 2 minutes under high pressure

Steaming:
Medium small white, whole, peeled (2 ounces each): 10 to 12 minutes

Orange Peel: See PEEL.

Oregano: A wonderful seasoning for Mediterranean and Mexican dishes, oregano marries especially well with GARLIC and TOMATO. There are two varieties of oregano: The Mediterranean variety is milder than the Mexican. The recipes in this book call for leaf oregano; if using ground oregano, reduce the quantity by half. Add oregano with discretion as too much can give a medicinal taste to a dish. See HERBS.

Pacific Coast Ocean Ribbons: This brownish-green sea vegetable, normally sold in thin dehydrated strips, is a member of the KELP family. The ribbons are sweeter than KOMBU (a popular type of kelp) and cook more quickly. They can be used in any recipe calling for kombu or WAKAME. See SEA VEGETABLES.

Paprika: A red powder that comes in sweet or hot versions, depending upon variety of peppers used. The recipes in this book all call for sweet paprika. Sprinkled lightly on top of purees and spreads, it makes a striking garnish. Paprika is a characteristic seasoning of Hungarian and Spanish dishes. See SPICES and Flavorprints, page 4.

Parsley: Fresh parsley is so readily available that I never use the dried form. I prefer FLAT-LEAF parsley for its more intense flavor, but the CURLY-LEAF variety is more widely available and can be substituted. Chewing on a fresh sprig is a great breath freshener, especially after eating GARLIC.

Select bright green bunches that show no signs of wilting or yellowing. *Store* in the refrigerator in a bottle of water, stems down and leaves covered with a plastic bag, for up to 1 week (the flavor diminishes after the first few days, so use slightly more than called for in the recipe). *Prepare for chopping* by rinsing then drying in a kitchen towel or salad spinner. Remove any thick stems and reserve them for stock. Chop the leaves and any slender stems. See HERBS.

Parsnips: I have a sweet tooth, which I try to satisfy in healthful ways. For this reason I love the whitish carrotlike roots called parsnips, which add a delightful sweet edge to a dish. I especially enjoy parsnips in soups and stews, and they are delicious pureed. Although parsnips cook fairly quickly, they hold their shape nicely in longer-cooking dishes. *Select* firm, young, slender parsnips; older, thick ones tend to be woody, with a hard central core. *Store* in the refrigerator in

a plastic bag for up to 2 weeks. *Prepare for cooking* by scrubbing well or peeling, if not organic. Trim tops and root ends. When cutting larger parsnips into chunks or slices, cut the wider-topped slices into 2 to 3 pieces.

Pressure cooking:
1-inch chunks: 2 to 3 minutes under high pressure
¼-inch slices: 10 to 60 seconds under high pressure

Boiling:
1-inch chunks: 5 to 6 minutes

Pasta: A mind-boggling array of whole grain and organic pastas has become available in recent years. For lovers of chewy *al dente* (firm to the tooth) pasta made of refined semolina flour, the mellow and sometimes sandy texture of whole grain pastas often leaves something to be desired. The good news is that there are some excellent pastas from which to choose.

For those to whom texture is a high priority, Eden Foods has come out with high-quality pastas in different shapes and "flavors," all using certified organic flour. Like more commercial pastas, these are made from the endosperm of durum WHEAT and not the whole grain. As a result, while they do provide protein and carbohydrates and are organic, these pastas do not contain the fiber, minerals, and B vitamins found in their whole grain counterparts.

There are also numerous whole grain pastas with quite pleasing textures, including buckwheat noodles called soba and whole wheat/brown rice udon. Pasta labels can be confusing and are easily misunderstood. The only way you can be certain if the whole grain is used is when you see either "whole" or "whole grain" in the ingredients list. The words "100 percent" are an indication that only one type of grain has been included to make the noodle but do not guarantee that the whole grain has been used. The word "sifted" indicates that the bran and, most likely, the germ have been removed.

As more and more people are discovering that they are sensitive to wheat, manufacturers have responded by producing a variety of nonwheat pastas, whose quality and texture have improved considerably in recent years. KAMUT and SPELT pastas are easily tolerated by many who are allergic to wheat. Rice bifun and mung bean HARUSAME are nonwheat clear noodles with a delightful resistance to the bite (if not overcooked!). They work very well in Oriental dishes. Starches such as kuzu, JERUSALEM ARTICHOKE, and POTATO are the main ingredients of other enjoyable pastas.

The quality and texture of these pastas vary considerably. Shop around until you find the kind you like or, better yet, hold a pasta tasting with friends.

See pages 159–161 and individual listings under BIFUN, HARUSAME, KUZU KIRI, RAMEN, SOBA, SOMEN, and UDON.

Peaches: Although there are many varieties of peaches, the most common type is the freestone, so named because it is easy to separate the flesh from the pit. Ideally, peaches are left to ripen on the tree before being picked, but most of us have to buy them slightly hard. Let them ripen at room temperature in a loosely sealed brown paper bag. *Select* peaches that yield slightly when gently pressed and are free of soft spots. Once ripened, *store* them in a plastic bag in the refrigerator. For best taste, bring the peaches to room temperature before eating.

Peanut Butter: Once a great favorite of mine. I have now switched my loyalties to other nut butters (crunchy almond and creamy cashew are current favorites) for reasons cited in the PEANUTS entry. If you are still hooked, opt for organic peanut

butter with nothing added except perhaps salt. See NUT BUTTERS.

Peanut Oil: An oil pressed from PEANUTS. It has a high smoke point and is therefore good for frying. See OILS.

Peanuts: Members of the legume family, peanuts are a good source of protein but, unlike other legumes, they are very high in fat. Seek out organic peanuts because, according to Rebecca Wood in *The Whole Foods Encyclopedia*, "peanuts are one of the most chemically adulterated crops" in the United States. This is because peanut crops are rotated with cotton crops, which are systematically treated with highly toxic chemicals that enter the soil. Peanuts are also prone to a carcinogenic mold called aflatoxin, particularly if they are harvested and stored in the humidity of the Southeast. (New Mexican peanuts, field dried in the arid Southwest, are generally free of aflatoxins. Westbrae's Valencia and Arrowhead Mills's Deaf Smith County peanut butters are made from New Mexican peanuts.) Unfortunately, the USDA considers a low percentage of aflatoxin to be acceptable, a fact that has encouraged me to transfer my affection for peanuts to other nuts. See NUTS AND SEEDS and PEANUT BUTTER.

Pears: My favorite pears for eating out of hand are the roundish, sweet, and juicy Comice—unless miniature Seckel pears are available. For cooking, try the long-necked Bosc, and for chopping and adding to a salad, the pale green or reddish Anjou is best. Peel skins before cooking, but if you're not going to use them immediately, cover the pears with water mixed with a few tablespoons of lemon juice to prevent browning. *Select* pears without bruises or soft spots. When ripe, pears will yield to gentle pressure at the stem end. If not sufficiently ripe, keep them at room temperature in a loosely sealed paper bag. Once ripe, *store* them in a plastic bag in the refrigerator. For optimum taste, eat them at room temperature.

Peas, Dried: There are three different varieties of dried peas: whole, split green, and split yellow. They are dried from the field pea, which is different from the common fresh green pea.

Whole Dried Peas: take twice as long to cook than split peas and tend to be mealy-textured. Although they could theoretically be cooked with a grain that has an equivalent cooking time, their looks set up the expectation of green-pea taste, which they don't deliver. They are not a favorite in my kitchen.

Split Yellow Peas and *Split Green Peas,* on the other hand, cook up in a flash to become luscious, thick soups and purees. Because their seed coats have been removed, both turn to mush quickly. They make superb soups but are not good candidates for salads. Because they create foam during cooking, it is essential to add a tablespoon of oil per cup of dried peas when cooking them in a pressure cooker. See BEANS and the bean cooking charts, pages 175 and 177.

Peas, Green (English Peas): Grown to be eaten fresh, these are one of the few vegetables that I like to keep on hand in the freezer. Frozen green peas don't require any cooking; just defrost them and toss into salads or add them at the last minute to stir-fries. *Select* fresh green peas in plump, shiny, tender pods. Thick pods indicate older starchy peas. *Store* the pods in the refrigerator in a plastic bag for up to 2 days. *Prepare for cooking* by shelling the peas. Reserve the pods for Pea Pod–Corncob Stock (page 29). Pressure cooking is not recommended because of the risk of overcooking.

Boiling:
2 to 4 minutes

Pecans: Pecans are absolutely delicious, in part because of their high fat content. For optimum freshness, purchase pecans in the shell and remove the nutmeats as needed. Next best, buy the nuts from a shop that refrigerates them (to prevent the oil from going rancid); store them in the freezer in a tightly sealed container for up to 3 months. See NUTS AND SEEDS.

Peel: Also known as zest, the peel called for in the recipes is the thin colored layer of skin on an orange or lemon that contains full-flavored citrus oils. It's best to use organically grown fruit to avoid pesticide residues.

For maximum yield, remove the peel in strips by using a sharp old-fashioned potato peeler. Use a gentle, sawing motion to avoid scraping off the white layer of pith underneath, which is bitter. Finely chop the peel by hand or use a minichopper. Extra peel is best frozen in strip form in a well-sealed container, but use 1½ times the amount called for as there will be some loss of flavor.

A less efficient but workable approach is to grate the peel on the finest side of a box grater. After the peel is removed, plan to squeeze out the juice from the fruit within 48 hours (it can be frozen) as the fruit quickly begins to get moldy.

One large lemon yields about 1 tablespoon of finely grated peel. One large orange yields 2 tablespoons of grated peel.

Pepitas: See PUMPKIN SEEDS.

Peppercorns, Black: Black pepper is the unripe fruit of a vine that is picked when still green. The immature berries are left to ferment briefly and then they are dried in the sun until they shrivel up and turn black. Although all black pepper is pungent, the complexity of taste varies according to variety and place grown; my personal favorite is Tellicherry, available in gourmet shops. Pepper is wonderful for adding vibrancy to a dish that lacks pizzazz. Just keep in mind that a little goes a long way. It's worth getting a good pepper mill: Freshly ground pepper is far superior to the commercially ground kind. See PEPPERCORNS, SZECHUAN; PEPPERCORNS, WHITE; and SPICES.

Peppercorns, Szechuan: Unrelated to black PEPPERCORNS, these reddish-brown berries have very rough skins that are split open. Discard any tiny black seeds that fall out of the berries as they can be quite bitter. Grind Szechuan peppercorns in a spice mill or crush in a mortar and pestle, and add a pinch to stir-fries or Cold Sesame Noodles (page 164) for a distinctively sharp taste. For enhanced flavor, dry-roast the peppercorns in a heavy skillet before grinding. They are sold in most Oriental groceries. See SPICES.

Peppercorns, White: Unlike BLACK PEPPERCORNS, which are picked when immature, white peppercorns have been allowed to ripen on the vine. After harvesting, they are soaked in water and their outer skins rubbed off before they are left to dry. White peppercorns have a milder flavor than black peppercorns, and are a good choice for people who do not like strong seasonings.

Peppers, Chili: See CHILI PEPPERS.

Peppers, Roasted: See ROASTED PEPPERS.

Peppers, Sweet (Bell Peppers): See BELL PEPPERS.

Pigeon Peas (Gandules): Sometimes called "no-eye peas," since they are "spotless," these roundish brown beans arrived here from Africa along with the BLACK-EYED PEA. They can be used to replace the latter in a Hoppin' John Salad (page 216). A popular item in Caribbean kitchens. See the bean cooking chart, page 175.

Pignoli: See PINE NUTS.

Pine Nuts (Pignoli): These luscious nuts are fairly expensive since it is very labor intensive to remove them from the pine cones. But because of their intense, sweet flavor and high oil content, a small handful adds remarkable elegance, particularly to grain pilafs. Roasting pine nuts brings out their unique flavor, and they make a delightful garnish. Pine nuts are quite perishable, so buy small quantities and store them in the freezer. See NUTS AND SEEDS.

Pink Beans: Best known in the Southwest, pink beans are often used instead of PINTO BEANS in making chili and refried beans. See BEANS.

Pinto Beans: These quintessential Southwestern beans were dubbed with the Spanish word for "painted" (*pinto*) because of their deep red-brown markings on a pinkish-beige background. Medium-sized pintos compete with red kidneys for center stage in chili. When cooked, they lose the painted look and become pinkish; for this reason, PINK BEANS are often substituted. See BEANS and the bean cooking charts, pages 175 and 177.

Pita Bread (Pocket Bread): A flat, round Middle Eastern bread that forms a pocket when sliced in half. Opt for pitas made of organically grown whole wheat. Cut in triangles, heat, and serve with Hummus (page 312) or Babaghanoush (page 317). Or cut in half and use instead of sliced bread for sandwiches. Use dried-out pita for making Middle Eastern Pita Salad (page 276), or bake small pita triangles at 350° until crisp, about 10 minutes, to serve as chiplike snacks.

Plantains (Cooking Bananas): You may have passed these by, thinking they were a strange mutant: Plantains start out looking like large green BANANAS, and as they ripen, they become yellow with large black spots. When green-skinned, plantains are bland and starchy. In the Latin American kitchen, they are peeled and fried or cooked in soups and stews—much the way we use POTATOES or other starchy vegetables. My preferred way to eat plantains is to let them ripen at room temperature until they are totally black. This may take as long as a week, but when peeled, sliced, and fried in this mature state, they become very sweet and creamy, with a firm bananalike texture.

To peel, cut shallow incisions down the length at about 1½-inch intervals and remove the skin. Then cut thin slices of flesh along the diagonal and brown the slices on both sides in an oil-brushed cast-iron skillet over medium-high heat. Warning: Ripe plantains burn easily. Serve hot. Very yummy.

Polenta: This CORNMEAL porridge is a regional specialty of Northern Italy. Cooked in the traditional way, it takes about half an hour of constant stirring to achieve the characteristic lump-free consistency. In my pressure cooker version (page 78), I use CORN GRITS instead of cornmeal (which doesn't cook well under pressure). The resulting polenta has more texture than traditional versions and tastes less porridgy. It has gotten rave reviews from all of the tasters.

Pomegranates: The pomegranate is about the size of a large onion, with a leathery red skin. It makes its dramatic appearance in the fall. To eat, cut into quarters (wear an apron and watch for spurting juice; it stains!). Bend back each quarter to expose the seed clusters. Either bite out a dozen or so seeds or gently pry them out with your fingers and gather them into a bowl. Pomegranate seeds make a beautiful garnish for boiled grains and green salads. To extract the juice, press the seeds against the sides of a mortar and use it instead of lemon juice or VINEGAR for an elegant magenta vinaigrette.

Popcorn: A variety of CORN whose kernels have very hard hulls. When heated, the moisture within each kernel becomes steam, forcing the kernel to expand until it pops and turns inside out, exposing the soft starchy center. Popcorn is a high-fiber, low-calorie snack food—only 25 calories per cupful when air-popped with 1 gram of protein and 1 milligram of calcium as bonuses. *Store* the unpopped corn in an airtight container in a cool, dry place for up to 1 year. Avoid refrigeration, which dries out the popcorn.

You can make popcorn without any special equipment by heating a tablespoon of oil in a heavy pot that has a lid. Stir in a cupful of dry kernels. Cover and shake occasionally, cooking over high heat, until you hear the first pop. Reduce the heat slightly, then continue to shake frequently until the explosions die down. Remove the lid and season, if desired, with salt, ground DULSE, or ground DRIED HERBS (such as OREGANO, THYME, and ROSEMARY). Alternatively, pour some TAMARI SOY SAUCE in a spray bottle and lightly mist the popcorn.

Poppy Seeds: Tiny blue-gray seeds that add a delightful crunch and nutty flavor to cakes and salad dressings. Like SESAME SEEDS, they are an excellent source of calcium.

Always buy poppy seeds whole and *store* them in a tightly sealed container in the freezer for up to 3 months. Because of their high oil content, poppy seeds quickly become rancid. For this reason, purchase them from a place that has quick turnover or that stores them under refrigeration.

Porcini: These dried Italian Boletus MUSHROOMS have an intense flavor. Because they are so expensive, I often use just a few at a time to replace double the quantity of supermarket dried mushrooms. *Store* in a well-sealed container in a dry place. Rinse well or soak to remove any sand.

Potatoes: Potatoes come in two basic types: thick-skinned and thin-skinned. Thick-skinned potatoes, like russets (Idahos), are best for baking and frying. Thin-skinned varieties, such as new potatoes or long whites, have waxy flesh and are well suited to steaming, boiling, and pressure cooking. Potatoes are a good source of potassium and vitamin C (if unpeeled). *Select* potatoes with no signs of sprouting, green eyes, or moldy areas. *Store* in a cool, dark place for up to 1 month. *Prepare for cooking* by scrubbing well and poking out any eyes or blemished areas. Peel thick-skinned potatoes, if desired.

New Reds, Long Whites, and Other Thin-Skinned Potatoes

Pressure cooking:
Whole, medium (2 ounces each): 7 to 8 minutes high pressure
Whole, small (1 ounce each): 5 to 6 minutes high pressure.
Peeling unnecessary. Before cooking, pierce in a few places to prevent the skins from bursting. Halve any potatoes heavier than 2 ounces.

Steaming:
Whole, medium (2 ounces each): 30 to 35 minutes
Whole, small (1 ounce): 15 to 20 minutes

Boiling:
Whole, medium (2 ounces each): 25 to 30 minutes

Russets (Idahos) and Other Thick-Skinned Potatoes

Baking:
7- to 8-ounce potato: 45 to 50 minutes at 400°
Scrub well and pierce in a few places before setting in the oven.

Potatoes, Sweet: See SWEET POTATOES.

Prunes: These dried plums are low in fat and are a fine source of fiber, iron, potassium, and vitamin A. See DRIED FRUIT.

Pulses: The dried seeds of legumes, such as beans and peas. See LEGUMES and individual listings.

Pumpkin: Resist the temptation to transform your jack-o'-lantern into pumpkin pie; the flesh of these large pumpkins tends to be both stringy and watery— not ideal for making a tasty puree. Instead, opt for small pumpkins (often referred to as "pie pumpkins") or other varieties of winter squash. However, a retired jack-o'-lantern, if still fresh, can make a beautiful serving tureen for a soup, pilaf, or stew. If cut-out features would cause serious leaks, just set the bowl of food inside the pumpkin. See PUMPKIN SEEDS and WINTER SQUASH.

Pumpkin Seeds: Usually sold with their white hulls removed to reveal the flat, olive-green seeds. They are available either raw, roasted, or spiced ("hot punks"). Pumpkin seeds are high in protein (29 percent) and a good source of iron. Pepitas, sometimes confused with pumpkin seeds, are actually taken from a particular variety of squash grown in Mexico.

To Roast Pumpkin Seeds: To roast your own unhulled seeds, first separate them from the clinging, stringy pumpkin flesh (a tedious job made slightly easier by swooshing in water). Pat them dry in a kitchen towel, then toss them in 1 tablespoon of oil and ½ teaspoon of SALT (optional) for every cup of seeds. Spread them out in a single layer (or a double layer, at most) in a large Pyrex dish and roast at 350°, stirring occasionally until toasted, about 30 to 40 minutes. See NUTS AND SEEDS.

Quinoa: Native to the Andes and about the size of SESAME SEEDS, quinoa (pronounced KEEN-wa) has a more impressive protein profile than that of wheat and contains numerous amino acids (lysine, cystine, and methionine) not normally found in grains. It's also very quick-cooking, delicious, and easy to digest.

Quinoa must be carefully swooshed in water and rinsed multiple times until the water runs clear (see page 95 for detailed instructions) to remove all the bitter saponin coating (believed to be a natural insect repellent). Packaged quinoa tends to be cleaner than quinoa bought in bulk. Rinse the quinoa just before cooking and drain it thoroughly. If the grain sits for 5 to 10 minutes in a moistened condition, the seeds begin to soften and this throws off the cooking time.

Plain-cooked quinoa has a slightly grassy taste, so I prefer to cook it in vegetable stock with a few cloves of GARLIC or perhaps a generous pinch of DRIED HERBS. I have experimented with toasting the quinoa before cooking, but I don't think it's worth the effort: The grain has a lovely nutty quality and slight crunch without any extra fussing.

The trick to preparing quinoa is to be stingy on the water and the cooking time: It can turn to mush in a flash. Be on guard! Properly cooked, it will be light, fluffy, and transparent, with a small white

filament (the sprout) dangling visibly. At the end of cooking time, if there's unabsorbed liquid in the pot and the quinoa is tender, simply pass it through a strainer.

Quinoa's mild flavor makes it a very versatile grain. Substitute it for BULGUR for a sensational Tabbouleh (page 107), or dye it scarlet with some raw beets (page 97) and serve it warm or at room temperature. It's also a natural cooked with corn, another native American (page 98). For a special treat, mail-order Ernie New's organic black quinoa (see page 476); it's gorgeous to look at, and has a delightful nutty taste. Warning: Ernie's black quinoa needs lots of rinsing and a minute or two more of cooking. See GRAINS and QUINOA FLOUR.

Quinoa Flour: Quinoa flour has a slightly grassy taste, which works best in small amounts in savory muffins and pie crusts. You can easily grind the flour as needed in a blender or spice grinder. Thoroughly rinse and dry the seeds before grinding. See QUINOA.

Radicchio (Red Chicory): These beautiful wine-red leaves with their bright white ribs and core look like miniature butterhead LETTUCE, but they have a characteristic bitter edge. Radicchio (pronounced rah-DEEK-ee-o) is usually eaten raw in salads, and the larger single leaves make beautiful "bowls" for a grain salad. Because it is considerably more expensive than lettuce, I use radicchio in very small quantities on special occasions, either as a garnish or in a mixed green salad.

Select small, tight heads with crisp leaves that show no signs of browning around the edges; the heads should have firm, unblemished white cores. *Store* unwashed in the refrigerator in a perforated plastic bag for up to 1 week, but use as soon as possible.

Raisins: Raisins are dried grapes, and are an especially good source of iron. I find raisins too sweet to eat out of hand, but love them in spicy stews, muffins, and desserts. Since grapes are a highly sprayed fruit, it's best to opt for organic raisins whenever they are available. Avoid golden raisins, which are Thompson grapes treated with sulfur dioxide to prevent them from darkening.

The small Thompson raisins are the most common, but try MONUKKA RAISINS because they are plumper, with more complex flavor. Muscat raisins are the sweetest of all. See CURRANTS and DRIED FRUIT.

Ramen: Thin, yellow Chinese spiral-shaped wheat noodles usually eaten in soups. Generally precooked, ramen are ready in minutes when plunged into boiling water—great for quick meals. Some varieties include grains other than wheat. For a very quick MISO soup, dissolve 1 heaping teaspoon of miso per cup of water and simmer for 2 minutes with a bit of freshly grated GINGER. Add a sheet of shredded NORI and simmer 1 minute. Stir in cooked ramen and simmer until heated throughout. Garnish with chopped SCALLIONS and a few drops of TOASTED SESAME OIL.

For an absolutely no-effort soup, you can buy ramen sold in a packet with an instant broth. It's not as tasty as the quick soup described above, but handy when you're in a hurry or on a camping trip. Opt for ramen made of whole grain flour and mixes that are free of preservatives. (For extra flavor, you can add some fresh ginger and scallions and a bit of MISO or TAMARI SOY SAUCE.) See PASTA.

Rapeseed Oil: See CANOLA OIL.

Red Cabbage: See CABBAGE.

Red Kidney Beans: See KIDNEY BEANS.

Rhubarb: Although considered a fruit, rhubarb is actually a vegetable with red stalks and *poisonous leaves*. Rhubarb is too tart to eat raw but, with added sweetening, it has a memorable and delicious taste. *Select* medium-thick to slender stalks that are crisp and firm. A light pink rather than a red color indicates hothouse-grown rhubarb, which is less stringy but also less flavorful. *Store* in a tightly sealed plastic bag in the refrigerator for up to 1 week. *To prepare for cooking*, rinse well and trim off ends. Slice as directed in recipe. Rhubarb contains a surprising quantity of water, so little to no liquid is required for cooking. One pound of rhubarb yields about 3 cups cooked. See Rhubarb Raisin Crumble (page 392) and Ginger-Poached Rhubarb (page 395).

Rice: Rice has become so commonplace in our diet that it may come as a surprise to realize that it's not a native grain. Introduced to the American South during the eighteenth century, rice is available in so many shapes, sizes, and colors that I will restrict this entry primarily to the types of rice normally available in health food stores.

One way to categorize rice is by color, the two main types being BROWN and WHITE. WHITE RICE has been stripped of its hull, bran, and germ to expose a starchy endosperm that has only a small fraction of the nutritional value of the original grain. (In some instances the white rice has been enriched to return some of the lost nutrients, but this strikes me as going a long way around the block.) The only two white rices you may find in health food stores are WHITE BASMATI and ARBORIO (see below).

There is a second distinction to be

made: Are the rice grains long or short? The difference is visible when you examine SHORT-GRAIN BROWN and LONG-GRAIN BROWN rices. The former is short, fat, and stubby, while the latter has long, slender grains.

The following list is alphabetical by type of rice. For information on purchasing and storing grains, see pages 62–65. For directions on cooking rice, see pages 118–120.

Arborio: Used to prepare the Northern Italian rice dish RISOTTO, these plump grains of white rice swell up with liquid, but don't break or become mushy when properly cooked. Traditionally the rice is not rinsed before cooking, since water would wash away the starch released during cooking that contributes to the characteristic creaminess. (Arborio rice is high in a type of starch called amylopectin, which contributes to its special consistency.) Arborio is available in gourmet shops, by mail order, and in some health food stores. You can substitute other Italian "superfino" grade rices, such as Vialone nano and carnaroli. Brown rice and domestic long-grain rices do not work as well in risotto recipes.

Basmati: Its name translates as "queen of fragrance" and you'll know why as soon as you cook up your first batch. Authentic basmati is imported from India or Pakistan and has a distinctively nutty aroma, a slightly chewy texture, and an appealing lightness. Health food stores generally carry domestically grown white and brown rices labeled basmati. These are varieties of aromatic rice and not true basmatis, but have quite pleasing aromas and tastes. Because it is so highly aromatic, I prefer white basmati to long-grain white for quick, easy-to-digest rice dishes (see recipes, pages 142–149). With its long, slender, and fluffy grains, brown basmati offers a pleasing alternative to long-grain brown rice, for which it may be used as a substitute.

Brown: SHORT-GRAIN BROWN RICE has short, plump grains slightly less than twice as long as they are wide. Most are buff-colored, and occasionally there is a pale mint-green grain. Short-grain brown rice has a characteristic chewiness, despite the fact that I usually give it at least 5 additional minutes over the flame (page 119). Because of this chewiness, short-grain brown rice always manages to maintain some texture, even when it is technically overcooked. Depending upon the ratio of water to rice, its consistency will vary from slightly stickier than long-grain brown rice to very sticky. The latter preparation is ideal for sushi (page 270).

LONG-GRAIN BROWN RICE has long, slender grains—at least three times as long as they are wide. It is less chewy and more fluffy than short-grain. Long-grain brown and brown basmati are the rices I now use the most. Experiment to discover your preference.

Texmati: A hybrid of long-grain and aromatic rices that to my palate is a watered-down version of its parents. Stick with the real thing.

Wehani: An interesting light-rust, long-grain brown rice, wehani was developed and named by the Lundberg Family, rice growers of Richvale, California. During cooking, wehani smells like popcorn, and it looks like and has the slight crunch of wild rice. To me, the flavor and texture of wehani are not satisfying enough to warrant serving this rice on its own. I prefer to mix it with long-grain brown rice in a ratio of 1 to 3 for appealing visual and textural contrast.

Wild Rice: Sometimes referred to as the "caviar of grains," this slim, elegant, blackish seed is expensive and often saved for special occasions or mixed with other grains for visual contrast and a nutty taste and crunch. Although not really rice (it's the seed of an aquatic grass native to the Great Lakes region), it will no doubt always be considered so. Wild rice is high in protein and a good source of B vitamins, iron, and other minerals.

I sometimes think they call it wild because the cooking time is so unpredictable, but in the pressure cooker it seems to butterfly (burst open) after about 22 minutes. For mixed-grain dishes, I prefer to cook wild rice separately and then toss the grains together. Cooked wild rice can be refrigerated for up to 5 days and frozen for 3 months.

Only about 20 percent of the wild rice sold is actually harvested in the traditional way, primarily by the Chippewa of Minnesota; the remaining 80 percent is cultivated in paddies, mainly in California. The rice is graded by its length and the number of broken seeds it contains, becoming more expensive in the range from Select (short) to Extra-Fancy (medium) to Giant (long). Since taste and nutritional value remain the same for all grades, I usually choose Select or Extra-Fancy wild rice if available. Wild rice seems more affordable when you remember that it expands 3 to 4 times during cooking, so that 6 ounces (1 cup dry) serve 3 to 4 people.

Rice Cakes: The heavier the rice cake, the more RICE and the less air it contains. At best, rice cakes are a benign snack food; they don't offer much nutrition, but they have almost no fat and do manage to satisfy the desire for something crunchy. There is a startling variety of taste and texture among brands; I favor the Lundberg Family's organic unsalted popcorn rice cakes for crispness and good flavor. Mini rice cakes are handy for hors d'oeuvre.

Rice Flour: See BROWN RICE FLOUR.

Rice Syrup (Brown Rice Syrup): This "liquid sweetness" (as the Japanese call it) is a thick, amber syrup traditionally made by combining sprouted BARLEY with cooked brown RICE and then storing the mixture in a warm place. As fermentation occurs, the starches in the rice are converted to maltose and a variety of other complex sugars. Complex sugars enter the bloodstream more slowly than simple sugars (like refined sugar and MAPLE SYRUP), thus providing a more steady stream of energy.

The number of domestic brands of rice syrup that are available differ in mode of manufacture (some contain barley enzymes rather than sprouted barley), sweetness, flavor, and baking properties. Whole grains baking expert Meredith McCarty favors the Sweet Cloud/Tree of Life brand, made from organically grown rice and sprouted barley. The distributor of this brand, Great Eastern Sun, can be reached at 800-334-5809. Do not be tempted to substitute rice syrup for maple syrup in baked goods, as they have different moisture contents.

Measure the syrup from an oiled spoon or cup to avoid messy cleanup. Although an opened jar of brown rice syrup can be stored at room temperature, I prefer to keep it in the refrigerator. However, it's easier to spoon out when it's at room temperature.

Risotto: The generic term for a very creamy and slightly soupy Northern Italian rice dish traditionally made with a particular type of short-grain white rice, such as Arborio. The perfect risotto (pronounced rih-ZOT-oh) should be slightly soupy and chewy, with the rice offering a pleasant resistance to the tooth. See RICE, ARBORIO, and recipes, pages 151–158.

Roasted Garlic: See GARLIC, ROASTED.

Roasted Peppers: It's amazingly quick and simple to roast peppers to add wonderful flavor to salads and sauces. You can even do a few at a time if your hand-eye coordination is good.

Just set one washed-and-dried pepper on the grid covering the gas burner. Turn the flame to high and roast the pepper until it is completely blackened and charred on the underside. Give the pepper a quarter turn with a pair of long tongs (avoid long-handled forks or skewers, which prick the pepper and release juices) and continue to roast the pepper until it is charred on all sides. This process will take about 4 to 5 minutes total.

Place the pepper in a brown paper bag (make sure there are no live embers), fold over the top, and let steam for 15 minutes. Peel off the charred skin as you dunk the pepper up and down in a bowl of water.

Halve the pepper and remove the seeds. (Do this on a platter to catch any juices.) Cut into strips and proceed as directed in individual recipes. Extra roasted peppers can be refrigerated in a small jar, with a thin layer of OLIVE OIL and a clove of crushed GARLIC (if desired). Two large roasted peppers yield approximately 1 cup of puree; see Roasted Red Pepper Sauce, page 301.

Rosemary: A highly aromatic herb with pine-shaped pointed leaves. Used with discretion, rosemary adds extraordinary vibrancy to cooked dishes and baked goods. Used with abandon, it tastes like bad medicine. Try rosemary with EGG-PLANT, BEETS or SUMMER SQUASH. Also makes a fine seasoning for a bean salad. The recipes in this book call for whole dried leaves; halve the amount if using ground rosemary.

Rutabagas (Swedes): Large, roundish root vegetables with earthy brown skin that has golden splotches. The flesh is yellow-orange. Rutabagas are full-flavored, loved by some and despised by others. I find a happy compromise is to puree them with an equal amount of steamed POTATOES. Diced steamed rutabaga is delicious drizzled with MAPLE SYRUP. *Select* firm, smooth-skinned, heavy specimens. *Store* unwrapped in a cool, dry, dark place for up to 6 weeks. *Prepare for cooking* by peeling off the (usually) waxed skin.

Pressure cooking:
½-inch dice: 5 to 6 minutes high pressure

Steaming:
½-inch dice: 8 to 10 minutes

Baking:
½-inch dice: 35 to 40 minutes at 400°

Arrange in a shallow dish. Drizzle on about ¼ cup water or APPLE JUICE. Cover tightly.

Rye Berries (Whole Grain Rye): The whole grain with just the outer inedible hull removed. Rye berries are chewy even when thoroughly cooked. They are slightly more full-flavored than WHEAT BERRIES, with the faint sour taste of rye. It's fun to make "Rice and Rye" by substituting 25 percent of rye berries that have been soaked overnight for an equivalent amount of uncooked brown rice. Cook like Basic Brown Rice, page 119.

Rye Flakes: Rye's equivalent of rolled oats, the whole RYE BERRIES are briefly treated with dry heat to soften them, then they are passed between heavy rollers and crushed into flakes. Rye flakes make a quick-cooking, soft, tasty breakfast cereal (toast them first for added flavor), and are a welcome addition to Triple Grain Granola (page 370).

Rye Flour: A heavy flour made by grinding RYE BERRIES. Suitable for breads and savory muffins when heartiness and the characteristic rye flavor are desired. See FLOUR.

Safflower Oil: An oil expressed from the seeds of the safflower. It is odorless and tasteless, which makes it a good oil to use in baking or for light salad dressings. Because of its high smoke point, safflower is also a good choice for frying. Safflower oil lacks the vitamin E characteristic of many other oils. See OILS.

Sage: The musty flavor of sage is a fine complement to GRAINS and BEANS. Use sage with discretion, as too much of it can easily dominate a dish and make it taste medicinal. Recipes in this book call for leaf or rubbed sage; halve the amount if using ground sage. See HERBS.

Saifun: See HARUSAME.

Salt: Salt is taken so much for granted that we can easily overlook the fact that all salts are not equal. If you purchase salt at the supermarket, take a look at the label. You may be surprised to learn that the salt contains additives. (Up to 2 percent of additives is permitted by the USDA!) If the salt is iodized, a form of sugar called dextrose is added to stabilize the potassium iodide. Sodium bicarbonate is included to prevent discoloration. Toss in magnesium carbonate and sodium silico aluminate or another anticaking agent to keep the salt flowing, and you have more than you bargained for.

I now buy unrefined sea salt, which is free of additives and contains dozens of the trace minerals destroyed during the processing of ordinary table salt. Unrefined sea salt is usually available in coarse and fine grades. I prefer the fine grade, which is more convenient for use in cooking. Two excellent brands are Lima and Si Salt.

Scallions: These elegant, slender members of the onion family have delicate white bulbs and long green leaves. I treat them as two vegetables, using the stronger-tasting white bulbs in cooked dishes as I would ONIONS, and reserving the more delicately flavored leaves for tossing raw into salads. Sliced scallion greens also make a great garnish for soups. *Select* scallions with perky leaves and white, unblemished bulbs with moist roots. *Store* in a plastic bag in the refrigerator for up to 5 days. *Prepare for use* by removing any brown or wilted leaves. Trim off the root or wash it thoroughly to remove the sand and chop it along with the rest of the bulb.

Sea Vegetables (Seaweeds): These exotic vegetables—harvested from the sea coast and surrounding rocks—are high in protein and loaded with minerals. Although relatively little known in this country, they are prized in many parts of the world as an inexpensive source of good nutrition.

Sea vegetables are now readily available in health food stores. They are generally imported from Japan, where they are regularly used in elegant preparations such as sushi.

Select sea vegetables whose sources are clearly identified and whose distributors indicate that their products have been tested against possible pollutants. Favor domestic brands harvested on the Pacific and Atlantic coasts and encourage your local health food store to carry them. North American harvesters are dedicated to keeping their harvesting areas pollution-free. Many domestic brands can be mail-ordered (page 478). *Store* sea vegetables in well-sealed containers in a cool, dry place; they seem to last indefinitely.

Prepare for cooking by rinsing and soaking (see next page). Though most packaged sea vegetables have already been cleaned, check carefully for any clinging periwinkles. Sea vegetables purchased in bulk require more keen attention. Don't be alarmed if your sea vegetables are covered with white spots or a thin white powdery film: These are deposits of natural salts that form on the surface as they dry and are easily rinsed away.

Some recipes call for presoaking the sea vegetables before cooking. Soaking softens them, reduces their salt content, and tones down the flavor. (You can feed the soaking water to your plants.) Once rehydrated, sea vegetables can be refrigerated in the soaking water for up to 1 to 4 days.

To create small bits of dry sea vegetables, first break or tear the large pieces or snip them with scissors. Once soaked, sea vegetables are easily chopped with a sharp knife. See AGAR, ALARIA, ARAME, DULSE, HIJICKI, KELP, KOMBU, NORI, PACIFIC COAST OCEAN RIBBONS, and WAKAME.

Seaweed: See SEA VEGETABLES.

Seeds: Seeds are powerhouses of nutrition. They are a good source of protein and minerals, most notably calcium. Because of their high oil content, seeds are highly perishable. *Select* unbroken seeds that look clean and taste vibrant, preferably from a shop that refrigerates them. *Store* seeds in a well-sealed container in the freezer for up to 3 months. For toasting, see NUTS AND SEEDS. See also POPPY SEEDS, PUMPKIN SEEDS, SESAME SEEDS, and SUNFLOWER SEEDS.

Tamari-Roasted Seeds

Here's a quick technique for salting and flavoring seeds. Try it with pumpkin or sunflower seeds for a garnish or a snack.

Use 1 teaspoon of TAMARI SOY SAUCE per ¼ cup of seeds. Place the seeds in a small bowl and drizzle on the tamari. Stir

to coat. Transfer the seeds to a pie plate or toaster-oven tray and toast as directed in the entry for NUTS AND SEEDS. When done, remove the seeds immediately from the tray or they will stick.

Seitan (Wheat Gluten): Also known as "wheat meat," seitan is an ancient Oriental food made of chewy WHEAT GLUTEN. Fresh seitan is quite bland, so it is traditionally marinated in TAMARI SOY SAUCE and SPICES. It is usually sold in 8-ounce plastic tubs and can be found in the refrigerated section of most health food stores; be sure to check the expiration date. (Seitan imported from Japan and sold in jars is very expensive and often rather salty.)

Seitan is low in calories, easy to digest, and an excellent source of protein (a 4-ounce portion contains 15 grams). *Store* until the expiration date marked on the package, usually no more than 10 days from purchase. *Prepare for cooking* by draining the seitan (reserve the flavorful marinating liquid for stir-fries) and slicing it into "fillets" or dicing it. Add seitan at the last minute to stir-fries, vegetable stews, or PASTA dishes for a meatlike texture. You can use it as a substitute for marinated TOFU or TEMPEH. Seitan is definitely an acquired taste, but those who love it *really love it*.

Sesame Butter (Tahini): A paste made of calcium-rich ground SESAME SEEDS that enriches and flavors dips, spreads, baked goods, and icings. It is one of the characteristic ingredients of the Middle Eastern CHICK-PEA spread Hummus (page 312). The bottled sesame butter sold in health food stores is made of unhulled seeds and is usually toasted. The canned tahini available in Middle Eastern markets and some health food stores is made of hulled and untoasted seeds. The latter is more delicate in flavor and not as rich in fiber.

Black sesame butter has a slightly more intense taste and is very elegant to behold, but is only occasionally available for purchase. See NUT BUTTERS.

Sesame Oil: A light, delicately nutty oil that is delicious for use in salad dressings. See TOASTED SESAME OIL and OILS.

Sesame Seasoning Salt: Often referred to by its Japanese name, *gomasio*, this seasoning is one I've grown so fond of that I usually take some with me to restaurants to zip up bland dishes. Because it is so full-flavored, sesame seasoning salt may help you cut down on your straight salt intake.

Numerous brands of prepared gomasio are available at health food stores. Although most of them are quite tasty, a homemade version is fresher and at least twice as flavorful. Besides, filling your kitchen with the aroma of roasting SESAME SEEDS is right up there with the joy of sniffing an oven full of freshly baked bread.

I make about a cup of gomasio at one time and refrigerate it in a glass jar. Then I transfer it to a small shaker, and use it as needed.

The following recipe can be doubled or tripled. For a more colorful gomasio, use half white and half black sesame seeds. Using 2 teaspoons of salt results in a lightly salted condiment. Add more salt to taste, if desired.

Makes 1 cup

1 cup unhulled sesame seeds
2 to 4 teaspoons sea salt, or to taste

Rinse sesame seeds carefully and drain well. Set in a 10- or 12-inch skillet (I prefer cast iron). Roast over medium-high heat, stirring constantly, until the seeds begin to give off a rich toasted aroma and most of the seeds have darkened slightly, about 8 to 12 minutes. (If the seeds start acting like firecrackers

and fly from the pan, lower the heat slightly.) Stir in the salt for the final minute of browning.

Transfer the mixture to a food processor or blender. Use an on-off pulsing action to grind until the gomasio becomes a coarse powder. Taste and add more salt, if desired. Cool completely and transfer to a tightly sealed jar. Refrigerate until needed.

Variation: For NORI-SESAME SEASONING SALT, blend in a sheet of toasted nori that has been reduced to tiny flakes in a spice mill.

Sesame Seeds: These tiny beige seeds are packed with good nutrition and fine flavor. They are 35 percent protein—among the highest for seeds or nuts—and very high in iron, calcium, and numerous other minerals. Although black sesame seeds are sold in Oriental groceries and some health food stores (I keep them on hand for garnish), the white seeds are more readily available. Buy them unhulled for maximum freshness and to preserve the fiber and minerals in the hull. (Hulled sesame seeds are available for those who are concerned that the oxalic acid in the hull inhibits calcium absorption.) Because they are about 50 percent oil, sesame seeds are *very* perishable. *Store* in a tightly sealed container in the freezer for up to 6 months. *Select* seeds that have not been preroasted as they are more prone to rancidity.

The paste made of ground sesame seeds is often referred to by its Middle Eastern name, *tahini*. See SESAME BUTTER, SESAME OIL, and SESAME SEASONING SALT.

Shallots: These diminutive members of the onion family are usually expensive, so I buy them as a special treat or when I see a small basketful at a farmers' market. Like GARLIC, they have multiple cloves and are a bit pesky to peel, but their unique mild onion flavor sings gaily in sauces and dips. *Select* firm shallots that show no signs of sprouting. *Store* in a paper bag in the refrigerator for up to 1 week.

Roast shallots as you would garlic (page 425) to bring out their sweetness and dull any sharp edges. They are especially delicious in Roasted Shallot Cream (page 303). For sautéing, ONIONS can be substituted. For roasting, substitute pearl onions.

Shiitake (Oriental Black Mushroom): Shiitake have become increasingly popular in recent years and come dried and packaged in almost any health food store. These expensive, large-capped MUSHROOMS have such intense flavor that a few will perfume a potful of steamed RICE or soup. They are highly esteemed by the Japanese, who believe that they have extraordinary healing properties.

Although many whole foods cookbooks tell you to soak shiitake 3 to 4 hours or overnight, this is not necessary if they are to be cooked. Soak them until soft in boiling water to cover—about ½ hour. Pull out the stem and reserve it for stock. Cook the cap whole or in slivers, using the flavorful soaking water as part of the cooking liquid. (The soaking water rarely requires straining, since most shiitake are cultivated on artificial logs and are therefore not sandy.) *Store* dried shiitake in an airtight container in a cool, dry place. Fresh shiitake can be selected, stored, and cooked like ordinary button mushrooms.

Shiso (Beefsteak Leaf): This reddish-leafed herb, popular in the Japanese kitchen, is often used to color UMEBOSHI PLUM PASTE and pickles. It is also dried and ground and added to seasoning salts. Shiso is rich in iron and calcium.

Shoyu: The term shoyu is a confusing one because it is both the generic Japanese word for soy sauce and a specific type of traditionally made soy sauce whose distinguishing characteristic is that its fermentation starter includes CRACKED WHEAT in addition to soybeans. In *Cooking with Japanese Foods*, Jan and John Belleme explain that the finest shoyu is made of whole (rather than defatted) SOYBEANS, naturally fermented for 1 to 2 years, and then aged in wooden vats. For optimum flavor, add shoyu at the end of cooking. See SOY SAUCE.

Snow Peas: Available year round in Oriental markets, these sweet and crunchy peas are delicious in stir-fries and bean or grain salads. *Select* crisp pods that are free of blemishes. *Store* in a plastic bag in the refrigerator for up to 2 days. *To prepare for cooking*, pinch the brownish tip with an upward motion and pull off the attached string that runs along the upper side of the pod.

Young, tender snow peas can be eaten raw, but their color and flavor are enhanced by 2 to 3 minutes of stir-frying or a 1- to 2-minute plunge in boiling water (after cooking, strain and refresh immediately under cold water). Beware of overcooking as snow peas become soggy and lose their lovely green color.

Soba: Noodles that contain BUCKWHEAT FLOUR. In general, the higher the buckwheat flour content, the more expensive the noodle. (Some varieties contain less than half buckwheat flour.) Other ingredients are sometimes added, such as Eden Foods' wild yam (said to promote strength and vitality), or iron-rich mugwort-leaf soba. Cha-soba noodles are flavored and colored with green tea!

For optimum texture, follow the Japanese technique of adding ½ cup of cold water to the boiling water twice during the cooking time. This allows the central core of the noodle to cook thoroughly before the outside becomes soft and gummy.

Soba are normally sold in 8-ounce packages, each of which serves 2. Soba can be stored for up to a year, well sealed, at room temperature.

Somen: Thin, pure white noodles made of wheat flour, somen cook very quickly. Traditionally, the Japanese serve cooked somen in a bowl of ice water, with a dipping sauce on the side.

Sorghum (Milo): Although a major food source in many parts of the world (including Asia and Africa), almost all of the sorghum grown in the United States is fed to cattle. I've never seen this grain in a health food store, but if you find it, first make sure that it was grown organically. If so, then cook it as you would WHEAT or RYE BERRIES. See the grain cooking chart, page 67, and GRAINS.

Sorghum Molasses (Syrup): This is the sweet liquid extracted from the stalks of the cereal grass SORGHUM. It is similar to MOLASSES and quite popular in the southeastern United States. Sorghum contains sucrose, a simple sugar that is absorbed more quickly into the bloodstream than complex sugars. This is why I use BARLEY MALT SYRUP as a sweetener instead.

Soybeans: Soybeans on their own are rather bland, and many people find them difficult to digest. The great majority of soybeans are grown for use as animal feed or are processed into soy products, such as SOY SAUCE, TEMPEH, and TOFU. They are not intended to be eaten on their own. However, if you wish to eat beige soybeans *au naturel*, opt for organically grown beans to ensure the highest quality and best taste.

When pressure cooking soybeans, add 2 tablespoons of oil per cup of dry beans to keep foaming under control.

Since soybeans ferment easily, presoak them overnight in the refrigerator.

Better yet, pass up beige soybeans altogether, and opt for black soybeans, which have good looks, silken texture, and complex taste. See SOYBEANS, BLACK, and the bean cooking chart, page 175.

Soybeans, Black: I can't claim to have done a comparison tasting of the thousand or so varieties of soybean, but this one is well worth going out of your way for. Black soybeans are nationally distributed and available at most health food stores. At a quick glance, the beans could be mistaken for black turtle beans until you notice their very round plump shape and glossy skin. Because their skins are very fragile, black soybeans require both soaking and cooking with salt. See pages 191–192 for complete cooking instructions.

Soy Cheese: At first glance, this "cheese" might be considered a boon, especially to lovers of pizza who avoid dairy products. But check the label. Soy cheese is a highly refined product that often contains artificial flavors and some added starch for texture. In addition, many varieties contain casein and calcium caseinate, both derived from milk. If you have a craving for cheese, you just might be better off with the real thing.

Soy Flakes: Uncooked SOYBEANS are toasted with dry radiant heat and then pressed into flakes resembling fat, golden OATMEAL. The flakes are simmered in boiling water until tender, about 45 minutes. (You can halve the cooking time by soaking them overnight.) The skins rise to the top and can be removed or stirred back in. Soy flakes are an impressive source of protein and iron, and the taste and texture are reminiscent of cashews. Add the flakes to breakfast porridge and grain salads, or serve them on their own with some chopped PARSLEY and a vinaigrette dressing.

Soy Flour: A flour ground from hulled, cracked, and toasted SOYBEANS. Soy flour creates a dense, heavy texture in baked goods and can dominate other flavors. See FLOUR.

Soyfoods: A generic term referring to a wide range of foods derived from processed SOYBEANS, including MISO, SOY MILK, TEMPEH, and TOFU.

Soy Grits: The good news is that these grits are quick-cooking and about 50 percent protein. The bad news is that they are the by-product of soy oil extraction, made from crushed SOYBEANS that have been treated with a hexane solvent. SOY FLAKES and BLACK SOYBEANS are more healthful sources of soy protein.

Soy Ice Cream: In recent years, the market has exploded with a variety of cholesterol-free soy-based frozen desserts. Take care to read labels; some of these desserts are full of artificial ingredients, while others are more wholesome. While these soy ice creams may provide welcome alternatives to milk products, they are not necessarily healthful.

Soy Milk: This rich liquid is extracted from SOYBEANS that have been soaked in water, ground into a puree, cooked, then pressed dry. Soy milk is richer in protein than cow's milk and is high in iron and B vitamins. The taste and richness (dependent upon oil content) of soy milk vary dramatically from brand to brand. Some brands contain grain sweeteners. Experiment with several types to determine your favorite. See SOY POWDER.

Soynuts: SOYBEANS are soaked in water, then roasted and tossed in TAMARI SOY SAUCE to create a high-protein peanutlike snack. Some people find them difficult to digest.

Soy Oil: Extracted from SOYBEANS, this oil must be highly refined to remove the strong soy flavor. It has a high smoke point and is therefore good for frying, but because it lacks the versatility of SAFFLOWER or CANOLA OIL, I don't stock it in my kitchen. See OILS.

Soy Powder (Powdered Soy Milk): You can use this dehydrated soy milk powder to make soy milk at home. Just mix the powder with water. The milk is a bit grainy (unless you strain it through a double layer of cheesecloth) and not as rich as purchased soy milk, but the financial savings and reduction of packaging wastes are dramatic. Soy powder is especially useful as a replacement for soy milk in baking. See Onion Upside-Down Cornbread (page 323). See SOY MILK.

Soysage: A sausagelike patty usually made from okara (a soy pulp by-product of TOFU), nutritional yeast, WHEAT GERM, oil, and SPICES. "This food reeks of the sixties," comments a natural foods expert and friend, "but unlike granola, should be buried."

Soy Sauce: The difference between the commercial soy sauce carried by supermarkets and the traditionally brewed soy sauce found in health food stores is like the difference between a cheap cooking wine and a fine wine.

Traditional soy sauce is the product of the natural fermentation of SOYBEANS, SALT, water, and sometimes WHEAT. Because soy sauce contains both salt and glutamic acid, it acts as a flavor enhancer. The finest soy sauces are aged for a year or more. Commercial soy sauce is produced in a matter of days from a synthesized soy-based ingredient called hydrolyzed vegetable protein. Its dark brown color usually comes from caramel and its sweetness from corn syrup.

There are two main types of soy

sauce available in health food stores: Ta-mari and Shoyu. The main difference be-tween them is that the fermentation of shoyu is initiated with a wheat-soybean starter, while tamari's starter is prepared exclusively from soybeans. Although there are subtle differences in taste, ta-mari and shoyu can be used interchange-ably. Experiment among the different brands and types. I like tamari, which has a fuller flavor. A special favorite is organic MANSAN TAMARI, which is brewed in cedar kegs and blended with a small amount of the sweet Japanese wine MIRIN. Once the bottle has been opened, be sure to tighten the cap after each use and store in the refrigerator to preserve optimum flavor. See TAMARI SOY SAUCE and SHOYU. Those who cannot eat fer-mented foods will find a tasty alternative in BRAGG LIQUID AMINOS.

Soy Yogurt: I haven't had much luck finding soy yogurt in my local health food stores, so I tried making my own, follow-ing the directions in the definitive *Book of Tofu* by William Shurtleff and Akiko Aoyagi.

To make the starter I boiled 1 cup of water with ¼ cup of SOY POWDER and added 2 teaspoons of MAPLE SYRUP. I left the mixture, uncovered, in a warm spot until it soured, about 48 hours. I then added a quart of SOY MILK and let the mixture sit, uncovered in a warm spot for 14 hours and voilà, yogurt. A quicker method is to mix 1 teaspoon of dairy yo-gurt or yogurt starter (available in some health food stores) into the soy milk and let it sit for 14 to 18 hours. The longer it sits, the tangier it becomes. However, don't let it sit too long, or it separates into Miss Muffett's curds and whey. Soy yogurt is cholesterol-free and a good al-ternative for those who have lactose in-tolerance.

Spaghetti Squash (Vegetable Spa-ghetti): I find spaghetti squash rather bland and disappointing, but some people enjoy its unusual spaghettilike strands. Spaghetti squash has bright yellow skin and an oval shape. *Select* a firm squash without bruises or soft spots, and one that is heavy for its size. *Store* in a cool place for up to 3 weeks or at room tem-perature for 1 week. *Prepare for cooking* by gently scrubbing the skin. Pierce the skin in a few places with a paring knife. Put the squash in a large shallow baking dish.

Baking:

Bake about 1 hour at 350°. Turn once during cooking. The squash will yield to gentle pressure when done. To serve, cut the squash in half and remove the seeds. Use a fork to lift out the strands. Toss with a little light SESAME OIL and season with SALT, if desired.

Spelt: One of the most ancient grains, spelt is an ancestor of contemporary strains of WHEAT. Its taste and texture are similar to wheat, but its genetic makeup is slightly different. This latter fact is of special interest to people with wheat sensitivities who often find that they have a better tolerance for spelt. Spelt flour and pasta are now nationally distributed.

Spices: It's hard to imagine cooking with-out spices, those highly aromatic season-ings that come from the seeds, roots, bark, and buds of trees and plants. (HERBS, on the other hand, generally de-rive from leaves and stems.) The most important fact to remember about spices is that they become either bitter or taste-less when stale. Most whole spices have a shelf life of about 6 to 8 months while ground spices begin losing their potency almost immediately. For this reason, it's advisable to purchase whole spices in small quantities and grind them as needed. With the exception of DRIED GINGER, MACE, and TURMERIC, it's quite easy to purchase whole spices. To grind spices, a small electric coffee grinder works most efficiently. Small berries like ALLSPICE and CORIANDER can also be ground in a pepper mill. Resist the temptation to display spices in decorative clear jars or bottles near the stove; *store* them in a cool, dry, dark place, ideally in dark bottles. If your current supply of ground, dry spices has a very faint aroma or smell slightly musty, it's time to replace them. For two excellent mail-order source of spices, see page 477. See ALLSPICE, ANISEED, CARAWAY, CARDAMOM, CAYENNE, CELERY SEEDS, CHILI PEPPERS, CLOVES, CUMIN, CURRY POWDER, FIVE-SPICE POWDER, GINGER, JUNIPER BERRIES, MACE, NUTMEG, PAPRIKA, and STAR ANISE.

Spinach: I learned a while back that the roots of young spinach are quite edible. Just swoosh them in water vigorously along with the leaves to get rid of all of the sand. Spinach is a good source of iron; it is also high in potassium and vitamin A. *Select* spinach with small, young leaves, if available; they cook very quickly and their flavor is exquisite. Avoid spinach with wilted or yellowing leaves. *Store* spinach, already washed and spun dry, in a clean kitchen towel in the vegetable bin for up to 3 days. Frozen leaf spinach is an acceptable substitute for adding to soups and stews when you cannot find fresh spinach. I do not recommend pressure cooking spinach, since it cooks so quickly. To avoid discoloration, do not cook spinach in an iron or aluminum pan.

Steaming:

Place spinach in a large pot with only the rinse water clinging to the leaves. Cover and steam over high heat until wilted and tender, but still bright green, about 2 to 3 minutes. Lift out of the pot with a slotted spoon. A bit of freshly grated nutmeg is very nice on spinach.

Sprouts: When BEANS and SEEDS are soaked in water, they soften and send out edible shoots. As this happens, they become more digestible, sweeter, and richer in protein and vitamins. Sprouts are extremely simple to grow and "harvest" at home; see pages 287–289 for complete directions and serving ideas. ALFALFA SPROUTS are readily available. *Select* sprouts that are perky and show no wilting or browning. Eat them as quickly as possible. *Store* them in a plastic bag in the refrigerator for up to 3 days.

Squash, Summer: See SUMMER SQUASH.

Squash, Winter: See WINTER SQUASH.

Star Anise: A beautiful, brown star-shaped seed from China that has a sweet and fragrant aniselike flavor. It can be used as a substitute for anise in recipes, but keep in mind that its flavor is more intense. See SPICES and Flavorprints, page 4.

Steel-Cut (Irish or Scottish) Oats: Lovers of OATMEAL will discover that steel-cut oats are packed with sweet, wholesome flavor, have a mild chewiness, and a minimum of gooeyness. Although steel-cut oats take longer to cook than oatmeal (rolled oats), preparation time can be dramatically reduced by soaking the oats overnight and pressure-cooking them.

To make steel-cut oats, the groats are toasted and then cut into bits with steel blades. If you have a grain mill, you can do this at home for maximum freshness. See GRAINS.

String Beans: See GREEN BEANS.

Sucanat: This is a trademark—an acronym for SUGAR CANE NATURAL—for evaporated and granulated sugar cane juice. Less refined than standard white sugar, it contains some trace minerals and has not been chemically processed. Those who opt to keep some sugar in their diets may find it a viable alternative. Sucanat can be substituted in equal amounts for granulated sugar; its light brown color darkens baked goods somewhat.

Sugar Snap Peas: One of the enchantments of spring, these sweet, crunchy peas are eaten, pods and all, after a 2- to 3-minute steaming, or raw if they are really fresh. *To prepare*, pinch off the ends and remove the strings from both top and bottom. I like to eat them out of hand, but they are also good when cut in thirds and tossed into grain salads.

Summer Savory: Slightly milder than WINTER SAVORY, this herb tastes somewhat like a delicate form of THYME.

Summer Squash: Soft-skinned squashes with edible seeds, such as ZUCCHINI and YELLOW SQUASH. They cook very quickly and are nice when sliced and added to stir-fries or steamed whole (to preserve flavor). *Select* small (about 4 inches long), firm squashes that are heavy for their size. *Store* in a plastic bag in the refrigerator for up to 4 days.

Prepare for cooking by trimming off the ends. Rinse lightly (do not scrub with a vegetable brush as the skins are tender and bruise easily). For the most intense flavor, steam or pressure-cook small summer squash whole.

Pressure cooking:
Whole, small: 1 minute high pressure
½-inch slices: 2 to 3 minutes total cooking time

Steaming:
Whole, small: 9 to 10 minutes
½-inch slices: 5 to 7 minutes

Stir-frying:
¼-inch slices, cut on the diagonal: 2 to 3 minutes

Sun Chokes: See JERUSALEM ARTICHOKES.

Sun-Dried Tomatoes: Sun-dried tomatoes come either dehydrated or marinated in olive oil. The dry-pack tomatoes are excellent for making homemade Tomato Paste (page 306), or to impart a rich tomato taste to soups and stews. Marinated sun-dried tomatoes are probably too intensely flavored to eat out of hand, but are excellent to mince and toss in bean and grain salads. They add a punch of saltiness and nice specks of color. Use the tomato marinating oil to sauté onions when making RISOTTO.

Sunflower Oil: Extracted from SUNFLOWER SEEDS, this oil has a nutty flavor and a low smoke point, which limits its primary use to salad dressings and some sauces. See OILS.

Sunflower Seeds (Sunnies): Although they have hard black-and-white zebra-striped shells, sunflower seeds are usually sold already shelled. These tasty beige seeds are high in protein with noteworthy amounts of iron, calcium, and numerous vitamins, including vitamin E. Great to eat as snacks and to add crunch to pie dough, muffins, and salads. Like all nuts and seeds, they are high in fat, but the vitamin E is an antioxidant, giving them a slightly longer shelf life than most seeds. *Select* unroasted sunnies, which will last considerably longer than roasted ones. *Store* them in the refrigerator or freezer for up to 4 months. Their flavor is considerably enhanced by toasting, which you can do at home, but heat destroys some of the vitamins. For optimum freshness, refrigerate toasted sunnies and eat them within a few days. See NUTS AND SEEDS and SUNFLOWER OIL.

Sushi Daikon: See DAIKON PICKLE.

Swedes: See RUTABAGAS.

Swedish Beans: See BROWN BEANS.

Sweeteners: There is a wide range of sweeteners to use as alternatives to refined white sugar. The advantage to some of them is that they are made up of complex sugars that enter the bloodstream more slowly than refined cane sugar. See individual entries under BARLEY MALT SYRUP, CAROB, MAPLE SYRUP, RICE SYRUP, SORGHUM MOLASSES, and SUCANAT.

Sweet Glutinous Brown Rice: See RICE.

Sweet Potatoes: There are two types of sweet potatoes. The one I prefer for baking has bright orange moist flesh and skin that ranges from reddish brown to purple. This variety is often as sweet as candy; it is frequently referred to as a YAM. The other type of sweet potato has dry, yellowish flesh and lighter-colored (often tan) skin. This variety is preferred for moist cooking, such as boiling or pressure cooking.

Baked sweet potatoes make a great snack. I prepare a few at a time and reheat them as needed. *Select* slender specimens for baking as they cook much more quickly than chubby ones. (Do not pierce them with a fork, or you will end up with caramelized drippings to clean up.) *Store* them unwrapped in a ventilated spot at room temperature for up to 10 days.

If boiling or pressure cooking, peel first. (I often find it easier to use a paring knife than a traditional potato peeler.)

Pressure cooking:
Large, quartered: 5 to 7 minutes high pressure
¼-inch slices: 2 to 3 minutes high pressure
Boiling:
Large, quartered: 10 to 12 minutes

Baking:
Slender potatoes: 25 to 30 minutes at 400°
Chubby potatoes: 45 to 50 minutes at 400°

Swiss Chard (Chard): These large leafy greens resemble SPINACH and can be quickly steamed or stir-fried in much the same way. I particularly like to add chopped chard to soups at the end of cooking, for a splash of color and earthy taste. The ivory (or red) stalks look a bit like emaciated CELERY; they are more fibrous than the leaves and, unless very young and tender, need about 4 to 5 minutes more cooking time. Chard is a fine source of vitamin A, iron, potassium, calcium, and vitamin C.

Select crisp, vibrant leaves. *Store* them in a plastic bag for up to 2 days in the refrigerator. *Prepare for cooking* by swooshing in water to release any sand. Cut the leaves from the stems and strip any large stems of strings (as for celery). To avoid discoloration, do not cook chard in an iron or aluminum pan. See Basic Sautéed Greens, page 254.

Tahini: See SESAME BUTTER.

Tamari Soy Sauce: A fermented soy sauce made from SOYBEANS, SALT, water, and a soy-derived starter called *koji*. According to Jan and John Belleme, authors of *Cooking with Japanese Food*, traditionally tamari was made from the dark liquid that pooled on the surface of fermenting MISO. Nowadays, the production of tamari is similar to that of SHOYU except that the fermentation process is initiated with a wheat-free starter. Tamari is fuller-flavored than shoyu and contains more amino acids. It may be added either during or after cooking. See SOY SAUCE and SHOYU.

Tarragon: A magnificent herb, especially when fresh, and beloved by those partial to its delicate anise flavor. Because of its assertive flavor, a little goes a long way. Used with discretion, tarragon offers a lilting elegance to VINEGAR, mayonnaise, a TOFU dip, or a summer grain salad.

Teff: The staple grain of Ethiopia, teff is an ancient pinprick-sized seed with an impressive nutritional profile. It is now being cultivated in the United States. Because of its diminutive size—150 grains equal the weight of a whole wheat berry—it is not practical to strip off the hull, which is a blessing since the hull contains noteworthy quantities of protein, iron, and calcium. Teff is grown in three varieties: white, red, and brown.

Teff Flour: You can easily make teff flour by grinding the tiny seeds in a spice grinder. The flour lends a nutty flavor to baked goods and pancakes and is easy to work with as a thickener for soups and stews. Teff contains a natural yeast and when mixed with pure spring water and left at room temperature, it will begin to bubble. This fermented batter is used to make the crepelike Ethiopian bread called *injera* and can also act as a sourdough starter. See FLOUR.

Tempeh: This traditional Indonesian soyfood is made by splitting and cooking SOYBEANS, which are then inoculated with a starter. As the tempeh incubates, a fuzzy white mycelium of enzymes develops on the surface, rendering the soybeans more digestible and providing a range of B vitamins.

Tempeh has recently become very popular in the United States and is available in a wide variety of styles, some much more full-flavored than others. You will find them either in the refrigerator or freezer section of your health food store. I prefer the tempeh made with grains as well as soybeans, since the fla-

vor is milder. For additional information on selecting, storing, and cooking with tempeh, see pages 227–228.

Thyme: This potent gray-green herb is associated with the cuisine of the Mediterranean countries, especially France and Italy. It adds a pungent, aromatic flavor to foods and works especially well with TOMATOES, EGGPLANT, and GREEN BEANS. OREGANO can be substituted for thyme. Recipes in this book call for leaf thyme; halve the amount if using the ground herb. See HERBS.

Toasted Sesame Oil (Oriental Sesame Oil): An intensely flavored oil extracted from toasted SESAME SEEDS. A few drops drizzled onto cooked GRAINS, BEANS, or PASTA add marvelous flavor and make an instant sauce when combined with TAMARI SOY SAUCE or BRAGG LIQUID AMINOS. Toasted sesame oil burns easily, so avoid using it for sautéing, or proceed with great caution. Toasted sesame oil has a shorter shelf life than many oils; refrigerate after opening.

Tofu (Bean Curd, Soy Cheese): Judging by its availability in supermarkets and corner groceries, tofu is fast becoming the yogurt of the nineties. Tofu is an ancient food made by coagulating SOY MILK, then draining it and pressing the curds into a cake. It is an inexpensive and versatile form of high-quality protein, rich in calcium and cholesterol free. For information on selecting, storing, and cooking with tofu, see pages 218–219.

Tomatoes: It sure is hard to buy good tomatoes nowadays. The best revenge is to grow them yourself. Failing that, plum tomatoes offer the best flavor and texture. These egg-shaped fruits (the tomato is actually a fruit) have fewer seeds and more flesh per square inch than watery beefsteak tomatoes. I prefer them for cooking and eating raw—unless a vine-ripened beefsteak is available. Firm, sweet cherry tomatoes are also delicious. *Select* pliant but firm tomatoes that are heavy for their size. If they need further ripening, put them in a paper bag away from the sun. Once ripe, eat them right away or *store* them unwrapped in the vegetable bin of the refrigerator for up to 3 days. Refrigeration diminishes flavor. *Prepare for cooking* by washing and removing the core. The pressure cooker does a nice job of softening tomato skins in dishes that cook for longer than 10 minutes under high pressure. If using a standard stovetop cooking method, peel the tomatoes before combining them with other ingredients.

To peel tomatoes, submerge them in boiling water for 20 seconds. Lift out with a slotted spoon and set them immediately in a bowl of cold water. When cool enough to handle, remove them from the water and slip off the skins.

Triticale Berries: Triticale's name comes from the Latin *triticum* for wheat and *secale* for rye; this new hybrid grain has a better balance of amino acids than either of its "parents." Hulled triticale (pronounced triht-ih-KAY-lee) berries have a slightly sweet, nutty flavor and the characteristic chewiness of whole grains. To cut cooking time roughly in half, crack the berries in a grain mill or a good blender in the manner of STEEL-CUT OATS. It's also nice to use triticale berries in grain salads. See TRITICALE FLAKES, TRITICALE FLOUR, and the grain cooking chart, page 67.

Triticale Flakes: These are hulled TRITICALE BERRIES that have been toasted and then pressed thin between heavy rollers. They make a nutritious, quick-cooking breakfast cereal.

Triticale Flour: This flour is made from finely ground hulled TRITICALE BERRIES. You can substitute small quantities of it

for whole wheat flour. However, since the flour contains more BRAN than pastry flour, it will make the final product slightly heavier.

Turmeric: This root, a member of the GINGER family, gives CURRY POWDER its characteristic bright yellow color. It is occasionally available fresh in Oriental markets, but is most commonly sold in its dried, ground form. I like using turmeric to "dye" TOFU yellow in stir-fries, but since it is pungent and has a natural bitterness, sprinkle it on cautiously at first—about ¼ to ½ teaspoon—adding a bit more if needed.

Turnip Greens (Turnip Tops): These tasty greens have a slight bitter edge. *Select* bright green, perky leaves that show no signs of wilting or yellowing. Eat them the same day, if possible, or *store* them, trimmed and washed, wrapped in a kitchen towel in a plastic bag for 1 day. Cook them as you would SPINACH.

Turnips: This whitish, globe-shaped root vegetable with its pale purple cap is sweetest while still small. *Select* unblemished small turnips that feel heavy for their size. If the TURNIP GREENS are attached, they should look lively and bright green with no signs of yellowing. Remove tops, if any, and *store* in a plastic bag in the refrigerator for up to 24 hours. *Prepare turnips for cooking* by peeling. All but the smallest, freshest turnips have bitter skins.

Pressure cooking:
Medium-large (4 ounces each), quartered: 3 to 4 minutes high pressure
Small, whole (1½ ounces each): 7 minutes high pressure
¼-inch slices: 1 to 2 minutes high pressure

Steaming:
Small, whole (1½ ounces each): 20 to 22 minutes
¼-inch slices: 3 to 5 minutes

Baking:
¼-inch slices: 35 to 40 minutes at 400°
Spread out in a shallow baking dish. Add ⅓ cup water or APPLE JUICE. Cover securely.

Turtle Beans: See BLACK BEANS.

Udon: These flat whole wheat noodles, are nice to serve as Cold Sesame Noodles (page 164) or in recipes calling for linguine. Udon made of brown rice flour combined with WHOLE WHEAT FLOUR have an especially pleasing taste and texture. Udon are generally sold in 8-ounce packages (1 package serves 2 to 3) and can be stored for up to a year, well sealed, at room temperature.

Umeboshi Plum Paste (Pickled Plum Paste): A puree made of UMEBOSHI PLUMS, this flavor-packed condiment makes a delicious addition to sauces and salad dressings, but use it sparingly because it is very salty. My favorite use of plum paste is to spread a very thin veneer of it on toasted NORI when making sushi rolls (page 270).

Umeboshi Plums: These Japanese pickled plums have a sweet and fruity taste and are *very salty*, having been pickled in a salt brine for about a year. In Japan, umeboshi are served as a condiment, often with RICE, and are sometimes eaten straight to cure a wide range of ailments—from acid stomachs to migraine headaches. The plums are red because they are pickled with the red SHISO leaf, which adds iron and vitamin C. Umeboshi plums make good preservatives: Poke a piece of one in the middle of a ball of sushi rice, wrap it in a sheet of NORI, and take it on your next camping trip; it will last for 2 to 3 days.

The flavor of the plums varies considerably, depending upon quality and brand; health food store umeboshi tend to be of more reliable quality than those sold in Oriental groceries, which are sometimes dyed red with chemicals and not traditionally processed.

Umeboshi Plum Vinegar (Umeboshi Vinegar): A salty vinegar based on pickled umeboshi plums. See UMEBOSHI PLUMS and VINEGAR.

Vanilla (Pure Vanilla Extract): This smooth, slightly smoky flavoring is made by extracting the essence of vanilla beans and preserving it in alcohol and water. Pure vanilla extract is expensive, but a little of it goes a long way. It's simple and cost-efficient to make your own: Split a good-quality (dark brown and supple) vanilla bean down its length and set it into an 8-ounce jar with vodka or brandy to cover. Seal the jar tightly and let stand for 6 months to age. You can leave the vanilla bean in place as you use the extract.

Do not be tempted to buy imitation vanilla, which is made from a synthetic product called vanillin (a by-product of papermaking).

Vegetable Stock: A broth made by cooking vegetables until they have released their flavor and nutrients into the water. The most flavorful stocks are made from a variety of vegetables and HERBS. The broths lose about 30 percent of their flavor when frozen, so try to use them fresh. See various vegetable stock recipes, pages 21–29. See also box on instant vegetable stocks, page 27.

Vinegar: You are in for a treat when you begin to explore the world of unrefined vinegars with complex and mellow tastes—there is nothing harsh or puckery about them. A well-stocked health food store should carry a wide variety of high-quality vinegars. *Select* those whose labels read "organic," "raw," "unrefined," or "unpasteurized." *Store* vinegar, tightly capped, in a cool place for up to at least 6 months. Many vinegars will last considerably longer, but it's a good idea to date the bottle once opened and taste the vinegar before using after 6 months have elapsed.

Here is a description of my favorite vinegars and their best uses. I like to keep them all on hand to stimulate my creative juices.

Apple Cider: For a relatively inexpensive fruity vinegar, this is my choice. Try to get raw vinegar apple cider made by the traditional process of aging cider for at least 6 months in cypress and cedar casks.

Balsamic: An Italian vinegar made from white Trebbiano grape juice that becomes deep amber when aged in wood barrels. The finest balsamics are very slightly sweet, syrupy, and expensive; brands vary widely in taste and quality.

Brown Rice: Traditional brown rice vinegar takes more than 12 months to prepare. There are two types: One is made from unrefined sake (Japanese rice wine), water, and a vinegar "mother" (a mixture of enzymes or bacteria). The second is made from cooked rice, rice koji (a fermentation catalyst), water, and a vinegar "mother." Both vinegars are brewed traditionally in earthenware crocks. The vinegar is filtered and then aged in casks until the flavor is mellow and the color is deep amber.

Raspberry: I consider this vinegar optional, but love it for its delicate fruity taste, considerably milder than apple cider vinegar. I generally purchase an imported French brand based on white wine. Since it lasts such a long time, I don't mind the relatively high expense. Available in gourmet shops.

Tarragon (or Other Herb): Herbal vinegars are based on a mild white wine vinegar infused with a fresh branch of HERBS. They add sophistication to salad dressings, especially when fresh herbs are not readily available. Gourmet shops generally carry them.

Umeboshi Plum: This bright fuchsia vinegar has been a regular resident in my pantry since I discovered it a few years ago. Made from the liquor that rises to the surface of pickled UMEBOSHI PLUMS, it has all of the sweet fruitiness of a good wine vinegar, the puckeriness of lemon, and the saltiness of the sea. In addition to making a superb instant vinaigrette (page 210), a dash of umeboshi stirred at the last minute into a flat-tasting sauce, soup, or stew brings it to instant life. As natural foods cookery expert Mary Estella once commented: "Umeboshi is natural foods' answer to MSG."

Wakame: A traditional addition to MISO soup (see RAMEN), this sea vegetable can be softened in water for 5 to 10 minutes—there is some variation among brands—and cut into slivers for addition to a green salad. Any stiff midrib should be cut away once the green has been softened in water, unless the wakame is to be cooked. See SEA VEGETABLES, for general storing and cooking instructions; see also ALARIA.

Walnuts: Opt for organic walnuts sold by a merchant you trust. Commercially processed shelled nuts are treated with a variety of chemicals to give them a longer shelf life and uniform color. For optimum freshness, *select* unshelled nuts, *store* in a cool, dry place, and crack open as needed. If you buy shelled nuts, select refrigerated whole nuts rather than unrefrigerated broken bits, which are more likely to be stale. See NUTS AND SEEDS.

Wasabi: Often referred to as Japanese HORSERADISH (although not botanically related), this gnarled, potent root is most commonly sold in health food stores in powdered form—in small tins or individually wrapped foil envelopes. Choose wasabi in the foil envelope, since exposure to air results in a rapid loss of flavor and pizzazz. Check the label; usually the wasabi has been blended with horseradish or DAIKON root. (Some commercial brands contain green food coloring, which is best avoided.) Although I prefer UMEBOSHI PLUM PASTE for making sushi rolls, wasabi is more traditional. To make a paste, add a few tablespoons of warm water to 1 heaping tablespoon of wasabi powder and stir. Let sit at room temperature for 10 minutes before using.

When fresh horseradish is not available, replace with a pinch of wasabi powder in recipes.

Watercress: It may not surprise you that watercress is a member of the MUSTARD family, for it sometimes has quite a bite. (Young, tender watercress is often milder in flavor.) *Select* bright green, perky bunches; avoid those with very thick stems or a large number of withered or yellowing leaves. For salads and cooking, use only the leaves and the thinner stems; reserve any thick stems for stock. Chopped watercress can be added to a soup or stew at the last minute for a nice touch of green. It is also tasty stir-fried—but figure on using 1 bunch per person as it shrinks dramatically. *Store* watercress in a plastic bag in the refrigerator for 1 to 2 days—or for 3 to 4 days with the stems submerged in water and the leaves covered by a plastic bag. Rinse and spin-dry (for salads only) before using.

Watermelon: Perhaps no fruit signals relief on a sizzling summer day more than a slice of cool, crisp watermelon. And here's how to enjoy a watermelon feast and leave no garbage behind:

Watermelon seeds are delicious. In Asia, they are roasted and eaten as snacks. (Follow the instructions for roasting pumpkin seeds, page 446.) After roasting the seeds, you can pickle the rind.

If you buy a whole melon, *select* one that has clear skin without any soft spots and sounds hollow when gently tapped. If the melon is sold in halves or quarters, opt for a piece with brightly colored flesh and black seeds. Pale flesh usually indicates pale flavor. Lots of white seeds indicate that the melon was picked prematurely.

Wehani Rice: See RICE.

Wheat: The king of grains in this part of the world comes in three main varieties: bread wheat, cracker (soft) wheat, and durum. It can be further classified by the season in which it grows.

Winter wheat, which is planted in the fall, tends to have a higher gluten content.

Spring wheat, which is sown in springtime, typically has a lower gluten content and is ground into whole wheat pastry flour, used in making pie crusts, cookies, and cakes.

Wheat Berries (Whole Grain Wheat): The whole grain of WHEAT with only the outer hull removed. Wheat berries are quite chewy, even when thoroughly cooked, making them interesting candidates for grain salads and hearty vegetable stews. It's best to soak them to avoid long cooking. See CRACKED WHEAT and the grain cooking chart, page 67.

Wheat Bran (Miller's Bran): Just below the outer hull of the wheat berry lies a protective layer called the bran. In addition to its indigestible cellulose (which adds bulk and fiber to the diet), bran is rich in nutrients. Always buy bran "unprocessed" and pure. Bran cereals are often loaded with unhealthful ingredients.

Wheat Flakes: In a process similar to making oatmeal from OAT GROATS, WHEAT BERRIES are first steamed and then rolled flat. They make a flavorful quick-cooking breakfast cereal but are less chewy than BARLEY FLAKES. Try using them in Triple Grain Granola (page 370).

Wheat Germ: Wheat germ is what every good baker in the sixties put into cookies to boost their nutritional value—and what a shame it wasn't WHOLE WHEAT PASTRY FLOUR or sprouted WHEAT BERRIES instead. Because wheat germ is the embryo of the grain, as soon as it is exposed to the air, its nutritional value plummets. A high oil content causes wheat germ to go rancid quickly. If you like to spike your granola or cookies with wheat germ, be sure to store it in the refrigerator.

White Beans: A generic term for many types of white bean, including NAVY, GREAT NORTHERN, and CANNELLINI. They are all good for making baked beans and marinated bean salads. Check the bean cooking charts (pages 175 and 177) for timing.

Whole Wheat Flour: Flour ground from a type of whole grain wheat that is high in gluten and therefore suitable for making bread. Purchase stone-ground wheat flour when available and, if possible, from a health food store that refrigerates whole grain flours. It *cannot* be used interchangeably with WHOLE WHEAT PASTRY FLOUR. See FLOUR.

Whole Wheat Pastry Flour: Flour ground from a type of whole grain wheat that is low in gluten. It is more finely milled than WHOLE WHEAT FLOUR and is preferred for making cookies, cakes, and pie crusts. It *cannot* be used interchangeably with whole wheat flour. See FLOUR.

Wild Rice: See RICE.

Winged Beans: Extremely nutritious and versatile beans that grow in tropical climes. The winged bean has been touted as an important "future food" and one of the answers to the world hunger crisis, since its edible tubers are high in protein and the bean can be processed into TOFU, TEMPEH, and SOY MILK.

Winter Savory: An aromatic herb that is somewhat suggestive of a mild THYME. Winter savory has a more assertive taste than SUMMER SAVORY. It is delightful added to soups or cooked with vegetables. Use it with discretion, since too much adds a medicinal taste. See HERBS.

Winter Squash: These squashes—including ACORN, BUTTERCUP, BUTTERNUT, DELICATA, HUBBARD, KABOCHA, PUMPKIN, SPAGHETTI, and other hard-shelled varieties—store well through the winter and early spring. *Select* those with unblemished skins and no soft spots (which can be cut away if they develop after purchase). Protected by their hard skins, winter squash can be *stored* unrefrigerated in a cool, dark place.

When pressure-cooking organic butternut, kabocha, or delicata squashes, I don't peel them; other winter squash have tougher skins and should be peeled before or after cooking. Most winter squash are fine sources of vitamin A and fiber. The seeds of all varieties can be cleaned and roasted; see PUMPKIN SEEDS for instructions.

Pressure cooking:
Acorn, halved: 6 to 7 minutes high pressure

Butternut, ½-inch slices: 3 to 4 minutes high pressure

Pattypan, whole (2 pounds): 10 to 12 minutes high pressure

All winter squash, 1½-inch chunks: 3 to 4 minutes high pressure

Boiling:

½-inch slices, covered, in 1 inch of water: 6 to 8 minutes

Baking:

halved, seeded, unpeeled, placed cut side down in a baking dish, covered: 30 to 40 minutes at 350°

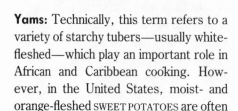

Yams: Technically, this term refers to a variety of starchy tubers—usually white-fleshed—which play an important role in African and Caribbean cooking. However, in the United States, moist- and orange-fleshed SWEET POTATOES are often labeled yams, much to the confusion of all who are concerned about such matters. See SWEET POTATOES.

Yellow Squash: A variety of summer squash whose shape resembles ZUCCHINI. Its flavor is milder than that of zucchini, and it has lots of edible seeds. I prefer zucchini when given the choice. See SUMMER SQUASH.

Zante Currants: See CURRANTS, DRIED.

Zest: See PEEL.

Zucchini: A mild-tasting summer squash that can be eaten raw or cooked. Zucchini doesn't have much personality on its own. It's cooked to best advantage by being stir-fried in olive oil with lots of garlic. *Select* the smallest zucchini you can find; they'll be less watery and more flavorful than larger specimens. See SUMMER SQUASH.

Find the shortest, simplest way between the earth, the hands and the mouth.

—Lanza del Vasto, quoted in Wendell Berry,
The Unsettling of America (San Francisco: Sierra Books, 1986).

Further Reading and Resources

The following listing is in alphabetical order by subject.

Community-Supported Agriculture

By purchasing advance shares in a farmer's harvest, you enable small farmers to grow organic produce: Then you reap what they sow. To learn about a community-supported farm near you and to request a catalog of books on related subjects, write to Biodynamic Farming and Gardening Association, P.O. Box 550, Kimberton, PA 19442. Tel.: 215-935-7797.

Cookbooks and References

The following titles were extremely useful in the preparation of my book, and I recommend them to anyone wishing to explore their subject areas more fully.

BAKING

Uprisings: The Whole Grain Bakers' Book, by the Cooperative Whole Grain Educational Association (Summertown, Tenn.: Book Publishing Company, 1990). An imaginative selection of recipes for breads, muffins, and cakes, many of which are dairy-free.

Baking for Health, by Linda Edwards (New York: Avery, 1988). A fine book for those on a diet free of white flour, refined sugar, dairy, and salt.

VEGETABLES

Raw Energy, by Leslie and Susannah Kenton (New York: Warner, 1984). A good primer on raw foods, with a section on sprouting and some recipes.

The Victory Garden Cookbook, by Marian Morash (New York: Knopf, 1982). An invaluable basic reference and cookbook; some recipes use animal products.

Uncommon Fruits and Vegetables, by Elizabeth Schneider (New York: Harper & Row, 1986). A fine encyclopedia of the unusual ingredients that are becoming more commonplace in our produce markets; some recipes use animal products.

GRAINS

The Complete Whole Grain Cookbook, by Carol Gelles (New York: Donald Fine, 1989). Fine background and basic recipes for cooking grains of all kinds; some recipes use animal products.

MISCELLANEOUS

FRESH from a Vegetarian Kitchen, by Meredith McCarty (Eureka, Calif.: Turning Point, 1989).

The Natural Foods Cookbook, by Mary Estella (New York: Japan Publications, 1985). Both the above books have delicious dairy-free vegetarian recipes with a macrobiotic slant.

Cooking with Japanese Foods: A Guide to the Traditional Natural Foods of Japan, by Jan and John Belleme (Brookline, Mass.: East West Health Books, 1986). Good background on various Japanese ingredients that have become commonly available in health food stores; some recipes are included.

The Book of Tofu, by William Shurtleff and Akiko Aoyagi (New York: Ballantine, 1988). The classic on the subject, with excellent background information and lots of good recipes.

The Whole Foods Encyclopedia, by Rebecca Wood (Englewood Cliffs, N.J.: Prentice-Hall, 1988). A lively alphabetical reference to the ingredients in a whole foods diet.

Ecology

In Context is a "Quarterly of Humane Sustainable Culture" that provides highly perceptive and inspirational articles devoted to subjects like "What Is Enough," "Earth and Spirit," and "Global Climate Change." Highly recommended. Annual subscription rate is $24. Write to In Context, P.O. Box 11470, Bainbridge Island, WA 98110.

State of the World, by Lester R. Brown, et al. (New York: Norton, 1992). This book is considered the most definitive guide to the world's resources and how they are being managed. Updated annually by the research team of the Worldwatch Institute, it is available in bookstores, but free to members of the Worldwatch Institute, 1776 Massachusetts Ave., NW, Washington, DC 20077-6628.

Diet for a Small Planet (20th Anniversary Edition), by Frances Moore Lappé (New York: Ballantine, 1992). This fully revised edition brings us up-to-date on Lappé's understanding that the essential cause of world hunger is the lack of democracy world-wide. For further information, write to the Institute for the Arts of Democracy, 700 Larkspur Landing Circle, Suite 199, Larkspur, CA 94939.

Thinking Like a Mountain, by John Seed, et al. (Philadelphia; New Society Publishers, 1988). A slim but powerful manual for developing a sense of "deep ecology," which is the ability to experience the interconnectedness of all life forms.

Silent Spring, by Rachel Carson (Boston: Houghton Mifflin, 1962 and 1987). The classic on the subject; an eloquent plea to cease poisoning the earth with chemicals.

Diet for a New America, by John Robbins (Walpole, N.H.: Stillpoint, 1987). Documents the devastating impact on the environment of a meat-based diet and the large-scale cattle raising required to support it. Robbins's new book, *May All Be Fed: Diet for a New World* (New York: William Morrow, 1992), amplifies these themes with up-to-date research, and it offers practical suggestions for implementing changes in our daily lives. Both books are available in bookstores and through EarthSave, "a nonprofit environmental and health educational organization dedicated to helping the Earth restore its delicate ecological balance." Write to EarthSave, 706 Frederick Street, Santa Cruz, CA 95062. Tel.: 408-423-4069.

Energy Saving in the Kitchen

The Smart Kitchen, by David Goldbeck (Woodstock, N.Y.: Ceres Press, 1989). The author fulfills the promise of the subtitle, which reads "How to Design a Comfortable, Safe, Energy-Efficient, and Environment-Friendly Workspace." This paperback can be mail-ordered from Ceres Press, Dept. SKB, P.O. Box 87, Woodstock, NY 12498 for $15.95 plus $2 shipping.

Solar Box Cookers International, 1724 Eleventh Street, Sacramento, CA 95814. Tel.: 916-444-6616. Promotes the use of solar cooking and sells instructions for building your own solar cooker.

Consumer Guide to Home Energy Savings, by Alex Wilson (Washington, D.C., and Berkeley: American Council for an Energy-Efficient Economy). An annual survey of the most efficient products you can purchase, including cooking appliances, refrigerators, and dishwashers. It also gives excellent tips for saving energy (and money!) in your kitchen. For further information, write to the American Council for an Energy-Efficient Economy, 1001 Connecticut Avenue NW, Suite 535, Washington, DC 20036. Tel.: 202-429-8873.

Food and Health

Food and Healing, by Annemarie Colbin (New York: Ballantine, 1986). A fascinating study of the relationship of food to health written by the founder of the Natural Gourmet Institute for Food and Health. For a free brochure on classes, write to the Institute at 48 West 21st Street, 2nd Floor, New York, NY 10010. Tel.: 212-645-5170.

Nourishing Wisdom: A New Understanding of Eating, by Marc David (New York: Bell Tower, 1991). A thoughtful and beautifully written selection of essays that explore how our attitude to food reflects our attitude to life and vice versa.

The Power of Your Plate, by Neal D. Barnard, M.D. (Summertown, Tenn.: Book Publishing Company, 1990). A selection of essays by physicians, each addressing how diet can effectively control particular illnesses.

Food Safety

Safe Food: Eating Wisely in a Risky World, by Michael F. Jacobson, et al. (Los Angeles: Living Planet Press, 1991). Practical advice on making safe food choices and maintaining a safe kitchen, plus recommendations for taking political action on such issues as food labeling and restricted use of food additives. Americans for Safe Food, which can be reached at 1875 Connecticut Avenue NW, Suite 3000, Washington, DC 20009, publishes a list of mail-order organic food sources. See also *Nutrition Action Healthletter* under NUTRITION.

Poisons in Your Food: The Dangers You Face and What You Can Do About Them, by Ruth Winter (New York: Crown, 1991). Excellent coverage of the "hidden ingredients" in food and how you can avoid them.

For Our Kids' Sake: How to Protect Your Child Against Pesticides in Food, by Anne Witte Garland (San Francisco: Sierra Club Books, 1989). Practical advice and tools for taking action offered by Mothers and Others for Pesticide Limits, an organization under the auspices of the National Resources Defense Council, 40 West 20th Street, New York, NY 10011.

Green Consuming

The main goal of the green consumer is to cut back on consumption altogether. When making any purchases, your choices are equivalent to casting votes for a better environment. Guides to green consuming abound. Here are two I have found useful.

Non-Toxic, Natural, & Earthwise, by Debra Lynn Dadd (Los Angeles: Tarcher, 1990). A listing and brief description of environmentally friendly products by category; contains a useful chapter on organic food, with an excellent listing of mail-order sources.

The Green Consumer Supermarket Guide, by Joel Makower with John Elkington and Julia Hailes (New York: Penguin, 1991). Useful advice on packaging, eco-labeling, and earth-friendly selection of food and nonfood items sold in supermarkets.

Nontoxic Cleaning

Clean & Green, by Annie Berthold-Bond (Woodstock, N.Y.: Ceres Press, 1990). This extremely useful book contains 485 recipes for preparing your own nontoxic household cleaners. I have made the author's versions of Fantastic and Windex, and have been using them with great success for months. The convenience and savings are dramatic! The book can be mail-ordered from Ceres Press, Dept. SKB, P.O. Box 87, Woodstock, NY 12498 for $8.95 plus $2 shipping.

Nutrition

Nutrition Action Healthletter is a lively, highly informative publication of the Center for Science in the Public Interest, a consumer activist group that lobbies in Washington,

D.C., for improved labeling, restrictions on unsafe additives, and many other fine causes. The newsletter is published ten times per year and is free to members of CSPI. Write to CSPI, 1875 Connecticut Avenue NW, Suite 3000, Washington, DC 20009.

Vegan Nutrition: A Survey of Research, by Gill Langley (Oxford, England: The Vegan Society, 1988). A no-nonsense report on studies in the field. Available by mail order through the American Vegan Association (see VEGETARIANISM).

Vegan Nutrition: Pure and Simple, by Michael Klaper, M.D. (Umatilla, Fla.: Gentle World, Inc., 1987). Practical advice on balancing a vegan diet. Available by mail order from EarthSave (see ECOLOGY).

The Nutrition Debate: Sorting Out Some Answers by Joan Dye Gussow and Paul R. Thomas, eds. (Palo Alto: Bull Publishing, 1968). Straightforward essays on the RDAs, natural versus organic, dietary goals, and food safety.

Organic Gardening

How to Grow More Vegetables Than You Ever Thought Possible on Less Land Than You Can Imagine, by John Jeavons (Berkeley: Ten Speed Press, 1974 and 1991). The classic primer on the Biodynamic/French Intensive method of gardening. For information on training programs and a catalog of related books, organic seeds, and gardening supplies, write to the organization Jeavons founded: Ecology Action, 5798 Ridgewood Road, Willits, CA 95490.

Designing and Maintaining Your Edible Landscape Naturally, by Robert Kourick (Santa Rosa, Calif.: Metamorphic Press, 1986). Grow a gorgeous garden that you can eat.

The New Organic Grower: A Master's Manual of Tools and Techniques for the Home and Market Gardener, by Eliot Coleman (Post Mills, Vt.: Chelsea Green Publishing Company, 1989). A fine basic primer.

A magazine devoted to the subject is *Organic Gardening*, Rodale Press, 33 East Minor Street, Emmaus, PA 18098. An annual subscription is $16.95.

For information and catalogs on heirloom seeds, write to Peace Seeds, Dept. GM, 2385 SE Thompson Street, Corvallis, OR 97333, and Seed Savers Exchange, Rural Route 3, Box 239, Decorah, IA 52101. The latter publishes a Garden Seed Inventory ($17.50 postpaid) of 215 United States and Canadian mail-order seed catalogs, with emphasis on heirloom and regional varieties.

For details on the development of urban and suburban rooftop agricultural systems to provide organic produce all year round, write to the Gaia Institute, Cathedral of St. John the Divine, 1047 Amsterdam Avenue at 112th Street, New York, NY 10025. Tel.: 212-295-1930.

Organic Products

The Organic Food Production Association of North America (OFPANA) is working to establish national standards for produce labeled organic. For more information and publications, write to OFPANA, P.O. Box 31, Belchertown, MA 01007. Tel.: 413-323-6821.

The Committee for Sustainable Agriculture (CSA) sponsors Organically Grown Week each September and acts as a clearinghouse for updated information on organic certification and products. For details write CSA, P.O. Box 1300, Colfax, CA 95713. Tel.: 916-346-2777.

Vegetarianism

The American Vegan Association, 501 Old Harding Highway, Malaga, NJ 08328. Tel.: 609-694-2887. A clearinghouse for information on vegan nutrition and a life-style that promotes nonviolence and avoidance of all animal products. It is an excellent mail-order source of books, and publishes an informative quarterly newsletter for its members.

Vegetarian Times, a monthly magazine devoted to subjects of interest to vegetarians. Subscriptions are $24.95 per year. Write P.O. Box 446, Mt. Morris, IL 61054-8081.

... For those who care about how their food tastes and the ways in which preparing and sharing it resonate through their lives and communities, modern agricultural practice and the food it produces seem to have brought about plenty at the price of both private pleasure and the public good—food that fills the stomach but starves the soul.

—Robert Clark, ed., *Our Sustainable Table*
(Berkeley: North Point Press, 1990).

Mail-Order Sources

General

The following sell a wide range of organic products. The sources in this section will send a free catalog on request.

Gold Mine Natural Food Company
1947 30th Street
San Diego, CA 92102
800-475-FOOD

Natural Lifestyles Supplies
16 Lookout Drive
Asheville, NC 28804
800-752-2775

Mountain Ark Trading Company
120 South East Avenue
Fayetteville, AR 72701
501-442-7191

Walnut Acres
Walnut Acres Road
Penns Creek, PA 17862
717-837-0601

Neshaminy Valley Natural Foods Distributor, Ltd.
5 Louise Drive
Ivyland, PA 18974
215-443-5545
Minimum order $100

Specialty

Most of the following will send catalogs by request. For further information on specific items, a valuable resource is *The Catalogue of Healthy Food*, by John Tepper Marlin (New York: Bantam, 1990).

BEANS

Bean Bag
818 Jefferson Street
Oakland, CA 94607
800-845-BEAN

Dean & DeLuca
560 Broadway
New York, NY 10012
800-221-7714
Both sources sell boutique beans harvested within the past year.

BLACK QUINOA

Ernie New
White Mountain Farm, Inc.
8890 Lane 4 North
Mosca, CO 81146
719-378-2436
Subject to availability.

CHILI PEPPERS

Los Chileros de Nuevo Mexico
P.O. Box 6215
Santa Fe, NM 87502
505-471-6967
Also carry various other Southwestern specialty ingredients, including chicos.

CHINESE

The Oriental Pantry
423 Great Road
Acton, MA 01720
800-823-0368
A good source of fermented black beans; minimum order is $10.

DATES

Ahler's Organic Date Garden
P.O. Box 726
Mecca, CA 92254
619-396-2337
Specify a 5-pound minimum order.

DRIED FRUIT

Timber Crest Farms
4791 Dry Creek Road
Healdsburg, CA 95448
707-433-8251
Also sell dried tomatoes.

HERBS AND SPICES

Frontier Cooperative Herbs
Box 299
Norway, IA 52318
800-669-3275

Spice House
P.O. Box 1633
Milwaukee, WI 53201
414-768-8799

INTERNATIONAL CONDIMENTS/VINEGARS, ETC.

G. B. Ratto & Company
821 Washington Street
Oakland, CA 94607
800-325-3483

MAPLE SYRUP

Uncle Joel's Pure Maple Syrup
Route 1
Hammond, WI 54015
715-796-5395

ORGANIC SEEDS FOR SPROUTING

The Sproutman
P.O. Box 1100
Great Barrington, MA 01230
413-528-5200

PORRIDGE, CEREAL, AND OTHER BREAKFAST FOODS

Fiddler's Green Farm
RFD 1
Box 656
Belfast, ME 04915

SEA VEGETABLES

Mendocino Sea Vegetable Company
P.O. Box 372
Navarro, CA 95463
Specialize in Pacific sea vegetables harvested off the coast of northern California.

Maine Seaweed Company
P.O. Box 57
Steuben, ME 04680
207-546-2875
Northeast coast harvester Larch Hansen prides himself on writing personal letters to each of his customers. There is a 3-pound minimum.

SEEDS FOR GROWING

See Further Reading and Resources under ORGANIC GARDENING.

SPICES (SEE HERBS AND SPICES)

WHEAT FREE/GLUTEN FREE

Allergy Resource
195 Huntington Beach Drive
Colorado Springs, CO 80921
719-488-3630
Also carry unusual flours and pastas.

WILD RICE

Black Duck Company
9640 Vincent Avenue South
Bloomington, MN 55431
612-884-3472
Fine quality with substantial savings over standard retail prices.

Index

Barbecue(d) (*cont.*)
  -style tempeh sauce, 231
  tofu, 222
Barley
  about, 72
  basic (as for wheat berries), 101
  flatbread, crunchy rye-, 325
  with a Mexican accent, 86
  muffins, chive-flecked, 336–337
  pilaf
    mushroom, 72–73
    mushroom pearl barley, 73
    shiitake mushroom, 73
  salad with carrots and dill, 74
Basic
  arame, 266
  buckwheat, 76
  bulgur (cracked wheat), 104–105
  couscous, 109
  greens, boiled, 253
  greens, sautéed, 254–255
  hijicki, 264–265
  Job's tears, 83
  polenta, 78–79
  quinoa, 95
  rice
    brown, 119–120
    white, casserole-steamed, 144
    white basmati or extra-long-grain,
      142
  vegetable stock, 21–22
  wheat berries, 101–102
  wild rice, 139
Basil grain salad, 112
Basmati rice. *See* Rice
Bean(s). *See also* individual bean
      listings (and Ingredients A to Z):
      Aduki; Black; Black-eyed peas;
      Chick-peas; Kidney; Lentil;
      Lima; Red; Tempeh; Tofu;
      White
  about, 171–178
    cleaning, 173
    fat-free cooking, 178
    pressure cooking, 173–175
    pressure cooking chart, 175
    shopping for, 172
    soaking, 173
    storing uncooked, 172
    stovetop cooking, 176–177
    stovetop cooking chart, 177
  amaranth and corn medley, 71
  black-eyed peas, Pat's spicy,
      178–179
  black soybeans, 191–192
  burritos, 196–197

Bean(s) (*cont.*)
  chili "barbecued" beans, 200–201
  chili, triple bean maybe it's, 186–187
  Chinese-style and greens, 198
  empanadas, 206
  ful medames, 193–194
  and greens Italiano, 199
  and not dogs, 202–203
  red and chicos, 194–195
  salad
    about, 208
    aduki watercress with horseradish
      dressing, 212
    black bean with coriander pesto,
      213
    and grain, what's available, 209–210
    hoppin' John, 216
    lentil-quinoa with curry vinaigrette,
      214
    potato–green bean, 281
    red bean olé, 215
    slaw, chili, 285
    southwest, 211
  skordalia, 316
  soup
    about, 40
    aduki with chestnuts and apricots,
      42
    aduki-corn chowder, squash-, 45
    black bean, hot and zesty, 55–56
    black-eyed pea, and collards, 41
    chick-pea with greens, garlicky,
      43–44
    lentil, with chestnuts, quick, 53
    lentil, fruited, 52
    lentil, Italiano, 54–55
    lima bean vegetable, 47–48
    miso with ramen, 448
    multibean minestrone, 50–51
    split-pea with parsnips, green, 48
    split-pea with squash and raisins,
      curried yellow, 49
    stock, bonus, 26–27
    white bean with escarole, 46
  turnovers, savory, 206–207
  wheat berry–bean stew, 102–103
Beet(s)
  dip, brilliant, 319
  pickled, quick, 241
  potato salad, 280
  puree of, and parsnips, 242
  quinoa, scarlet, 97
  risotto with pine nuts and currants,
      crimson, 155–156
Biscuits
  chive, 329